ALSO BY STEVE ENG

■

A Satisfied Mind: The Country Music Life

of Porter Wagoner

The Man from

Margaritaville

Revealed

■

STEVE ENG

St. Martin's Griffin

New York

JIMMY BUFFETT: THE MAN FROM MARGARITAVILLE REVEALED. Copyright © 1996 by Steve Eng. All rights reserved. Printed in the United States of America. No part of this book may be used or reproduced in any manner whatsoever without written permission except in the case of brief quotations embodied in critical articles or reviews. For information, address St. Martin's Press, 175 Fifth Avenue, New York, N.Y. 10010.

Design by Songhee Kim

Library of Congress Cataloging-in-Publication Data

Eng, Steve.
    Jimmy Buffett : the man from Margaritaville revealed / by Steve Eng.
      p. cm.
    Discography: p. 323
    Includes bibliographical references and index.
    ISBN 0-312-16875-6
    1. Buffett, Jimmy.   2. Country musicians—United States—Biography.
      I. Title.
ML420.B874E54   1996
782.42'164'092—dc20   96-20428
[B]   CIP
                                        MN

First St. Martin's Griffin Edition: November 1997
10 9 8 7 6 5 4 3 2 1

TO THE PARROT HEADS

WHO GROW UP AS WELL AS OLDER

■

Contents

■

Part One: Norfolk Island and Nova Scotia

Part Two: Gulf Coast Origins

Part Three: The Fall and Rise of Jimmy Buffett

Part Four: Where is Jimmy Buffett?

Acknowledgments: Changes in Contributions, Changes in Attributions

■

Many, many people have helped this author, often rendering more assistance than was ever expected.

Libraries come first, since they are always there: Betsy Fisher, Ron Perry, Bernadette Wessels (Ben West Public Library, Nashville); Kent Henderson, Paul Kingsbury, Ronnie Pugh (Country Music Foundation Library, Nashville); Theresa Hambrick (Tennessee State Library and Archives); Paul Wells (Center for Popular Music, Middle Tennessee State University, Murfreesboro, Tennessee); Else Martin, Betty Rodgers, Jean Strickland (Jackson-George Regional Library System, Pascagoula Public Library, Genealogy and Local History Department, Pascagoula, Mississippi); Harry L. Simmons (Mississippi Room, Southern Station, Hattiesburg, Mississippi); Irene Wainwright, J. Rodney Smith (New Orleans Public Library); Mary Ann Drinkard, Holly Rowland, George H. Schroeter (Mobile Public Library, Local History and Genealogy, Mobile, Alabama); Michael Thomson, Charles J. Boyle (Thomas Byrne Memorial Library, Spring Hill College, Mobile, Alabama); Miami Dade Public Library; Linda M. Huey, Thomas L. Hambright (Monroe County May Hill Russell Library, Local and State History Department, Key West, Florida); Multnomah County Public Library, Portland, Oregon; The Chicago Public Library; Barbara P. Andrews (Nantucket Atheneum, Nantucket, Massachusetts).

Historical sources: Arthur Mora, Mickey Quillen, Aaron Zahide (Epsilon Nu Chapter, Kappa Sigma, University of Southern Mississippi, Hattiesburg, Mississippi); W. A. Helms (Old Spanish Fort Museum, Pascagoula, Mississippi); Jazie Torjusen, Thomas Wixon (Pascagoula, Mississippi); Charles J. Torrey (Museum of the History of Mobile, Mobile, Alabama); Eleanor Benz (McGill-Toolen High School, Mobile, Alabama); Lisa Baldwin (University of Southern Alabama, Mobile, Alabama); Wayne Penney (Dad's Old Book Store, Nashville); Emma Walling; Gerry Pitchford (Auburn University, Auburn, Alabama).

Music informants: Katherine W. Lippincott (BMG Music Publishing); Drew Gilmer, Glenda Hart (BMI Nashville); Chet Flippo (*Billboard*); Meredith Stewart (Curb Records); Doyle Davis (The Great Escape, Nashville); Jeff Tamarkian (*Goldmine*); Stacy Harris; John D. Squires (J.D.S. Books); Sarah Brosner (MCA Nashville); Sam Knight (Margaritaville Records); Leslie Smith (New Orleans Connection); Keith Spera (*Offbeat*); Allenette Douglas, Mike Smyth (Phonoluxe Records, Nashville); Gino Di Pasquale (Record & Tape Traders Inc.); W. "Buddy" Kalb (Ray Stevens Music); Evelyn Birnal (*Rolling Stone*); Lee Hubner (Song Music); John and Marie Hartford; Robert R. Martin (Your Songs).

Governmental cooperation: Susan Haberle, Danny L. Kolhage, Sandra Madiado (Circuit Court, Monroe County, Key West, Florida); Jane Jasewic (Circuit Court, Sanford, Florida); Eva Smith (Jackson County Court House, Pascagoula, Mississippi); P. Boyd (U.S. District Court, Los Angeles, California); Los Angeles Supreme Court.

Media assistance: Tom Powell (*Amusement Business*); Michael Jernigan (*The Auburn* [Alabama] *Alumnews*); Dan Lyke (*The Auburn Plainsman*); Ann Meador Shayne (*BookPage*); James Plath (*Clockwatch*); Sandra Baker (*The Hattiesburg American*); Mike Hentz, Vernon Silver (*The Key West Citizen*); Bill Ede, Jean Metcalfe (*Louisville Music News*); Gary Holland (*The* [Pascagoula] *Mississippi Press*); Carol Cain, Judy Rojeski (*Mobile Press Register*); Tom C. Armstrong (*Nashville Life*); Jeanette Stark (*The* [Miami] *Post Herald*); Lon Ormanian (*Parrot Press*); Scott Bradford; Craig Wills (ProPhoto, Nashville); Nancy Sadusky (*Save the Manatees Club Newsletter*); Skip Allen (*Southern Boating*); Mark Saucier (*The* [Gulfport, Mississippi] *Star Journal*); Jean Prescott (*The* [Biloxi] *Sun Herald*); Phyllis Hill ("The Nashville Network"); Patsi Cox; Susan Collier (Liberty Records); David J. McDade (*The Tale Feather: Newsletter of the Detroit Parrot Head Club*); Walt Trott (*Entertainment Express*); Dave Vincent (WLOX-TV, Biloxi, Mississippi); Art Bastian, John Lynch (Vanderbilt Television News Archive, Nashville, Tennessee re: Spar Studio).

Discography contributors: Jerrett Campbell; Otto Kitsinger ("The Nashville Network"); Jon Lautieri; Bill Kehoe; Michael Richards (Music & More, Hendersonville, Tennessee).

Others who shared information, including published material, photographs, audio and video cassettes: Kenneth Booker; James E. Bronstein; Jay Curlee; Nicole George; Stu Gittelman; Jerry M. Gilbreath; Bill Hart; Brent Howard Holcomb; Christy Howell; Robyn Lee; Wade Lloyd; Jane McDonald; Jason Matson; David H. Sanders; Virgil Wilhite; Ron Stacey; Emma Walling; Rich Williamson; Jeff Toth; Lew Woodard, Jr.; Charlyn Zlotnik.

Finally, the 107 interviewees, many of whom also offered media material: Joe Allison; Ron Allred; Vernon Arnold ("Austin Church"); Linda Barnard; Thelma Bass; Bill Beasley; Dennis Beasley; Richard ("Rick") Bennett; Jimmy Bowen; Charlotte Bowles; Melle Brauderick; Hal Breland; James Hal Breland; Ruby Breland; Mark Brewer; Milton L. Brown; Raymond Bryant; Richard Bryant; Alan Bubis; Nancy Buchan; Al Bunetta; Tom Bush; George Cain; Buzz Cason; Barry Chance; Ron Chancey; Marshall Chapman; William R. ("Bill") Combs; Bob Cook; Daniel Cooper; Tom Corcoran; Don Cusic; John Dilbone; Tommy Ellis; Jim Foglesong; Ronnie Grant; Chris Gantry; Chuck Glaser; Tompall Glaser; Kevin Gottschalk; Lucas P. Gravell; Tom Hackett; Beverly Iturbe; Nelson Iturbe; Trey Iturbe; Phil Kaufman; Bill Kehoe; William E. ("Bud") Kirkpatrick; Tim Krekel; Don Lewis; Don Light; Patricia Lumpkin; James Kelly Lyons; B. J. McElwee; Tom McEntee; Maureen Maclay; William ("Wiley") Magee; Sam Malvaney; Owsley Manier; Ken Mansfield; Bob Mayo; Kevin Meyd; Jake Mladinich; Kim Nelson; Jimmy C. Newman; Scott Nickerson; Chuck O'Brien; Max Pace; C. Dianne Petty; Gordon Pike; Cecil R. Phillips; Katherine Phillips; Ron Phillips; Gordon Pike; Loretta Pitt; Jean Prescott; Marie Ratliff; Bob ("Robbie") Robison; Chris Robinson; Curtis Rockwell; William Scarborough; Mike Shepherd; H. W. Slater; Ron Stacey; Michael Stark; Keith Sykes; Capt. Tony Tarracino; Phil Tenney; John Ed Thompson; Henry Torjusen; Mitchell Torok; Travis Turk; Paul W. Urbahns; Paul Vermilyea; Brother Victor; Tom Walls; Brent Webster; Doug Weston; Bergen White; Howard White; Ruth White; Mark Will; Benny R. Williams; Nelson Williams; Jim Witzel; Gerry Wood; Reggie Young.

Preface: Some People Claim That There's a Biographer to Blame

■

9 September 1994

Dear Steve,

I have heard your footsteps in the far corners of my world, I felt it's time to set a few things straight after reading the note which was passed on to me by one of my employees.

I start this letter with a sense of controlled anger that I hope doesn't spill over into the pages. I understand that you are a writer and I appreciate the fact that you have treated me kindly in some of the things that have been brought to my attention, but that is where my compliments must stop. To cut to the chase, I would like to ask you to abandon the idea of writing an unauthorized biography. It is not for any reason of hiding skeletons in my closet or not wanting something said about me that hasn't already been said. Part of being a celebrity is shouldering the responsibility that comes with the life you have chosen. That responsibility also goes for journalists too. I know, I am both. I am more than capable of writing my own autobiography. I don't need any help or third-person interpretations. It is my life. I live it. I am a writer and if anyone should care to read about my life, then I should be the one to write it—not you. It's that simple. For the record, I plan to do an autobiography when I am about eighty-six, by then I should be ready to reminisce but right now, I am still too busy living. So you see any attempt at biography by you or anyone else can only be categorized for what it is—self-promoting hack writing to make a few bucks.

I am sure there are a lot of other people out there in Nashville or wherever who feel that the time is right for their story to be told and you might be the guy to do it—but as Bob Dylan wrote, "It Ain't Me Babe." I can't stop you from doing this project and I can only ask you to try to have some integrity. There is little left out there in journalism these days, but I would respect you a lot more and would be happy to buy you a beer the next time I am in Nashville. If you go ahead with it, then this will be the last you ever hear from me. Live your own life and stop trying to figure out mine. I leave you with a parting couplet that I believe comes from Shakespeare. "Isn't it the way of the mongrels, to gnaw at the tails of the champions." Let me know what your intentions are.

Sincerely,
Jimmy Buffett

P.S. If you do go ahead with this project, I hope you have the balls to start your book with this letter. I would happily grant you permission to print it "verbatim."

■   ■   ■

20 October 1994

Dear Jimmy,

Thanks for the letter postmarked September 19, from Long Island, in the Key West envelope (and for asking me to respond). My wife read it to me over the phone when I was in Mobile. Please note *my* new address and phone.

Since your career has been in motion for over a quarter of a century, a biography is obviously overdue. In no way should it impinge upon an *auto*biography, such as you propose for the far-distant future. *Your* memoir—full of stories, insights and opinions—will make its separate impact upon the readers. Meanwhile, an interim project can preserve information and present perspectives that might otherwise be lost forever. Such as locating the studio in Mobile where you recorded "Abandoned on Tuesday," or identifying your homes in Nashville. This research can only complement your own future effort, and hopefully, trigger memories for you when the time comes.

As soon as St. Martin's confirmed my proposal, I approached your management in writing (February 22) with my suggestion that the book be "authorized." I sent two packages—one for them, one for you, filled with past writing and credentials. Over the past several months I have reiterated (again in writing) my hope that this project be "authorized," with the emphasis on your career.

Your management, I am sure, is bombarded with projects and opportunities ... with your latest album going to Number 5, no doubt your organization has never been busier.

But your letter doesn't indicate that you ever received my full package—so here it is again. I trust that this letter will not be separated from the accompanying material.

By the way, I am interested in your creativity, and your literary tastes, and not so much in your "celebrity." Your better work will be around when you are not, so in part, this is for posterity.

Cordially,
Steve Eng

Introduction: But Why, Jimmy. . . ?

■

Jimmy Buffett is, sooner or later, worth it.

■   ■   ■

"Thank God no one was hurt," exclaimed Jamaican police commissioner Col. Trevor MacMillan on January 17, 1996. Jimmy, who loves the song "Jamaica Farewell," had landed in his seaplane near the coast of Jamaica the day before, only to get shot at by the fast-gun officials suspicious of *ganja* (marijuana) trafficking. "It was an incident we regret most sincerely," MacMillan said with a sigh.

Jimmy's "A Pirate Looks at Forty" (1974) is certainly his nostalgic smuggling anthem. Now, after his blasted plane episode, he provided "Jamaica Mistaica" for his 1996 *Banana Wind* album, joking about "dodgin' cannon balls" fired by "some asshole," while making it clear that he was *not* a cocaine cowboy armed with guns and an alibi.

■   ■   ■

Having switched from albums to book writing for a few years, now he has switched back, making up for lost time with annual compact discs full of new songs.

As always, his concert career persists. Though his boyhood hero was Jean Lafitte—and his song's pirate was "born two hundred years too late"—Jimmy reflects modern progress. Why, at his concert in Columbus, Ohio, on May 29, 1996, CompuServe offered Jimmy and his Coral Reefer band performing live, "on-line," to computer customers! How many of today's pop (or "new country") acts will be on-lining when *they* are forty-nine years old?

And how many will be encouraging ticket "scalpers" in the far future? Jimmy's tickets sell out in less than ten minutes—in 1994 this author bought the next-to-last ticket in the parking lot of Nashville's Tower Records. On Murfreesboro Road, ticket scalpers kept trying to wave down us motorists on the way to his concert at Starwood Amphitheatre, flashing their overpriced tickets.

CONCERT—
JIMMY

BUFFETT

4 tickets, $60/ea.
(901) 683-7917

After all, in 1993 Jimmy was handed a Key to the City by Mayor Phil Bredesen, who named the June 25 sell-out date "Jimmy Buffett Day in Nashville." That year, Nashville lady Kim Nelson confirmed how she'd been to at least four Starwood Concerts in a Sixties-style bus named Godzilla, motored by a "designated driver." She said, "Our blood alcohol level is higher than our IQ. When you hear Buffett, you're not going to have a care in the world for the next three hours."

■   ■   ■

But was Jimmy worth researching?

On August 24, 1994, driving to Florida, this author stopped for coffee at a Georgia market. There was Jimmy by the door, staring out from the front page of USA Today: JIMMY BUFFETT MAY SET SAIL FOR BROADWAY, read the headline for an article that went on to report his zeal for co-writing a musical based on the novel Don't Stop the Carnival (with its author Herman Wouk). The very next day his plane crashed in Nantucket, Massachusetts, and he swam for safety, winning a news story in The Miami Herald. That night in Key West, his longtime friend Captain Tony Tarracino was hosting riverboat gambling on board the FunKruz. But with the news of Jimmy's crash, suddenly all the roulette wheels stopped spinning. "The whole night was ruined," said Captain Tony. "I can see what the whole world was going to be like without Jimmy, 'cause one day we're all going to die. When I left the club, we went to Margaritaville [the restaurant] and found out he wasn't dead." Captain Tony says ninety percent of his customers weren't Buffett followers—yet "he became a symbol of some sort. He always protected his personal life."

More exciting than Jimmy Buffett, however, was Fidel Castro. Throughout this author's week in Key West, hordes of Cuban refugees made international news. Jimmy's milder Save the Manatees Club was certainly not geared up to rescue over two thousand Castro escapees washing ashore in one day. Unfortunately for this researcher, there were no thrilling Cuban scenes on exotic Duval Street—the only visible Cubans were on the front pages of every day's paper. The histrionic press inadvertently helped wreak Castroian vengeance for the 1961 Bay of Pigs invasion. Tourism was falling in Key West, down almost twenty percent! "Key West has now become a base of operations for reporters," reported *The Miami Herald* on August 31. "Never a dull moment in Key West," this writer suggested to local history librarian Thomas L. Hambright, who confirmed, "Well, there's always something happening." Pause. "After all, it's the end of the world," he said, noting that Florida's governor Napoleon Bonaparte Broward had earlier been a gun runner to Cuban rebels in the 1890s.

■　　■　　■

Back home, it was nice to find that Jimmy used to frequent Elder's bookstore, across from his old club The Exit/In, in search of Faulkner first editions.

Books are where you find them.

This author would not have acquired *his* book opportunity without the indirect help of novelist Ralph Compton and his ally Bob ("Robbie") Robison. Agent Ethan Ellenberg has shown more faith than I deserve, and editor Jim Fitzgerald has granted patience and assistance beyond belief. His co-editor Meg Drislane has done superlative work, and assistant Regan Good, publicist Claudia Riemer, and attorneys Paul Slevin and Surie Rudoff have provided warm support. *Thank you.*

And ultimate gratitude to my wife, Anne, and children, Mary Rose, Michael, David, and Natalie.

Steve Eng
Nashville
July 23, 1996

Norfolk Island
and
Nova Scotia

■

In our passage we touched at Pitcairn's Island for refreshments. The inhabitants being in want of some person to teach them to read, and write . . . [I] was discharged and went on shore.

> —John Buffett, "A Narrative of Twenty Years'
> Residence on Pitcairn's Island," *The Friend*
> (Honolulu), vol. 4, 1846

[Captain James Delaney Buffett] was an old sailing-ship man. He was originally from Nova Scotia. I don't know how he settled in Mississippi . . . that's one thing I wanted to ask him before he died. He went to sea for years.

> —Jimmy to Robert W. Morgan, radio interview at
> Louie's Backyard, Key West, March 1, 1980

Pitcairn Island Prologue: The Trips and Trials of John Buffett

■

After Mr. Hill's beating me over the head, breaking it in two places, and likewise my finger, I was suspended by my hands in the church, and flogged until I was not able to walk home.

—sailor John Buffett, letter, 1834

If man cannot find happiness on an island paradise, where can he find it?

—Marlon Brando, in *Brando: A Life in Our Times* by Richard Schickel (1991)

"Y ou all are *everywhere*, honey," said television host Whoopi Goldberg in September of 1992, joking about the prolificness of the Buffett family.

"We were very promiscuous during the Inquisition," answered Catholic Jimmy Buffett.

"I guess you were!" said Goldberg. "I'm going to cross my legs right here." And she did . . . having earlier speculated that there must be *black Buffetts* as well.

Jimmy's garrulous grandfather, Captain James Delaney Buffett, had often told him, when he was a boy, about the Polynesian Buffetts. But as Jimmy grew older, he wondered, "Is there really a string of Buffetts out in Polynesia—or is it just the old man fooling around during the Big War?"

Once after a show in Hawaii, Jimmy idly looked in the phone book—and behold, there were many Buffetts! He impulsively called one . . . only to learn that the Buffetts came from Tahiti. Then, after a show in Tahiti, he took some of his Buffett billboards and began tacking them to palm trees. Here he discovered the legend of John Buffett, from Pitcairn Island. Since John Buffett had migrated to Norfolk Island, that was Jimmy's next genealogical stop.

On his way to an Australian tour, he took his mother and father and flew the long way to distant Norfolk Island. "There was this huge clan of Buffetts . . . they were all there."

■　■　■

But back when Jimmy was thirteen, had he but peeked into the October 1960 issue of *National Geographic,* he would have stumbled onto some of the same lore. He would have been pleasantly shocked to see a portrait of none other than Mrs. Colin Buffett (and her daughter Alma) of Norfolk Island. This might have inspired him to forage further . . . toward Pitcairn Island, the haven (but not always heaven) of the immortal *Bounty* mutineers and their descendants. John Buffett had been their friend, their historian . . . and lover of perhaps too many of their women.

Jimmy would have been enchanted to trace a posthumous, family link to the infamous 1789 shipboard revolt . . . and later island exile. Which in turn had fostered three famous novels by Charles Nordhoff and James Norman Hall in the 1930s: *Mutiny on the Bounty, Men Against the Sea,* and *Pitcairn's Island.* The first one became a film in 1935, starring Charles Laughton as the tyrannical Captain Bligh and Clark Gable as mutinous hero Fletcher Christian. Then, in 1962, Marlon Brando, playing Fletcher Christian (versus Trevor Howard as Bligh), remade the film (somewhat cumbersomely). Jimmy Buffett the novelist (*Where Is Joe Merchant?*) could easily have been inspired by this classic *Bounty* trilogy.*

As for Mrs. Colin Buffett, she was pictured examining the Ten Commandments, carved in wood by surviving *Bounty* mutineer John Adams (Adams had been a hero to later Pitcairner John Buffett, who was, in a way, Adams's authorized biographer)—though on Pitcairn Island, at times, the Ten Commandments had been easier to carve than to obey (e.g., "Thou shalt not kill," "Thou shalt not commit adultery," not to mention "Thou shalt not covet thy neighbor's wife").

* Like Jimmy, author Nordhoff had a sailor grandfather, also named Charles Nordhoff, a journalist who wrote books about his ocean days on whaling and fishing ships.

But who was John Buffett . . . whom Jimmy claims as a distant sea-borne kin . . . whose connection he first revealed to Whoopi Goldberg?

John Buffett was born in Bristol, England, on July 16, 1797. He was a sailor on the English whaling ship *Cyrus*—and it landed on Pitcairn Island on December 10, 1823. John Evans, son of a London watchmaker, accompanied him. Already John Buffett had an incredible survivalist record, having withstood "ferocious storms" at Manila Bay and in the Moluccas, plus a shipwreck in the Bay of St. Lawrence (forty-two deaths!), as well as a shipwreck south of Boston. Scholar Peter Clarke types Buffett as an "adventure-toughened seadog [who] appears to have come across as a mild, soft-spoken scholar"—in short, in many ways a forebear, at least figuratively, of Jimmy Buffett, the writer who survived a plane crash in 1994.

Now, back in 1790, mutineer Fletcher Christian and his eight accomplices had sailed from Tahiti to rocky, uninhabited Pitcairn Island. They brought along Polynesian women, plus men destined to be "servants." Allegedly they abused the latter (such as commandeering one of their black wives), who purportedly retaliated, shooting the English dead. Only one survived, John Adams, nicknamed "Alexander Smith" (unaware of the United States President's name, till someone inconveniently told him). Adams was not alone—with eight or nine Tahitian women, and around twenty-five children. ("Love quarrels" had triggered some of the murders, and the widows preserved their late husbands' skulls.)

John Adams was John Buffett's future patriarch.

■   ■   ■

Jimmy Buffett has often pined, nostalgically, for a hypothetical career as a seaman, centuries ago. But how would he react to the 1821 report to the British Admiralty titled *Statement Respecting the Prevalence of Certain Immoral Practices in His Majesty's Navy?* The complaint itself indirectly helps explain the social stresses on Pitcairn Island. The document asserted that when British ships docked in port, the navy invited aboard "as many prostitutes as the men." (Though when there was a whore shortage, and maybe only three hundred female guests on board for five hundred sailors, why, they generously shared them!) Thus did ships of war, while in port, become

> a continual scene of riot and disorder, of obscenity and blasphemy, of drunkenness, lewdness, and debauchery . . . married seamen are frequently joined by their wives and families (sometimes compromising daughters from ten to fifteen years of age), who are forced to submit to the alternative of mixing with these abandoned women, whose language and behaviour are usually of the most polluting description; or of foregoing altogether the society of their husbands and parents. . . .

These women are examined at the gangway for liquor, which they are constantly in the habit of smuggling on board. . . . [Below decks] it is impossible to describe—the dirt, filth, and stench; the disgusting conversation; the indecent, beastly conduct, and horrible scenes; the blasphemy and swearing; the riots, quarrels, and fightings. . . .

But at least when John Buffett landed with Evans, the "simplicity and harmony of the little colony" appealed to him—so he asked to be permitted to stay. (Whereas Evans had to jump ship.) Buffett was moderately educated, and Adams made him the island leader—at least for a while. He preached sermons, taught children (and helped establish a school), and instigated *The Pitcairn Island Register.* Jimmy Buffett would have identified with these last two duties of John Buffett, especially running the *Register,* a faint parallel to his own journalism career (*Amusement Business, Billboard, The Coconut Telegraph,* etc.). John Buffett's effort was the literary ancestor of the *Book of Records of Pitcairn Island.*

In fact, John Buffett was "much respected and trusted," so his stories of John Adams were treasured, and in many instances are the "authorized" accounts. He told how Adams once refused to mend his fence, so his hogs invaded Fletcher Christian's garden. Christian threatened to shoot them—Adams promised to shoot Christian in return. So some of Christian's friends tied him up and were about to set him adrift in the ocean, when Christian intervened. Ever after, Buffett reported, Adams revered Fletcher Christian.

In 1825 Captain F. W. Beechey dropped into Pitcairn Island and attended a church service. Adams read the prayers; next came the hymns; then "a sermon followed, which was well delivered by Buffett." In case anyone might forget any of it, he delivered it two more times! ("The service thus performed was very long.") And yet the service was held *five times* every Sunday. Adams said there were sermons against gluttony, "eating being one of the sins of the flesh, like copulation and boozing."

But, as Pitcairnologist Harry L. Shapiro observed, "Despite its isolation a century ago, life on Pitcairn was far from dull." Buffett's *Register* recorded births, deaths, marriages—but Shapiro says, "The question naturally arises whether illegitimacy may not be present here. . . . No doubt that little monkey running up and down the branches of a family tree can do considerable damage."

As Beechey found out, John Buffett was a happily adulterous married man. Just nine weeks after arriving, he had married Dorothy ("Dolly") Young. His extra marital activities included Mary ("Big Melly") Christian, Fletcher Christian's granddaughter, as well! When Captain Waldegrave tried to learn how many people lived on Pitcairn (in 1830), he met resistance—nor was he granted *all* the parents' names ("It would be wrong to tell my neighbors' shame," someone whined). Shapiro says

Buffett "was the father of at least one of these two illegitimates"—and scholar Sven Wahlroos makes him the clandestine father of one son and two daughters, courtesy of Big Melly, surmising that *Bounty* survivor Adams "may well have regretted that Buffett had stayed on the island."

A later visitor, Captain Freemantle, decided that the Pitcairners needed *another* clergyman:

> The Englishmen who have been on the island have on the contrary done much harm, particularly Buffett, who, although a married man, seduced one of the young girls, by whom he has two children.

In 1798 one of the islanders, William McCoy, had achieved a cultural breakthrough. Having once worked in a Scottish distillery, he produced (on April 20) an actual bottle of liquor. Such maintenance of a still presages Lord Buckley's "God's Own Drunk" recitation-song, so often performed by Jimmy Buffett. McCoy was a drunk, and John Buffett would later defend the islanders' right to slurp alcohol. One of Buffett's colleagues, George Nobbs, was in fact "habitually drunk." Perhaps alcohol led to illegitimacy ("Why don't we get drunk and procreate?").

In 1831 the Pitcairners evacuated to Tahiti, including John Buffett and his official family. But the transplanted colonists frequently got drunk—and worse, disease began killing some of them. So the Buffetts, and other survivors, returned home.

The final solution to the Pitcairn pathology arrived in 1832, in the form of the elderly Joshua Hill. He was armed with "spurious" (forged?) letters supposedly annointing him as governor. Quickly he formed a temperance society to "eradicate the growing practice of imbibing intoxicants." To help persuade the colonists to adapt alcohol control, he implemented gun control . . . by bringing a loaded musket to church. He passed a Treason Act, aimed at ridding the island of "lousy foreigners." Nobbs and Buffett were both adjudged to be traitors—and sentenced to be flogged with three dozen lashes on "bare back and breech." Buffett's offense was, of course, his liaison with Big Melly. Hill personally shed his jacket and lashed John Buffett bloody, right there in church! (Supposedly with only two dozen whip strokes.) Buffett lay abed for two weeks, then boarded the whaler *Tuscan* with Evans and Nobbs and headed for Tahiti in March of 1834, with legal sanction.

He was further fined by the court to pay up "three barrels of yams or potatoes . . . [and] with or without your family, you are to leave the island by the first vessel that may present herself."

Buffett and Evans wrote righteous letters to the British government, and on September 16, 1834, Buffett returned to Pitcairn with his family, with dictator Hill soon to be ousted. Thanks to Buffett and his allies, Pitcairn Island became seemingly the first community in the world to grant female suffrage (1838), and was probably the first to make education mandatory—something "Southern" Mississippi graduate Jimmy Buffett should be distinctly proud of.

John Buffett even turned journalist momentarily, writing a memoir for the Honolulu Quaker magazine *The Friend* in 1846. His empathetic, islander prose anticipated that of *The Coconut Telegraph* newsletter a century later. Speaking of the whaling business (which baptized Jimmy's grandfather into seamanship): "Should whaling fail, we must go back to our old custom of dress. Shirts, pantaloons and jackets must be exchanged again for the 'Maro' [native island costume], and ladies' gowns for the native petticoats, which will be a great change indeed, for the young ladies and gentlemen of Pitcairn's!" This dichotomy—of professional sailing versus beach lounging—sums up Jimmy's own cultural schizophrenia. And in the next paragraph, John Buffett offers a handy coconut recipe.

As he said of his Pitcairn years: "My residence has convinced me that human nature is the same throughout the world." And his name survives on a 1973 Pitcairn map identifying "Buffett's Red Dirt" on the northeast side of the island, a quarter of a mile from where the *Bounty* had been burned.

In 1856 the British government moved all the Pitcairners to Norfolk Island (discovered by Captain Cook in 1774), including John Buffett. It had been a fairly gruesome British penal colony for a time, but T.C. Roughley in *National Geographic* (October, 1960) rejoiced that the "hardy settlers" transformed it into "a Pacific paradise." James A. Michener, author of Jimmy Buffett's beloved *Tales of the South Pacific,* called it "a speck under the forefinger of God." Some Buffetts returned to Pitcairn in 1863—but John Buffett died on Norfolk on May 5, 1891.

∎ ∎ ∎

As for Pitcairn Island, the *Bounty* mutiny itself is a cult phenomenon whose commemorative bicentennial—April 28, 1989—was celebrated on a reconstructed *Bounty* ship near the rock volcano Tofua, as well as at the National Maritime Museum in London, displaying artifacts like John Adams's pigtail. A veritable *Bounty* following persists and, like Jimmy's Margaritaville empire, not all in one place—from the library at Sydney, Australia, to Hollywood's film archives.

Jimmy, who complains tirelessly (and tiresomely) about not getting a *Margaritaville* film offer, should consider shifting his film gears and attempting a *Bounty* sequel. There have been at least five *Bounty* films, and even if Brando's was a business fiasco, there is still hope.* In 1962 a *Bounty* museum opened in St. Petersburg, Florida, and publicity efforts

---

* The film cost $27 million (and the script alone $327,000), and this in 1962 dollars. But Brando had not wanted to play Fletcher Christian—he had wanted to play John Buffett's icon, John Adams, instead.

sounded faintly like Jimmy's Margaritaville merchandising—including table decorations of coconuts and melons, raw fish recipes, and Tahitian drums and songs.

But the first *Bounty* film, in 1916, was filmed partly on Norfolk Island. Alas, only a few stills remain (it was initiated in Australia), but maybe, just maybe, there was a Norfolk Buffett in it somewhere.

If only as an extra.

From Canada to the Gulf of Mexico: Captain Buffett's Exodus

■

And the sturdy fishing schooner sways so lazily, to and fro; Nova Scotia is my sanctuary, and I love it so.

—Hank Snow, "My Nova Scotia Home," recorded 1959

[A] poor simple sailor, just like me,
Must be tossed and driven on the dark blue sea;
Farewell to Nova Scotia, the seabound coast,
Let your mountains dark and dreary be.

—"Farewell to Nova Scotia," traditional folk song recorded by
George Hamilton IV, 1973

Jimmy Buffett's grandfather, Captain James Delaney Buffett, hero of "The Captain and the Kid," was born while Pitcairn Island alumnus John Buffett was still alive—on November 9, 1887. His birthplace was Rose Blanche on the southeast coast of Newfoundland ("The New Founde Land"). Rose Blanche became "an important fishing settlement," despite its tiny population of only a few hundred. Distinguished by white granite (*roche blanche*, for "white rock" in French), Rose Blanche lies twenty miles east of Port aux Basques—and about a hundred and twenty miles from Glace Bay, separated by Cabot Strait.

The family eventually moved to Glace Bay.

The town was incorporated in 1901. Its name, translated literally, means Glacier Bay (from the French *glace* for "glass"). The town is icebound most of the year. Located on Cape Breton, it's a coal-mining and deep-sea-fishing center. Two years before James Buffett left, the immortal Marconi (in 1902) engineered the first "official transatlantic wireless connection with Europe," from Table Rock, just above Glace Bay. (At least Buffett's grandson Jimmy would one day utilize Marconi's invention—radio—for fun, profit, and eventual petulance.)

■ ■ ■

The Buffetts are of Welsh descent. But *Nova Scotia* means "New Scotland"—and was so named 152 years before the Highlanders came to stay, when it was still possessed by the French and Indians. To imaginative brains, Nova Scotia on a map resembles a lobster, at least in its contours—and Cape Breton Island (home of Glace Bay) looks like the *claws* of a lobster. Fittingly ... since by 1940, Nova Scotia was the world's leading source of lobster. Jimmy Buffett's humorous, fish-eating persona evokes his grandfather's Nova Scotia background. On the coastline, tuna fish weighing from a hundred to nine hundred pounds regularly feed on mackerel and herring—and one fish plant at Halifax was processing *fifty million* pounds of fish a year. (A single fisherman caught twenty-one giant tuna in eight days—"tuna by the ton"; 3,677 pounds, to be exact.)

Halifax was where country singer Hank Snow lived in the 1930s. Jimmy's song "The Wino and I Know" features an ice-cream man—"a hillbilly fan" who collects 78 rpm records by Hank Snow. Snow's own "My Nova Scotia Home" recalls that the "fragrance of the apple blossom sprays the dew-kissed lawn" of his homeplace. And Snow's many nautical songs like "Bluebird Island" anticipate Jimmy's—as do his Caribbean songs, explicated by Mark Humphrey in his authoritative *Jimmy Buffett Scrapbook*.

Like Jimmy's grandfather, Hank Snow was a Nova Scotia sailor, starting at age twelve in 1926. He worked on sailing ships, sometimes playing harmonica, acoustic guitar, and tap-dancing—as well as listening to country songs over the static-filled radio. Hank went ashore in time for the Depression, and Jimmy—forever joking (and singing) about dope smuggling—would be proud to note that Hank Snow was, briefly, a rum-running bootlegger. Mark Humphrey says that Snow's "greatest pre-Buffett country tropicana came in the form of such Caribbean-flavored riches as 1951's 'The Rhumba Boogie' [Number 1], and 1954's 'That Crazy Mambo Thing' [Number 10]." (Snow even did a show in Glace Bay, Nova Scotia, around 1960.)

And like Jimmy, Hank Snow endured his own Nashville debacle, being kicked off the slippery deck of RCA records after forty-five years and swimming ashore to the touristy island of Opryland, where the loyal natives applaud him to this day.

∎ ∎ ∎

Jimmy's Margaritaville record company promoted the Cajun girl band Evangeline from New Orleans. The name Evangeline has its own Nova Scotian origins. The French settlers, called Acadians, were run out of Grand Pré by the British in 1755—and immortalized by Henry Wadsworth Longfellow in the narrative poem *Evangeline*. An Evangeline statue was erected at Grand Pre.

The Catholic Acadians migrated to Louisiana, where they were called Cajuns . . . and Cajun music became one of Jimmy's biggest influences.

∎ ∎ ∎

At age sixteen, in 1904, seaman James ("Jimmie") Delaney Buffett left Nova Scotia to become a whaling-ship cabin boy. He was looking for his older brother John—a rumored shipwreck victim.*

He finally ventured down to the Gulf Coast in 1916, if not earlier (one news story says 1911), making his home base the seaport of Pascagoula. In 1917 two shipyards were established there by the United States Emergency Fleet corporation. One of them had been owned by the Krebs family, related by marriage to the Flechas and Seymour families.

James Buffett began staying at a boarding house down on the beach in Pascagoula. Located on Beach Boulevard on the east corner of South Pascagoula, it was probably owned by a man named Hollister, but it was run by a lady—Condalaura (Flechas) Seymour, born in Pascagoula in November of 1873, daughter of Joseph J. Flechas and Condalaura (Villar) Flechas. Her father died in 1883, leaving the schooner *Sea Horse,* along with three barges; her mother died in 1908.

Condalaura Flechas married Norman M. Seymour (born 1869) in 1896, but she filed for divorce in 1916. He had trouble paying his seven-dollar-a-month alimony, since the butcher shop he was running eventually folded when the International shipyard closed down. Condalaura Seymour was a hardworking woman on the beach. Her teenaged daughter, Hilda Seymour, would eventually catch the eye of Captain James Delaney Buffett.

---

* An early U.S. Buffett was "Josiah Buffett, mariner," from the eighteenth century. Family tradition makes him a Long Island farmer (town of Huntington) who resisted the British loyalty oath—had his farm seized during the American Revolution—and was taken prisoner but escaped, visiting his family by night, till he sneaked across the frozen Sound and made it to Connecticut, with countless other refugees. (In 1913 genealogist Frederic Gregory Mather traced twenty-six Buffetts in this locale.)

Gulf
Coast
Origins

■

The curving shore of the Gulf of Mexico, even that part within the confines of the United States, is not all of one piece. Geologically it represents several methods by which the land areas of the globe have been built up. Historically its culture, now under a single flag, is underlaid with a mosaic of varied influences—Spanish, English, French, Early American—each of which left its fingerprints on this cup that holds the warm waters of a Southern sea.

—Leonard Ormerod, *The Curving Shore: The Gulf Coast from Brownsville to Key West* (1957)

I had very ordinary children who turned into extraordinary adults.

—Loraine "Peets" Buffett to Becky Gillette, "Stories to Send You," *Mississippi* magazine (March–April 1993)

Son of the Singing River

■

I got a doll in Pascagoula,
I got a jewel in Gulfport,
And both of them more warm-blooded
Than any woman I've met up north.

—Larry Kingston, "Biloxi" (Number 10 country hit for Kenny
Price, 1970)

The day the squirrel went berserk
In the First Self-Righteous Church
In that sleepy little town of Pascagoula

—C. W. "Buddy" Kalb, Jr., and Carlene Kalb, "Mississippi Squirrel
Revival" (Number 20 country hit for Ray Stevens, 1984)

Condalaura Seymour operated a
mariner's hostel, a haven for Gulf Coast sailors, whose ships were loading
and unloading lumber around twelve miles away, off Horn Island.
Daughter Hilda had been born October 30, 1897—"a dark-haired
beauty," says Jimmy Buffett's mother, Loraine. She was quite taken with
this latest lodger, Jimmie Delaney Buffett, even though he was ten years
older than she was. His supper-table talk was romantic and exotic,
combining "strange people and far-off places." In 1986 Jimmy Buffett
reminisced to Helen Bransford in *Interview:* "He'd talk about places
like Madagascar and Mozambique." He told Bonzai (in *Mix*) that his
granddad had "seen everything but he was never a wise-ass. He'd listen

to other people telling stories when he'd seen ten times as much, but he'd only interject when he had something funny or useful to say."

Jimmie's boardinghouse sojourns were brief, sometimes six months apart, so "for a while he continued to have a girl in every port, like seafarers the world over." He even seemed to ignore young Hilda, other than giving her "a polite hello," so she slipped a note into a book he was reading, asking him to talk some more since "you always sound so good."

It worked.

On August 12, 1918, he and Hilda slipped over to Gulfport, Mississippi, in Harrison County—and got married by a justice of the peace at the Circuit Court. Presumably Hilda was Catholic (her family was), but Jimmie was Episcopalian. They didn't own a car, and Pascagoula (then as now) was quiet, so the newlyweds' favorite recreation was walking on the beach. . . .

■ ■ ■

Pascagoula may have been tepidly tranquil, but at least its history was distinctive.

The "only natural seaport" in Mississippi, its name came from the "Bread People" Indians. Journalist Arthur Smith called Pascagoula "beautiful to pronounce, spell and visit." Its official, non-Indian history began in 1718 with the erection of a cypress-and-pine building that came to be called the Old Spanish Fort, set back upon a hill amid pecan trees. The French were in control, and it wasn't Spanish and wasn't a fort. It still stands (with a museum, at 4602 Fort Street).

The British took over in 1763, then the Spanish in 1789. Pascagoula joined the new state of West Florida in 1810, and the following year, Mississippi Governor Claiborne (a former Tennessee judge) established the parish of Pascagoula.

The Old Spanish Fort housed the German immigrant Krebs family from the 1730s until 1930. They became the leading family of Pascagoula since they "multiplied the fastest." Patriarch and land baron Hugo Krebs seems to have invented a cotton gin twenty years before Eli Whitney. Their adjacent graveyard is the oldest still in use in the Mississippi Valley. The Krebs clan started a shipyard—as did the Flechas family, whom they married into. Family ties, from Krebs to Flechas to Seymour to Buffett, connect Jimmy Buffett with Pascagoula's "first family" of Krebs. Early maps even termed Pascagoula "Krebsville." And modern-day shipbuilder Roy Krebs fashioned the *Blue Seas* schooner, which transported President Kennedy to the Caribbean.

■ ■ ■

Amusingly, in this period *another* Buffett slipped through Pascagoula—a fact seemingly unknown to Jimmy Buffett's family.

Way back on May 12, 1804, a real-estate witness named Peter Buffett had been "declared not to know how to write," so had to sign an X to a sales contract of land in Pascagoula. His name was discovered in 1994 by library researcher Betty Rodgers, a descendant of one of the witnesses: "My ancestors interacted with many people along the Coast (there weren't a lot at this time period) . . . as we changed governments: French, Spanish, English, Spanish, and Mississippi territory. He must have moved on as he appears in no other records that I have."

■   ■   ■

In November 1814, Nashville's Andrew Jackson, applauded for his recent Creek Indian victory, crossed the Pascagoula River. The following January, a share of Pascagoula boys aided Jackson in his resounding victory of the Battle of New Orleans. He utilized the services of Jimmy's boyhood idol, pirate-patriot Jean Lafitte—plotting their victory at Maspero's Exchange, a New Orleans coffeehouse in the French Quarter, not far from Jimmy's nightclub venue, the Bayou Room. (Maspero's still operates today at 440 Chartres Street.) Some of Jackson's cannons still stand outside the Old Spanish Fort.

Mississippi entered the Union in 1817, and appropriately, as historian Jay Higginbotham points out, the county surrounding Pascagoula was named Jackson. The town flourished, a three-story hotel, manned by slaves, symbolized its rise.

■   ■   ■

In the 1830s, James Copeland, Pascagoula's most rebellious citizen until Jimmy Buffett, shot his way into fame. Copeland was the star of the entertaining Copeland Clan, robbing stores in Mobile and stealing slaves in Louisiana and horses in Texas. He also drugged an Irish trader, then hatcheted him to death and stole his boat. (Such a combination of drugs and piracy would have made a nice, macabre folk song!)

But Copeland delivered his finest performance at Old Augusta on the upper Pascagoula River in 1857. Thousands of "gallows head" spectators appeared at his final show, "thrilled to the bone," according to Jay Higginbotham, as "the body of James Copeland fell through the trap door and with a sickening twang dangled in mid-air."

Sheriff J. R. S. Pitts, who fitted the rope around Copeland's neck, published his client's posthumous memoir. Sheriff-author Pitts was arrested for libel, then jailed in Mobile. From the author's Appendix:

> Many devoted friends have endeavored to persuade him from the pres-
> ent object of publication, because of the dangerous elements in high
> life which affect society, but, for life or death, "the die is cast." . . .
> The author has studiously avoided tinting any of his observations with
> preferences in favor of either of the conflicting political parties of the
> day.

Like any self-respecting unauthorized biographer, Pitts was willing to risk his life! His *Life and Confessions of the Noted Outlaw James Copeland* still survives, having been published in 1858, 1874, 1909, 1980—and 1992, the same year Buffett published *Where Is Joe Merchant?* Professor John D. W. Guice, from Jimmy's alma mater, the University of Southern Mississippi, states in his introduction that mimeographed and Xeroxed copies of the 1909 edition circulated "with as much caution and excitement as bootleg whiskey!" (Five thousand copies were reported stolen from a Hattiesburg warehouse.)

Thus far, James Copeland is Pascagoula's longest-running author. From his harbor haven in pirate Hades, he might be proud that his better-selling successor, Jimmy Buffett, wrote that shoplifting classic of misdemeanor music, "Peanut Butter Conspiracy"—as well as his story-song of a felony fiasco, "The Great Filling Station Holdup."

■ ■ ■

Some time before the Civil War, Henry Wadsworth Longfellow, author of *Evangeline,* may well have visited Pascagoula. From his poem called "The Building of the Ship":

> *Timber of chestnut, and elm, and oak,*
> *And scattered here and there, with these,*
> *The knarred and crooked cedar knees . . .*
> *Brought from Pascagoula's sunny bay . . .*

Skeptics say he never went to Pascagoula—but to play it safe, there's a Longfellow House (3401 Beach Boulevard), just in case he did.

After all, Pascagoula was "held together by a lotus-eating philosophy. History here becomes an old wives' tale as full of legend as of fact," rhapsodized the Federal Writers' Project historians in 1938, since around the "wharves and the aged fort the marsh grass and Spanish moss grow as they have for centuries."

Admiral David Farragut grew up in Pascagoula. In 1864 he invaded his old home port as Commander of the Federal Navy. A boyhood friend—and a Confederate—tried to stop him. Farragut threatened to kill him, so the fellow instantly decided to join the Union forces . . . and renew his old Farragut friendship.

As for Longfellow, he had the shipbuilding theme correct. At some point, the "first yellow pine log" was felled near the riverbank, then floated downstream to Pascagoula. The first ship was built in 1772, to transport corn and deerskins, and a shipyard was started in 1838. Shipbuilding inflated the population (1890–1906), and Pascagoula ships earned renown for being able to traverse the Gulf all the way to Mexico. The town exported pecans, deep-sea red snapper, shrimp, and oysters.

■　■　■

By 1911, 291 ships were generating over $8 million worth of imports and exports at Pascagoula. The following year, Nashville's *Cumberland Telephone Journal* ran a three-page feature touting the town as the nation's gateway to Panama. A confederation of Gulf Coast businessmen convened at Biloxi in 1913, "to boost the Gulf Coast as a whole."

Then World War I inspired the U.S. government to commission ten 9,000-ton steel ships to be built at Pascagoula, and the local shipbuilding payrolls leapt up to $80,000 a week. (And the population rose to 3,375.) Soon, the first steel ship built in Mississippi was launched from this seaport.

■　■　■

By the time of Jimmie and Hilda's marriage, the International Shipbuilding Yards had consolidated with the federal government, but with the war's end, the business declined, "leaving the hulls of unfinished schooners half submerged in the river to mock the town's industrial death."

Fortunately, the deadly armistice was encored by the beneficial Volstad Act—banning alcohol. Prohibition fostered one of Jimmy's most nostalgically revered professions: smuggling. Rum-running was an honored Pascagoula enterprise, as the bay became a nautical chamber of covert commerce. The shipwrights were routinely persecuted by the puritanical federal prosecutors. Then, when the U.S. Coast Guard set up its base in 1927, they further stifled the honest bootleggers.

At least Pascagoula can boast that Al Capone, most respected of all American gangsters, was reputedly one of their rum-running patrons. Sometimes the smugglers would loan their boats to respectable shrimpers, in exchange for the fishermen's boats, where they'd stash their rum under the oysters and shrimp. The town also earned international recognition when the British and French governments protested, in writing, that the U.S. Coast Guard had grabbed 2,400 cases of liquor from a friendly Canadian smuggler.

The death of Prohibition in 1933 dealt a business blow from which Pascagoula (like Chicago) only slowly recovered.

■　■　■

Jimmie and Hilda lived in the boardinghouse until 1926. Significantly, considering the career of their grandson Jimmy, the Seymours' hostel stood near to the esoterically named Singing River.

Therein lies the mythological source of Jimmy Buffett's career.

Since the early nineteenth century, residents and visitors claimed to have heard music rising from the river's waters. Supposedly, the ethereal music would cease once a fisherman jumped overboard or splashed the water with an oar. For those who like to read sheet music, the actual notes were reprinted in *The Popular Science Monthly* in 1890. Charles Darwin, in his *Descent of Man,* said that fishes could make musical noises. Or it could be the grinding of sand on slate. Or water sucked by an underwater cave. Or natural gas leaking out. The more accepted, scientific explanation, however, features *ghosts of Pascagoula Indians* who drowned rather than submit to the tyrannical Biloxi Indians. Other explanations included (1) the death sounds of two Indian children dying in the river; (2) the sounds of Catholic church bells shipped from France on a vessel that sank; (3) the sound of a drowning Indian maiden named Tallulah; or (4) the sound of a mermaid ghost from 1541 witnessed by explorer De Soto.

In 1925 Sir Arthur Conan Doyle—English spiritualist (and authorized Sherlock Holmes biographer)—was invited to Pascagoula to crack the case. He declined. At least the federal government rallied in 1937, by subsidizing a WPA painting of Pascagoula Indians singing their death chant, to be hung in the post office.

The river splits into two banks, one at Pascagoula and one at Gautier, to the west. (Some old-timers in 1987 protested the erecting of a Singing River sign that gives Gautier credit for music that is only heard on the Pascagoula side!) There are poems and even songs about the Singing River. The press boasted in 1977 that "it was the only spot in America where these melodious fish concerts are heard."

In 1967, when Jimmy was in school at Hattiesburg, country-music singer Kenny Roberts recorded "The Singing River" in Nashville on the Starday label. The song was written by Mrs. Edgar M. Lane of Jackson, Mississippi—even as *Outdoors* magazine for that year encouraged tourists to come *hear* the Singing River: "After all, what mortal can argue with a legend?"

■ ■ ■

In the early years of their marriage, Jimmie Delaney Buffett left again and again for the sea, as Hilda hung on at the rooming house, raising children. James Delaney Buffett, Jr. (Jimmy Buffett's dad), was born on November 25, 1919. And Patricia Buffett was born on August 3, 1921; Catherine Buffett, August 19, 1923; and Billy Buffett, July 16, 1926 (dissolute hero of Jimmy's song "The Pascagoula Run," and short story of the same name).

■ ■ ■

The last wooden ship to be built at the International Shipyard was the *Monfalcone,* in 1922, and its first master was . . . James Buffett. The 2,400-ton five-mast Gavrentine was built to haul coal from Virginia to Italy, but it was never used for this. Captain Buffett took the 372-foot ship (with 90,000 square yards of sail) to New Orleans, where (at the St. Andrews dock) it was loaded with three million feet of lumber.

Destination: Havana.

"I took with me on that voyage my wife and baby," Captain Buffett said in 1943. He and Hilda—with young James Jr.—had posed on deck for a news photograph. "I could tell you about a tropical hurricane we ran into three days out of New Orleans that was a beauty, but the good ship behaved swell, and we came through okay." The cargo was the largest load of lumber ever brought to Havana, but when they arrived, all the banks were closed. Buffett had to "put up the lumber for bond" in order to return home. (The consignee had left town.)

While they were waiting for their money, the cook prepared a festive cake for little James's birthday. Mother Hilda dressed up James ("J.D.") in a white sailor suit "with blue braid around the wide collar and a star on each corner." Thus, on the deck of the *Monfalcone* in Cuba, did Jimmy Buffett's father take his "first tottering steps." Captain Buffett raised his ship's flags—and soon, reportedly, *all* the ships in the Havana harbor had raised their flags in Happy Birthday celebration.

In his story "Hooked in the Heart" in *Tales from Margaritaville*, Jimmy alludes to this episode, and recalls pouring over his grandfather's logbooks and journals. Later, in his Key West period, he listened wistfully to the tales of Havana's "old days"—when the ferryboats bore people, each day, across to the gambling casinos and "art-deco hotels."

In 1948 J.D.'s brother and Jimmy's uncle, Billy Buffett, was in Havana, and retraced his father's footsteps, through restaurants, bars, and "who knows what else" from his father's career. Billy reported back to his family where the best food could be bought, and where the prettiest girls could be found. Captain Buffett's Cuba visit was echoed, somewhat, in Jimmy's novel, *Where Is Joe Merchant?*

■ ■ ■

In all, Captain Jimmie sailed the *Monfalcone* for three years, until it was sold to a canning company in Long Beach, California. They turned it into a gambling boat—until it finally burned up.

The *Monfalcone* was the sister ship of the five-masted barkentine *Marsela,* which Captain Buffett termed "one of the most beautiful and best ships I have ever sailed."

■ ■ ■

After Billy was born in 1926, the family moved into a rental house on the seafront, on Beach Boulevard. Hilda's mother accompanied them, helping to raise the children and cook and clean. Several times, Hilda sailed with Captain Buffett as he transported lumber in the Caribbean.

One destination was the Turks and Caicos Islands, a southeast extension of the Bahamas. Captain Buffett took his family there on the sailing ship *Chickamulla* around 1928, and then north to New York. In his story "Life in the Food Chain" (*Tales from Margaritaville*), Jimmy tells how the voyage became a calamity, when, due to the lack of wind, the boat was halted for twenty-eight days. Thirsty and hungry little James Buffett found a can of evaporated milk rolling around in the galley, opened it, and was draining the can when the black cook intervened. He wanted his father to punish him, but Captain Buffett refused—what *else* could his ravenous son do? Miraculously, another ship rescued them with food supplies in a few days—and they became a news feature on the front page of the *New York Herald Tribune*.

That was Captain Buffett's last sailing-ship trip. The *Chickamulla* was discarded, off Highway 90 in a bayou near Mobile. "I saw it every time I crossed the bay," remembers Jimmy. In 1969 Harry McDonnell of the *Mobile Register* spotted the charred remnants of the boat below Spanish Fort Hill, along Battleship Causeway in Baldwin County. It had been used as a temporary lodging by the workers who had laid the causeway, until years later "a pyromaniac touched a match to the dry timbers just to see flames leap into the sky."

One of Jimmy's favorite authors is William Faulkner, a fellow aviator. He lived repeatedly in Pascagoula, starting in the summer of 1925, when he courted an ex-Nashville debutante, writing her a book of fifteen sonnets. Faulkner's beach-boy casualness was partly Buffett-esque—he went unshaven and wore a rope instead of a belt, yet he usually wore white duck trousers and a white shirt. The girl spurned him.

Faulkner was back in 1926, then again in 1927, right after his *Mosquitoes* novel was published. He had written it in Pascagoula. Set in the French Quarter (the Vieux Carré) of New Orleans, it celebrated the bohemian literary and artistic life there—and deeply influenced Jimmy Buffett, due to his own New Orleans tenure in the 1960s. Faulkner honeymooned in Pascagoula in 1929, and he and his bride rented a home on the beach, where she almost drowned herself—was it a suicide attempt . . . ?

■　■　■

Captain Buffett's son, young J.D. Buffett, was educated at the Pascagoula high school, and his father is variously listed in the school records as a "shipman" and "navigator." J.D. and his friend Henry Torjusen both played alto saxophone in the high-school band around 1941, and had something else in common as well—fathers who were seldom home. Henry's father, Charles, was also a sea captain. Speaking of Captain Buffett, Torjusen says, "He was a great man. He was gone almost all his life. He didn't spend too much time at home with his family." Typical voyages were nine months to a year. (Henry Torjusen himself became a ship pilot for years, even once going to Pitcairn Island to pick up their mail!)

■ ■ ■

In 1938 Robert Ingersoll Ingalls (named after Robert Ingersoll, the evangelistic agnostic) arrived. With Hitler invading Poland, he sensed that Pascagoula would undergo an economic renaissance—an encore to its World War I glory. Ship production commenced in 1939, and SS *Exchequer* was the world's first ship to be totally welded, instead of riveted.

Mississippi's state economic assistance, plus World War II, was helping to expand the Pascagoula shipyards, and the town's population jumped from 5,900 in 1940 to 25,000 in 1942.

■ ■ ■

In 1940 Vernon Presley—a Mississippian fresh out of "jailhouse rock" prison—moved to Pascagoula with wife, Gladys, for a six- to eight-month stay. They lived with Vernon's cousin Sales Presley in a one-room shack with screen walls—and both men worked in the shipyard. Then they moved back to Tupelo, where son Elvis Presley could start in the first grade. In the 1950s, Elvis would work at a club in nearby Biloxi.

■ ■ ■

A nineteen-year-old girl named Mary Loraine Peets was working as a secretary at Ingalls in 1941. Born on August 14, 1921, she lived in nearby Gulfport (approximately thirty miles to the east) with her mother, Bessie Thompson Peets. The origin of the family's name was Welsh. They were from Meridian, Mississippi, birthplace of "The Blue Yodeler," Jimmie Rodgers. Her father, Thomas D. Peets, Sr., still lived there.

In August, "Peets," as she was called, began dating J.D. Buffett. One day they visited J. H. Pelham's seafood restaurant at 380 Front Street along the river. (Pelham was in the oyster and shrimp business.) Here they met Captain Buffett on one of his precious returns from the oceans. The whole family was swayed by his commanding presence, especially the enchanted young Peets. This woman, whose last name doubled as her first, inspired Captain Buffett to laugh, "What kind of name is *that?*" Peets was particularly wooed by his gray-blue eyes . . . which never seemed to stop twinkling.

Captain Buffett was now in charge of the *Delmundo,* a Mississippi Shipping Company cargo vessel carrying goods from New Orleans to South America.

■ ■ ■

Peets had her share of female colleagues. At Ingalls, a woman's work had just begun. The Pearl Harbor bombing of 1941 showered the shipyard with government contracts—and women worked next to the men in the machine shop. Their dark-glassed helmets concealed their gender, but they wielded their welding tools and lathes as well as the men. A posted sign said:

> **BEWARE OF THE MACHINISTS**
> **WHEN PANTS TOO LOOSE**
> **BEWARE OF THE MACHINES**
> **WHEN PANTS TOO TIGHT**
> **BEWARE OF THE MACHINISTS**

Women welders could often outweld the men. A champion lady welder was flown in from Oregon, but was defeated by local girl Vera Anderson, "Champion of America."

On the more arcane side of the ladies' life at Ingalls hovered the menace of the Phantom Barber. In 1942 the nocturnal assaulter began attacking Pascagoulan women at night—to cut off their hair with his scissors. Ingalls workmen began staying home to protect their wives. Finally, a suspect was arrested. (When he asked to see the warrant, they threatened to shoot him.) He was a Harvard-educated metal salvager, suspected of Nazi connections (maybe plotting to blow up the Ingalls shipyard, fancied the public), and earned a ten-year penal sabbatical.

∎ ∎ ∎

At the local courthouse on May 6, 1942, J.D. and Peets were married. Their wedding was sanctified the following day by Catholic priest P. J. Carey at Our Lady of Victory Rectory. On Saturday, May 9, a wedding celebration was held for the couple at the local Comet Club, and the next day, they had a chicken-dinner picnic in Gautier.

Meanwhile, on May 7 and 8 occurred the first all-air fight in naval history: American and Japanese ships in the Coral Sea, near Australia and the Solomon Islands, held their fire and let the airplanes blast each other. The Japanese lost one hundred planes, two ships, and three thousand men; the U.S. lost twenty aircraft, two ships, and five hundred men. The Battle of Midway followed on June 4 and 5, another naval victory for the U.S. Commander in Chief Roosevelt, a wheelchair paralytic, who became "the first President to fly in an airplane while in office and to leave the country during a war." He left Miami by plane in January 1943, heading for Casablanca—scene of the Humphrey Bogart and Ingrid Bergman film of that same year, one of Jimmy's favorite movies.

At some point, Captain James Buffett joined the U.S. Army Air Corps and became a repairer of airplanes. His son Billy joined the U.S. Navy, and would become a thirty-one-year member of the U.S. Merchant Marine. And Jimmy's daddy, J.D. Buffett, joined the Army Air Corps.

Back when they got married, Peets and J.D. had received a letter of congratulations from J. B. Converse, the president of a Mobile, Alabama, shipbuilding company, along with some money as a wedding gift. Perhaps J.D. and Peets suspected that one day they might move to Mobile. Naturally, the town's shipyards were thriving on the wartime demands. (But when twelve black shipworkers were promoted in 1943, they were attacked, beaten, and hospitalized.)

Interestingly, Hank (né Hiram) Williams worked at the Alabama Dry Dock and Shipbuilding Company in Mobile in 1942, 1943, and 1944. He and wife Audrey toiled together with their blowtorches. Hank preferred to make music in the honky-tonks at night, and they finally went back to Montgomery, Alabama.*

■ ■ ■

World War II was a period of musical change that would seminally affect Jimmy Buffett's career—and anyone else's, south or west of Tin Pan Alley. Country music would soon be published as well as recorded at Nashville, even as black blues and eventually rock 'n' roll would accomplish the same in Memphis and elsewhere. Jimmy would weave in and out of those fields, as well as others, including the nostalgic, respectable pop music of the wartime period.

Now, back in 1940, the radio stations had refused to renew their agreement with ASCAP (the American Society of Composers, Authors and Publishers), the song vendors' union founded in 1914. They balked at ASCAP's $9 million shakedown for their use of ASCAP songs for twelve months. No pay, no airplay—so everyone expected to hear the sound of silence. But the stations covertly founded BMI (Broadcast Music, Inc.), and glommed 36,000 new copyrights, opening the door to "hillbillies" and "niggers" (to use the colloquially correct terms of the times). After ten months ASCAP capitulated—and the musical Civil War between the South and Tin Pan Alley was momentarily at truce. Important to Jimmy's future, Latin music also now had more radio vogue.

Jimmy's first cult success was on jukeboxes with "Why Don't We Get Drunk" (1973). Yet James C. Petrillo, godfather of the musicians' union, who was "leery of mechanically reproduced music," loathed the nation's forty thousand jukeboxes because they played those records that he hated so much. So he called a twenty-seven-month strike in 1942, which only incited more "indie" (independent) or little record companies to sell "folk" as well as "race" (black) records. (Jimmy's first commercial records were for an indie label named Barnaby.) Petrillo's unwitting contribution to Southern music should earn him at least a plastic plaque in the Rock and Roll—and the Country Music—Hall of Fame.

Country boys, white and black, had donned the same color—khaki—

---

* When Jimmy Buffett arrived in Nashville in 1969, the pathetic Audrey Williams was still in town, forming an all-girl band and drinking the rest of her life away.

and were off to war. Jimmy's future employer, *Billboard* magazine, woke up. In 1942 it launched the "Harlem Hit Parade," evolving into "Race Records" by 1945, then "Rhythm & Blues" (R&B) in 1949. In 1945 a black serviceman from Nashville, Cecil Gant ("The G.I. Sing-sation"), briefly charted "I Wonder" in Pop. And *Billboard* had begun listing "Folk Records" in 1944 (momentarily "Hillbilly" in 1947), finally calling them "Folk (Country & Western)" in 1950.

A disgusted ASCAP renegade, Fred Rose (cowriter of Sophie Tucker's "Red Hot Mama"), went to Nashville in 1942 and founded the Acuff-Rose BMI publishing company with Roy Acuff. They signed Hank Williams in 1946. Rose, an ex–piano plinker who had written for Gene Autry, had been everywhere—blues, country, pop, Western—and died in 1954. Had he lived, he would have well appreciated Jimmy Buffett's latter-day versatility, for under Jimmy's beach-boy facade lurks some "big band" empathy, exemplified by his 1980 rendition of "Stars Fell on Alabama" (*Coconut Telegraph*). Jimmy knew the song as a boy, and according to his *Parrot Head Handbook* (1992), he grew up enjoying the better Tin Pan Alley songs of the Forties. But the big bands were largely defeated by World War II—thanks to the draft, too many of their musicians had to lay down their instruments and pick up weapons.

■ ■ ■

After the war, many Ingalls warships were being converted back to cargo carriers. By now, pretty Pascagoula had its tidy, shady streets (overhung with oak and pine trees, decorated with magnolias and azaleas) built up with government-funded "Navy houses," such as the one at 2218 Tyler Street, where J.D. and Peets Buffett lived.

The year 1946 inaugurated not only the postwar consumer binge that so empowered the entertainment industry, but also the profitable (for a while) Cold War, which ultimately sundered American culture into ferocious factions by the 1960s.

Before the war, workers' wages had averaged twenty-five dollars a week, but by Victory Day they had risen to $44.39. In 1946 automotive, steel industry, and coal miner strikes (infuriating President Truman) had symbolized this wage earners' upsurge.

And on March 5 British Prime Minister Winston Churchill proclaimed that an "Iron Curtain" separated the capitalist West from the communist East. On April 30 an atom smasher was announced at the University of California at Berkeley (ironically, the Berkeley campus would become the Lexington-Concord of the American Hippie Revolution in the Sixties). On July 1 a nifty atom bomb was plopped near Bikini Atoll in the Pacific. According to country singer–songwriter Fred Kirby, the atom bomb had been given to mankind "by the mighty hand of God"—and his song "Atomic Power" went to Number 6 for the Buchanan Brothers.

(Jimmy opposes nuclear weapons, as does his preferred President, Bill Clinton.)

■ ■ ■

Military blacks, returning home to civilian life, found all too little had changed, especially in the South. *Billboard* flaunted a front-page feature on December 7—"Where Does Show Business Stand on Intolerance?"— condemning racism ("Everything we have ever stood for, and died for, is raped by intolerance").

The same issue advertised a new release of "Stars Fell on Alabama," as well as Frank Sinatra's holiday recordings, with Columbia Records claiming that "Santa Claus Is Sinatra." Forty-eight Christmases later, in 1994, Sinatra's *Duets II* album would include a duet track with Jimmy Buffett.

For Christmas of 1946, J.D. and Peets got a gift in the form of James William Buffett, born at the Jackson County Hospital in Moss Point, adjacent to Pascagoula. Today Jimmy Buffett's birthplace is the Chateau De Ville Nursing Center.

Jimmy is astrologically a Capricorn—like Dolly Parton (born the previous January), a sun sign purportedly adept at accumulating money. Other music folks born on Christmas Day include jazz trombonist Kid Ory and singers Cab Calloway and Tony Martin.

Moving to Mobile

■

The quaintness and mellowness of the old Mobile is submerged beneath the bustling commerce of a busy seaport. Whirring factories, mills and a hundred varied industrial plants are sinking their roots into the deep, rich soil, and ships of all nations plow their heavy laden routes between Mobile and the four corners of the world.

—Marian Acker Macpherson, *Glimpses of Old Mobile* (1983)

Once again, as in the rum-running Twenties, Pascagoula suffered the pains of peace after the war shut-down. Ingalls sunk into a deep relapse.

At its wartime peak, the shipyard had employed 11,000 workers. They would arrive in shabby cars, or by train or by bus, or simply by the strength of their thumbs, hitchhiking. There was such a shortage of milk, adults would often do without to provide for their children. Tent cities had sprouted up, along with a village of a thousand trailers beside a lake. One such workman griped, "These people in houses think trailer people are vermin." The 1940 population had been 5,000, and it rose to 35,000 during the war.

Then it plummeted, down to 10,000. Few if any government contracts continued. And more than 800 federally built apartments were torn down—though another 1,125 were left standing. "Before long it looked like a ghost town as hundreds of abandoned shacks were observed, shacks that had been hastily constructed during the war," said historian Higginbotham.

Pascagoula paid its personal price for World War II's economic harvest. Around seventy of its servicemen came home, including one who was wearing a Bronze Star—Donovan Gautier, veteran of the Bataan Death March and three years of Japanese imprisonment. Several others did not come home alive.

■　■　■

It was in 1947 that Bob Ingalls, owner of the shipyard, bought the home which he named the Longfellow House, to cash in on Longfellow's possible—if improbable—visit to Pascagoula. An angry business competitor opened a jukebox joint next door, derisively called the Shortfellow House. One would hope that Jimmy Buffett's hedonistic uncle Billy Buffett patronized the place, enjoying "its purple rum and loud honky-tonk music." Then on September 19, 1947, a devastating hurricane struck, wrecking thirty-seven homes, even killing people at Gulfport and Biloxi. Shortfellow House at Pascagoula met its demise: "Beer cans, broken bottles, garbage, splintered pilings, oyster shells, and pieces of chairs lay strewn over the lawn and beach."

Coincidentally, perhaps, at the end of 1947, J.D. Buffett and Peets were contemplating a move to nearby Mobile, only around thirty miles to the east. With good reason—there had been at least two rounds of layoffs at Ingalls. Somehow they scraped up the money for house payments, and began shopping for a new home in Mobile.

■　■　■

Musically, 1947 was a year when rhythm and blues was increasing its volume, yet it seemed mostly in the hands of Louis Jordan, singer-saxophonist. He had three Number 1's, all of them making it onto the pop charts, too.

In pop music, Guy Lombardo had a Latin hit, "Managua, Nicaragua." But the biggest pop record of the year was "Near You" by Francis Craig (vocal: Bob Lamm), which spent an unbelievable seventeen weeks at Number 1. "Near You" was the first important hit on an independent label—Bullet Records, founded by James Bulleit. (It was recorded in the city where Jimmy Buffett would start his own indie label—Nashville.) Milton Berle would sing it as the closing number on his television show, and it became a Number 1 country hit for George Jones and Tammy Wynette in 1976, but more important, it triggered Nashville's first record-pressing plant, Southern Plastics. "Everything in Nashville has been an accident," observes thirty-year music veteran Ruth White (everything from Strobel's Music Shop in the Arcade to WSM, from songwriter Carmol Taylor to Porter Wagoner). "WSM was an accident, and so was the Opry. Nashville's recording and publishing was an accident. Music Row was an accident."

■ ■ ■

J.D. Buffett planned to go to work at the Alabama Dry Dock & Shipyard Company on Pinto Island. Historian Richard R. Lingeman said its "great cranes towered starkly against the skyline, dominating the city." During the war, the company had hired upwards of 40,000 workers, and a worker might make $1.17 an hour. Wartime Mobile produced 196 tankers and freighters and seven destroyers. The population doubled (from 115,000 to 250,000)—and when the Buffetts arrived in early 1948, at least 25,000 shipworkers were still employed. Unlike Pascagoula, which had run out of government contracts, postwar Mobile was staying in business, big business.

The wartime influx had its rowdy social effect. Long lines would form outside the Mobile theaters and liquor stores and restaurants, where "once inside people fought for the waitress, likely a cute blonde trick from East Jesus, Texas, who told you only the chicken croquettes were left and got fifty-cent tips from the sailors." Lingeman figured the waitresses had run away from home to follow a serviceman boyfriend. One 1940s journalist, Max Lerner, typed the Mobile shipyard gals as "New Amazons" who could "outdrink, outswear, outswagger the men." (Peets Buffett was not exactly in *this* group—an office girl from Ingalls, she would one day hold a secretarial position at the Alabama Dry Docks.)

John Dos Passos said the streets of Mobile in the 1940s featured "stout women with bundled-up babies, lanky backwoodsmen with hats tipped over their brows and a cheek full of chewing tobacco"; young men without hats, wearing open-necked, colored sports shirts; and "countrymen with creased red necks and well-washed overalls," as well as stocky businessmen, smoking cigars . . . and high-heeled girls in bright dresses, their hair piled up high on their heads.

Dos Passos also thrilled at the hoary romance of Mobile's yesteryear, symbolized by century-old buildings with tall, shuttered windows and wrought-iron balconies overhung with vines. The "buildings once housed a roistering assembly," wrote poet-folklorist Carl Carmer. "The crews of ocean windjammers found liquor here in gilded saloons." Steamboats had traveled from Mobile to Selma, Montgomery, Demopolis, and Gainesville, from the 1820s into the twentieth century, according to historian Virginia Van der Veer Hamilton. In 1835 there were forty-three three-masted schooners anchored in the bay.

By 1948, the city was one of the world's biggest seaports, something like a "gigantic construction camp," or even "more like a Western mining camp than a Southern seaport town."

Since 1928, Mobile had been renowned for its Alabama State Docks, which converted 540 acres of swampland into more than thirty cargo piers, jutting into the Mobile River above the city. Huge quantities of freight would arrive by railroad, only to be stored in sheds until loaded onto the ships. The State Docks had spent a million dollars on the Mobile Seaman's Club, a wondrous venue for family socializing.

■   ■   ■

On May 1, 1948, James D. Buffett, Jr., bought a house at 3157 Ralston Road in the Westlawn subdivision, for $7,650. Near the small house lay a large vacant-lot park, where Peets could stroll with baby Jimmy. No doubt she marveled at the 1946–51 expansion of Mobile—new churches, homes, public buildings, and especially, *new schools*. (Back during the war, the U.S. Office of Education had denounced Mobile's school system as being the nation's worst.) The rather ecstatic Mobilians hyperbolically proclaimed their postwar city to be "the Greater Gulf State."

Boyhood by the Bay

■

Back to Mobile Bay . . .
Magnolia blossoms,
Cool summer nights,
Warm, rolling seas . . .

—Curly Putman and Dave Kirby, "Mobile Bay" (Number 60
country hit for Johnny Cash, 1980)

Life is an experience, and it's meant to be lived. I knew that from
childhood. Fortunately, I come from a family of travelers, gypsies, and
sailors. When I was five years old, I was already thinking of getting
out of Mobile, Alabama.

—Jimmy to Terry Rose, interview at radio station KIRO-FM
Seattle, August 1992

When they moved to Mobile, they
didn't have a car," remembers Jimmy's aunt Patricia Lumpkin. Her
brother was Jimmy's father. Patricia's mother, Hilda Seymour Buffett,
and her father, Captain James Delaney Buffett (if he happened to be
home from the sea), would "go and pick them up there on Ralston
Road, and they'd come back nearly every weekend [to Pascagoula], or
every *other* weekend."

Jimmy never had a brother, but his fraternal surrogate over the years
was Baxter Lumpkin (born January 1945), the son of Roy and Patricia
Lumpkin. Jimmy and Baxter would play on the weekends, and as they
grew older, "Jimmy would stay down here all summer long. He loved
it down here. We called him a 'Rube Goldberg.' You remember, [Rube]

always had those inventions, they were so crazy," Mrs. Lumpkin laughs, recalling the cartoonist whose zany protagonists would usually contrive an eccentric, complex machine for performing some simple function.

"My daughter had a stuffed monkey somebody had given her. We had gotten a movie camera for Christmas. So Baxter and Jimmy got together and they'd *hang* the monkey. They would show the monkey [on film], and the next thing you knew, the monkey was hanging from the tree. Jimmy always had good ideas . . . well, *he* thought they were good ideas!"

The most enchanting family member was, of course, Captain Buffett, of 1017 Parsley Avenue in Pascagoula (renumbered later as 1810). As Jimmy said on Biloxi television (WLOX) in 1989, on the *Great Mississippians* show:

> That's one reason I wanted to travel—when I'd listen to my grandfather's travel, he'd lighten my imagination. From the little bayou behind his house on Parsley Street [sic], you can go to Mississippi Sound and trace your way around the world if you want, if you're brave enough and have enough imagination. . . . I could not envision myself living away from the water. It's part of my makeup, being able to grow up, especially on the Gulf Coast in the South. I've traveled all over the world, [but] it's still a very special spot—there's not many places like it. There are some interesting places that come close, but it's a very unique place. It's a real part of my heritage.

And as he told Noel Coppage in 1974 (*Stereo Review*): "As a child, I always traveled right along the Coast, probably never went ten miles north of Mobile—never went to upstate Alabama at all."

And vicariously, he would sail the seven seas with his granddad. "When he'd come back, I'd go down and listen to all of his stories," Jimmy told Helen Bransford in *Interview*, so many of which were about far-off tropical islands. "To an eight-year-old, they'd just ring, they were so exotic. So I knew the first opportunity I had, I was going to sea."

Of all his songs, Jimmy's personal favorite is probably "The Captain and the Kid," in which he nostalgically relives his childhood reverence for James Delaney Buffett. He'd climb on his grandfather's knee and, figuratively, "we'd go sailing back on barkentines and talk of things he did." The captain had regressed—from commanding ships to raking leaves in the back yard. He never quite adjusted to living on the land.

"He was a character. . . . He had yarns and tales, he was a great storyteller, he had a sense of humor," Jimmy told the *Great Mississippians* audience in 1989. He trained Jimmy to not merely spin yarns, but *to listen to them.* Jimmy told Helen Bransford that "to be a good writer you have to be a good listener." Grandfather Buffett's raconteurship was underscored by another, later influence—Ernest Hemingway, who said: "Either write what you know about or write what you've heard about."

So thanks to Captain Buffet, Jimmy would go sailing whenever he could. "Later I used to jump boxcars and ride them from my mom's house to my grandmother's, forty-three miles away in Pascagoula." Boxcar riding was good training for the music business, since perpetual motion largely determines the troubadour's vagabond emotions. One of the first country-music recording artists, Harry J. "Haywire Mac" McClintock, who wrote "Big Rock Candy Mountain," was a professional railroader as well as hobo ("Hallelujah! I'm a Bum"). He was followed on RCA-Victor by Jimmie ("Waiting for a Train") Rodgers, whose idolater Hank Snow cut train-bumming songs like "Hobo's Last Ride." Contemporary star Boxcar Willie keeps the hobo music tradition alive.

Singer-songwriter Rod McKuen wrote "The Art of Catching Trains" for his verse collection *Lonesome Cities* (1968). Jimmy's recollections parallel, somewhat, those of McKuen, as young Rod jumped onto trains after school, when they slowed down at the trestles (or at whistle-stops to pick up the mail), and dove through an open boxcar door ("Then standing in the doorway you're the king / as crowns of hills and towns go by . . . "). (Jimmy, though, might not agree with McKuen that "Baseball's just a sissy game / to anyone who's waved at passing trains.")

So, as Jimmy had implied, Captain Buffett's legacy wasn't merely seamanship—or even storytelling—but traveling itself. For Jimmy, the entertainer's highway became his ocean, and the concert halls his safe harbor ports of call. (And Jimmy's wives might identify with his grandmother Hilda Seymour Buffett, whose captain husband was seldom in the home harbor.)

■　■　■

The Buffetts' move to Mobile had been motivated by J.D.'s boss at Ingalls, Paul Keith. He had left in disgust over flagging business in postwar Pascagoula. The Buffetts followed in Keith's path, straight to the Alabama Dry Docks and Shipyard.

Mobile City directories list J.D. as an "engineer," a "mechanic," and finally as a "supervisor." Peets is variously a "clerk," a "stenographer," and an "office secretary." Eventually she worked in labor relations at Addsco, as the company was called.

Addsco had started back in 1916. Mobile's "cotton dynasty" had collapsed, but a band of visionary businessmen pulled four separate companies together (two dry docks, an ironworks, and a boiler plant) into a consolidated whole. Cornering the market on ship repair, Addsco throve on the demands of World War I. Instantly it trained more than four thousand workers.

Despite the postwar reduction in business—followed by the 1930s'

Depression—Addsco became the foremost ship repair firm on the Gulf Coast. In World War II, it fixed more than two thousand ships which had been "either bombed or torpedoed with ferocious intent" by enemy ships and submarines.

After the war years, Addsco bought up equipment from the Navy and Marines and expanded into a 426-acre operation, complete with every service (carpentry, blacksmithing, pipe fitting, copper and sheet-metal welding, etc.). Its headquarters was on Pinto Island.

Mr. and Mrs. Buffett had a guaranteed career for the rest of their working lives.

■ ■ ■

If Jimmy's birthplace of Pascagoula had been a microcosm of the Gulf Coast, then Mobile was the macrocosm. Of Alabama's 362,000 acres of salt water, 252,000 acres constituted Mobile Bay. By 1975, it was the twelfth-largest seaport in the nation, and in the words of author Maureen Maclay, "a boundless wellspring of wonder," celebrated for its "history, natural beauty, and old-world charm. With its pristine beaches, miles of waterways, centuries-old live oaks, temperate climate, friendly people, and village-type atmosphere."

Like Pascagoula, over the years Mobile passed from lover to lover (France, Britain, Spain, and finally the United States—including its umbilically connected twin, the Confederacy). The French founded the city in 1702, and in 1704 the Bishop of Quebec dispatched a ship, the *Pelican*, with twenty-three girls from France, each equipped with a trunk called a *cassette*, containing their marital dowery. Termed the "Cassette Girls," they dutifully—and promptly—married the wedding-hungry men, "and soon there were new families in the town." (But in their Petticoat Rebellion, they staged perhaps America's first sit-down strike—squatting on their rears, in protest against "corn bread," till their husbands agreed to plant "French bread.")

By 1776, Mobile was in British hands, so when some covert copies of the Declaration of Independence began circulating from Virginia, the residents looked at the British bayonets and declined to buy a ticket to the American Revolution. Then the Spanish captured them in 1780, and finally, in 1813, U.S. General James Wilkinson seized Mobile in the War of 1812.

With six rivers converging in the bay, Mobile began flourishing as a cotton-trading seaport. Slavery was crucial to the town's economy (not to mention its social status—slaves helped masters get dressed in the morning!). Mobile had more than one thousand free blacks, who sometimes bought slaves themselves.

The city was boisterous and boozy. Historian Virginia Van der Veer Hamilton says to compare it "with her sister cities in Alabama is to liken a full-blown, worldly Creole courtesan to a group of prim, Anglo-

Saxon girls. Perhaps the prevailing breezes from the ocean helped to melt the ice of Puritanism as it seeped down from the north . . . travelers found Mobile distinctive by reason of a joyous, unbounded appetite for food and drink."

Jimmy told Arts and Entertainment television host Elliott Forrest in 1994 that "New Orleans is the only city in America that has a European feel to it." Well, Mobile itself used to invite exotic comparisons. In 1861 a British visitor called it

> the most foreign city I have yet seen in the States. After dinner, we walked through the city which abounds in oyster saloons, drinking houses, lager-bier and wine shops, and gambling and dancing places. The market was crowded with negroes, mulattoes, quadroons, and mestizos [racial mixtures] of all sorts, Spanish, Italian, and French, speaking their own tongues, or a quaint lingua franca, and dressed in very striking and pretty costumes.

Other British tourists commented on all the alcohol in Mobile. With grog shops on every corner, politicians made local election days festive days ("Why don't we get drunk and vote?") Jamaican rum was a staple, and yellow-fever epidemics were combated with claret and mint julep. Seacraft workers frequented "coffee saloons" for cakes and pies.

■ ■ ■

In early 1858, William Walker came to Mobile. Born in Nashville in 1824, he grew up about a block from the site of the Grand Ole Opry's Ryman Auditorium. Walker was a lawyer, a doctor, and a New Orleans (and San Francisco) journalist. He was also a perpetual south-of-the-border invader (Baja California, Sonora), and during one revolution, even became President of Nicaragua. Some of Walker's coconspirators were banished to Jimmy Buffett's future home of Key West; he himself was arrested at Mobile, but the charges were dropped. His book, *The War in Nicaragua,* was published there in 1860, the same year he invaded Honduras from Mobile. A firing squad canceled his career, but not before he converted to Catholicism.

Men like Walker were called *filibusters* (from the Dutch word for "freebooter"), and they used Nashville, Mobile, Natchez, and New Orleans for their invasions of Texas, Cuba, and points south. They were land pirates lusting for territory, not just gold.

With a slight stretch of language, we might term Jimmy Buffett a musical or literary filibuster, especially considering his novel *Where is Joe Merchant?*

■ ■ ■

The Civil War intervened, and ex-Pascagoulan Admiral David Farragut guarded Mobile Bay, uttering the immortal, "Damn the torpedoes! *Full speed ahead!*" The Confederates lost their ironclad *Tennessee,* but their admiral Raphael Semmes still managed to sink at least fifty-five Union ships. The Admiral Semmes Hotel opened in Mobile in 1940, and its Admiral's Corner lounge was where Jimmy pressed his solo performing career. Semmes himself was a popular nautical author—*Service Afloat and Ashore in the Mexican War* (1851) and *Memoirs of Service Afloat During the War Between the States* (1869), among others. He died across the bay at Point Clear in 1877, and is buried there in the Catholic cemetery (Jimmy's sister Lucy has lived at Point Clear).

■ ■ ■

After Mobile surrendered, Yankee and Rebel generals sat down together and drank champagne, toasting one another with typical Gulf Coast conviviality ("Why don't we get drunk and Reconstruct?").

Jimmy Buffett's Margaritaville restaurants, in Key West and New Orleans, had their predecessor in Festorazzi's post–Civil War coffeehouse on Royal Street, where marble-top tables supported the elbows of politicians and merchants. Observes Virginia Van der Veer Hamilton, "Mobilians combined a love of spicy repartee and an ability to laugh at themselves."

Jovial Mobile was something of an entertainment mecca, welcoming stars like actress Sarah Bernhardt—and Oscar Wilde, who arrived in 1882.

The Irish-born poet, already well-known for his "long hair, long legs, large teeth, dreamy posturing, singsong speech patterns, and arch cleverness," gave a lecture at the Mobile Theater. His pithy and subtle message was offset by his wild clothing and erratic vocal diction. Similar to Jimmy Buffett's Margaritaville merchandising, Wilde's performance had its own show *business* backup—hawking "Baker's cocoa, vanilla chocolate and Mack's milk and chocolate," as well as "handsome summer suits." Historians William Warren Rogers and Robert David Ward summed up Wilde's Mobile performance: "Alabamans, like other Southerners, admire courage, and it took courage to dress in outrageous costume and appear in public."

■ ■ ■

In the spring of 1994, Jimmy Buffett was spotted rolling down the street in Mobile on a Mardi Gras float. He was reportedly sponsored by the local mystic group, the Knights of Revelry (founded in 1874).

"He was there, trying to be low-key and have a good time—he was a joy to be around. I got to talk to him for a couple of minutes," recalls Trey Iturbe. "I asked him if he remembered my uncle from high school, and he did . . . Nelson Iturbe." Nelson Iturbe's wife, Beverly, says her seventeen-year-old teenaged daughter managed to shake Jimmy's hand.

The Mardi Gras has often been cited as the blueprint for Jimmy's own concert-tour career. New Orleans is the Mardi Gras's biggest home today. But the festivities still persist in Mobile, and for good reason. The Mardi Gras was born there—in 1704 on Twenty-Seven-Mile Bluff, up the Mobile River from the site of the city today. French colonist Nicholas Langlois instigated an eating-drinking-singing-dancing jubilation, led by around 250 masked revelers, whose faces had been painted red.

Their parade made hedonistic history. Such carnival masquerading was a paganistic spurt of wanton pleasure, eventually scheduled for the day before Ash Wednesday, the first day of Lent. (*Mardi Gras* is French for "Shrove Tuesday," or "Fat Tuesday.") Mardi Gras today starts weeks before Ash Wednesday, and has become a luscious feast of frolic, to be gobbled up before the virtuous Lenten famine sets in, when the pious diet of prayer and fasting inflicts the total abstinence of sensuality. Today's tourist attraction of Mardi Gras notwithstanding, originally it was not so much an orgy of ecstasy as a relief value pressed by the Gulf Coast working class to relieve their yearlong pangs of labor.

So the Parrot Head followers of Jimmy Buffett—in their gaudy colored shirts and feathered parrot masks—ought to tip their red, orange, or magenta baseball caps in obeisance to Mobile. After all, their distant ancestors were the Boeuf Gras Society of 1711, which used a giant bull's head to lead its procession. The bull's head lasted until 1830 (presumably preserved taxidermically!), when it was replaced by a papier-mâché substitute, shipped over from France. It took fifteen men to lift it.

When some paraders broke into a hardware shop in 1830 and stole some cowbells, this led to the "Cowbellions" mystic society. They were enticed over to New Orleans in 1852, and to this day, Mobilians claim *their* Mardi Gras is the more sincere, that New Orleans's bigger, bolder version is *just* for the tourists.

After the Civil War, an ex-Confederate named Joe Cain rode through town in a charcoal wagon, dressed like a Chickasaw Indian, urging people to shed their post–Civil War melancholy and renew their Mardi Gras devotion to public ecstasy. It worked. Balls, parades, and marching bands have made the Mardi Gras Mobile's biggest annual event. And the whole scenario is promoted by an amusing conspiracy of secret, mystic societies.

■ ■ ■

In 1948, the year the Buffetts arrived in Mobile, Peets was pregnant again. She returned to Pascagoula to deliver Loraine Marie Buffett on December 2.

In 1953 they sold their Ralston Road home, and that year lived in two apartments. One, 1800 Hunter Avenue (160 Stonewall Place today), number 162C, was a humble upstairs apartment—an eerie reminder of how far their son Jimmy has climbed on the ladder of life. They were living at 2704 Briley Street when Jimmy's second sister, Lucy Ann Buffett, was born on October 10, 1953.

In January 1954 they purchased an attractive brick house in the Sunset Hills subdivision, at 4623 North Sunset Drive. It lies to the east of University Boulevard, right below the University of South Alabama (where one day Peets would go back to school for an English degree), and near Spring Hill College, a Catholic school of considerable future importance to Jimmy Buffett.

The most recent owner of the house, Mary McKay, dug into the attic in 1994 and found some of Jimmy's high-school homework papers— *and* a copy of a 45 rpm single, "Abandoned on Tuesday," written and recorded by Jimmy on a forgotten label, Audio Mobile.

In Mobile, music is where you find it.

"Heroes and Crooks"

■

The six-stringed Spanish ancestor of the modern guitar, called the "vihuelas de mano" or possibly the four- or five-stringed guitar, could have been the first musical instrument in Mobile.

—"Was Guitar First Mobile Instrument?" *Mobile Press*, August 14, 1960

It was the worst time of my life. I was in school and I just hated school.

—Jimmy to Natt Yancey (Associated Press), *Chattanooga News Free Press*, March 30, 1975

Six String Music" is one of the stronger songs on Jimmy's 1994 *Fruitcakes* album. It ridicules the "crap" on television and recommends ignoring the telephone in favor of acoustic guitar picking, accompanied by singing.

But Jimmy's mother told Becky Gillette of *Mississippi* magazine that while he sang when he was very young, he stopped when he entered school "because he was very shy." In grammar school in Mobile, Jimmy played trombone—but "never even tried to sing in high school." His parents bought him a twenty-five-dollar guitar and lessons to go with it. "He probably doesn't even remember this," reflects Peets. "He only lasted a couple of weeks."

Yet Mobile's own musical tradition extended back to the arrival of

Spanish settlers, who discovered that the Creek, Choctaw, and Cherokee Indians used earthenware drums, gourd rattles, and reed flutes for their dances. Presumably the immigrants, in "the Golden Age of Spanish Music," knew the organ and lute music of their own home-country composers. On the Gulf Coast, slave chants, folk songs, and military music were the norm—and Catholic church music. The first mass in the Mobile vicinity was chanted in 1540. Researcher Frances Beverly speculates that while the Spanish probably "brought their guitars and other musical instruments," they most likely didn't use them since "the only damsels whom they met were the Indian squaws, and there was always a brawny Indian, handy with a bow and arrow, in the offing, so conditions were not conducive to music and romance."

Ultimately, Mobile's multicultural milieu absorbed various strains of European music: minuets, French ballet or opera, French (or Spanish) harpsichord, and—more in Jimmy's vein—English and Scottish folk songs such as "The Elfin Knight," "Barbara Allen," and "Hangman, Slack on that Line." (The latter resurfaced as "Hangman," with Jimmy's beloved group, the Kingston Trio, in 1961.)*

Jimmy always admired pirate Jean Lafitte, one of whose men lived near Mobile at Coden, and fiddled and played a "reed fife" to entertain the Creoles, the early settlers, and especially the fishermen.

Two of Jimmy's musical heroines are female troubadours Joni Mitchell and Marshall Chapman (a one-time Coral Reefer band member), so he might be amused to read that in Alabama "the guitar was the rage in the 1850s, and no young lady was considered 'accomplished' unless she could play 'The Spanish Fandango.' "

The Civil War period was, somewhat literally, a dead musical epoch— except for wedding ceremonies and funeral numbers. ("It was said that the very sound of the beating of a drum would send the women into hysterics.")

Mobile's progress into the modern musical age was conventional, and mostly classical, reinforced by colleges like Spring Hill, founded in 1830 and instigator of the Mobile Music Association. (Jimmy would marry a Spring Hill graduate, Margaret Washichek, who became a music-industry employee, and whose second husband is a Buffett ally to this day.)

■ ■ ■

Jimmy went to St. Ignatius grade school, in a large, two-story wooden house on Spring Hill Avenue at Tuthill Lane. Founded in 1952 by the Jesuits at Spring Hill College, it first enrolled 104 students. Additional buildings were constructed over the years.

---

* Standard entries in Francis James Child's authoritative *English and Scottish Popular Ballads* (1882–95).

Catholic education had begun in Mobile in 1833, when forty students enrolled under the Visitation Sisters. By 1851, an all-Creole Catholic school had been started (Creoles being a mixture of white, black, and sometimes Indian), but in Jimmy's schooldays, in the 1950s and 1960s, the classes were virtually all white. Catholics held back on integration because they feared they would lose their students, who might then migrate to the segregated public schools. They initiated, instead, black Catholic schools and black Catholic parishes. Catholic schools began integrating in the 1960s (and one white Mobile priest left his vocation to marry a black student).

Jimmy's interest in people—and not in their pigmentation—is exemplified by his performing with the Neville Brothers, and by his song "African Friend" (1978), about a black French-speaking Haitian with whom he gambles (and who says they had one *hell* of a good evening— it was truly their night to win).

■ ■ ■

Schoolboy Jimmy was intellectually sharpened by his mother. "She taught me that reading is the key to everything," he told Becky Gillette. "Reading as a child expanded my imagination, and when I grew up I looked at the literature I enjoyed the most, and asked why." In his song "Son of a Son of a Sailor," he claims to have read "dozens of books about heroes and crooks," and learned much from both.

What were the books?

"My mother used to make me read the classics," he said, such as Robert Louis Stevenson's *Treasure Island*—like millions of boys for over a century, Jimmy identified with hero Jim Hawkins. In fact, his *Margaritaville* movie script—which has never been filmed—is a musical comedy, a "*Treasure Island* updated, young Jim Hawkins." His other favorite book was Mark Twain's *Huckleberry Finn*. Both reinforced his feeling for water.

"I grew up on Mobile Bay," he told *Islands* magazine, "where the water was rather dull-looking and all the cypress trees around gave it a reddish color." So in his imagination, Jimmy fancied he was somewhere else—afloat on water clear and white, near sandy beaches. One day he would discover it for real, in Key West.

Who was his hero?

"When everybody else was studying generals and American war heroes, Jean Lafitte was my hero," Jimmy told Elliott Forrest. "Son of a Son of a Sailor" extols the venerable profession of smuggling—loading the last ton of contraband, "one step ahead of the jailer." Other kids were building plastic model battleships, but Jimmy was assembling a plastic version of Lafitte's *Black Falcon*. Pirates "looked a lot more adventurous than the people that lived in Sunset Hills in Mobile. . . . I think it just kindled that spirit that had always been there from my family heritage. We're all seamen." In "Son of a Son of a Sailor" the contemporary seafolk ride the wind that had carried their ancestors before them.

Speaking of Jean Lafitte to *Interview*'s Helen Bransford, Jimmy said, "I grew up in a seaport town with a rough waterfront . . . smugglers were always prevalent within that cultural system—only the contraband changed [from Civil War blockade running to Depression-era rum-smuggling to marijuana smuggling in the 1960s] . . . It was the life that few people ever lived or dared to live. There was something very romantic and swashbuckling about it. And there still is."

Indeed, one of the United States' Founding Fathers, John Hancock, whose signature was the biggest and boldest on the Declaration of Independence, had been accused by the British of smuggling wine, and he and his comrades burned a tax collector's boat, almost a case of piracy.

The new United States had banned the importing of slaves in 1808, so—as in Prohibition in the 1920s, this was a blessing to Gulf Coast smugglers. Jean Lafitte (born circa 1780) bought slaves for around a dollar a pound ($150 to $200), then sold them for $600 to $700 in New Orleans. He stiffly claimed that he was no "pirate," only a "privateer" or "corsair" (that is, a patriotic pillager of enemy ships). Known affectionately as a "gentleman smuggler" in New Orleans, Lafitte "wore a mustache now and then," according to his biographer, and was deemed an epicure. "He loved fine silver and fine appointments for his table and his home; and he loved to entertain." Of his stolen silks and linens, he kept the best for himself.

While Lafitte's pirate persona inspired young Jimmy, his entrepreneurial achievements ought to have earned the respect of the cagey, middle-aged merchant James William Buffett. The distant predecessor of Jimmy's New Orleans French Quarter Margaritaville store (One French Market Place) might be Lafitte's shop on Royal Street (between Bourbon and Chartres streets). Lafitte also ran a warehouse down in the swamps called the Temple, offering tariff-free goods at a discount—a kind of Byronic, buccaneer Wal-Mart. "Smuggling, as well as privateering," wrote historian Grace King, "had always been a regular branch of the commerce of Louisiana."

Lafitte's home base was Barataria Bay, a colony of homeless nautical brigands. The benevolent Lafitte helped his pirate guests fix the prices of their stolen goods, for mutual economic benefit. Lyle Saxon said that "while the men slept through those torrid afternoons, Jean Lafitte swung lazily in his hammock upon the veranda overlooking the Gulf. Sometimes he scanned the far horizon with the telescope which stood beside him." Lafitte was proud of his career, and of how his convivial, criminal community was prospering.

No one knows when (or how or where) Lafitte died. Pascagoulans—who like to think he was born there—love to dig (in vain) for his treasures. As for Jimmy, he and some friends would reenact the Battle of New Orleans at the E. R. Dickson schoolyard, and he would play the part of Jean Laffite.

■ ■ ■

Mobile afforded Jimmy ample excursion onto the water: "I sailed on just about everything," he told *Motor Boating and Sailing* magazine in 1982. "Stars, a Crosby Cat, yacht-club boats, you name it."Encouraging his watery wanderlust even more was the musical comedy *South Pacific,* as produced by the Catholic Theater Guild of Mobile. Jimmy was taking piano lessons at the time, when his teacher "played 'Bloody Mary' and sang 'Bali Ha' i' with a strong Southern accent." The mystique of the Tahitian island of Bora Bora haunted him ever after.

Jimmy gives credit to *South Pacific* in his "Walkabout" introduction to his book *Tales from Margaritaville.* The book itself is obviously inspired by James A. Michener's *Tales of the South Pacific* (1947), the source for *South Pacific.* Michener's book won a Pulitzer Prize for fiction, and though ostensibly a short-story assemblage, its interlocking tales have the effect (and reputation) of a novel. (To save money, the publisher started the next story on the same page where the last one ended, which helped create the "novel" image!) While the book was technically never a bestseller, its abridged, paperback version (Pocket Books, 1948) sold a nice two million copies.

Michener's life and career parallels Jimmy's, to an extent (and maybe his father's, grandfather's, and Uncle Billy's as well).

Like Jimmy, Michener grew up loving *National Geographic* magazine—and most coincidentally, in the "Mutiny" chapter of *Tales of the South Pacific,* he relived his World War II visit to Norfolk Island. There he saw "faded photographs of long-dead Christians, Buffets [sic]," as well as a petition signed by the same islanders stating that since God had brought them there, they wished to plant "an avenue of pine trees," and if they didn't "live to see them tall, our children will."

Michener also noted a white gravestone: "Adams Buffet Quintal, Aged 1 Yr."

South Pacific opened on April 7, 1949, at the Majestic Theater on Broadway, and lasted for 1,925 performances. Several songs from the show were recorded by pop artists and charted in *Billboard* ("Bali Ha' i" had five hit versions; "Some Enchanted Evening" had seven). In those days, songs were deemed more important than singers, and melodies the public cared about were more important than production technique.

Richard Rodgers said something with which every Parrot Head must agree: "Boys in the Navy are boys in the Navy, and there's not much that you can write for them except songs that are fun for them to sing."

South Pacific, then, is certainly one of the greatest seminal influences on Jimmy's performing career.

As for Michener, he was in Korea in 1952 when a *Life* magazine representative hunted him up. They wanted him to write a blurb for a new book that would be published in its entirety in one issue. It was Jimmy Buffett's future favorite, *The Old Man and the Sea* by Ernest Hemingway.

■ ■ ■

Jimmy's song "Life Is Just a Tire Swing" (1974) extolls the Hank Williams bayou classic "Jambalaya"—supposedly, it was the only song Jimmy could sing. He said he'd never been west of New Orleans, nor east of Pensacola—which rhymes with "RCA Victrola"—his only contact with the outer world. Noel Coppage of *Stereo Review* quoted Jimmy in 1974: "Hank Williams—I could sing a few of his songs."

But country music was largely for adults, with hard-hitting lyrics like "It Wasn't God Who Made Honky-Tonk Angels" (sung by Kitty Wells) and Hank Williams's generally morose numbers like "I'm So Lonesome I Could Cry." Jimmy told Noel Coppage: "You know what's weird? As a kid I loved Mitch Miller and the Mills Brothers. Loved those 'Sing Along with Mitch' albums, maybe just because I loved to sing." Ironically, Miller went to the sing-alongs out of disgust over the 1950s' rock 'n' roll cataclysm. (Rock wasn't "immoral," Miller said—just *monotonous*.)

Miller had been everywhere, almost, from big bands to Sinatra to Guy Mitchell. It was Mitch Miller who had rapport with Nashville's Fred Rose, getting Hank Williams songs into the throats of Columbia Records pop singers (Tony Bennett, Frankie Laine, Jo Stafford). Miller claimed to have witnessed the first "echo chamber"—a microphone dangled into a toilet bowl—and strove for a live effect, coming from the days of one-track recording. ("People had to know their business. If you didn't get it on the take you were doing, you had to throw it all out and do it again.") The best country music of yesteryear—and Jimmy Buffett to this day—sounds live even though recorded in the studio.

As for Hank Williams, he was called a "folk" artist in the trade publications. Other forms of folk music made their occasional appearance, though rarely on the radio. The left-wing labor movement (with communist connections) had fostered Woody Guthrie, and his friend Pete Seeger exerted leadership in a group called the Weavers. Their 1949 hit "Goodnight Irene" sold two million copies, written by the late Huddie Ledbetter, an ex-convict blues singer from Louisiana known as Leadbelly. (There were many other simultaneous chart versions, from Dennis Day's to Red Foley's with Ernest Tubb.) The Weavers were boycotted during the age of McCarthyism, but folk music kept popping up, as when Harry Belafonte's hit "Jamaica Farewell" was released in the fall of 1956.

Onstage, cutting his live *Feeding Frenzy* album in 1990, Jimmy followed "Margaritaville" with "Jamaica Farewell." He told the audience he wanted to take them "back to the beginnings," when he first heard the song and it "got me out of Mobile, Alabama. . . . Thank you, Harry Belafonte, I hope you like what we've done to your song."

"Margaritaville" itself is as Caribbean, and as singable, as "Jamaica Farewell." While not overtly derivative, still no song is closer to it. "Jamaica Farewell" moves forward with a gentle storyline and an unforgettably catchy chorus. Only weeks later, in early 1957, Belafonte's "Banana Boat (Day-O)" charted—as did numerous other versions. Both songs had been on his *Harry Belafonte—Calypso* album (1956), making him RCA's first million-selling album artist. Jimmy has often praised calypso music, yet Belafonte grumbled: "My two big records right now aren't calypso at all—even though everyone seems to have hung that tag on them. One is a West Indian ballad ["Jamaica Farewell"], the other is a West Indian work song ["Banana Boat (Day-O)"]." (A group called the Tarriers had liked Belafonte's album, and beat him to the charts with their "The Banana Boat Song" single.)

Calypso music itself had been born in the working fields of Trinidad— and World War II helped give it a beat, by supplying oil barrels, which became drums. In 1945 "Rum and Coca-Cola" was a calypso hit for three acts (Number One for the Andrews Sisters). William R. "Bill" Combs grew up at 4619 Sunset Drive next to the Buffett family. Speaking of his playmate Jimmy: "*He loved calypso*—he wore calypso pants when they were in style."

Alabama Altar Boy

■

*We are building schools so that our children may be lifted up to the
Kingdom of Grace.*

—Bishop Fulton Sheen, dedication speech, McGill Institute High
School, Mobile, October 29, 1952

My *God!* What does that do for
our children?" Jimmy asked onstage at the Marine Stadium in Miami
around 1985. He was introducing "We Are the People Our Parents
Warned Us About." And he answered his own question with "Let's find
out"—then lurched into the irreverent song. The lyrics laugh at how
his own parents hoped he would become a Jesuit priest—*or,* perhaps,
a Naval Academy graduate. He also introduced "Why Don't We Get
Drunk (and Screw)" as an "altar boy dream." (The whole show forms
his *Live by the Bay* video.)

While attending St. Ignatius grammar school, Jimmy had become an
altar boy at mandatory mass, held at the St. Joseph Chapel on the Spring
Hill College campus. Altar boys tend to enjoy their role—especially

when they get out of class to serve at a wedding or a funeral (and in the process, earn some token pocket change).

Catholic school children are required to perform modest charitable acts, from collecting donations for the needy to visiting the sick or unfortunate. Such experience over the years instills humanitarian benevolence into young hearts. Jimmy Buffett—composer of "My Head Hurts, My Feet Stink and I Don't Love Jesus" (1974)—has managed to obligate his over-sixty Parrot Head groups to charitable commitments. Whether helping the homeless or visiting nursing homes, the Parrot Heads *must* enact *some* regular good deeds . . . if they wish to get Saint Jimmy's blessing for their organization (and his sacred imprimatur on their newsletters!).

The St. Joseph Chapel was built in 1910, in the Gothic style of the Middle Ages. Fittingly, ex–altar boy Buffett would get married in the same Spring Hill chapel in 1969.

"He sang in the church as an altar boy," remembers former neighbor Bill Combs. "I was a Methodist," says Combs, but "he took me to an altar boys' picnic," where there were contests and games. "He said if I *won,* he would get *half* my prize. At one altar boy picnic, there was a place called Dead Man's Coffin, with a tub where you'd bathe off before you'd go swimming in the lake, which was so cold, you'd turn blue."

Catholics weren't supposed to eat meat on Fridays. "He came over to our house one Friday," says Combs. "We were eating hot dogs—he made himself *throw up.* He was *devout* about everything he did! For Lent, he would give up his Hershey bars for *forty days.*"

In 1955 Bill's uncle Gordon Wood came to Mobile, looking for a job. He had Jimmy wash his truck for him, and paid him twenty-five cents!

Bill's brother Bobby Combs remembers them hanging around the edge of golf courses and possibly stealing golf balls. But who can be sure? After all, it was around forty years ago! At least, Billy says, "I never heard him get into any kind of trouble. His father kept him under his thumb. . . . His mama took us to the [Mobile] Mardi Gras. The Buffetts would stay at the Battle House Hotel."

The Battle House Hotel is no longer open today. It stood on the site of Andrew Jackson's headquarters (1814), and the first version of the hotel was built in 1852. It burned down in 1905; the one where the Buffetts liked to stay was built in 1908. But from the nineteenth century forward, the Battle House was at the center of Mardi Gras festivities. Its ballroom was a showplace for celebrations by mystic societies; in 1935 it was built into a miniature Western town, so that an unmarried "Spinsters" act could ride around on their "Golden West" ponies.

In the 1940 and 1950s, the dance bands of Jan Garber, Guy Lombardo, Cab Calloway, and Duke Ellington appeared regularly in Mobile for the Mardi Gras, and "When the Saints Go Marching In" became Mobile's Mardi Gras theme song.

Jimmy's Mardi Gras holidays at the Battle House Hotel with the Combs brothers furthered his carnival education. As Mardi Gras memoirist Emily Staples Hearin remarks, a Mardi Gras parade "takes just three Mobilians—two to march, one to watch." The Battle House itself was undoubtedly a monumental model for Jimmy's later Margaritaville nightclub–restaurant–Parrot Head product establishments.

■   ■   ■

Billy Combs remembers that Jimmy came back to Sunset Hills around 1974 and "brought his bus into the neighborhood. It had a big sunrise painted on it." Pause. "Mobile didn't help him."

Jimmy's song "Saxophones" (on the 1974 album *Living and Dying in ¾Time*) complains about not getting airplay in Mobile for his acoustic recordings, whereas, if he'd had a saxophone on his songs, they might have played them.

More to the point was the overall snobbery in the higher quarters against popular music when Jimmy was growing up. Mobile's music historian Robert Allen Kennedy in 1960 conceded that while "harmonica, guitar, and barbershop quartet music is far better than no music at all," it just might lead the listener to "a more respectable kind of art music"—that is, classical music. He quoted historian Francis Butler Simkins, who condemned "the musical shortcomings of the Southern people . . . [their preference for] ragtime, jazz, and hillbilly tunes. The jukebox with its raucous rhythms attained undisputed dominion over the dance halls, and the radio became supreme in the home. Radio programs originating in Southern stations were invariably of an inferior order." Simkins decided that the South's "culture was too rustic and new" to develop an urbane, sophisticated musical milieu.

Meanwhile, Elvis Presley was gradually winning Jimmy over with his 1958 New Orleans movie, *King Creole*. Jimmy eventually began performing there. "I think it was all Elvis's fault," he told Elliott Forrest, "'cause I remember the scene from *King Creole* when Elvis comes down Bourbon Street and the crawfish lady's singing. I knew at that point I wanted to go to New Orleans and I wanted to sing and live in New Orleans." The film was directed by Michael Curtiz, who had done *Casablanca* (Humphrey Bogart and Ingrid Bergman), and fittingly, Elvis (as Danny Fisher) is opposed in New Orleans by gangster Maxie Fields, played by Walter Matthau. New Orleans is historically noted for its venerable Mafia heritage. In this turbulent Fifties period, with actor James Dean dead (and Buddy Holly and numerous other entertainers eventually dead or maimed in their rock 'n' roll odysseys), Elvis Presley was a surviving rebel *with* a cause. The cause was *music*—music of irrepressible country origins with a blues beat, served up to teenagers everywhere—including thirty-five chart records on black rhythm-and-blues radio through 1963.

■ ■ ■

There's a recurring rumor that Jimmy was once kicked out of high school. Brother Victor (Brothers of the Sacred Heart) pooh-poohs this. He was Jimmy's counselor and English teacher at the Catholic boys' school McGill Institute. "He had all male teachers, very, very strict. I *still* have people coming and asking me, '*When* was he kicked out of school?' It kind of gets on my nerves, and I say, 'What are you talking about? He was the most meek, mild person you'd want to meet.' A little bitty guy, you know, and he'd always keep his hair crew-cut. He never gave any trouble to anybody, because those guys were afraid of the Brothers, anyway. When the Brothers said 'Frog,' they *hopped*.

"I can say this right off the top—he was a very modest, a very humble person. Always interested in the water—surfing and stuff like that. He came from a very pure and devout Catholic family." (In 1994 Brother Victor was still having a monthly lunch with Peets and J.D. Buffett in a local restaurant.) "I think Jimmy is still strong in his faith, even though he may not be a practicing Catholic."

Jimmy does list his religion as Catholic in *Who's Who in America*. Says Brother Victor, "I'm sure he puts down 'Catholic' anytime he's asked to. I know a lot of people who don't *practice* their religion— which means they don't go to church every Sunday, or holy days—but in their hearts they believe in the main tenets of the Catholic Church."

Brother Victor acknowledges Jimmy's sometimes flippant reactions to the nuns and priests of his boyhood schooldays. He cited "Grapefruit— Juicy Fruit" from his *A White Sport Coat and a Pink Crustacean* album (1973), where at the drive-in, a couple guzzles some gin, then commits a mortal sin, in a nice rhyming triplet.

"We all go through a period where we drop our faith," Brother Victor concedes, "and some of us have a schedule and some of us don't. We *were* a little hell fire and damnation—maybe too much of it at the time. We were preaching more from *fear* than love. Then after Vatican II [1962–65], a lot of people were leaving the convents and the monasteries because they realized the fear tactics were not the right way to go about it.*

"It should be more of the love tactic. That's what the New Testament is all about. The Old Testament is about fear and not love. Jesus uses the Old Testament to build on, as a foundation."

---

* Vatican II modernized the Church, discarding its mandatory Latin Mass; permitting meat on Fridays (cheeseburgers were no longer in purgatory); allowing women to go without hats and veils when attending mass; encouraging folk-style acoustic guitar music in church; and—most important to the Parrot Heads—asking Catholic laypeople, in the pews, to provide clothing, food, and lodging to the less fortunate. A folk song flourished (echoing Jesus from Matthew 25:40) with the lyrics "Whatsoever you do to the least of my brothers, that you do unto me."

Brother Victor says Jimmy sent him copies of his two adult books. And while Jimmy is mostly restrained and polite, "he can get his ire up when he needs to. I've seen him at concerts get really upset with the drunk kids who get up onstage. He controls the crowd. . . . He turned forty-eight this Christmas [1994], and he sends word to me that he's growing old, and here I am . . . *sixty-six!*"

He remembers that Margie Washichek graduated from the all-girl Bishop Toolen High School across the street from McGill. In 1958 the high-school bands were combined, then in 1973 the schools themselves consolidated as McGill-Toolen. McGill had been founded in 1896 to provide education for poor boys and to win them over to the priesthood. The present institution was founded in 1952.

Brother Victor also notes that next door to McGill was St. Mary's Parish, where Father Abram Ryan, "the poet-priest of the South," was once a pastor (1870–78). Earlier, Father Ryan had preached at St. John's in Edgefield, today's east Nashville, site of Holy Name Church. Jimmy lived in east Nashville, circa 1970–71, and recorded later at the Woodland Sound Studio.

Father Ryan was something of an entertainer—two thousand people might show up to hear him preach, and he traveled widely. His book *Poems*(1879) went through forty editions. He had been a freelance Confederate chaplain who had rescued Confederates *and* Unionists wounded or dying on the battlefields.

Nashville's Father Ryan High School was near some of Jimmy's favorite early-Seventies locales: his performing venue, The Exit-In, Elliston Place Soda Shop, and Rotier's Restaurant, which Jimmy likes to advertise from the stage at Starwood Amphitheatre when he performs in the Nashville area.

■   ■   ■

"We developed some talent up there," recalls Mark Will, one of Jimmy's McGill teachers. "He was a junior and we were in the penthouse above the top floor of the school. That's where the art department was, and I taught him mechanical drawing and art. He's creative, let's face it. And that's a good atmosphere to work in, and to nurture that ability in an art course. That part of your brain is already working, so it's natural to explore that end of it.

"He brought his guitar several times up to the art room," Mark Will adds. "We were able to hear his presentations." (Elvis Presley had also performed with his guitar at a high-school talent show in Memphis—and at the homeroom picnic in Overton Park he would perform . . . mostly for himself.)

"He was a cheerleader in high school," remembers Chuck O'Brien, one of his friends when they were sixteen to eighteen years old. "Margie [Washichek] was a cheerleader, also." Cheerleading may be the best possible training for an entertainer—Grand Ole Opry star Skeeter ("The End of the World") Davis was a cheerleader in Dry Ridge, Kentucky ("I was a much better cheerleader than I am a singer"). Cheerleader Jimmy is portrayed in a *Parrot Head Handbook* picture.

O'Brien lived at Point Clear on Mobile Bay, a resort center since the nineteenth century, when city folk would ride steamboats across the bay, dancing in the moonlight to the ship's orchestra. A former Civil War hospital became a super-social center, the Grand Hotel, where Chicago millionaires would come, oblivious to the Confederate flag flying high overhead. Speaking of Point Clear, "Jimmy's parents used to rent a house every summer," says O'Brien. "Mobile Bay—no addresses. One side of the road is woods, one side is houses."

He remembers Jimmy's music: "He bought himself a twelve-string guitar and only learned himself one song, 'Tom Dooley.' He would sit on the wharf and start playing that one song."

Twelve-string guitars sound superficially good, with all the harmonic strings, but they're hard to play well and especially to record. The first twelve-stringer of note was Huddie "Leadbelly" Ledbetter—but he never charted a song on the radio himself.

As for "Tom Dooley," it was a sanitized version of "Tom Dula." Dula, a Confederate war hero, was hanged on May 1, 1868, in Iredell County, North Carolina, for murdering "a discarded sweetheart," Laura Foster. Supposedly she had infected him with venereal disease, which he passed on to her successor, mistress Ann Melton. According to an earlier version of "Tom Dooley," he picked his banjo before the hangman's rope simultaneously cured his genital ailment and his psychic guilt.

Ninety years and six months after Dula's final performance (which netted two news stories and two songs), in November 1958, "Tom Dooley" went to Number 1 for the Kingston Trio. Their primitive, impassioned singing—and eclectic instrumentation—gave them the success the Weavers had missed due to Pete Seeger being blackballed for his politics. Scholars were fond of snubbing the Kingston Trio, forgetting that folk music, like any other music, is going to be shaped and bent to fit the market.

The hyperflexible Trio could shift from Irish ballads to country music, from Mexican to Caribbean. Members Bob Shane and Dave Guard grew up in Hawaii. Shane's father was a Hawaiian distributor of toys and sporting goods; Guard's was a civil engineer and an Army Reserve colonel. In college they met Nick Reynolds, born in San Diego (like Frank Bama of Jimmy's *Where Is Joe Merchant?*), whose naval-captain dad brought home "the songs of the lands in which his ship had made port." He played guitar, so the captain and his kids staged what Reynolds called "international family songfests." When Reynolds got married, he and his wife lived in a houseboat and could water-ski off their front porch. Their publicist, Frank Werber, had escaped with his parents from a Nazi concentration camp, and sneaked from Marseilles to Martinique, hidden in a French fishing boat.

The Trio had studied the right subject in college: not music, but *business* (like Garth Brooks). Folk purists detested the Kingston Trio for bringing so much pure fun to their audiences and making so much pure money. By 1959, they'd sold eight million records, and their collegiate crew-cuts and buttoned-down collars reaped them disdain from the Greenwich Village crowd that worked for pass-the-hat tips and maybe ten dollars a night. Robert Shelton said the market became "glutted with folk music that was distorted, hoked-up, disguised, and distorted." Even John Stewart, who replaced Dave Guard in the Trio, admitted they fueled themselves with cocktails before facing an elitest audience at Greenwich Village's Folk City: "It terrified us. These were people who thought we were bullshit and in many cases were right." As an anticipation of Jimmy's commercialism, Stewart says, "There was always a rivalry of us defending 'good-time' folk music and them defending serious folk music." But Jimmy's next role model, Bob Dylan, confessed: "Yeah, it was the Trio who got me started."

The Kingston Trio charted seventeen *Billboard* singles from 1958 to 1963 (and nineteen Top 40 albums by 1964). Like Jimmy, they had the right formula: *music, water* (they collected songs in Tahiti), and *money.*

Gulf Coast Collegiate

■

I was not a good student, I didn't have much school spirit—I was there because I had to be, because if I wasn't there they were going to send me to Vietnam because I was so bad.

—Jimmy to Marcia Hill, *Our Finest Hour: Great Mississippians* (WLOX-TV), Biloxi, Mississippi, October 1, 1989

I grew up on the water near Mobile Bay. It always has been the most relaxing place and it's where I write the best," Jimmy told Johnny Carson on the *Tonight Show* on May 5, 1981.

But Pascagoula was still his home, too. In "Life is Just a Tire Swing," he reminisces about going off to summer camp with his cousin Baxter, from Pascagoula, and sleeping in a pup tent with a lamp. (The site was Camp Graveline at Bellefontaine, a tiny town on the old Grenada Trail founded in the 1840s.) He also recalled eating Easter dinner with his "crazy old uncle and aunt"—Billy Buffett and his wife. He told Noel Coppage in 1974 that "Aunt Coo was just nuts. She died of some incurable brain disease, and my uncle, he was an alcoholic." In the song,

Jimmy mentions their antebellum house "across the old bayou," and he has said that after his aunt's death, Uncle Billy sold their mansion for "like, four cases of Budweiser and a fifth of wine."

"Is Uncle Billy a renegade?" asked television interviewer Marcia Hill in 1989.

"Absolutely" was the answer. (Uncle Billy died on October 26, 1991.)

"My childhood was spent on the Gulf Coast," Jimmy told her. He had come back to Pascagoula in the spring of 1989 to attend his grandmother's funeral, and as he drove around town, he realized that Mississippi "will always be home. . . . I went out to the cemetery, and I drove around—and my secretary was with me—and it was the first time I had gone off the beaten path . . . and it *lit up* some real memories of childhood."

"Are you sentimental about Mississippi?" asked Hill.

Jimmy said he basked in the "the aura of being a Southern writer," while laughing sardonically about Mississippi being "the whipping-state of the nation," thanks to its racism. He had to "sort of defend being from there. . . . People always thought of Southern people as being so colloquial and so localized. And it's just not true.*

"I could not envision myself living away from the water," Jimmy told Marcia Hill. "It's part of my makeup. All those anthropological studies that say that coastal, Neanderthal men were of a gentler breed than the meat hunters and the trackers—'cause the ocean provided everything for them, you didn't have to go out and kill to live. I think it all probably goes back to that. Coastal people *are* a gentler people—it's a wonderful, warm kind of existence. And I don't know many people that wouldn't take two weeks and go to the beach, anywhere. . . . And being able to grow up on the Gulf Coast—I've traveled all over the world and it's still a very special spot. There's not many places like it. There are some interesting places that come close. But it's a very unique place—it's a real part of my heritage."

"Just growing up here, everyone knows he is from here," comments Curtis Rockwell, photographer and sports editor for Pascagoula's *Mississippi Press*, "just knowing that someone who made it big, just might have done the same things that you did." (Rockwell has enjoyed dozens of Buffett concerts.)

"You've got water everywhere," says Rockwell, "and water's just *in* you, if you're down here. You just try not to have the water inbred in

---

* "There's an old saying about how, when you enter Mississippi, you should set your watch back 100 years," joked journalist Joe Rogers in 1995. "Make that 130 years." Mississippi-born Rogers, writing for *The* [Nashville] *Tennessean,* was amused that the Mississippi legislature was finally planning to ratify the Thirteenth Amendment to the U.S. Constitution—outlawing slavery—in February 1995. (Back in the 1980s they had been preoccupied with trying to adopt the Nineteenth Amendment of 1920, granting women their voting rights.)

you. When I went to college, I wasn't 'Curtis from the Coast,' I was 'from the Coast and I was Curtis.' You get infatuated with the Coast life down here."

Indeed, at the start of his high-school senior year in 1963, Jimmy sat down by the water and wrote an amusing, aquatic essay titled "My Fatal Mistake." He confessed to a "silly and stupid" mishap that was simply killing him! On Labor Day he and some friends had wanted to go water-skiing . . . then noticed that their boat had several holes in the bottom. So Jimmy went over to the marina, looked for some plastic wood—but mistakenly bought rubber cement instead. Predictably, his patchwork repair job was blown out by the water and the boat capsized, so he and his pals had to sit waiting for the Coast Guard to rescue them from their "unsinkable" craft!

■ ■ ■

Even before college, Jimmy kept trying to play music. Nelson Iturbe recalls, "I remember in high school, Jimmy would bring his guitar to school. He would be by himself, just composing, picking on his guitar. His music's unbelievable."

As Jimmy told Noel Coppage, "There was nothing before music but school. I *hated* high school. It was the most miserable time of my life." He expounded to Mobile journalist Natt Yancey in 1975, "For the majority of people, the best time of their life was high school. They had the big fling, the proms, and the class favorites, and then it was gone. They hit the rut at about twenty-five."

In 1964 Jimmy was graduated from McGill Institute. Onstage in New York City in 1981, he alluded to his Alabama upbringing on the "redneck Riviera," where his "Catholic school was responsible for *everything*." The audience exploded with applause. "Having spent fifteen years in those places, I couldn't wait to make up for lost time." More, extended applause.

In the same month of his graduation, on June 21, 1964, three civil-rights workers—Andrew Goodman, Michael Schwerner, and James Chaney—arrived in Philadelphia, Mississippi, outraged by a Negro church burning. Since one of them was black and another one Jewish ("nigger-lovin' Jewboy"), they were tossed in the local jail, then released. Forty-four days later they turned up murdered. The convicted killers received modest sentences, and several others indicted were acquitted. The film *Mississippi Burning* (1988), starring Gene Hackman and Willem Dafoe, is a macabre melodrama of these Mississippi misfortunes.

■ ■ ■

That fall Jimmy enrolled at Auburn University in Auburn, Alabama, and stayed in the Plainsman Apartments. Years later, the resident manager told Nelson Williams and some other followers that Jimmy "lived like a bum in his apartment. He was always smoking dope, always drinking beer, and never went to class. And always playing his guitar, late at night." Williams and his friends answered, "You know, this guy is famous now."

The manager didn't believe them. "Uh-uh. This guy was a *bum*."

Auburn was founded in 1836. One of its pioneers' girlfriends had been reading Oliver Goldsmith's eighteenth-century poem "The Deserted Village" and urged him to name it after "Sweet Auburn, loveliest village on the plain." The Methodists established East Alabama Male College in 1856. It closed for five years during the Civil War, but Confederate General James H. Lane, youngest brigadier general in the war, taught at Auburn later. It became coeducational in 1892.

Jimmy's mother told Becky Gillette that "Auburn is where he learned to play guitar," which Jimmy confirmed: "Women are more attracted to guys with guitars than guys with typewriters." In his *Interview* interview, Jimmy said that he was a shy altar boy, devoted to skin-diving and sports. At a social event, all his fellow fraternity "pledge swaps" sat around and "scratched their asses"—but the girls all kept their distance, while haughtily straightening their brassieres. The only classmate to win their attention was Johnny Youngblood, and he earned that with his guitar. He explained to Jimmy that all it took to entice a girl was just three chords. "Teach me," pleaded Jimmy. "And that was the start of my professional career. For no other reason than to meet girls." Three weeks later he was entertaining the girls with G, C, and D.

Of course, he had already begun picking in high school, but he played enough at Auburn to change his college priorities. "He flunked out," his father said, beaming, to Becky Gillette, but his mother amended: "He was on academic probation when he left."

Jimmy himself set the record straight on April 18, 1979, telling an Auburn concert crowd (dressed in Hawaiian shirts and straw hats) that "I left here with a .32 overall, and I haven't been back since." At least he earned a nice, honorary, postgraduate headline: AFTER FLUNKING OUT IN '64, BUFFETT GETS HIGH MARKS FROM AUDIENCE." Journalist Ford Risley said, "We can only hope, as Buffett said, that it will not be another fifteen years until he returns to Auburn again."

When Jimmy came back and performed at Auburn Coliseum on January 25, 1990, fraternity brothers Tom Hackett and Troy Teal fueled themselves with margaritas, then yelled across the street at some girls, who shouted back, "Get away from us!" So they ran across the street, pulled the girls to the concert—and one of them, named Karen, married Tom Hackett in 1993. For the Hacketts, Jimmy's annual concerts in Atlanta are a kind of "mini-anniversary."

At least Jimmy Buffett's legacy to Auburn is social, if not scholastic.

■ ■ ■

"I had flunked out of school earlier—Auburn—and I had been banished to Poplarville [Mississippi] and gone to Pearl River [Junior College]," Jimmy told Marcia Hill in 1989. "And I said, 'Hell, I'm going to join the Navy or the Army, and get out of here. *I'm useless.*' Just about that time, I started playing music . . . and it probably saved my life."

The tiny logging town of Poplarville had been home of the colorful politician—and dedicated Southern racist—Theodore Bilbo. Pecan orchards and "tung" trees characterized Poplarville (the latter supplied oil from its nuts). The tung trees' white blossoms have a Chinese look to them.

But a mere six years before Jimmy moved to Poplarville, in 1959, a young black man had been accused of rape and was locked in the city jail. Then a lynch mob dragged him from the jail and shot him to death on a bridge near Bogalusa, Louisiana. Civil-rights historians Seth Cagin and Philip Dray say that the lynchers included a former deputy sheriff and a preacher, and that virtually everyone knew who they were. *Nothing was done about it.* In June 1964, the black defense attorney for the lynched man was speaking at Oxford, Mississippi, and in the evenings the civil-rights workers played their guitars and sang the newly fashionable "freedom songs." Weeks later, the FBI forces would be searching Pearl River for the bodies of three missing civil-rights workers.

■ ■ ■

Jimmy rented a room at the home of Hal and Ruby Breland, on old Highway 11 within the city limits of Poplarville. Jim Wetzel, a friend of Jimmy's mother, checked out the apartment one Sunday, and Jimmy moved in the very next day. The Brelands' son, James Hal Breland, was only fifteen and was enchanted with his parents' new tenant.

"He had a six-string and a twelve-string," James Breland recalled. "He would get tired of the six-string and would pull out the twelve-string. He took turns playing each one. He would play all the time—up to and including three o'clock in the morning. That's when Dad would get upset and come down the hall. He would play all the time back then."

His father, Hal Breland, confirmed this: "I wanted to throw him out of the house on many a night—"

"But I wouldn't let him," interrupted Mrs. Breland.

Hal Breland laughed. "Oh God, he'd be back there and me trying to sleep at two and three o'clock in the morning. He be picking on a guitar, playing 'When My Sailboat Comes Sailing In.' He used to pick on that thing *all* night long, back then, and I'd give him fits."

"He was pleasant, and was a good boy," added Mrs. Breland. "I would go in and listen to him and encourage him. It was so pretty, his playing and his talent. It would be his own songs. He'd write on his tablet. Then he'd go a little further, and I'd say, 'Oh, that's *pretty*, Jimmy, that sounds *so* good.' . . . He would laugh a lot, silent-like."

Their son remembers that when Jimmy was at the library studying, he would hurry home to watch his favorite television show—*Batman*. "When the weekends came around, he'd hit the road. No telling where he went when he left. . . . He always wore Hush Puppies, he loved those Hush Puppies. He had to hoof it; he didn't have a car. What dating he did do, we'd let him use our car.

"He'd have friends over, and sometimes they'd get a little rowdy—Dad would have to straighten them out. He used to sing all the time. He would have all the kids in the neighborhood. He'd sit on the back swing—they'd all come in to listen to it. The one he'd sing quite a lot was 'Where Have All the Flowers Gone?'"

That song had gone to Number 21 for the Kingston Trio back in 1962. Written by Pete Seeger, it was reminiscent, slightly, of the sad soldier-poems of the late Victorian poet A. E. Housman. Like a good short story, it ended where it had begun, amid the flowers, which initially the girls had picked for their soldier boyfriends, and which ultimately decorated the soldiers' graves. The song came true for around 58,000 soldiers of Jimmy's generation.

Pete Seeger had been stationed in Biloxi, Mississippi, in 1943, as an Army private at Keesler Field. In 1956 he was harried by the House Committee on Un-American Activities, for refusing to answer Commie folk queries, and for some reason, the phrase "long time passing" bubbled up in his troubled brain. Five or six years later it blossomed into "Where Have All the Flowers Gone?"

In July 1963, Seeger was in Greenwood, Mississippi, with Bob Dylan, performing in a field with hundreds of "freedom fighters." In August of the following year, he was in Hattiesburg, Mississippi. Black and white civil-rights workers were mad at each other, and local white racists were adding fuel to the flames. Then Seeger unslung his guitar and "brought a truce. . . . Everyone sat down together." The next day in Meridian, Mississippi, in the middle of his concert, someone handed him a note announcing that the bodies of the civil-rights workers—Goodman, Schwerner, and Chaney—had been found in a swamp. Seeger began singing about a "healing river," whose water would "wash the blood / From our sand." That summer, thirty-five black churches were bombed or burned, for supposedly good reason—Mississippi blacks were daring to vote.

Like Jimmy, Pete Seeger had hoped to be a journalist, but settled for music instead. He wore colorful stage clothes (aqua and tangerine) and, like Jimmy, entertained a concert cult following in lieu of radio listeners (he was blacklisted). Seeger also ferreted out Caribbean music and, like

Jimmy, eventually became an environmentalist (cleaning up the Hudson River with the help of singer-songwriter Don McLean).

In 1966 Jimmy himself went to Hattiesburg. He enrolled in the University of Southern Mississippi—or "Southern," as it is affectionately called. Why? Because a fellow musician, Doug Duncan, went there. So did Duncan's girlfriend, Susie Pittman. Already the three of them had formed a little folk group trio, to play on the weekends while Jimmy was at Pearl River. Now up at Southern, the trio wore "navy blue shirts and matching belts and ascots," Jimmy told journalist Frederick Burger in Palm Beach, Florida, in 1979, in an unpublished interview. "We played little fraternity things and coffee houses in Mississippi at this time."

From Kappa Sigma
to Trader John's

■

Honey, life's just a great big piano, and everybody's playing his own little tune.

—black servantwoman's philosophy embraced by Hattiesburg college girls in the 1920s

The Choctaw Indians surrendered four million acres east of the Pearl River in 1805. By 1830 President Jackson was antagonizing the Chickasaws into leaving Mississippi. (God bless Caucasian America!)

After the Civil War, New South railroading brought in the pioneers. The site called Gordonville—75 miles north of the Gulf Coast, 90 miles south of Jackson, 105 miles north of New Orleans—became Hattiesburg. It started as a railroad depot, then became a town in 1884. It was named for Hattie Lott Hardy, wife of the founder, lumberman Captain William H. Hardy.

Hattiesburg, on the "longleaf pine belt," became a lumber and railroad town, and industrial plants balanced its economy as well, creating a "noisy factory district, from which rise the pungent odors of turpentine and cut pine." The town has grown from a population of 240 to 40,000 in over a century.

Jimmy's alma mater, the University of Southern Mississippi, descended from Mississippi Normal College, a teachers' school founded in Hattiesburg in 1910. When the board of trustees met for a banquet that year, their menu included "lake shrimp cocktail" and "baked snapper turtle." Pigs even had their place on campus—the college paper in 1920 declared that swine were "an accepted institution," and students would be "lonesome without their presence and their cheerful grunts." The school president managed to ban cigarettes (he himself was a tobacco chewer and spitter). And the school's female literary society was determined *not* to create "a band of cultivated freaks," but to foster ladies loyal to the Old South—and ready for the New. In nice, quaint anticipation of Jimmy's hippie sixties, in the 1920s the humorous Bolshevik Club voted to stop the campus cooks from "washing the mackerel before serving, since water destroys its greatest quality—fragrance." A bizarre women's pageant of over three hundred girls, dressed up as birds and rabbits, was filmed and shown as an advertisement for the school.

In the 1930s, the school president decreed that "academic training without manhood or womanhood is worthless," and touted "a high standard of morality" for the students. Not until 1940 was "legalized dancing" permitted at the college—"with grace and rhythm and in every respect in good taste."

Interestingly, by the 1950s Mississippi Southern College offered courses in radio. Recreation on campus in the Fifties included Sadie Hawkins Day dances, and good ol' panty raids. The music department flourished, flaunting a nationally famous girl dance troupe, the Pride and Dixie Darlings—the same department that would rebuff Buffett in the 1960s.

The times changed in many ways. Jimmy often jokes about his Hattiesburg shoplifting escapades commemorated in his "Peanut Butter Conspiracy" song (1973). Back in 1959 a black student, Clyde Kennard, had tried unsuccessfully to enroll—later he was imprisoned for stealing three sacks of chicken feed, and died in prison. In 1962 Governor Ross Barnett raised Southern from its college status to university status. Barnett was a fervid Mississippi racist. That same year Barnett opposed black enrollee James Meredith at the University of Mississippi ("Ole Miss"), till thousands of federal troops escorted Meredith, whose enrollment cost two lives. The next year, his pal Medgar Evers was shot to death in his own driveway. In 1964 Forrest County (including Hattiesburg) had a sixty-seven percent black population—but only *one percent* black registered voters.

In 1965, the year before Jimmy entered Southern, two blacks were admitted without any ruckus. (But downtown, White Knight racists firebombed the home of civil-rights leader Vernon Dahmer, who responded with his shotgun, then died from fire in his lungs.)

■ ■ ■

Jimmy entered in 1966, and his ultimate double major was history and public affairs (journalism).

He joined the Epsilon Nu chapter of the Kappa Sigma fraternity. This college-boy society was founded in 1869 at the University of Virginia at Charlottesville. Today Kappa Sigma has more than 250 chapters, and around 185,000 members. National Kappa Sigma "Men of the Year" include journalist Lowell Thomas (Lawrence of Arabia biographer), newscaster Edward R. Murrow, former U.S. Senator from Tennessee Estes Kefauver, songwriter-pianist Hoagy Carmichael ("Stardust"), and former U.S. Senator Robert Dole. As late as 1992, Kappa Sigma advised its pledges that "certainly cutoffs and sweatshirts do not coincide with many people's image of a true gentleman—nor do seven-inch-wide ties that match your purple shoes." Yet in the same book appeared a picture of Jimmy at the Kappa Sigma house—as well as three pages of instructions on how to tie a necktie.

■ ■ ■

Television interviewer Marcia Hill says that Jimmy "admits academics *weren't* a priority." Jean Prescott, journalist for the Biloxi *Sun-Herald*, confirms this assessment: "All Jimmy wanted to do was noodle around with that guitar, and he didn't care much about going to school. Not that he was a bad student, but it just wasn't that important to him."

One of Jimmy's classmates told her an anecdote from around 1966. He had gone into the student union right before Thanksgiving. "There was this empty student union and the last people were leaving for the holidays, and the only person in there was Jimmy, sitting on the stage, not sitting on a chair on the stage—nothing but a six-inch riser—just sitting there apparently writing songs on the guitar. Because he wasn't performing somebody *else's* tune. He was in there alone, and may have stayed the whole holiday alone, but he was also great for hitchhiking up and down Highway 49."

Jimmy told Marcia Hill, "I was a complete social outcast in Hattiesburg. . . . Ha-ha. . . . Why are you laughing at that?"

"Why doesn't that surprise me?" retorted Hill.

Jimmy told her that one year he spent more time in New Orleans and Biloxi, Mississippi, than he did at school. "I took night classes two or three days a week, and I was working on weekends. By that time, I had been bitten by the music bug and I was performing. I started out doing my first show in Biloxi—years ago, when it was a folk club."

"That was where his first shot was, working for me," remembers Jake Mladinich, retired owner of Trader John's at Biloxi. Mladinich knew

Jimmy's father when "he worked for the Mississippi Power Company and they lived in Moss Point, Mississippi, about twenty-six miles east of Biloxi"—apparently an interim job during an Ingalls employment hiatus.

Biloxi had been a recreational town for many decades. The Federal Writers' Projects in the 1930s called Biloxi a shrimp and oyster paradise, with "sunshine on blue-green water, white sands, and tall green longleaf pines," whose cosmopolitan, romantic immigrants (Poles, Austrians, Czechs, Yugoslavians) thrived on the summer fun of boating, swimming, racing, and dancing. The local clubs offered free admission to the ladies and free beer for everyone at election time, and the residents played "almost as much as the tourists." Jean Prescott contrasts Biloxi's coastal conviviality with the inland territory: "Even today, you go ten miles north of the Interstate, I-10, and it's like you're on a different planet. It's almost outback, redneck, or white trash as they come."

Remembers Jake Mladinich: "I owned several nightclubs, and restaurants and hotels. Trader's [Trader John's] was all 'folk' in those days, what we called 'folk music.'"

Mladinich had seen, or rather heard, it all.

Back in the Fifties, someone had phoned from Nashville, seeking help for a stranded, broke musician named Elvis Presley. Mladinich hired him to play at his Fiesta club, but the older clientele disliked Presley, so he moved on to other venues. Eventually Mladinich's friend, actor Robert Mitchum, told "Colonel" Tom Parker, a music manager up in Madison, Tennessee, about Presley, and Parker got Presley signed to RCA records.

Jean Prescott says that back in the Fifties, club owners in "dry" Biloxi would pay $250 for illegal liquor licenses, and then "you would get a telephone call forty-eight hours in advance that the feds were coming and you would lock all your good stuff up." Clubs would close for six days, then reopen: "So they kept the preachers happy—and they also kept the people on the Coast, that wanted to drink and gamble, happy."

Numerous Gulf Coasters recall how hard the Mafia worked to provide alcohol, gambling, and other recreation. These modest Sicilians seldom get their deserved credit from regional historians. The Mafia always did a good job on keeping clubs orderly and safe, coming down hard on impolite customers.

Presley also entertained at Keesler Air Force Base in Biloxi. In 1957 a Marine trainee at Keesler named Lee Harvey Oswald studied radar and aircraft surveillance . . . and read a lot of books in his room. On April 24, 1960, blacks attempted to enjoy the Biloxi beach to the south of Highway 90, then were run off by white teenagers. Property owners on the north side claimed the beach was private property. That night, black cars were bombarded, and blacks and whites were wounded by bullets and pellets. It took years for a federal lawsuit to open the sands to everyone.

By the early 1960s, Jake Mladinich was sending his Coventry Singers and other folk acts to the ABC-TV show *Hootenanny* (1963–64), run by Art Linkletter's son Jack. *Hootenanny* needed outside help, having blacklisted Pete Seeger and the Weavers, and earning boycotts by Joan Baez, the Kingston Trio, and Peter, Paul and Mary. In retaliation Mladinich also got some of his acts into Las Vegas.

Mladinich had been running auditions on Monday nights. Folk music was "strictly the instrumentation and vocals—there were no 'acts' at all in that folk era. No comedian or joke-teller . . . I remember Jimmy because he had a lot of personality and everybody liked him."

"Hey, Buffett's playing at Trader's tonight. Let's go down there," people would tell Jean Prescott. "There weren't that many clubs where you could really catch a lot of live entertainment at the age we were at the time. I never met him—I never sat down and had a beer with him personally. But it was unfortunate, 'cause people would laugh and talk. . . . It was almost like background music sometimes. He had a good rapport with the audience. I don't mean getting into a confrontation with a heckler—well, nobody heckled him. People would yell stuff up at him, and he would yell back at them—maybe in the middle of a song. He was a fun guy to go and see performing 'cause he would horse around and . . . *you* know!"

Prescott figures that there were illegal minors in the clubs. While the owners didn't want an entertainer "talking about 'unlawful carnal knowledge' onstage," it didn't matter if *Jimmy* did it, " 'cause he had that wicked little-boy smile on his face and everybody knew there was no malice there. And everybody thought it was funny, whereas, somebody else couldn't have gotten away with it."

Sometimes onstage, when introducing "God's Own Drunk" (by Lord Buckley), Jimmy will jokingly mention Bob Cook and Brent Webster, two of his New Orleans music friends. Cook and Webster liked to do "God's Own Drunk," and Jimmy learned it from them. Cook made his own debut at Trader John's. He was so enchanted with the club, he went out and bought a forty-dollar guitar, learned to play it, and in two or three months was performing. He and Webster were playing there one Monday night when in came Jimmy at "hootenanny" time. "He had probably the cheapest guitar you could find," Cook believes. "You tune it up, but with high action [strings high above the neck], it pulls out of tune. I think you'd probably have to tune for every song if it's in a different key. He was *constantly* tuning. Jim was good about being able to change his string and not even stop singing—he would reach back and get one out of his pocket, and put it on the guitar while he was still playing."

Webster left Biloxi in 1965, and he believes Jimmy may have first come there as early as 1964. "He wasn't doing much. He just had a horrible guitar." Webster remembers how badly Jimmy wanted to get into the music scene: "The impression was, he was trying too hard. His exuberance preceded him." Once he even performed at the Fiesta, the club where Elvis failed to woo the customers—ironic, considering Jimmy's idolatry of "The King" and his film *King Creole.*

Trader John's is gone today, along with Mladinich's three other clubs. Demolished. But he was paid millions of dollars to accommodate the Biloxi Belle Casino (857 Beach Boulevard). It floats on the water and "looks like a three-deck Spanish galleon. It was done by the same architectural firm that did Disneyland . . . so that's in the place where Jimmy worked."

On Jimmy's landmark album, *Changes in Latitudes, Changes in Attitudes* (1977), appears a song by Jesse Winchester, "Biloxi," which extols sisterlike pretty girls swimming in the ocean, observed by a boy who is filling his pail with salt water, and who digs a hole in the beach and allows fantasy creatures to flourish out of his daydreams.

Reminisces Jean Prescott: "A lot of the people who are crazy about him—even if they never met him, even if they're not the age he was, they know what he is talking about. He never comes to Biloxi without singing 'Biloxi.' This isn't Margaritaville, and I'm sure he wasn't writing about here, but I know *nine thousand people* that are exactly like the guy in 'Margaritaville.' *They just can't get off their asses.* They would rather sit on the beach—I'm serious!—they wear flip-flops and wait for somebody *else* to finish boiling shrimp or crawfish, back up on the kettle on the grass side of the highway."

Speaking of the song "Biloxi," Jimmy says that Jesse Winchester songs "just put you where you would like to be"—such as New Orleans, where (in the song) the storms blow, the sun sets, and the sky reddens. New Orleans, a much better destination than Saigon, Vietnam . . . or Canada, where Winchester (born in Shreveport, Louisiana) had fled to dodge the draft in the late 1960s.

The Upstairs Alliance

■

Before "Margaritaville," there was the Pizza Hut and USM in Hatties-burg.

—Becky Gillette, *The* (Hattiesburg) *Advertiser News*,
September 1, 1993

I was nineteen years old and I would have been right in the middle of the Vietnam era," Jimmy told Marcia Hill in her in-depth television interview. "At Camp Shelby they were training men to go to Vietnam. . . . I'd have been a helicopter pilot . . . at nineteen; I would have been dead, I really believe that."

He was reliving the year of 1967.

"And I started playing music and it gave me something in my life that was more important. I was working at a place in Hattiesburg, it was a pizza place in downtown. . . . I will never forget, I had to play this bar and there were these guys—it was the first wave of people coming back from Vietnam, who were training other ones to go. And they all hung out at this bar, so you can imagine—here are kids who are on their way to war, which nobody knew what the hell was going on anyway—and the people coming back were the interesting ones.

"Because I had huge guilt about the fact *I* was in school, and these other guys were going to die for this useless cause."

But the men returning from Vietnam told Jimmy, "Whatever you do, *don't* go over there. It's not what you think it is."

"God, I feel bad about this," Jimmy answered.

"Forget it. It's useless, it's a waste of everything. It's an old man's war. *Whatever you do, don't do it.*"

So Jimmy would play in the Pizza Hut, "full of drunk soldiers coming and going to Vietnam. That was the toughest crowd I ever worked in my life. . . . The jukebox was in the back room, and I had to go shut the jukebox off before I could start playing. Inevitably, I'd turn the jukebox off . . . I'd get a couple of beer cans thrown at me. I'd walk back to the other room, start playing—and the jukebox would come back *on* in there, and I'd have to go back in there and turn it off. And here's some poor drunk soldier—on his way to God-knows-whatever rice paddy, halfway around the world—and *I'm* the one that's got to turn his jukebox quarter off! *That* gave me some stamina and some stability." Pause. "That was probably the highlight of what I learned in Hattiesburg."

Jimmy also told Marcia Hill that he was "working intermittently," dropping out of school at times, to work in New Orleans. "So going to school was more of a base of operations to me, it was a necessity to be in school because I was really at that point committed to playing music." At any moment he feared being drafted. When he would go and keep registered, someone would tell him, "Not only are you going to get drafted when we get you, but you're going directly to Vietnam."

"Oh yeah? You watch," Jimmy would answer back.

"I really thought if I didn't go over there and waste my life, I could make a lot of people happier by continuing being in music. It was a strange feeling at the time. But I'm glad I made a decision. . . . A lot of people who didn't go to Vietnam had a lot of guilt about that, which you've got to work out.

"I go to Washington, and play every year, and go by the Vietnam [Veterans] Memorial, and I think it absolutely should be *required* for the people that make foreign policy for this country to have to walk by that monument on the way to work. For it is a very powerful thing to see. And it was a very powerful part of my life, though I never went."

■　■　■

President Lyndon Johnson, a one-time schoolteacher (who stole his 1948 primary election), said that "the answer for all our national problems comes in a single word. That word is *education.*"

The rapidly expanding University of Southern Mississippi was throbbing with growing pains. The Kappa Sigma fraternity house burned down in 1965 (presumably accidentally); the current building contains the room probably occupied by Jimmy in 1967.

On May 10, 1967, "student unrest" exploded. The ostensible causes were petty campus strictures—signing-out requirements, and curfew for dormitory women. A Fifties-style "panty raid" was halted by Hattiesburg police, aided by Sixties-style riot dogs. The students responded by screaming and flaunting a few pairs of girls' underwear . . . accompanied by flung rocks and bottles, breaking some car windows. And, strangely, a large wooden cross was set afire outside the ruins of the Kappa Sig house. The next night, a mob of fifteen hundred threw eggs and killed some ducks, and about twenty boys were arrested. The students were demanding a "voice" in campus affairs.

Back in 1964, Barry (*Why Not Victory?*) Goldwater became the campus hero. And in 1966 hundreds of Southern signatures were gathered to support Lyndon Johnson's war in Vietnam. But the 1967 student tensions had their undercurrents—maybe some racial friction, but more likely, a mounting distrust of the war.

An "old man's war" it was indeed.

Its instigators, John Foster Dulles and Allen "The Gentleman Spy" Dulles, had been Nazi business traffickers in the 1930s from their Wall Street law firm. In the Fifties—as Secretary of State and Director of Central Intelligence respectively—John Foster Dulles and Allen Dulles propped up puppet Ngo Dinh Diem in South Vietnam, to oppose the northern forces of Ho Chi Minh, which had vanquished the French. Diem was inept (like his sponsors), and gradually American troops were sacrificed as "advisers"—though General Douglas MacArthur had warned against letting U.S. men set foot in a "land war" in Southeast Asia.

President John F. "*PT-109*" Kennedy, meanwhile, violated international neutrality, permitting the Bay of Pigs Cuban invasion (from Jimmy's future home of Key West) in 1961. Its secret plotter, Allen Dulles (with United Fruit Company bank ties), was off playing golf at the time, and quirky Kennedy yanked the air cover, letting more than one hundred troops die.

Kennedy sunk himself deeper into Vietnam—and in Dallas, Texas, in 1963, died of natural causes of a political nature (bullets), possibly from the Bay of Pigs veterans association. His Vice President and successor, Lyndon Baines Johnson, tried to excel Kennedy, by lunging deeper into the Vietnam jungle. The war was merely "a conflict"—and when Eisenhower pleaded that the war be legally declared (in 1967), he was spurned. The U.S. Congress didn't want to be held responsible for the dead boys returning home, since their parents were voters (5,008 dead in 1966). Besides, American businesses continued to trade with the Soviet Union, selling them military computers and setting up huge trucking plants. The Soviets, of course, abetted the North Vietnamese.

Jimmy's storytelling hero, James A. Michener, complained that "our democracy lacked the courage either to declare war against the Communists or to mobilize the civilian economy in support of the quasi-war we were fighting." He said that we sent some boys to death and let luckier ones "remain home and earn a pile of money." Prophetically, he was condemning the earlier, Korean "conflict." Now in the Sixties, President Johnson—who was fighting for black civil rights at home— was shipping disproportionate numbers of blacks to their deaths in Vietnam (so when black singer Eartha Kitt protested the war to Lady Bird Johnson, federal thugs smeared her).

Thus did Jimmy Buffett major in club work, while loyally minoring in draft-ducking.

■ ■ ■

The University of Southern Mississippi, meanwhile, "was able to offer its students better and more varied entertainment," such as the collegiate-dressed, soft-pop group the Lettermen, who came every year in the early 1960s, or New Orleans jazzman Pete Fountain in 1965, as well as comedian Bob Hope, singer Glen Campbell, and blues-blasters Ray Charles, Ike and Tina Turner, and the Temptations.

In 1995 the Director of Public Relations at Southern was William E. "Bud" Kirkpatrick, but from 1958 to 1972, he had been the school's Director of Student Activities. One of his activities was getting Jimmy Buffett to perform in the student union "coffeehouse" (McLemore Hall today). It was nicknamed Nat's Nook. Jimmy starred at its grand opening.

"Jimmy sort of hung out at the union looking for band jobs. I'd get him to do little pieces of work whenever I had things to do," Kirkpatrick told Becky Gillette of Hattiesburg's *Advertiser News*. "We had peanuts on the table, and we just let the hulls fall as they may. After two or three weeks, it got to be quite an atmospheric-type place.

"Broke Buffett prevailed upon me to let him have that [gig], so he would play in there and sing two or three nights a week, and his girlfriend would take up the money. So he'd keep the money and provide me with a source of programming entertainment."

Like Jake Mladinich, Bud Kirkpatrick was an unsung Mississippi folksingers' guru. "There were a lot of acts out there who were good but couldn't get booked. They didn't have a record—they didn't have a phonograph record, they didn't have a track record," Kirkpatrick said in our interview. So the various colleges would team up and supply transportation for different acts and move them from campus to campus, giving them a week of free dormitory lodging and free food, and letting them play for the students. They called it "the Coffeehouse Circuit."

Kirkpatrick remembers visiting Greenwich Village's folk club the Bitter End, and he thinks it's funny they passed up on a duo called Simon and Garfunkel. "Buffett did it here, he never did get on the circuit, but he did that concept at our place. . . . Jimmy was an extremely likable guy, a dedicated member of his fraternity. He had a great love for 'Mom Reed' [Mrs. Reed Tyrone], the house mother."

Black folksinger Josh White, Jr., was one of their selected acts. White, whose father had once performed at the White House for President Roosevelt, now ended up at Buffett's Seventh Street apartment for a barbecue. "At that time, having a black person over in the proper white South was quite extraordinary," remarks Richard "Rick" Bennett, one of Jimmy's roommates and musicians. "What a night we had. Old Josh sitting there singing, and Jimmy and a bunch of us just picking away. It was quite moving for the fact it was so different." Bennett says that in those days, local racism was strictly "heavy-duty." (White wrote music for a 1967 documentary film *The Freedom Train*.)

"I did the obligatory fraternity dances with my rock 'n' roll band," Jimmy told television interviewer Marcia Hill.

Jill Easton, a Southern student at the time, attended a big Kappa Sigma party "with a live band, and many had been doing serious drinking," according to her interview with Becky Gillette. "It was late in the evening. Buffett was out in the middle of the dance floor, and he started taking off his clothes. When he got down to the bare essentials, several of the brothers picked him up and carried him out of the room, raised high above their heads. Jimmy was still struggling to remove the last item of apparel."

Easton also remembers Jimmy performing in a basement club named Grandma's: "It was sort of a black-light place. Just him and an acoustic guitar."

One of Jimmy's fraternity brothers, William "Wiley" Magee, lived off-campus with him and recalls: "We were in the same classes, business administration. I used to sing with him, I was in church groups. We had some little old places we would go out to, and just sing—one of 'em was downtown in Hattiesburg. He'd hock his guitar during the week, and we'd all pick up money and go get it on Friday afternoon. We had one of the best intramural softball teams. He was never a very good softball player, but he'd get out there and *try*. . . . He talked about being a writer, some [laughs], but we didn't pay no attention to it.

"We never had any money, but we had a darned good time. I used to go out and work a stockyard in Hattiesburg—I was from the country, and I knew how to work with cows. Buffett came out there one Wednesday and he gave up on the cow deal! None of us had a decent car to ride in, all of us was riding in clunkers."

Drummer Bill Kehoe, who played with Jimmy, remembers Buffett's tan Ford Falcon. "He called it 'the Tan Hopper'—it was his transportation. It had a standard transmission, but it was unique, because it didn't have first or third gear—or reverse! It just had second or fourth, and he had to be *careful* where he parked."

■   ■   ■

In July 1967 Jimmy's beloved musical, *South Pacific,* appeared at Hattiesburg on the Southern Stage. That summer featured other exciting performances, such as a Negro bus boycott, the blacks throwing bottles, breaking bus windows, and shutting down the local bus line—and Ross Barnett campaigning for governor in the *Hattiesburg American:* "The people of America are getting sick and tired of Martin Luther King." The paper announced that statistically Mississippi was the *worst* state in the nation for educating young children.

Also in July, the paper ran an editorial titled "Hippie Hooray?": "The hippie movement, no matter how you feel about it, is not without a bit of allure (they are outdoors a great deal and don't believe in work), but all is not flowers and belts and beads and suntan." Hippiedom led to hepatitis, venereal disease, amphetamine injection, and LSD, and not merely "tambourines and bangles."

An editorial the following month was titled "Negroes Hurting Themselves Most," and another, "You and the New Left," quoted FBI director J. Edgar Hoover saying that the radicals included not only students, but "college faculty members (mostly young), graduate students, guitarists [!], writers, intellectuals of various types, ex-students still 'hanging around' the campus, curiosity seekers, Communists and Trotskyites. Many of the New Leftists are merely intellectual tramps who seek the exotic and eccentric as emotional outlets." Hoover recommended that young people pay more attention to Jesus of Nazareth. (Two of Jimmy's favorite authors were subjects of Hoover's scrutiny: William Faulkner, who had an 18-page file, and Havana resident Ernest Hemingway, with a 122-page file proving that he was a drunk, with anti-Fascist opinions.)

Jimmy's former roommate and band member Richard Bennett thinks that the Hoover reference is funny. "Of course, now we know all about *him.* What's left to be said about *that?*"

Elsewhere, the summer of '67 was even hotter—by the end of July, eighty-three people were dead and thousands maimed in black "rebellions," mostly up North. That spring, *Ramparts* magazine had exposed the Central Intelligence Agency for having bribed the National Student Association. (One of *Ramparts'* editors, Ralph J. Gleason, moved on to the rock magazine *Rolling Stone.*) That October an Oakland, California, anti-draft riot unleashed tear gas and billy clubs, while tens of thousands of protestors in Washington, D.C., faced fixed federal bayonets on the steps of the Pentagon.

■ ■ ■

By contrast, Jimmy Buffett knew where *he* belonged in the Soaring Sixties and went there as often as possible. "Gradually I went on to New Orleans," he told Marcia Hill, "which was the next step in the ladder to success."

"I lost my virginity there, so I'm sort of visiting it to see if I can get it back," Jimmy said on Arts & Entertainment television in 1994.

"Good luck. Let me know if you do," responded a lady sitting at a table.

She was sitting in a patio at 616 Ursuline Street (the Casa Cassie apartments of the 1960s). "I lived right up in that apartment," Jimmy said, pointing up to Room 305. With program host Elliott Forrest, Jimmy entered the apartment and sat down and patted the bed for the national TV audience. "Well, this was the place. I was eighteen years old, an altar boy from Alabama, and I came here looking for fun and this is where I found it." (In an untelevised portion he said, "She knows who she is.")

Jimmy's pal Richard Bennett says, "I know how he lost his virginity. I'm the one who walked in and picked up the girl. It's a classic story. That place in New Orleans, we had everybody who would come and visit, sleep on the couch, sleep in the tub. I well remember *that story*."

And Elliott Forrest asked Jimmy if it was food—or water—that precipitated this erotic rite of passage.

"It was probably the water. That's as good a thing as any to blame it on." Though just in case Elvis Presley was watching the show, Jimmy told him that it was really *his* fault. (Another time he said he wanted to come to New Orleans and pretend he was living in a Tennessee Williams play.)

He told Forrest that he couldn't afford a balcony apartment—that a balcony was like a bird perch, a "panorama of life in general," where you could look down and watch the action on the streets in "other people's lives, and they didn't know you were there." He had hoped to make enough money to one day rent a balcony apartment.

And he spoke with pride about a haunted house in the same block: "I think I actually saw a ghost," thus evoking New Orleans's happy horror heritage (from voodoo queen Marie Laveau, to authors Lafcadio Hearn, Anne Rice, and necrophilist Leilah Wendell).

■ ■ ■

"My grandfather was a captain for Delta Steamship Lines," Jimmy told Hayes Ferguson of the New Orleans *Times-Picayune*, "and I remember as a child I used to come over from Pascagoula and meet his ship and have dinner at Tujague's," at 823 Decatur Street. (Jimmy has since had dinner with his daughter, Savannah Jane, at Tujague's, and she said, "Dad, this town is as much fun as any place I've ever been.")

Those early visits, at age eight or nine, inspired what he calls his "biggest memories." Jimmy told Elliott Forrest that because his grandfather's ship was always leaving New Orleans for Buenos Aires and Rio de Janeiro, he came to regard the Crescent City as "the northern edge of the Caribbean . . . the gateway out to the world."

So it became Jimmy's musical gateway, starting probably in 1966.

"Did you sing out on the street?" Forrest asked as they strolled along. Yes, he did—and "around four or five Mardi Gras ago," he borrowed a street singer's guitar, and started performing on the street once more. "I made around eleven dollars."

"New Orleans was just, to me, the haven of lunatics from the South," Jimmy told Keith Spera in 1993 for *Offbeat,* New Orleans's music magazine, "And I fit right into that category. . . . One of the great things about New Orleans is that its cultural thread has maintained through generations. That's what I really love about it." To which he added, to Elliott Forrest: "I never quit coming back here. It's kind of a great place that feeds your creative soul. I always find that I'm writing well when I come to this town, as it did to a long line of creative people. I don't think I'll stop coming back." (He told Robert Hilburn of the *Los Angeles Times* that New Orleans inspired him to be a writer of books, but that music interrupted this ambition for a while.)

■ ■ ■

In fundamental ways, New Orleans never changes. Back in the 1830s, blind men played fiddles on the streets and children danced for pennies— black boys still hop and skip for money on the French Quarter sidewalks today. When singer Jenny "the Swedish Nightingale" Lind performed twelve concerts in New Orleans in 1851, "Jenny Lind shirts" and "Jenny Lind cravats" were on sale in the stores—a faint harbinger of today's Jimmy Buffett T-shirts.

Historian Harnett P. Kane called New Orleans "a lady—part American, part Spanish, more French than either in her essential viewpoint. . . . She is considered a little shady, if not worse; she would be the first to admit she is no anemic Puritan. For she has seen a good deal in her day, and she doesn't shock easily." For example, in 1857 some brothels were first licensed, evolving into the beloved Storyville, where piano-playing facilitated the bordello business. In Storyville's legalized epoch (1898–1917), there might be fifty sexophonic musicians playing any single night.

Black musicians had already been constructing horns, flutes, drums, and "pebble-filled gourds, long whistles, pipes punched with holes, violins made from cigar boxes." Musicians were proud they could *not* read music, since after all, "Whadda we do when the lights go out?" In Mardi

Gras parades, everyone sang and danced, but black jazz-folk's highest moment was marching and playing for someone's funeral—"When the Saints Go Marching In" epitomized the movement, and prefigured rock 'n' roll. First charting for New Orleans–born Louis Armstrong in 1939 (at Number 10), as "Saints Rock 'n' Roll" it hit for rock pioneer Bill Haley and his Comets in 1956 (at Number 18).

Armstrong, as a child, had delivered coal to one of the Storyville prostitute's cribs and was seduced by the music. Storyville was in the larger French Quarter, home of jazz, ragtime, and Dixieland over the years, and considerable rhythm and blues, by Fats Domino (whose piano-playing and friendly singing inspired white cover versions by Pat Boone), Huey "Piano" Smith and the Clowns, among many. In "Saxophones," Jimmy says that he cut his teeth on "gumbo rock"—then he alludes to Benny Spellman, who used to perform with Huey "Piano" Smith and Ernie K-Doe, and who had a hit with "Lipstick Traces (On a Cigarette)" in 1962. He mentions, too, Dr. John, a white New Orleans–born blues-man (Malcolm John "Mac" Rebennack), Irma "the Soul Queen of New Orleans" Thomas, and Clarence "Frogman" Henry, whose comical "Ain't Got No Home" proved that he could sing like a girl as well as a frog. ("Frogman" Henry even performed at Jimmy's Margaritaville cafe in the 1990s.)

Back in the early Sixties, white blues singers Edgar Winter and Janis Joplin played on Bourbon Street, in the Dream Room. Joplin once went to New Orleans with a female friend who pushed her out a moving car, with her purse inside, so resourceful Joplin "did two tricks" to get back to Austin, Texas. Next door at Your Father's Moustache, Lamar Alexander played trombone—which he preferred "because it drowned out everything else"—and washboard in 1965. (Alexander was Governor of Tennessee from 1979 to 1987, U.S. Secretary of Education from 1991 to 1993, and a Republican Presidential candidate in 1996.)

Jimmy's chief New Orleans venues were next door to each other on Bourbon Street—the Bayou Room and Gunga Den. His band was named the Upstairs Alliance, and the band's official address was 616 Ursuline Street, apartment 60. Jimmy played rhythm guitar and sang, along with singer Bettye N. Bridges (from Louisville, Kentucky), lead guitarist Richard Fellom (from Hammond, Louisiana), bassist Richard "Rick" Bennett (from Ontario, Canada), and drummer Bill Kehoe. Fellom, Bennett, and Kehoe lived off and on with Jimmy at the Seventh Street apartment in Hattiesburg. Sometimes Jimmy's future Key West comrade Vic Latham would play harmonica with the group.

Jimmy says he was "thrown into the spotlight of the band" because he was the only member who had credit at Werlein's—and he could go and buy the sound system. He claims that all he really wanted to do was be a backup singer and bass player, "but then I had no choice."

Bettye Bridges was the lead vocalist on Kehoe's surviving tape, and in other memories as well.

The band sang current popular songs to entertain the liquor-bar customers. Original songs that no one has heard before don't sell many drinks—the key to nightclub-musician survival is not "art," or even "talent," but rather the cash register. Some club owners never listen to their acts but rely solely on their bartenders' reports.

"We were the first group on Bourbon Street to do a long [Beatles] Sgt. Pepper medley, and we did a Rolling Stones medley," recalls Bill Kehoe. "Other musicians would come and hear. We started out with 'Sgt. Pepper's Lonely Hearts Club Band,' 'With a Little Help from My Friends,' then 'Lucy in the Sky with Diamonds,' and ended it with 'A Day in the Life.'" We did a lot of Beatles songs, a lot of Byrds songs. Jimmy was a big Gordon Lightfoot fan—he would do 'Early Morning Rain.' . . . He did some Dylan—'It's All Over Now, Baby Blue'—we did a three-part harmony arrangement. We did the Jefferson Airplane's 'White Rabbit,' Kenny Rogers and the First Edition's 'Just Dropped In (To See What Condition My Condition Is In),' the Mamas and the Papas' 'California Dreamin' and 'Monday, Monday' . . . 'Tobacco Road' [the Nashville Teens], Vanilla Fudge's 'You Keep Me Hangin' On.'" (Bettye Bridges would often sing "Different Drum," the pop hit for Linda Ronstadt and the Stone Poneys.)

Richard Bennett, who started with a stand-up bass and then went electric, remembers when they started in the Bayou Room, the manager used to call them "Strike Three," and stick them far in the back of the room, and yell, "Strike three!" at them. "We used to get hecklers, like you wouldn't believe. Finally we got a guy who was an actor, who later became our close friend—Steve Pirnie ['the Pirnie Bird']."

Sometimes they would catch Fats Domino at Al Hirt's club with the revolving stage, and they would also go and see Clarence "Frogman" Henry—Bennett says that his song "Now She's Gone" was one "we tried to do all the time."

A private source remembers that they did rhythm and blues songs like "Knock on Wood," at the Gunga Den, and would alternate with another band, trading sets. The other band would do all R&B. They were white, however, since the Mafia gangsters who ran the club didn't like Negro performers on the premises.

Since Louisiana's climate was similar to Sicily's, Mafia scholar John H. Davis says, "Sicilian immigrants preferred New Orleans to all other American cities." The *Saturday Evening Post* called it "Cosa Nostra's Wall Street" in a 1964 major article.

Up Bourbon Street was the Sho-Bar club in the 1960s. It was owned by Pete Marcello, of New Orleans's most prestigious Mafia family.

His colorful brother Carlos joked, "Sure, I used to be involved in the rackets. . . . But the Mafia—I don't know a thing about it. . . . I've never heard of anything like that in Louisiana." A reformed bank robber, Carlos Marcello once did a year in prison for selling marijuana. At the Sho-Bar in 1962 appeared Jada, "the hottest stripper in town," and she impressed Dallas nightclub operator Jack Ruby so much that he recruited her for his Carousel Club in Dallas, Texas . . . where she was reportedly dancing when President Kennedy was assassinated. Attorney General Robert Kennedy had kicked Carlos Marcello out of the country, to Guatemala—but he returned, since he was a loyal American gambling provider and political supporter of Lyndon Johnson and Supreme Court Associate Justice Tom Clark. One of Marcello's employees was former pilot David Ferrie, suspect in District Attorney Jim Garrison's Kennedy assassination investigation. (The patriotic Mafia was a Cold War contractor for Castro-killing plots.)

When asked whether or not the Sho-Bar was run by the Mafia, Richard Bennett laughs, "Which one *wasn't,* back then?" Bennett became a partner of comic actor John Candy, who "was like my kids' godfather. And when he did *JFK* with Oliver Stone [about the Kennedy assassination], we got sitting and talking about those days in New Orleans. I said, 'You've got to believe, this was closer than you think it was. Because Ruby *was* there.' In New Orleans, everything becomes kind of mystical and magical . . . and just bends over the edges of design . . . which is wonderful."

Today the Sho-Bar occupies the old site of Buffett's club, Gunga Den, at 325 Bourbon Street. An onstage girl dancer gyrated in pathetic, pelvic pirouettes, during our interview with the genial bartender, who alluded to Marcello. (Blues harpist Vic Latham told Buffetophile Mark Humphrey that next door to the Bayou Room was a "strip joint," offering a wide selection of hookers as well.)

Jimmy told Johnny Carson on the *Tonight Show* in 1990 that he worked in a "numbers place," whose manager represented "that organization that ran clubs in New Orleans." Imitating the man's Italian accent, Jimmy quoted him: "You break so many strings, I'm going to *fire* you if you break any more strings! *Loosen 'em up,* and you won't break any!" Jimmy didn't argue . . . and loosened his strings at the expense of his music: "Hell, I needed the money!"

Jimmy's friend Bob Cook, himself a comedian and singer, says that the Bayou Room's bartender "was a judo expert, an Italian-looking guy, short and squat. He was kind of our mentor. He would say, 'Don't do this, the boss doesn't like that, he loves it when you do this.'

"Larry Lamarca was the Bayou Room owner," says Cook. "One night somebody came in and tossed a glass at the stage in disgust—and somebody said something onstage—so they took him out the back and he never came back, so they must have beat the shit out of him. You're in trouble, if you got in trouble there. They had doormen who'd go down the street and just *pick* fights. They just *love* fights. They were expecting trouble, and when trouble came, they were in there in a second, and the person was usually out there, *hurt*."

Brent Webster never smoked marijuana, but he remembers one night in the Bayou Room when some customers had set fire to some straw hats made of hemp and it smelled like marijuana. Next thing he knew, Larry Lamarca had slammed him into the "bayou" tree and said, "If I ever catch you doing that shit in my bar again, you're a dead man." Webster hadn't done anything, but being a comedian, he was *the* prime suspect. He knew Lamarca *meant* what he said.

"The guy who ran the Bayou Room was stereotypical," adds Webster, "slick hair, fat, shiny suits, and all that shit. We actually went to Carlos Marcello's house—he was the banker of the Mafia. I was over there when Jim Garrison was doing all that crap, too. It was all over the place. Being street people, you were privy to it. Being street people, what a community that is! Everyone protects you and knows you—and you get into places—but I don't know if I would ever be comfortable being a tourist down there."

Bob Cook returned to Bourbon Street in the 1980s and discovered the Bayou Room had been replaced by a venue for female impersonators. "And damned good ones, I might add. They'd dance in front of you with harsh lights on them, and you couldn't see they were hiding anything. They were really good, they looked like women—queen of the crop."

Another Buffett site was Love Shop on Decatur Street, operated by Quint Davis. It was a "head shop," and Keith Spera of *Offbeat* rhapsodizes: "In the waning moments of the Sixties, the laissez-faire attitudes of Bourbon Street forged young Buffett's musical persona." In fact, "fellow hippie" Quint Davis has become executive director of New Orleans's Jazz Fest, encouraging Jimmy's Margaritaville record label.

Jimmy also told Johnny Carson that once "a gentleman walked through the door of a club I was working at in New Orleans. He looked like Roger McGuinn of the Byrds, and he professed to be. We were so desperately looking for a break, we wanted him to be Roger McGuinn."

Johnny: "You got taken?"

"Yeah, we got taken." They hoped he would get them to Hollywood. They even brought him back to Hattiesburg to live with them. "We had to defend this guy, because he had curlers in his long hair . . . this was Mississippi in the mid-Sixties. It was great going into restaurants with this guy."

Richard Bennett says that even "a goatee was looked on with disdain" in Hattiesburg. And this fellow was "walking around with a wolf hat and long hair." Finally they looked into his wallet.

"Ricky, this guy isn't who he's supposed to be!" cried Jimmy.

They called the man's mother. "It became such a tangled mess. A small town in Mississippi is *ready* for tangled messes. We had him perform at Nat's Nook, and he was so bad—he was such a fake—he was just terrible. He couldn't remember the words to 'Mr. Tambourine Man.' "

Bennett drove him to the Laurel airport, even as the police were headed for their apartment to arrest him for being an impostor, frantically trying "to get him out of our life before the world falls down. We were harboring him. It was touch and go. Me and Buffett at that time, we were just coming natural—we were not smart enough to plan *anything.*"

Another impostor hustled them in a New Orleans bar, claiming he was from RCA-Victor and suggesting that maybe he could get them onto RCA Records. He would buy Bettye Bridges gowns. "It turned out he was selling *RCA appliances!* He strung us good. That was a classic joke."

By contrast, Jimmy encountered some genuine artists at 601 Bourbon Street, in the Ivanhoe piano bar: two members of the Neville brothers group. As early as 1960, Aaron Neville had charted an R&B hit, "Over You," and "Tell It Like It Is" went to Number 2 in pop in 1967. His brother, keyboardist Art Neville, formed the Meters, a hit record group that one day toured with the Rolling Stones. In 1977 Art and Aaron Neville (with two other brothers, Charles and Cyril) formed the Neville Brothers—in 1988, they sang backup on Jimmy's *Hot Water* album. As early as 1957, Art and Aaron had backed up Larry Williams on "Short Fat Fanny" and "Bony Moronie." Over the years, one or more of the Nevilles has worked with acts as diversified as Allen Toussaint, Patti Labelle, and even country's Tammy Wynette. Today, like Jimmy, they are a high-selling cult concert show.

Another positive influence was . . . Uncle Billy Buffett. "He went to sea all his life," Jimmy told Marcia Hill. "He would always come through New Orleans when I was there, and he would bring me exotic things from all over the world, like carved teak tables—or the first Sony tape recorder I ever saw in my life . . . reel-to-reel." Pause. "He was out there on the edge . . . *he lived it.* I didn't really see him around that much, 'cause he was moving—but when Billy was around, you knew he was there." And as his aunt Patsy Lumpkin affirms: "When Jimmy was trying to make it big in New Orleans, pluckin' on that guitar, he saw some lean times. My brother Bill would come in, and if Jimmy was playing, he would get all of his *crew* there." Laughs. "Jimmy would have a *full* meal!"

■ ■ ■

Monday night was a school night. But fortunately, perhaps, Jimmy wasn't home on Monday, November 28, 1967, so when the phone rang at Gunga Den around midnight, Bill Kehoe remembers their mutual dismay . . . *despair.*

Rick Bennett says they jumped into their car and drove frantically home to Hattiesburg in the middle of the night.

The Fall of the House
of Hattiesburg

■

"You earn your living, don't you?" "Yeah, that's part of it. . . ."

—interview with District Chief Richard Bryant, Hattiesburg Fire
Department, July 9, 1994

J immy, Rick Bennett, and Richard
Fellom made it home at four A.M. Not a good morning . . . maybe the
worst in Jimmy's life.

■ ■ ■

At around 11:32 P.M., a horrified neighbor had called the fire department.
The house at 3202 West Seventh Street was in flames!

"The alarm came through on our switchboard," remembers District
Chief Raymond Bryant, Jr., who was a firefighter with his twin brother,
Richard, in 1967. (Their father, Ray Bryant, was Hattiesburg's fire chief.)
"This has been thirty years ago, but I've got the scars to show it. . . .

"They said somebody was in there, when I and this other firefighter entered this carport." It was in flames. "We went in through the back door, and the carport fell on me—and that was *it*, for me!"

When the carport collapsed, it crashed down upon a parked car, *and* upon Raymond, till his brother Richard and James Jackson miraculously lifted it off him. "There were nine men that *couldn't* lift that carport, when they tried it, next day—so whatever took place, took place."

"Burned his gloves off and everything," adds his brother. "They hauled his ass to the hospital . . . thirty-two days in the hospital." Six broken ribs, third-degree burns on his face, hands, and legs—and a dislocated hip. Says Raymond: "It was eight months before I could walk."

Immediately after the carport crash, fireman J. C. Lewis entered the front room. Of the seven tenants in the apartment, only one was home that night.

Frank Cain.

He had come back from a date at around eleven P.M. He probably went to bed, then awoke from the smoke—the unexplained fire had started in a utility room next to the carport. Frank's back bedroom was unharmed. He had probably tried to save his three cats, but there they were, lying in the front bedroom, dead, with their master lying on the floor also dead, three feet from the front door. Frank Cain had suffocated from the smoke. The paint on the floor had blistered around his body, leaving a macabre outline of his corpse.

On Wednesday a memorial service was held at the school auditorium, and the funeral on Thursday featured Kappa Sig brothers as pallbearers. Jimmy was most likely one of them.

∎ ∎ ∎

Who was Frank Cain?

He was from Panama City, Florida, a 1966 graduate who had majored in political science and minored in history, and now was in graduate school, working part-time as a political-science instructor. He'd held offices in various regional student government groups and campus political groups, and he acted in campus plays (as Sitting Bull in *Annie Get Your Gun* and Cardinal Woolsey in *A Man for All Seasons*).

Is truth really stranger than fiction? Certainly Frank Cain's death had some uncanny traces of synchronicity (like Southern Gothic horror fiction). At the beginning of the year, on January 25, the *Hattiesburg American* had carried almost the identical story, about a fire in Austin, Texas, where one boy suffocated in a dormitory and five others were injured. Nor was Cain's death the first such tragedy in his family: Two years earlier, his father had died when a gas tank exploded in the garage—and earlier, a brother had died in a car wreck. (His mother came up and visited Raymond Bryant, Jr., in the Forrest General Hospital.)

■ ■ ■

Hours after the fire, the morning paper (November 28) carried other, typical news of the time. Defense Secretary Robert McNamara was escaping from the Vietnam debacle he had incited, resigning to become president of the World Bank (a reminder that American patriotism supported international businesses). And the North Vietnamese Viet Cong were now inflicting "hit-and-run" attacks on southern air bases, slaughtering more American boys (of whom 9,400 died in Vietnam in 1967).

Jimmy rarely praises Hattiesburg, but the paper that morning gave him probably his first publicity notice: "Bennett, Fellom, and Buffett are musicians and were working in New Orleans at the time of the tragedy." And he got a front-page picture, albeit morbid, with Bennett, Fellom, and two other roommates (Fred Poteat and Keith Johnstone), standing and staring at the burned-out, collapsed carport.

If Jimmy had been home that night, doing his homework, maybe his career would have ended in flames. Or maybe Frank Cain would be working, today, for Margaritaville Records.

But the Upstairs Alliance was at the right place at the right time, on Bourbon Street where they belonged.

Stuck in Mobile with the
Nashville Blues

■

Sure, we are winning the war.

—Bob Hope, in the *Hattiesburg American,* January 1, 1968

My music is contemporary, along the line of John Hartford and Joni Mitchell. I would like to project a message that people will listen to and think about. And today, Nashville has become the center of the recording industry; I have always had intentions to go.

—Jimmy to Lee Haug, *Mobile Press,* July 21, 1969

I knew him very well. I didn't know he was going on to achieve the kind of fame he has," remarks history professor Dr. William Scarborough. "He was a good student, really. I remember him very favorably. He was interested in history."

But in the fall of 1967, Jimmy took a Civil War course and scored around 70 for his final average: D-plus. "Today it would be a C," says Dr. Scarborough. "He had quite a few absences, too. . . . I remember him as one who's not real comfortable taking orders from anybody. He was his own boss, and didn't like to conform to rules . . . like attendance, and stuff like that.

"Then for the winter of '67–'68, he had me for 'The Old South' and he made an A in that course. He only had one absence. So the fall must have been a bad time for him. He must have had some distractions. He had a kind of checkered record. But I remember he was enthusiastic about history. A lot of students pass through here, and you don't even remember them. But he's one I would have remembered even if he had not become famous—he was very interested in the class, and he joked a lot. I got to know him better than I usually get to know students. He had an outgoing personality and we got along very well together."

In fact, Jimmy was probably the top student in that class. (Even in grammar school Jimmy had read several of Bruce Catton's Civil War histories, not to mention books by Kipling.) And he would keep Dr. Scarborough informed of his progress with his band down in New Orleans.

"Now he doesn't have any great love for this university. I don't know what turned him off." Pause. "Tell him I think he should share a little of his loot with us."

■　■　■

Jimmy told the *Mobile Register* in 1970 that he took only one music course, with "too much theory and not enough feeling." But twenty years later, he told Marcia Hill that "they wouldn't let me take music classes at Southern because I wasn't a music major. And I wanted to take some theory classes. They had a real snotty attitude about it." He paused and jabbed his hand in jest—"*Take that!*"—and laughed. "And that made me mad. Because I was a working musician. It was like they looked down on me because I was working for a living."

Or, to quote William Faulkner in one of Jimmy's favorite novels, *Mosquitoes,* "Now, you lay off our New Orleans bohemian life; stay away from us if you don't like it. I like it, myself: there is a kind of charming futility about it."

■　■　■

Southern probably didn't know—nor would have cared—that singer-songwriter Van Dyke Parks had been born in Hattiesburg in 1943. The mostly obscure Parks had a strangely seminal influence, from cowriting with Beach Boy Brian Wilson, and playing piano on records with the Beau Brummels, Judy Collins, Tim Buckley, Randy Newman, Phil Ochs, and the Byrds, among others, to producing a Caribbean album in 1971 for the Esso Trinidad Steel Band. Like Buffett, Parks was a watery music pioneer, whose own *Discover America* album (1972) has been called a "potpourri of Calypsos."

As for Jimmy, Southern's best classroom contribution to his music career was poetry. He studied poetry "just for rhyme schemes and things like that," he told dopezine interviewer Bob Anderson (*High Times*) in 1976. "I've always been interested in poetry. If I ever studied anything in college that I retained, it was that. Poetry."

Rhymed and metered poetry, however, had disappeared from main-stream magazines, and arty poetry journals had virtually banished lyric verse. Edna St. Vincent Millay and Robert Frost (who read at President Kennedy's inauguration) were the last major American lyric poets, themselves often grudgingly accepted by the academic critics. But the song-writing Sixties, with talents like Donovan and Eric Andersen, resembled London in the 1890s, when poet Ernest Dowson came up with "hook" phrases like "gone with the wind" and "the days of wine and roses."

Before Jimmy could combine poetry and guitar-picking—and transport his lyrical wares to Nashville—he first had to get out of school.

When? is the question. Some wonder if he actually got his diploma, but USM confirms that he did, in 1969.

"He graduated in 1968," says Rick Bennett, while admitting that the records show they officially graduated in 1969, since they forgot to file for graduation. "We both got caught up in anything that had to do with that registration shit." Pause. "We both had '69 graduations, but we both graduated in '68—if you know what I mean. I didn't know you *had* to file for graduation—we had better things to do, in our minds. They wanted to throw us out of school, because we had goatees."

Jimmy explained to Marcia Hill how he diplomatically handled his diploma problem: "I went through the motions of going to school. They wouldn't let me out when I graduated, because I had four hundred dollars' worth of parking tickets."

Which Rick Bennett confirms: "The Tan Hopper was always getting ticketed."

"And I paid 'em and I graduated," said Jimmy, "and got the hell out of there, and went to New Orleans."

Jimmy is also remembered for his local shoplifting, celebrated in "Peanut Butter Conspiracy." Alumni director Ron Phillips says, "They'd go in there and they'd steal peanut butter to survive on—he'd go in with a friend. It was called the Mini-Mart, back then."

In spite of the song's promise that once the thieves came into some money, they would repay the proprietor, Jimmy told Marcia Hill's television audience: "I never paid the Mini-Mart back, either."

■　■　■

Upon finishing school in 1968, Jimmy probably went home to Mobile.

At some point his friend from Biloxi and New Orleans, Bob Cook, met him in Mobile at the Admiral's Corner lounge at the Admiral Semmes Hotel. Cook's Artists' Corporation of America booking agent from Milwaukee had gotten him the gig. Cook was a former glee-club singer who hadn't even bought a guitar until he was twenty-five. "When I was home, my mom would come listen to me, and Jimmy would come and sit in, and his mom would come in. Sometimes I would play upright bass—I was playing a Guild six-string." Cook remembers Jimmy playing Beatles songs, and Simon and Garfunkel songs, like "Mrs. Robinson": "It was just when they were starting to turn to folk electrified—and Jim picked up on that.*

"I was doing a lot of comedy. I was there around five or six nights a week, and he would normally come in Friday or Saturday night. It was just a nice get-together. Sometimes his mother and my mother would be the only people in the audience, late at night. It wasn't that big a traffic area." (Jimmy credits hotel manager Frank Taylor with having given him this first big break.)

The twelve-story hotel is fairly close to the ocean. By the sea, at the end of Government Street, stands a bronze statue commemorating Admiral Ralph Semmes. The hotel itself was built in 1940. Among its many famous guests were Eleanor Roosevelt, Gene Autry, Carol Channing . . . and Elvis. Jimmy's friend John Ed Thompson remembers he was performing for "$125, plus a room—if you didn't take the room, you got $150. Since his parents lived here, he got $150, he stayed at their house. That's a treat."

Jimmy admitted to Marcia Hill that his parents "suffered much grief" as he struggled with his music, but that they were supportive, when they didn't have to be. Yet some of his own successful friends have parents who "won't even admit their children were actually in show business." His mother still has Alabama friends who ask, "When's he going to give this stuff up and get a *real* job—and come home and do something *decent* with his life for a living?" His mother confirmed that some friends would say, "What's he doing, playing guitar instead of studying?" Yet she and her husband would occasionally catch their son at a "dive in New Orleans," or at the piano bar in Hattiesburg—or at the Admiral Semmes.

Even Jimmy's former McGill High School teacher Mark Will used to drop into the Admiral Semmes on his way to Mardi Gras balls, and noticed that his former student had "been in there playing from time to time." Jimmy's high-school friend Nelson Iturbe remembers him across the street in a little club called the Prince's House, frequented by wrestlers. Iturbe's wife, Beverly, would counsel Jimmy about his ponytail hairstyle: "You'd better loosen your rubber band, it's too tight." Iturbe says, "Long hair was just getting into style, here in the South."

The bartender at the Admiral Semmes was Jean Harrison—still working there in 1995, as Jean Mabile. She remembered Jimmy well, playing

---

*Like Jimmy, the Beatles' John Lennon had a childhood seaport background—in Liverpool. He told *Rolling Stone* editor Jann Wenner that "it's an Irish place . . . where the Irish came when they ran out of potatoes. . . . It is cosmopolitan, and it's where the sailors would come home with the blues records from America on the ships. . . . There were established folk, blues, and country and western clubs in Liverpool before rock and roll and we were the new kids coming out."

in the piano-bar area, sometimes during the week, but mostly on the weekends from seven or eight P.M. to one A.M. His following included "a lot of college kids. The place was packed on Friday and Saturday," remembers Jean Mabile. "He and Bob Cook used to play together. 'Big Bad Bruce' was a song he and Bob would sing. They would sing real funny songs. He was always good to the waitresses. . . . He used to talk about his granddaddy a lot—he said he instilled a lot of stuff in him. His dad and mom would bring groups of people in to see him from the shipyards."

He used to play two Peter, Paul and Mary hits from 1963, "Blowin' in the Wind" (Number 2) and "Don't Think Twice, It's All Right" (Number 9), both written by Bob Dylan. "He used to talk about him all the time," says Jean Mabile.

"Blowin' in the Wind" condemned racism as well as perpetual warfare. Dylan's "Masters of War" (1963) cursed the military-industrial complex which President Eisenhower had warned against in his farewell address. Even Jesus would never forgive the bureaucrats who hid behind their desks while young people's blood flowed in the mud, harped Bob Zimmerman, the Jewish gypsy from Minnesota, who adopted Dylan Thomas's first name for his own last name. And the Cuban missile crisis inspired his even more scathing "A Hard Rain's A-Gonna Fall" (1963), drawing a line in the sand between his college generation and their Cold War parents, who were being heated up by the secret, illegal war in Laos.

To fledgling songwriters like Jimmy Buffett, Dylan's artistic versatility was more powerful than his politics—from Old Testament–style anthems like "The Gates of Eden" and Coleridgean drug fantasies like "Mr. Tambourine Man," to eventual Tin Pan Alley–quality mainstream numbers like "If Not for You," for Olivia Newton-John (1971). Dylan's seminal influence on Nashville was profound—new writers like Roger Miller, Willie Nelson, Tom T. Hall, and Bobbie Gentry wrested unusual songs out of the subconscious, instead of looking over their shoulders to Hank Williams's ghost for inspiration.

Bob Dylan recorded his milestone double album *Blonde on Blonde* in Nashville in 1966. "He was the first young outsider to record in Nashville," claimed his producer, Bob Johnston, "and it was Bob Dylan who eventually opened the door for everyone since."

By 1968 Nashville was definitely reaching a turning point. That year its historic past was further severed from its uncertain future, by four deaths—those of former Grand Ole Opry host Red Foley; Opry founder George D. Hay ("the Solemn Old Judge"); folk revivalist "Pop" Stoneman; and RCA country producer Steve Sholes, who had signed Chet Atkins and Elvis Presley to the label.

■ ■ ■

Nineteen sixty-eight was a traumatic year in many other places.

That January, the *Hattiesburg American* reported that in New Orleans a Kennedy assassination witness had been mysteriously thrown through a glass door (he had heard four shots, not three, and not from the Book Depository). In March, U.S. troops secretly killed countless children and women in the village of My Lai. In April, the Reverend Martin Luther King, Jr., was assassinated in Memphis. Jimmy's idol Harry Belafonte made the funeral—and King's killer, James Earl Ray, had earlier claimed to have worked in the same shipyard as Jimmy's daddy—Ingalls, at Pascagoula. King opposed the Vietnam War, as did Presidential candidate Robert F. Kennedy, assassinated in Los Angeles that June. President Johnson refused to run for reelection, and the thrilling Democratic convention that August in Chicago featured violent police attacks on incorrigible demonstrators. Richard Nixon became President.

Even Jimmy's family's faith of Catholicism was somewhat sundered by the Vietnam War. "Christ's war . . . a war for civilization," decreed Cardinal Spellman; and ex–altar boy William E. Colby sponsored the Phoenix Program, which sent thousands of Vietnamese civilians to rest in peace—disapproved of, later, by *Washington Star* journalist Mary McGrory, who was raised as a Catholic. In 1967 the once-Catholic magazine *Ramparts* had its Kennedy files burglarized, and the Berrigan Brothers priests were arrested in war protests. The following year, Catholic Senator Eugene McCarthy ran for President against the war.

■ ■ ■

By 1969 Bob Dylan was back in Nashville (*Nashville Skyline*). Sweeping the floor in the studio was songwriter Kris Kristofferson. Kristofferson's country hit "Viet Nam Blues" had sniped at some hippies for touting Ho Chi Minh in front of soldiers in Washington, D.C. (The song went to Number 12 in 1966 for Dave Dudley.)

■ ■ ■

It seemed inevitable that Jimmy would head for Nashville. New Orleans had been "an incredible melting pot of musical talent," he told Richard Harrington of the *Washington Post*, but "you had to face the facts and realize that you'd have to go to New York, Los Angeles, or Nashville."

But first he cut a single in Mobile, at the upstairs Product Sound Studio. The studio had been set up by Nick Panioutou, with John Ed Thompson, Travis Turk, and Milton L. Brown. Says Thompson, "We had a Greek, a Jew, and a Methodist. We were an ecumenical recording studio." They originally wanted to cut an album of Civil War songs by Milton L. Brown.

The studio was above a dentist's office, so they could only record at night—or every other Saturday, when the dentist wasn't there. Laughs Thompson, "We had low rent, low equipment, we just did what we could." Their equipment was so "rinky-dink" that when engineer Travis Turk (a WUNI disc jockey at the time) would bring in a potential customer, people would look at the studio "and kinda frown." Then Turk would say, "Let me play you something that we cut last night," and they'd respond, "You got *that* out of *this* room?" (Despite their modest equipment, Turk would mix the tracks over at his radio station.)

Their partner, Milton L. Brown, was a University of Alabama graduate who had started with a ten-dollar pawnshop guitar. Eventually he entered the Alabama Music Hall of Fame, for having written Eddie Rabbitt's hit "Every Which Way But Loose," the title song for Clint Eastwood's 1978 film. Recalling Jimmy Buffett in 1978, Brown said, "Mobile has the ideal laid-back atmosphere. It has one of the most creative atmospheres I have ever known." On Brown's real-estate office wall—along with countless music mementoes—is an autographed picture of Jimmy inscribed, *Milton, would you buy a used car from this man?*

Jimmy's song "Abandoned on Tuesday" is a lovelorn lament, a nice middle-of-the-road song, sung with open, urban diction. Some pretty, jazz-derived major-seventh guitar chords embellish the instrumental tracks (major sevenths had been popularized by Bob Lind's "Elusive Butterfly" and John Hartford's "Gentle on My Mind"). The flip side, "Don't Bring Me Candy," is in the same tone—friendly pop. The label was Audio-Mobile, and the BMI publisher was Top Drawer Music; Jimmy was sole writer of both tunes.

Thompson thinks it's amusingly prophetic that Jimmy Buffett, of "Come Monday" immortality, recorded his "Abandoned on Tuesday" in their studio.

■ ■ ■

Besides having his music—and enough credits for graduation—Jimmy now had a girlfriend, Margaret Louise Washichek, born in Mobile on May 3, 1947. She was popular, pretty—and smart as well, remembers Beverly Iturbe, whose husband, Nelson, used to date Margie.

And what did Margie think of Jimmy's music? "I'm fairly critical," she told Lee Haug of the *Mobile Press* in 1969, "so Jimmy plays his songs for me first, and I tell him what I think of them. But, of course, his word is final." She said she lent him moral support—she was certain that his talent would make him "a great success in the field of music."

When they fell in love, Margie was attending Spring Hill College, a Catholic school that her family had been identified with for over half a century. Her grandfather, Francis Washichek, had blown into Mobile in 1906, in the midst of a hurricane. Born in Czechoslovakia, he was a graduate of the University of Chicago and had come to teach at Spring

Hill. He knew five languages, and this multilingual heritage had its effect on Jimmy's girlfriend. "My father and my uncle Phil often swam in the Spring Hill lake where they discussed and learned languages from Brother Eaton, who was on the faculty," she said in 1966. Greek and Latin, Spanish, French, and even Japanese, permeated the Washichek clan.

Since Jimmy had been a Spring Hill altar boy, and Margie had graduated from Toolen, the girl's school next to Jimmy's high school (which have since combined), they had probably known each other awhile. "Over the years," Margie said in 1966, "in one way or another—studying, teaching, attending Mass, swimming, hiking—our family has spent a lot of time on the Spring Hill campus. For us, in many ways, it has been like a second home." Margie was ecstatic, having just received the Azalea Trail scholarship to Spring Hill. She posed in the *Mobile Register* with a picture of her grandfather.

Margie was also an Azalea Trail maid. The Junior Chamber of Commerce (Jaycees) sponsors the award, with the approval of the Highway Department, according to Jimmy's former teacher, Mark Will, honoring "the famous tourist trail of beautiful azaleas we grow so plentifully around here. It's easy for the tourists to follow the pink line of azaleas around the city." Marian Acker Macpherson wrote that the azaleas turned the town into a "fairyland for the six weeks of its reign. Each year thousands of visitors storm the city" to wander down the forty-mile Azalea Trail "and drink in the unbelievable beauty and color. The brilliant starlike blossoms are everywhere—against the fresh cream brick of a new home—against the blue-gray flagstone of the old."

Margie had also been Gayfer's Teen Board model—as well as the first Miss USS *Alabama*—and, according to the *Mobile Press* in 1969, Jimmy's "number one fan."

Margie's college was founded in 1830 and taken over by the Jesuits in 1847. By recruiting students from the West Indies and Mexico, Spring Hill helped make Mobile one of the most-known American cities in Latin America. The school stayed open during the Civil War, despite the New Orleans blockade, and the Union capture of Mobile (their soldiers slept on the campus). Margie told the story of her uncle Bernard, who was a class valedictorian—he had a "balloon-shaped face" when he gave his address, having been stung badly by bees the day before!

She didn't mention that her baby brother had been killed in 1951 when a milk truck jumped off the street and into the family's front yard.

Her father, Paul, was a warehouse manager of the Marine Junk Company. Foreshadowing her own long career in the music industry, in 1966 Margie was working in public relations at Spring Hill.

Amusingly, in November of 1968, Timothy Leary had been invited to the campus to give his side in a drug debate. Leary had convinced a generation that LSD was a better choice than Vietnam, and the students raised $1,200 to consider this psychedelic option. "Since drug research is of vital importance to the intelligence agencies of this country, you'll be allowed to go on with your experiments as long as you keep it quiet," Leary's drug partner Mary Pinchot Meyer had told him back in 1962. Her secret lover was John F. Kennedy, who smoked marijuana with her. Her estranged husband was Cord Meyer, Jr., a CIA operative, and after her mysterious murder in 1964, one of his colleagues lock-picked her house in search of her diary. (Meyer also messed with the National Student Association, then in 1971 tried to bully Harper and Row into surpressing Alfred W. McCoy's *The Politics of Heroin in Southeast Asia,* which became a Cold War classic.)

Since Margie's man Jimmy would soon be co-writing and recording a song called "Ellis Dee," it was ironic that Bishop Toolen opposed Leary's "philosophy of life" from being uttered on campus. Six hundred outraged students staged an orderly demonstration, with a wooden coffin, symbolizing (in their minds) the death of free speech at Spring Hill.

■ ■ ■

Milton L. Brown and Travis Turk had a Nashville friend, James E. "Buzz" Cason, a singer for Spar Records. "One weekend Travis [Turk] was already in Nashville," recollects John Ed Thompson, "and Milton [Brown] and I, and Buffett went up for the weekend. . . . We cut about ten or twelve songs in one night. All, you know, with no money spent— we got it gratis, and didn't hire any musicians. Milton played piano, Travis played drums. And Buffett played rhythm, I think. We tried to get the bass sound out of a regular guitar, and we couldn't get a bass sound. So . . . Buffett lay down on the floor and played the foot pedals on an organ, for bass."

The session led to two singles being cut for Par-T Records in Atlanta. On three of the cuts, Milton Brown is singing lead, and on one of them Jimmy is singing lead. The "group" on the label is "Sun and the Tan Band," and three of the songs were "May the Bluebird of Happiness Dump His Load of Happiness on You," "Everything I Touch Turns to Poppy Doo," and "Look at Them Toe Suckers, Ain't They Sly?" (with Jimmy singing, "Look at them nose pickers, ain't they sly? / Picking them boogers and letting 'em fly"). "You gotta remember," says Thompson, "we were drinking Boone's Farm."

But what about Jimmy's songwriting?

"I've got this friend from Mobile, we've got some songs coming up," Turk told Cason. "I'd like to cut him, if you'd produce him."

Cason signed Jimmy on a paper napkin at Lum's restaurant. His formal production deal with Cason was dated June 17, 1969, and Jimmy's home address was still his parents' house in Mobile. In July he signed a contract with Russell-Cason Music Publishing.

With his typical ambivalence, Jimmy told Noel Coppage of *Stereo Review* in 1974: "The Gulf Coast is sort of keyed to New Orleans. It's a Catholic-based culture, Creole and Cajun . . . not a redneck culture at all. I listened mostly to gumbo rock out of New Orleans. I was never into country. I don't even know why I went to Nashville."

He underscored this in 1978, for *Music Journal,* saying that he had worked in Mobile shipyards, and tended bar, as well as forming a "hard-core Jefferson Airplane copy band"—the Upstairs Alliance, no doubt. He said he wanted to go to California, "but I didn't have enough money to get there. And I had enough to go to Nashville," adding, with his usual contempt, "A country nightclub is something I wouldn't play in for a million dollars." (Supposedly, Jimmy had an offer from Johnny Rivers's Soul City record company in Los Angeles.)

On July 19, 1969, he and Margie married in a "folk mass." Officially, both of them were living at home with their parents on their wedding day. The ceremony was in the St. Joseph Chapel at Spring Hill, where Jimmy had once performed as an altar boy. As his high-school teacher Brother Victor remarks: "Every town has a place where people like to get married because of its architecture and its beauty—you know, the ambience. A lot of people—not even Spring Hill graduates—try to get that chapel to get married in." Student Joseph P. Newsham described it thus in 1910:

> As we open the door a flood of golden light from the manifold amber windows surrounds us. The walls are all cream and white. Overhead the groined vaults spread, crossed in mystic array, by the arch ribs which spring from the foliated capitals of the double row of reeded pillars. The balustrade of the organ loft is a miniature Gothic arcade. The sumptuous quartered oak pews are decorated with Gothic panels. . . . [T]he three splendid gift altars . . . are all done in veined Italian marble, Mexican onyx, and pure white Carrara.

On the same day of the marriage, Senator Edward "Teddy" Kennedy drove his car off a bridge, and his lady passenger wasted away at Chappaquiddick, Massachusetts. The following day, Neil Armstrong landed on the moon. The following month, musician-occultist Charles Manson killed Sharon Tate, and more than a quarter million Woodstockers made history in New York State with music, dancing, marijuana, hippie clothing, and no clothing.

Unable to join the raucous, rocking hippie world of music, Jimmy had to settle momentarily for a job writing for *Billboard* magazine—in Nashville.

He and Margie moved to an apartment in a house in west Nashville, at 410-A Chesterfield Avenue. Recollects Milton Brown: "I remember going there and he looked at it as acceptable, realizing that it was not going to be the Taj Mahal. I remember the graffiti when I went in there—that was before they all kind of ganged up to keep graffiti out—and saying, 'Wow! This is definitely a starting spot.'"

As Lee Haug proclaimed in the *Mobile Press:* "Jimmy Buffett will busy himself in Nashville with writing and recording . . . some day soon Mobile will see his face and name on record-album covers, and perhaps even watch him perform on television. It's not easy to beat a winning team." The article itself was captioned "A Winning Team," and the accompanying photo showed Margie, beaming, with her hands on Jimmy's shoulders, captioned "All Set for Nashville."

The Fall
and Rise of
Jimmy Buffett

■

When Jimmy Buffett migrated from Mobile to Nashville in 1969, full of piss, vinegar, and talent, he unknowingly helped form the vanguard of the new Nashville sound. Did this multitalented writer-performer quickly turn Music City U.S.A. on its ear? Well, no . . .

—Gerry Wood, *The Coconut Telegraph*, September
1986

Everybody in the Keys has had a beer with me. You can print that.

—Jimmy to Betty Williams, *The Key West Citizen*,
January 27, 1985

The Media of Music Row: *Amusement Business* and *Billboard*

∎

The real strength of Nashville is the concentration of thousands of talented music people . . . a great sea of surviving songwriters kicking and gouging, fighting for their professional lives each day . . . abuses and humiliations, real or imagined, that turn reasonably sane folk into textbook paranoids. . . . Into this vital, volatile, hustling world go you, armed with nothing but a few reels of tape, a few pieces of paper.

—Michael Kosser, *Bringing It to Nashville (1976)*

Jimmy's *Billboard* boss, Bill Williams, had told him many years ago that he knew he would make it in music. Jimmy quoted him on the back cover of his 1981 album, *Somewhere over China,* which he dedicated to him as well. Williams was an exemplar of the music industry's struggling attempt to legitimize itself to the often ambivalent—and once hostile—Nashville media community. "One day I'm going to write a book," Williams told Jimmy. "They'll all sue me, but it'll be the goddamned truth!" (Alas, he never did.)

The founder of the Grand Ole Opry (in 1925), George D. Hay was once a journalist for the Memphis *Commercial Appeal* ("I covered 137 murders in one year—it was the human interest in it that I loved"). In fact, his newspaper had let him run a radio show as "radio editor" in

1923. But as the Opry progressed in the 1930s, both the *Nashville Banner* and *Tennessean* avoided covering country music out of jealousy for radio, not even printing local radio schedules for many years.

Jimmy's journalistic grandfather was perhaps Charlie Lamb, who first hired Bill Williams to write stories. Lamb may well have been Nashville's first national music journalist. During World War II, he was stationed at the Keesler Field air base near Biloxi. Around 1951 he was offered fifteen dollars a week by *Cash Box,* out of New York City, to write a column—and sell advertisements and subscriptions. Lamb couldn't afford a hotel room, so would type by the side of the road on his portable typewriter and shave in a cold-water creek outside of Nashville. He paid a parking-lot attendant twenty-five cents a day to answer the pay phone by the Ryman Auditorium (home of the Opry) and say, "Charlie Lamb Agency."

Lamb's *Country Music Reporter* (then *The Music Reporter*) became a Hollywood-quality journal (1956–64), and according to retired songwriter Gary ("Trade Mark") Walker, operator of the Great Escape record-store chain, Lamb should be in the Hall of Fame. He hired Williams around 1957. And singer Faron Young's *Music City News* was started in 1963—its circulation today is 200,000. (One of its Sixties writers, Dixie Deen, married story-songwriter Tom T. Hall.)

But the local, snobbish disdain for country music had been profound. Vanderbilt University professor Edwin Mims predicted musical success for the city in 1929—due to *opera,* not Opry, connections. Hank Williams, the most famous country singer (and songwriter) of all time, earned only four known mentions in the Nashville press in his ragged lifetime, since, according to biographer Colin Escott, "newspapers, even in Southern towns, tended to concentrate on the goings-on among society's grandees"—and even "trade-paper coverage was a random affair edited out of New York or Chicago, often with more than a touch of condescension." Latter-day *Tennessean* reporter Jack Hurst said the public viewed the music people as "boobs or hypocrites, who played to the low tastes of the one-gallus, bib-overall crowd and made enough money to gold-plate their Cadillacs and shame the fine city they had taken over."

By the Sixties, though, Nashville was starting to grudgingly acknowledge its music industry's impact. Money talks, even to (especially to) west Nashville's Belle Meade elite. In his history of the city, Alfred Leland Crabb complained that country music made *too much money,* giving it one curt paragraph while writing over a page on the Nashville Symphony Orchestra. But when WSM radio announcer David Cobb idly called Nashville "Music City, U.S.A.," the hyperbolic nickname stuck.

An archetypal newcomer by then was Bill Anderson, who scored countless hits, became a television star (from the 1960s into the 1990s), wrote songs for others ("City Lights" for Ray Price), and was an astute businessman. He had a journalism degree from the University of Georgia, and since the early Seventies has maintained a column in *Country Song Roundup.*

Another prose writer–turned–songwriter was Kris Kristofferson. Not a journalist, but an aspiring novelist, Kristofferson was from Brownsville, Texas (the western extremity of the Gulf Coast). He studied creative writing, won the top four out of twenty *Atlantic Monthly* short-story prizes, then ricocheted through Oxford University as a Rhodes scholar and the U.S. Army as a helicopter pilot, finally crashing in Nashville as a starving songwriter with a dying marriage. His parents used to send him newspaper clippings about classmates who had become successful. Kristofferson's hits finally got him out of his twenty-five-dollar-a-month apartment. His first big successes coincided with Buffett's Nashville tenure, 1969 to 1971.

Kristofferson's desperate example offered hope to the literate, Dylan-esque types, who just knew they could force their poetic lyrics down country chord progressions (if they didn't mind sweeping floors for a while, like Kristofferson). It didn't occur to them (or to Jimmy) that Kristofferson's affectionate lover's adieu, "For the Good Times," would come true for hundreds of busted-marriage Nashville songwriters, musicians, and other writers. (Jimmy's friend Aaron Neville recorded "For the Good Times" in Nashville in 1995.)

Nostalgically, Jimmy used the title of Kristofferson's 1970 song "Blame It on the Stones" (written with Bucky Wilkin) as the title of Chapter 52 in his novel *Where Is Joe Merchant?*

■ ■ ■

Jimmy's debut was apparently with *Billboard*'s subsidiary magazine, *Amusement Business*—quite fittingly, since *Amusement Business* covers live entertainment, from carnivals and circuses to theme parks and civic centers. From elephants to Parrot Heads.

In 1983 *Amusement Business* editor Tom Powell was out at Fan Fair, looking for the stage manager. He thought he'd spotted him, wearing Bermuda shorts and a white T-shirt, and asked, "Aren't you the sound-and-light man?"

"No, I'm not the sound-and-light man."

So who was this character? "Oh, that's Jimmy Buffett," someone told Powell. Embarrassed, he went back to Jimmy and apologized—and took his picture, admitting that Jimmy probably had never had his picture in *Amusement Business* before.

Back at the office, Powell began leafing through the old bound volumes of the magazine, finding Jimmy's "Talent Traffic" columns—and his misspelled name on the masthead as "Jim Buffet."

Jimmy's name first appears on the November 15, 1969, masthead, right behind that of Bill Williams, both assigned to Nashville. The week before, in his *Billboard* column (November 8) Williams wrote: "*Jimmy Buffett* did a concert at Belmont College last week," referring to the stately school on the hill at the south end of Music Row. (Television host Ralph Emery studied there; singer Trisha Yearwood is a Belmont music business graduate; music biographer Don Cusic teaches there.)

Bill Williams was Jimmy's boss, and that same year (1969) had been elected president of the Country Music Association. Born in 1922 in Nebraska, he was a college graduate who started working in Nashville in 1951 at the Opry's radio station, WSM. He was a WSM newsman and Opry publicist. WSM's sponsor was National Life Insurance—and down in the company's lobby one morning in 1957, singer Ernest Tubb fired a .357 magnum bullet past Williams's head. "My God, I've shot the wrong man," apologized Tubb, who had missed Williams entirely. Police guided a drunken Tubb down to jail, whose intended target— booking agent Jim Denny—never received *his* intended bullet. Williams told both local newspapers that he had *nothing* against Tubb (front-page stories resulted)—but at least he was broadening his own communications experience, readying himself for *Billboard* in 1967, as the Nashville bureau chief.

Williams welcomed people like Buffett, because "Dylan, Buffy Sainte-Marie, and all those other stars coming in here to record narrowed the gap between pop and country." He knew there would "always be a Loretta Lynn, a Kitty Wells, a Roy Acuff, an Ernest Tubb," but pointed out that even Hank Snow had used horns and pop instruments on a recent record: "It's the difference between selling seventy-thousand singles and selling five hundred thousand singles. Money does it every time."

"Bill Williams, he was wonderful, absolutely wonderful," says former associate director of ASCAP (the American Society of Composers and Performers) Gerry Wood. An ex–public relations director at Vanderbilt University, Wood had come to ASCAP in 1969. He remembered hearing how journalist Jimmy went to Memphis "to cover some sort of carnival at the fairgrounds. Jimmy kept slipping away and *listening* to this music, instead of *reporting* on the music." Later Gerry Wood went to work for *Billboard* himself—"and here I am writing in *Billboard* about Jimmy. Just reversed around."

Ironically, Gerry Wood's ASCAP organization had rewritten its history with Orwellian verve. "We're not just whistling Dixie . . . we not only have Gene Autry, we have Bobby Russell," they boasted, alluding to Buzz Cason's partner. Cason was with ASCAP; so was Bob Dylan. ASCAP claimed to pay more than BMI.

Yet back in the Fightin' Fifties, in its pre-Nashville era, ASCAP had hated black *and* white Southern music equally—without discrimination—when Tin Pan Alley had sneered at its lowbrow competitor, BMI ("Bad Music Incorporated"). Elvis was the ogre, since he combined both genres. BMI offered quicker payment, since its rock—or "hick"—hits were only expected to earn money for a short while. But when ASCAP noticed that "six-week wonder" songs were still selling records a decade later, they began courting the very folks they had so long disparaged. In 1948 they'd had around ninety percent of the nation's songs, whereas by 1965, the loathed BMI held around eighty percent of the tunes!

ASCAP came to Nashville in 1962, and at its open house party, the country business guests gobbled up every hors d'oeuvre and slurped down every free drink, with the taste of sweet revenge!

Now in 1969 its secretary was ... Margie Buffett. And when her desperate songwriter spouse dropped by, Margie said to boss Gerry Wood: "This is my husband, Jimmy."

"We hit it off, and they came and visited us a lot," says Wood, "out at our cabin on the Davidson-Sumner County line" (northeast of Nashville, near Ashland City). Wood's wife, Ellen, had been a professional model, had won prizes for her paintings, worked for music publishers, and was a book editor (*Country Music Who's Who*). "We became fast friends and saw *2001: A Space Odyssey* together, and partied around quite a bit." (Today, Wood is the Nashville writer for *Country Weekly*.)

At one point, Margie Buffett also worked as the talent coordinator for the *Johnny Cash Show* (ABC-TV, 1969–71).

Wood calls Jimmy "an unknown singer-songwriter who impressed me even in his early efforts. . . . He wasn't writing mainline Nashville country music, that's for sure. His skewed perspective gave a fresh twist to any topic he tackled, and made it impossible [for him] to achieve any success at that time in Nashville."

■ ■ ■

Gerry Wood remembers hearing one of Jimmy's songs, called "The Captain and the Kid," back then.

On January 2, 1970, Captain James Delaney Buffett was dead on arrival at the Singing River Hospital in Pascagoula. He was eighty-two years old. Jimmy made it to the funeral, and the captain was buried at the Machpelah Cemetery. Standing in front of the captain's house on Parsley Avenue in 1994, his aunt Patsy Lumpkin said, "People all gather at one particular house after a funeral," and Jimmy walked around indoors, turning his grief into a song. He actually wrote it, however, back in his Nashville apartment.

"The Captain and the Kid" is one of his best, a personal folk song that still could have been a hit—like Loretta Lynn's "Coal Miner's Daughter." The song commemorates James Delaney Buffett's professional passage from sailing ships to raking leaves in a Pascagoula backyard, unable to fully adjust to living on the land. Remembers his daughter, Patsy Lumpkin: "Captain Buffett never learned to drive. He backed into Mother's pecan tree—then turned around and hit the house!

Then Mother picked up a piece of wood and came after him, saying she was going to *hit* him with her 'ugly stick.'"

The song has a happy, if spectral, ending: The captain lives on in the cosmic afterlife, and "the kid" will always feel close to him—as the captain waves to him from his Flying Dutchman–quality ship, out on the sea.

One record producer had more than a casual interest in the song but wanted Jimmy to change it. He claimed the ending was too sad because the man is dying (even though the lyric is ultimately happy). Maybe Jimmy could fix it and *not* let the old man die. "I can't do that," Jimmy said, "because he did." So he walked out, and claims to have never pitched a song in Nashville again.

"I just knew the timing wasn't right for him in Nashville. I remember that very frustrating era for Jim . . . to have all that talent, and not get the recognition. It had to be pretty tough," continues Gerry Wood, telling how Jimmy would come over to ASCAP. "We had a table—an antique table in the boardroom—and we had one of those big old hockey sets, those push-and-pull things. Jimmy and I would just spend hours playing hockey—we had every player named, we had our coaches named. We would trade players, we would fire coaches. We had these fictional characters—one of these coaches, whom we hired and fired, was named Rudy Breno, who appears in *Where Is Joe Merchant?*

"I think that was Jimmy's world then, he was getting away from all the frustration and he was just creating things. It became one of the most *real* things you've ever seen . . . and it scratched the shit out of the table! The president of ASCAP became very upset about that . . . especially after Jimmy left ASCAP."

∎ ∎ ∎

At least *Billboard* gave him some Nashville credibility.

Founded in 1894 in Cincinnati, Ohio, it progressed from covering troupes like Buffalo Bill's Wild West Show to logging sheet-music sales in 1913, which exceeded record sales for decades. But in 1917 *Billboard* admitted that the phonograph was the "greatest musical factor of all times," while complaining that the pop market had so much "drivel," and "so little class." Gradually *Billboard*'s journalistic columns increased, to complement all the advertising. A front-page headline in 1960 blared: NASHVILLE ON RISE AS HIT-MAKING HUB.

Starting on January 24, 1970, Jimmy began writing the Nashville section of the "Music Capitals of the World" column, under a byline. He cited as many non-country acts as possible—from a live Tennessee appearance by Josh White, Jr. (whom he'd met in Hattiesburg), and Steppenwolf, to some Nashville pickers backing up the Jewish-Catholic-bred poet-singer (and novelist) Leonard Cohen, and Fifties rocker Little Richard recording in Nashville.

And he would cover a live show at the Municipal Auditorium, where power failures caused a forty-five-minute delay, "which is nothing new to the facilities at the auditorium." (The Municipal Auditorium still functions—and still flounders—having been upstaged in turn by the Nashville Convention Center and by a gigantic arena.) The show featured Tony Joe White, who enchanted Jimmy with his "swamp rock" genre, and hits like "Polk Salad Annie" and "Rainy Night in Georgia." Such concert reporting would have its deep effect—in only a few years, Jimmy Buffett concerts would be turning up in the same *Billboard* "Talent in Action" section.

■ ■ ■

Nashville was definitely becoming more cosmopolitan, crossing over from country to pop, and from booze to drugs. As a veteran music publisher said to John Grissim (*Country Music: White Man's Blues*) in 1970: "If you want to talk about misbehaving, those rock and roll guys can't hold a candle to country music. Hell, most of these ol' Country boys who are still making a good living have been tearin' up bars, startin' fistfights, gettin' laid, breakin' up marriages and hittin' the whiskey bottle before these kids were born. Hell, talk about marijuana and pills, who do you think first brought that stuff across the border in the first place?" Pause. "The goddamn hillbillies, that's who!" (Amphetamines, after all, were a necessity for many entertainers—to keep their eyes on the road and their show on the road.)

Grissim wrote up the disc-jockey convention week, held each fall, with all its shows and meetings. He lamented the low-quality marijuana on the tables at some cocktail parties ("pathetic-looking joints . . . the dried-up old-graham-cracker variety") and noticed one entertainer wearing a woman's negligee, and a famous record producer who was unzipping, briefly, the dress of a "snuff queen" in the crowd, who was doubling as a lady journalist. (Grissim heard that good-looking girl songwriters utilized the couches in certain offices, and that some Music Row executives were called "closet fuckers.")

■ ■ ■

More respectable was the large *Billboard* section on April 25, 1970, to which Jimmy contributed, covering the city's music business. According to the lead article by Bill Williams, Nashville's first wedding in 1780 had utilized a shipment of Jew's harps from St. Louis; by 1830, no city of its size in the country had such interest in live music—organ, flute, violin, harp, and piano concerts—with minstrel melodies the most popular. Williams quoted the *Nashville Whig* (1857) concerning songwriting: "The song is generally about some maiden, who lives near some river, who did or didn't do something, who died somehow, and is supposed to be loved by the singer to the last pitch of distraction."

Jimmy's article, "The Studio That Jack Built," extolled the newly opened headquarters of Jack Clement—virtuoso producer, songwriter, and publisher. Jimmy's personal studio destination was 110 21st Avenue South, where similarly versatile Buzz Cason performed in a hot-selling, pseudo-group that was truly "a downstairs alliance."

Down in the basement of the Baker Building . . . at Spar studio.

The Nashville Sound of Sound-alikes
(You Can Be a Spar)

■

I'm sick of all these aggressive hippies or whatever they are, the Now Generation.

—John Lennon, *Lennon Remembers: The Rolling Stone Interviews*
edited by Jann Wenner (1971)

Isn't this kind of deceptive? What's going on?" Johnny Carson asked Jimmy on *The Tonight Show* in 1990.

Carson was describing the act Milli Vanilli, "two guys who apparently don't sing very well . . . doing concerts which they are up lip-synching." Carson said they had sold seven million records, and Jimmy agreed, "That was a lot."

The duo had won a Grammy for an album on which they hadn't really sung. They intended to sing on their next one, however, when the scandal broke—and their Grammy was revoked. They admitted having made "a pact with the Devil" for fame.

"Have you ever done anything like this before?" Carson interrogated Jimmy.

"I have to confess that a long time ago, when I was living in Nashville, I was a member of a group of people who did 'copy records.' You remember when they did the 'bargain records,' and you faked and sounded like the real artist? I think I was Ronny and the Daytonas."

(Indeed, Buzz Cason, Jimmy's first manager, had written "Sandy" for Ronny and the Daytonas with John "Bucky" Wilkin, which went to Number 17 on the pop chart in 1965.)

"I was very poor," added Jimmy. "I was a member of the Now Generation, and we did 'copy songs.'"

When he and Johnny Carson finished talking, Carson promised the viewers that there would be *no* lip-synching on *his* show!

Yet Buzz Cason himself, when he was in Nashville's Isaac Litton High School, had lip-synched doo-wop hits on Noel Ball's *Saturday Showcase* (WSIX-TV) in 1956. Cason's pseudo-black group was the Manhattans, and they would bring black records to dances and fake it—till someone told him, "Leave those damned records at home, and then you'll have to sing!" Cason says, "We were supposed to be the professional talent and we were usually worse than the amateurs."

Born November 27, 1939, Cason grew up on Ardee Avenue in the Inglewood suburb of Nashville (about a mile south of Colonel Parker's Elvis headquarters on Gallatin Road). "Nashville never has been a country town," Cason told Daniel Cooper of the *Nashville Scene* in 1995. "Nashville was a big-band town, and R&B." Certainly there has always been a dearth of live country clubs—a 1963 Esso city map doesn't even list one country-music site, not even the Ryman Auditorium, in its "Sight-Seeing Guide."

Like John Lennon, Cason was an art student—but "once I saw those cameras, it was over for me. I thought this might be better for me than doing artwork." Cason began playing guitar for the Casuals, backing up Brenda Lee. By 1960 he was in Los Angeles, and his Liberty record "Look for a Star" went to Number 16 in pop—it copied the British hit version by Garry Mills, only Cason's name on the record was "Garry Miles." Cason became one of the post–Buddy Holly Crickets, on the British hit "(They Call the Girl) La Bamba," milking the morbid memory of Ritchie Valens, who had the hit first, and died with Holly in the plane crash.

Thus was Jimmy's discoverer a versatile vagabond who boomeranged in and out of Nashville, via Los Angeles and London. As the British *Record Mirror* reported on March 27, 1965: "Cason, the Crickets' A&R [artists and repertoire] man, who accompanied them on their British trip last year, is reported to be working as an independent record producer."

Yes, Cason sang . . . played . . . produced . . . and published.

He had signed Jimmy to his company, Russell-Cason, which owned 1968 hits written by his partner, Bobby Russell: "Little Green Apples"

(Number 2 in pop; Number 6 in country) and "Honey" (Number 1 in pop; Number 1 in country). The two of them were sound-alike singers for Spar Records, for which Cason recruited Jimmy.

The phrase "Now Generation" was generic, aiming to stabilize and sanitize the rambunctious young pop, rock, and folk fans, who didn't obey many of their parents' rules, but didn't drown in drugged-out hippiedom, either. The Now Generation was a trendy name for a fake group, and Jimmy, who often complains (as well as boasts) about not having hits, would come closer to more hits in the underground Spar studio than he would on the ground floor of his future career.

Upstairs in the top of the Baker Building was the Top Billing booking agency, founded by Bill Graham, whose monumental Show-Biz Productions was down the hall (syndicated television shows: *The Wilburn Brothers, Porter Wagoner,* and so on). Down in the depths of Spar, co-owner Bill Beasley said, "We can do anything any other major recording studio can do." The *Tennessean*'s George Barker (in a 1965 article called "Listen to the Mocking Birds") called Beasley "neither a cool nor a hep cat. Beasley, they say, is a copycat." Beasley said, "We don't waste time or money producing songs that aren't hits. If a song isn't a hit, we don't record it." Someone else quipped: "How long will the public spend ninety-eight cents for a real Beatles single when they can buy a good imitation for thirty-nine cents?" Beasley's partner Alan Bubis thinks they sometimes outsold the originals—a country hit might sell only ten thousand or twelve thousand—but they might ship one hundred thousand.

Radio listeners might hear a hit but not know who recorded it, then, if they spotted the same title on a Now Generation album in the supermarket, for maybe half-price (with Jimmy Buffett wearing dark glasses in the group on the cover), they'd buy it. Cason and Russell did most of the singing—they possessed at least a dozen voices between the two of them. Russell could do Presley, Dean Martin, the Beach Boys, or Robert Goulet. "Sometimes a singer makes a mistake on a record," said Russell, "and that's real tough to repeat."

Jimmy Buffett is on at least two Now Generation albums, *The Now Generation Come Together* and *The Now Generation Hits Are Our Business,* both released in 1970 and produced by Tom Walls. At least Jimmy is on both covers, and some of the rest of the "group" was assembled for photo purposes only, out at Centennial Park (resembling such soft-pop groups as the Seekers or We Five). One of those portrayed is engineer Travis Turk. Exactly which tracks Jimmy was on is not known—the first album had five Number 1's on it, and the second album had seven (songs like "Honky-Tonk Women," "Last Train to Clarksville," "Suspicious Minds," "Down on the Corner," "Leaving on a Jet Plane," etc.).

■   ■   ■

Once at Spar they were cutting a Ray Stevens hit, "Ahab the Arab," and didn't know how to finish it. Miraculously, Stevens was in the building—and helped sing part of the sound-alike of his hit! Stevens had been a star on Monument Records, but had now joined an independent label, Barnaby Records, started by singer Andy Williams and his brother Don. Andy Williams was on Columbia, so Columbia was going to distribute Barnaby Records.

Maybe Cason could get Jimmy Buffett onto Barnaby. . . .

"The Christian?" Goes Down to Earth

■

He came up from Mobile, and I said, "Let's take a shot on him and see what we can come up with." The first album was Down to Earth, *cut over at a studio called Spar in the basement of the Baker Building.*

—Buzz Cason to Jay Orr, *Nashville Banner,* June 25, 1993

That may have been the downfall of Buffett, because I signed Buffett," laughs Mike Shepherd, former general manager of Barnaby Records. "The first time Buzz played me Buffett's stuff, I knew he was going to have a hit, sooner or later. The people in the record business may not know what a hit is, but they know what the potential is. I knew Larry Gatlin was going to have a hit, eventually, when I heard *his* first demos. And of course other people amaze you, when *they* have a hit, 'cause you didn't think they'd have one in a million years.

"Today, it's the same thing. Ninety percent of the people who come to Nashville can't even get in to see anyone."

Shepherd had been promotional director at Monument Records, itself a dynamic, independent company, created by the imaginative wizard Fred Foster. Monument had launched Roy Orbison, Boots Randolph, Jeannie Seely, Dolly Parton, Kris Kristofferson, and the comical Ray Stevens, with parody hits like "Gitarzan." ("Ray is a very nice guy to this day," Jimmy told journalist Frederick Burger in 1979.) Shepherd says, "Ray and I had become real close, and buddies. Then Andy Williams popped in and offered Ray a summer replacement show, and part of that deal was Barnaby Records, which Andy already owned." So Stevens and Shepherd left for Barnaby, and Shepherd began reissuing Everly Brothers songs from Williams's old label, Cadence. Barnaby opened its Nashville office at 1009 17th Avenue South, right next door to Porter Wagoner Enterprises.

Shepherd already knew Cason and Russell, whose Rising Sons label Monument had distributed (scoring a 1968 hit, "Everlasting Love," a pop standard cowritten by Cason). "Cason called me one day and told me about Buffett. I had met Buffett, and we had been playing tennis together at lunch time. . . . Ray's record ["Everything Is Beautiful"] was out, and was a smash, being distributed by Columbia—and it was a good place for an act to get a start."

Cason admits that his partner Russell "wasn't too interested; he sounded like a 'wacko folkie' to him." When he told Shepherd, "I've got this kid Buffett, he's got some songs," and let him hear some, Shepherd just "flipped out."

Shepherd says, "I particularly liked 'The Christian?' so I sent it out to Andy and Allen Bernard, Andy's manager, and said I wanted him on the label. I'm from New York . . . so I went to New York and saw Ron Alexenburg, who was the liaison between Columbia and the subsidiary label [Barnaby]. And we signed him."

Jimmy received five hundred dollars from Barnaby and bought himself a twelve-string acoustic guitar.

"The Christian?" and most (if not all) the songs for the first album were cut at Spar. "I heard that Buffett was cutting down there, but I was busy upstairs," chuckles Bill Beasley, who says, "Buzz Cason was one of the most talented men of that era." Beasley should know—back in the Fifties, he himself had cut Pat Boone's first singles ("like Perry Como, covering rock songs") and "Down Yonder" by Del Wood, a female piano-instrumental country hit and Opry standard. In fact, Spar was probably the first studio in town to install eight-track equipment—and maybe the first to ape Hollywood string effects, a harbinger of the eventually hated "Nashville Sound" of crossover mush.

Spar, at least, could do the most for the least money. Buffett's total first album cost around five thousand dollars to produce. Bob Cook played guitar, harmonica, and bass; Cason sang backup; Travis Turk was one of the drummers, not to mention the engineer *and* the producer. Cason figured that the sessions had produced pretty good demos, that they could recut them in time, but after Shepherd heard "The Christian?" he said, "Oh no, let's put it out."

"The Christian?" was co-written with Milton Brown, and has the "flattened seventh" chord progression, which gives it a bitter blues quality (like the chorus of Lynn Anderson's 1970 hit "Rocky Top"). Shepherd was a Catholic convert and "The Christian?" is an acerbic, highly moralistic song that ridicules pretentious, smug, churchgoing "Christians." The question mark in the title kicks hard. The lyric suggests that flaunting one's religion while looking out for oneself first doesn't necessarily woo Jesus. A true Christian needs more than flamboyant, self-styled faith, such as some good ol' archconservatives like to parade around.

Billboard gave "The Christian?" a "Special Merit Spotlight" notice on May 30, 1970: "Strong debut out of the Nashville scene is a potent piece of material with a biting lyric line and a top vocal workout. Could make it big." It was one of *Cash Box*'s "Picks of the Week" (August 1, 1970): "Jimmy talks about the 'Golden Rule' in this very strong gospel-aimed religious offer."

Gerry Wood supplied the photograph for the album cover. Jimmy wanted it to be titled *Jimmy Buffett Drives Religion and Politics into the Ground*. "So what do we do for an album cover with a title like that?" asked Wood. His own answer, that March, had been to row up the Cumberland River with Jimmy in his ten-foot aluminum rowboat, S.S. *Wood*, ballasted with rum and beer. When Wood spotted some junked cars dumped on the riverbank to prevent erosion, "I saw the album cover. A battered old car mostly buried by debris and river residue presented itself as the perfect representation of the title concept." While Wood readied his camera, Jimmy squirmed through the back window of the rusted car. . . .

"Hurry up and take that picture, goddamn it!"

"Hey, if you hear anything slithering around down in there, it's probably just a snake—a water moccasin—but don't worry, Jimmy, they don't bite if they're out of the water." Pause. "Or . . . maybe . . . they don't bite if they're *in* the water. . . ." Wood couldn't remember which.

"YOU TAKE THAT DAMNED PICTURE!"

At Barnaby, some "rocket-scientist music-biz chiefs decided on a shorter title," *Down to Earth*. The cover depicts Jimmy deep down in the earth, in the back of the ruined, half-buried car. The Nashville sound of existentialist angst, the singer literally half underground, on an album of mostly underground songs, cut below the street level of 21st Avenue South.

The album cover was briefly considered for a Grammy award.

■   ■   ■

Down to Earth was ahead of its time for Nashville in 1970, and still is today.

Its second song, "Ellis Dee" (written with Buzz Cason), has a sprightly, singable melody, jarringly at odds with its scathing lyrics. Ellis Dee is the nickname of a black dope addict whose son is aggrieved by his father's habit—and who makes a good target for the police. Jimmy damns the dope pusher on the street, a parallel to Hoyt Axton's "The Pusher" for Steppenwolf (1964). Housing-project drug trafficking and consequent gun deaths make Nashville's black low-income rentals Murder City, U.S.A. even today.

At the time the song appeared, J. Edgar Hoover's secret FBI program Cointelpro had been inciting violence between black militants, paralleling the CIA's Operation Chaos (followed by its pre-Watergate burglary in 1971). Ellis Dee, of course, stood for LSD (lysergic acid diethylamide), a Cold War drug promoted in a tax-supported whorehouse of un-American activities in San Francisco in 1955. As part of Operation Midnight Climax, prostitutes had lured in the subjects, who were slipped LSD, then watched through mirrors—later victims were given LSD and electric shock, to see how their brains worked (or no longer worked). In a macabre parallel to Jimmy's song, the CIA also prescribed LSD for black drug-addict patients in a Kentucky hospital for seventy-five consecutive days around 1959. The LSD "acid" might affectionately be nicknamed the Langley Secret Drug, since the CIA supported it until 1963, sometimes bribing victims with heroin if they would but *try* some LSD.

"The Missionary" is another religious polemic, about a preacher who has been vaunting American-quality peace overseas (swords into plowshares), helping naked aborigines to "distinguish right from wrong." Now he is demoralized, and embarrassed, by his nation's jungle warfare. America, morally, just ain't what it used to be.

The folkie ballad "Mile High in Denver" anticipates (maybe even inspired) John Denver's "Rocky Mountain High" hit of 1972, since its melody is good. "The Captain and the Kid," opening with acoustic arpeggios, completes Side One. Years later, in *Stereo Review,* Peter Reilly praised this "autobiographical ballad, radiating sunlit grace and tenderness," concerning the grandfather "who passed on his love of the sea and a sense of its mystical pull for those who journey upon it."

On Side Two, "Captain America" takes a stab at mediaphobic Vice President Spiro Agnew, as well as at Merle Haggard's hit "Okie from Muskogee," itself a philippic against antiwar kids. "Ain't He a Genius?" sounds like ironic wishful thinking—about a former underground weirdo who's now become a star, reaping the usual jealousy that success always brings. "Turnabout" is a love song about a girl from Mobile, enticing a boy living up North into returning to the bay.

"There's Nothing Soft About Hard Times" is an impassioned country-blues cut. Jimmy's marriage to Margie may be hinted at in "I Can't Be Your Hero Today," since the irritated man is a Capricorn, and his diffident lady is a Taurus—at least the zodiac fits the Nashville Buffett couple. "Truckstop Salvation" ridicules stereotypical Southerners who live off the Bible and moonshine whiskey, whereas the alternate world Buffett extols is not a "country fair sideshow."

Record World said that *Down to Earth* "has been reviewed as a country-pop presentation in the vein of James Taylor and Gordon Lightfoot." Jimmy's friend and backup musician Bob Cook believes the album was "banned in Boston," due to "The Christian?," and that "they wouldn't play it on the air for a while. It did sell some, and it was promoted. The fact that it was banned in Boston was a big booster for it and made it sell more."

Jimmy has always griped that it only sold 324 copies—he even told *Time* magazine in 1977, "It was a terrible record."

Gerry Wood says, "Nobody bought the album. Nobody bought Buffett. Jimmy's hopes for quick success were shattered." Buzz Cason received almost no money, though Bob Cook says, "I got residuals off that for years. I was just a player on it and a background singer—I was getting checks like $22.50 a quarter for a long time. It must have sold more than a thousand copies." Almost five years later, Cook was still getting smaller quarterly checks, down to around two dollars. In October of 1970, in an enthusiastic article, "Cason Enterprises Climbs," *Record World* declared that thanks to the album, "Buffett is presently preparing for a promotional tour which will include several syndicated television appearances."

One belated review by Chris Wohlwend, "Buffett Album Good Effort," in the *Knoxville Journal* (March 1, 1971), said that Jimmy "takes swipes at many of society's ills," but that his gibes were gentle, due to his "soft singing style" and the country-rock sound. Wohlwend praised the "haunting homesickness" of "Turnabout," where "he sings it like he means it." The review said that "in all songs Buffett's singing is very good," comparing him to James Taylor, and called the backup band good and effective as well. Jimmy played in Knoxville the following week.

Still, with its rebellious, folkie-leftist tone, *Down to Earth* must have been unwelcome in the Opry-oriented Nashville oligarchy.

■   ■   ■

Bob Cook was on the road in 1970, till Jimmy asked him, "Why don't you come to Nashville? We can get some free recording time with Travis Turk at Spar." (A *Country Song Roundup* article that fall, "Sooner or Later They All Come to Nashville," rattled off as many names of visiting celebrities as possible: singers Jose Feliciano, Arlo Guthrie, and Tony Martin, and actor Chill Wills.) So Cook rented a "dingy little apartment in a house" and began working in the lounge at the King of the Road Hotel (Day's Inn Nashville Central today). "When they had big shows upstairs, I would try to catch the overflow downstairs," he recalls. His humor tactics probably influenced Jimmy: "The first thing you've got to do is make them laugh their asses off. Then they'll listen to you. I gave them all the funny material I could collect along the way."

Cook began helping Cason work on his own new studio, Creative Workshop, in south Nashville (still in operation today). Jimmy helped too. "I was helping Travis to pull wires and solder and build," says Cook. "We were in there all night, pulling wires till our eyes crossed, and soldering blocks and things like that. Then we would play chess all night."

At least Cason's Barnaby achievement had triggered his new studio, which became a permanent Nashville music institution, including Southern Writers Group U.S.A. publishing. In fact, one of Jimmy's jobs was to promote Cason's publishing. But Cason still thinks he didn't get statements from Barnaby. "Back then, nobody got paid right, if you got paid at all."

■ ■ ■

At some point, Jimmy and Margie moved to east Nashville, into a log cabin at 1421 Porter Road—probably reassembled in 1943 from some ancient cabins in Kentucky. Supposedly it had been originally a tavern, almost certainly from the eighteenth century. Current owner Loretta Pitt says it has "cathedral beams" overhead, and "old wormy chestnut paneling." Referring to the cramped upstairs, Cason says, "That's where he cut his chops. He would sit up there in that heat all night and rehearse."

Jimmy was playing anywhere he could, colleges especially, and in any clubs he could find, such as the Exit/In, where the *Tennessean*'s Clark Parsons says he performed "his songs on short notice when big names canceled." Buzz Cason says Jimmy was the first to perform there when it opened in 1971. Remembers cofounder Owsley Manier: "We were building the place. I'd never heard of Jimmy Buffett, nor had anyone else. The stage was about half finished—two-by-fours, and some pieces of plywood. He walked in through the street door from the back, wearing cutoffs and a T-shirt, with a guitar, and auditioned right there in the afternoon, and I hired him. A lot of people that ended up being quite larger later [such as David Allen Coe] just kind of wandered in off the street, virtually unknown, and I hired them."

In the first nine months, the club seated around 120; then, in 1972, it expanded next door to around 240 capacity, and Jimmy played in the larger Exit/In several times as well (probably on trips up from Florida). "He did decent business. He went from that club to filling up Murphy Center [Murfreesboro, Tennessee].

"The biggie, then, was that song 'Why Don't We Get Drunk (and Screw)' which was sort of counter to the remains of the folk movement that was going on then—but that was just part of him."

Countless stars have played at the Exit/In throughout the past quarter century, from Dr. Hook, John Prine, Tom T. Hall, Jerry Lee Lewis, Delbert McClinton, Etta James, Waylon Jennings, and Chuck Berry, to Talking Heads, R.E.M., NRBQ, Lemonheads, and the Fleshtones.

■   ■   ■

"He wanted to find out what it was like on the road, and to be a traveling musician," says Bob Cook, who had moved to Iowa, "so he came to Des Moines, and he was supposed to play in the Wakonda Lounge. To do it, he had to borrow a Carmen Ghia from somebody. It did the job, and his first try was pretty frustrating. I talked to him at the motel, and he didn't *like* the road. He worked the job for a week or less, and said, 'That's it, I'm not going to do this anymore, it's too hard,' and he went on back to Nashville. He didn't finish the job on the road and didn't want to continue traveling. His original idea was 'I want to do this every night and sharpen myself,' but he found out he didn't like it every night."

In most clubs, there's no real "listening room"—just talking and drinking and dancing—and if you don't play "greatest hits" (like the Upstairs Alliance), you won't be invited back. Jimmy had outgrown lounge work, so with all his originals, and his new album deal, he desperately needed *concerts,* not barroom, background music gigs.

"Jimmy used to come back from some of his trips and play colleges, to increasingly larger audiences, maybe a couple hundred," says Gerry Wood. "But he also used to play in the basement of the Carmichael Tower at Vanderbilt, to maybe fifteen or twenty people. He would come back with different songs. One time he came back with 'West Nashville Grand Ballroom Gown'; another time he came back with 'My Head Hurts, My Feet Stink, and I Don't Love Jesus' printed on a T-shirt."

■   ■   ■

"In Hattiesburg, they had invited me back to play my alma mater," Jimmy told singer-songwriter Jerry Jeff Walker on the *Texas Connection* television show (TNN) in 1992. "But they had *no* idea what I had turned into . . . lyrically, that is." It was 1970, and Jimmy was playing at The Hub, in the student center: "It was charming . . . it was one of those magic nights in show business. I was playing between night classes, when all of these teachers would come take their classes . . . they were much older people. They had me in a corner, and I was singing one of those great truth-in-love songs of mine, 'Why Don't We Get Drunk (and "You Know What")'—for which I was immediately told I would *never* be invited back to my alma mater!"

Sitting with Jimmy and Jerry Jeff Walker on the TV show was Greg "Fingers" Taylor, Jimmy's Coral Reefer harmonica player. Jimmy was explaining how they first met this same night at Hattiesburg: "This young harmonica player came up. In any town there is *always* a harmonica player—or somebody's got a cousin who's a harmonica player: 'You should hear my cousin, he's the greatest'—and they get up there, and they're not what you would call virtuosos. But Fingers got up and I went, 'Well, he *is* sort of good.'"

Jimmy asked him, "You want to work, you want to leave college, you want to see the world?"

He nodded.

"Next thing I knew, he was out of the dorm, and we were in Jonesboro, Arkansas, for our first gig."

Taylor was from Jackson, Mississippi, and had started a rock band, the Immortals, patterned after the Beatles. On the USM campus he had played backup with Delaney and Bonnie and Friends (Delaney and Bonnie Bramlett), and the Nitty Gritty Dirt Band.

"I got Jimmy a date with a girl at Burger Town," Taylor told Frederick Burger (*Atlanta Constitution*) in 1985. He also said Jimmy had performed for "only a handful of appreciative coeds." He said that *he* offered his services to Jimmy first—that Jimmy was initially reluctant—but they ended up playing most of the week together. He drove Jimmy over to Mobile—"Driving along as the sun came up, Jimmy was playing his guitar, singing all his songs to me."

■　■　■

In November 1970, Jimmy was over in Cason's new studio cutting his next album, *High Cumberland Jubilee*. But the album was unreleased until 1977.

The opening track on Side One, "Ace," is about an illiterate, panhandling hobo from Mississippi (recalling the tradition of Hank Snow's "Hobo's Last Ride" and Bob Dylan's "Only a Hobo"). "Rockefeller Square" mocks a New York millionaire's son as he tries to become an underground renegade, and "Bend a Little" is another didactic lyric demanding that people be more open-minded; both songs were cowritten with Cason. The melodies are thus far indifferent, but "In the Shelter" is compellingly pretty, with a syncopated beat—about a girl with a confused personality, at odds with her father, who just cannot go back home. "Death Valley Lives" is a kind of sequel, about another beleaguered girl, and has an exciting melody.

The last cut is one of Jimmy's all-time best songs, "Livingston's Gone to Texas." The haunting melody starts with the dominant chord, to underscore the depressing theme: The girl's boyfriend has left for Texas. Like a good country song, it relies on inane understatement—"Nothing here is different, nothing's changed at all"—and Livingston will be "gone awhile." Ernest Tubb's "Walking the Floor over You" has the same Southern obliqueness that says nothing yet tells everything (he doesn't know why she's left, but he *does* know that she's gone). Jimmy's release (the bridge) has an uplifting melody. The poignant last line underscores

Livingston's long and painful absence: "the snow's about to fall." The song would soon come true for Jimmy and Margie.

Side Two opens with more of the same: "England" (written with Cason), about a girl who's flown to England to escape her lover. The title of one of the songs, "The Hang-Out Gang" (written with Cason), echoed the nickname for Jimmy and the musicians who hung around Cason's studio. "High Cumberland Jubilee/Comin' Down Slow," also written with Cason, starts with a pretty, Beatles-like melody, then shifts into a folkie, bluegrass sound. The double-song is over five minutes long.

■ ■ ■

Gerry Wood still likes three of the album's songs—"In the Shelter,""Livingston's Gone to Texas"—and "Travelin' Clean," from Side Two. It inspired him to write a screenplay with Jimmy: "a wacky tale of some weirdos taking a Scenicruiser bus from Maine to Key West, down U.S. 1, picking up oddball characters en route, and coming to a crashing finale as it plunges off the southernmost point into the southernmost seas."

They also wrote The Quitters together—"about everyone quitting, who becomes a national phenomenon, from airplane pilots, to the President—written before Nixon resigned!" Folk-pop singer Buffy Sainte-Marie, "wonderful woman that she is," had recorded in Nashville and told Wood, "Show these scripts to my manager—he might be interested." So he and Jimmy flew to Chicago, then took the Union Pacific passenger train, The City of Los Angeles, which was "yellow with pink stripes," out to L.A. They were on the train for two days, so they kept writing on one of the scripts.

Jimmy had one copy of Down to Earth with him, for Sainte-Marie's manager. In the dining car the first night was a father and his son, about ten or eleven, and they became excited that they were sitting across from a real recording artist. "Do you have an album?" they asked. "Yeah," said Jimmy, and ran back to his room for his only copy, which he gave to the strangers. When they got to L.A., they gave the manager the scripts . . . and never heard from him again.

"I feel somewhat responsible for getting him into trains," says Gerry Wood. On Valentine's Day, probably in 1971, they were supposed to go to Louisville. It was snowing so they took the train, and were working on a script—the train arrived in Louisville at five P.M., but Jimmy insisted they reboard the train. "My good friend Ricky Bennett lives in Cincinnati—let's go visit him." So they went to Cincinnati. The dining car closed down, then the train crashed into a parked station wagon—whose owner had gone to get a pizza. "We rescued the pizza," boasts Wood, "and got it into the dining car and ate it."

Back in Nashville, Margie and Ellen Wood were waiting at the station, in vain, for their husbands . . . for Valentine's Day dinner. The men called home, and "Ellen took it pretty good, and then Margie got on the phone and Jimmy got an earful. Then he put me on, and I got an earful. Ellen said, 'Gerry Wood, when you get back you'll have to do *all the dishes*.' We partied all night, and had about an hour's sleep and caught the next train back. When I hear that line in 'Come Monday,' about 'rented cars and westbound trains,' I know where *that* came from."

■   ■   ■

Jimmy's ex-drummer, Bill Kehoe, was still at Southern in the spring of 1971. He remembers the "Spring Fling" music show, when Jimmy showed up and gave him a copy of *Down to Earth*. "He told me I wouldn't find it in the record stores around here, it was just around Nashville."

Jerry Jeff Walker was there, too.

"We're going to sit and b.s. a little bit," said Walker at the opening of his 1992 *Texas Connection* TV show with Jimmy. "For us, this goes back about twenty years. We started on a stage together somewhere in Mississippi."

"Jerry Jeff was my *hero* then."

"It took about twenty-four hours to change that," added Walker.

Jimmy agreed: "It changed *real* quick. . . . 'I'm not sure I want to be like that.'"

Gerry Wood helped it happen. There was some sort of music conference scheduled—Wood drove to Memphis, took a train to New Orleans, then drove a rental car up to Hattiesburg. "Jimmy was there, and Jerry Jeff was there. I had been trying to sign him up for ASCAP, and I introduced them and Jimmy was awed at meeting a star."

Born Ronald Clyde Crosby in 1942 in New York State, Jerry Jeff Walker had touched down in Texas in 1966, moving there eventually. Walker wrote "Mr. Bojangles," a low-charting 1968 single for himself, but a Number 9 pop hit for the Nitty Gritty Dirt Band in 1971.

"Jerry Jeff was going out to California, to talk to someone about writing music for a movie," continues Gerry Wood, "and we drove to New Orleans together." Buffett said on TV that they rented a car, which they then "ditched," placing himself henceforth on the blacklist of the rent-a-car companies. Jimmy had used his credit card—Walker said, "It didn't matter"—and Jimmy said they'd better cowrite a song, to pay for the car. Wood remembers: "We all hung out all night long at the Cornstalk Fence Motel on Bourbon Street. We started at these bars, hatching this plan that we ought to take the Panama Limited back to Memphis, and they started putting funny little pills into my drinks." Someone was singing a song in a club that he said had been taught to him by Jerry Jeff Walker. Walker walked up and said, "I don't remember teaching you that song."

They got back to the Cornstalk Fence around five A.M., staying in the same room. Gerry Wood's train was leaving at seven A.M., and "I remember hearing a train whistle in my dreams, and waking up around noon." Wood, Walker, and Buffett went to the train at four-thirty P.M., and Walker said they couldn't board it without two bottles of Wild Turkey. "And here's the train about to leave, and it's literally moving as we jumped on. We had these double bedrooms, and they pulled out their guitars and the singing went on till about two or three in the morning. The conductor was threatening to throw us off the train if we made any more noise."

Then, either Jimmy or Walker came up with a line, "I met a railroad lady, just a little bit shady," and the two of them began trading lines back and forth, cowriting a new song. Walker and Jimmy knew that railroad services were being discontinued—they were upset that sweet "ladies of the night" would be out of work, who sold "party favors" for bank presidents and railroad officials. "That was our main concern," says Jimmy, "about the rail industry in America." When they said the lady was a "loner," Wood contributed "highballing," because to him, it was a double entendre: "She met a highballing loner who thought he could own her." Gerry Wood feels he is owed $1/192$ of the song royalties for supplying this one word.

The next morning in their train compartment, Jerry Jeff Walker sang "Mr. Bojangles" for the first time for Jimmy and Gerry Wood. "It was such a stunning performance. After it was over we couldn't say anything . . . we just went back to our rooms."

Soon they were back in Nashville. At one point, Walker dropped by Jimmy's Porter Road log cabin and they "partied." Walker attempted to make a long-distance call. The number wasn't visible on the phone—he didn't want to bother the Buffetts—so he tried to coerce the operator into making his call, without supplying the number. She refused. He shouted into the phone, so she "froze" the phone so he couldn't call out. The next morning she called back, asking Jimmy: "Are you ready to behave now?"

■ ■ ■

Back in his *Billboard* days, Jimmy's editor, Bill Williams, had telephoned booking agent Don Light to tell him about Jimmy. Light listened to his tapes and "thought he was unique, thought his songs were unique. Thought maybe I could help. Didn't know it would take so long." Light was a former Grand Ole Opry drummer and *Billboard* staffer who had opened his agency in 1965, handling acts as diverse as Governor Jimmie ("You Are My Sunshine") Davis, the Oak Ridge Boys, and the gospel family the Rambos. Buzz Cason also began talking to Light about Jimmy.

Jimmy wanted to work at the Bistro in Atlanta. Light got him a gig. One of his dates was New Year's Eve 1971—*not one person showed up to hear him,* but he persisted. One of his Bistro listeners was "Uncle Tom," a journalist for the youth tabloid *The Great Speckled Bird* (one of whose street peddlers was Mary Vecchio, immortalized in the Kent State shooting photograph, bending over a dead student). In July 1971, Uncle Tom said Jimmy's music "isn't hung in any one motif—he's folk, country, blues, and rock, and likes to share his small glories (like meeting childhood hero, Roy Rogers, snoring in a Nashville studio) from the stage." He compared him to Dennis Hopper and Peter Fonda in the film *Easy Rider* (1969), but said his lyrics weren't limited to "movements and fads." He said Jimmy didn't have a phony voice of "contrived coarseness to keep in the ethnic-Dylan bag," and that he was competent with both his six-string and twelve-string guitars. He complained that Jimmy's album was hard to find. "Despite its quality, *Down to Earth* hasn't sold for shit," and Jimmy hadn't helped Barnaby or the CBS distributors "become any richer." In fact, his next album was being offered to other companies—"both RCA and A&M are bidding for it, and Jimmy hopes to have it out in August or September."

Barnaby Records had accidentally buried *High Cumberland Jubilee* deep down in the earth. Mike Shepherd had left, and was unaware that Barnaby had told Jimmy that the master tape was "lost." Says Shepherd with regret: "If I had been there, I would have protected him all the way, up and down the line."

Cason took Jimmy to New York, and they were turned down by every record company.

"That was not the best period of Buffett's life," judges Gerry Wood. "Tapes lost. Marital—make that martial—trouble. No record sales. No radio airplay. And I was beating the hell out of him in tennis and table hockey." Jimmy told Chet Flippo in *Rolling Stone* in 1977 that after his first album came out, he "hired a complete band, went on the road, and was broke in two months. Went back to Nashville, and my wife and I split up."

■ ■ ■

Jimmy was running out of enthusiasm for Nashville since, for one thing, "his landlord didn't like the intensity of the purple paint that Jimmy had used to decorate his bedroom," according to Gerry Wood. "Buffett also didn't like the Nashville winters. And the Nashville music business." That year Nashville's "The Battle Hymn of Lt. Calley" was charting, out of sympathy for the convicted My Lai baby-killer—radio stations were flooded with hundreds of favorable calls.

One night, Jimmy was out driving in Margie's Mercedes-Benz with songwriter Donnie Fritts ("Alabama Leaning Man"), who is mentioned in the introduction of Kristofferson's "The Pilgrim." Gerry Wood says they were drinking as they drove, and "somehow the rear door became a detached part of the car. I think another car ran into it when they opened the door. Or maybe Jimmy or Donnie ran into it. Or they ran into another car which ran into the door." At least Jimmy slipped the door into the backseat, and drove it home and left it parked outside the cabin on Porter Road.

Jimmy often jokes about flying to Miami at this point, with his thumb over his expired credit card. Destination: Jerry Jeff Walker. Travis Turk remembers driving Jimmy to the airport, and within a day receiving a registered letter canceling his arrangement with Jimmy (ditto Buzz Cason). Cason had let Jimmy's contract expire, so Jimmy had moved on. He had already endured twenty-six record company rejections.

In a week or two he was back in Nashville and asked Turk, "What's going on?"

His comrades Cason, Wood, and Turk couldn't get him anything but a free meal now and then, and a couch to sleep on. They didn't know what the fuck Barnaby had done with *High Cumberand Jubilee*, though they would get to see it in 1977. Turk at least became a successful Nashville engineer and says engineering is an art: "Like a painter who takes a little bit of red, and a little bit of yellow, and a little bit of purple, and he gets a new color." A few years later, at Creative Workshop, Cason hung a picture of "a typically burnt-out Buffett in a yellow T-shirt with a dancing hula girl on the front." It was inscribed: *If you stay in show business too long, this is what it will do to you.*

"If I'd gotten big in Nashville, I'd be a total ass," Jimmy told Candice Russell of the *Miami Herald* in 1974, " 'cause I wouldn't have known better. I'd have a big ranch and play Las Vegas. I was thrown in with a manager who handles Andy Williams and John Davidson." To Judith Sims of *Rolling Stone* he said the next year: "I hated Nashville. It's too closed, too incompetent, and there's lots of nepotism. I was sick of it, so I moved to Key West."

To paraphrase a song on the "lost" Barnaby tape, Livingston had gone to Florida, where "he had a ball." You wonder—did he ever think "about the tears his woman cried"?

The Young Man and the Sea

■

Christ, this is fine country!

—Ernest Hemingway, in a letter to Mike Strater, May 13, 1928,
extolling Key West

*Key West is not only a place. It is also an attitude. . . . You can walk
or stagger to the bars and restaurants, always meeting people you know
or know about. . . . Characters were not only a few people; they were
many of the people in town. Someone commented, "It's the only island
insane asylum."*

—Lee Dodez, *Memories of Key West* (1994)

In 1972 Jerry Jeff Walker released
"L.A. Freeway," something of a definitive, pack-your-bags, evacuation
anthem. It became a Jerry Jeff standard, since it celebrates leaving your
key in the front-door lock . . . a pink slip in your mailbox . . . after
packing up all your dishes (which rhymes with those "sons of bitches,"
the landlords).

The lyric somewhat epitomizes Jimmy's frenetic departure from Nashville, right after the phone bill fiasco. Walker was living in Coconut
Grove, a Miami suburb, and said, "You ought to come down and visit,
it's really nice down here."

Jimmy flew down and lived there maybe six months. Walker advised
Jimmy: *"Follow your own weird. . . . "*

Back in 1960, would-be weirdo Ronald Crosby (the future Jerry Jeff Walker) had left New York State, with a Stella guitar on his back and "a tattered copy of Dylan Thomas's Welsh mysticism in his hip pocket." He told Thom Duffy of the *Orlando Sentinel* in 1986 that he "hitchhiked all the way through Central Florida. There wasn't anything down here then, just sunshine . . . long, tall grass . . . alligators—and not nearly as many mosquitoes." He played music on the beach for about three dollars a day "and all the suntan lotion I could rub on." Supposedly, he was going to "find himself, then slip into a respectable career."

Like his hero-worshiping protégé Jimmy Buffett, Walker was saved from the dire fate of respectability—by New Orleans. In the Crescent City, he became "Jerry Ferris" and used a fake ID card to get into bars until he was twenty-one. He played and sang on the sidewalks, and since every time there was a murder the police arrested all the street drunks, he was tossed in jail for four days. There, a black jailmate named "Mr. Bojangles" danced and entertained him. The resulting song has been recorded by everyone from George Jones to Sammy Davis, Jr. And yes, in 1968 Crosby became Jerry Jeff Walker.

Coconut Grove in Miami just might have been the perfect habitat for Jimmy Buffett. Decorated with banyan trees facing Biscayne Bay, the suburb was a haven for both "social recluses and the creative set." Inventor Thomas Edison had lived there, as well as politician William Jennings Bryan and authors Harriet Beecher Stowe, Zane Grey, and poet Robert Frost.

Miami itself features "Little Havana" on "Calle Ocho" (Southwest Eighth Street), home for Cuban refugees since Fidel Castro's takeover in 1959. Miami's street-dancing version of the Mardi Gras is Calle Ocho's Carnival. Amusingly, in the early Sixties, everyone in town seemed to know that Miami was a Cuban invaders' capital—a fact officially kept from the American public—with Zenith Technological Services at the University of Miami a "secret" government front. An espionage safe house was located in Coconut Grove. John Roselli, recruited from the Mafia to kill Castro, turned up floating in an oil drum off Miami in 1976, subsequent to his Senate testimony.

■ ■ ■

It was almost by accident that Jimmy and Jerry Jeff Walker left Miami. Supposedly a club date was canceled, and Jimmy was "too broke to go back to Nashville." So "one cold day in Miami" he tossed his guitar in the backseat of Walker's maroon 1947 Packard (with the license plate FLYING LADY), and, according to Gordon Chaplin in a 1977 *Washington Post* article, "fled down the Keys to where Highway 1 slips finally into the bloodwarm edge of the Gulf Stream. Key West was as far as he could go: the final hangnail of the country." On the cover of the 1993 revival of an early Barnaby recording, *Before the Beach,* Jimmy is sitting on the hood of Walker's car, in an old photograph.

Key West is 154 miles below Miami, and along the way is Key Largo, formerly Rock Harbor. It changed its name to exploit its tenous connection with the Humphrey Bogart–Lauren Bacall film *Key Largo* (1948). "*Key Largo* was the catalyst that sent me farther south," Jimmy said in 1985. "The temperature was about eighty-five degrees, and there was a sailboat race going on."

Chaplin said Key West was at the "end of a long trail of one-night stands in college coffeehouses all through the South." Jimmy told him: "It was a bad time, yelling at the college kids to shut up so I could hear myself play. Nobody in Nashville would give me a recording contract. I didn't even know if I wanted to go on with music."

One story has Jimmy visiting Los Angeles briefly, after Nashville, only to be turned down by the New Christy Minstrels. His arrival in Key West is often cited having been in November 1971; a Buffett gig was scheduled at the Flick Coffeehouse in Coral Gables in December.

Walker had his own fond recollections of Key West from the Sixties. "I spent two years lost down on the Coast at Key West, Florida," he told John Moulder in *Country Rambler* in 1976. "I was tossed in jail about once a week—I was usually just standing around when a fight broke out or something else funny happened."

"The most important thing about the place," Jimmy told Gordon Chaplin, "was that it was completely virgin territory, completely different than what I'd left behind. Incredible characters, great bars. A different form of life, almost."

Jerry Jeff Walker had tended bar in Oneonta, New York, and on his *Texas Connection* interview with Jimmy in 1992, he alluded to their mutual "running buddy," Phil Clark. Walker hadn't seen him in around fifteen years. "He was the bartender when we were first hanging out in Key West. He was a real pirate. We just knew it. He had that kind of breath and those eyes."

Jimmy then reminisced about how Phil had been so loyal to his local friends: "He would always get the tourists to check into the hotel—pretty gassed-up—and then he would charge all of *our* drinks to *them.*"

"Definitely a pirate," confirmed Walker.

"I *love* Americans. And he was really that. There was always *something* going on—he put words in my vocabulary that later became songs," such as "Nautical Wheelers," which mentions Phil, and "A Pirate Looks at Forty," the dope-smuggling anthem (both 1974). When Jimmy saw Clark sailing off with his girlfriend "to some exotic island," he mused, *Gosh! I wish I could grow up to be a pirate like him!* Jimmy never equaled Phil Clark in the smuggling profession, but at least he felt some Stevensonian, *Treasure Island* empathy for him: "I was always a Jim Hawkins fan. . . ."

Clark aired a "false Bahamian accent," according to Jimmy's photographer comrade, Tom Corcoran, who wrote a masterpiece memoir, *Wastin' Away in Marijuanaville.* Corcoran said Clark flaunted such trinkets as a "piece of treasure or fossilized shark's tooth, or brass turtle," on a chain around his neck—or whatever it took to help him in "balling a parade of earthy nineteen-year-olds." Clark liked to play "A Pirate Looks at Forty" on the Key West jukeboxes, but wisely behaved himself, remembering all too painfully his late 1960s arrest.

Gerry Wood calls Clark "a notorious smuggler, some kind of an advertising-agency guy who came down and got into the good life, back when marijuana was a fun thing to smuggle. He ended up drowning in Sausalito [California, in 1986]. I think he got drunk and hit his head on the pier."

Jimmy's friend Bob Mayo, proprietor of Bobalu Southern Café, used to employ Clark. He would visit him in the morning and "get his ass out of bed, kick him out on the street," and force coffee and toast down him. "I guess he borrowed two hundred and fifty five-dollar bills from me—*one at a time!*" Mayo recalls Clark passing through Georgia with a friend "on the run," and then later hearing from someone in California that he was dead. "We took up a collection at the [Full Moon Saloon] and had him cremated and sent down in a box—we took him around to the Chart Room and five or six bars." Since Clark's favorite drink was Black Jack, they toasted his ashes with Black Jack.

As Jimmy said to Jerry Jeff Walker, "I'll tell you what, if you'd like to see Phil, his ashes are in an urn atop the Full Moon Saloon cash register."

"All right, then I *have* seen him," answered Walker.

"He would laugh at this, believe me," said Jimmy.

So would some other people. Such as Gerry Wood, who says that "one night they got some of the ashes out and snorted them, when everybody was pretty high." The bartender at Louie's Backyard, Chris Robinson, confirms this, since Clark's friends were casting at least some of the ashes into the ocean. Clark's ex-fiancée, Carol Shaugnessy (founding editor of Jimmy's *Coconut Telegraph* newsletter), says they waved a pirate flag as they sprinkled the ashes into the sea.

Bob Mayo gets the last word: "I'll tell you honestly, I don't think he's dead. I *hope* he ain't. I hope I look up some night, when I'm real drunk, and he'll say, '*Hey, Bobby!*' I hope he's alive. He was, you know, 'Mother, Mother Ocean . . . ,'" quoting the opening line of the song.

Every Parrot Head sings along when Jimmy does "A Pirate Looks at Forty," which has become a happy elegy now that Clark is apparently dead. (While Clark was in hiding, Key West locals renamed it "A Pirate Looks at Five-to-ten.")

The song, written in the first person, has the protagonist bragging about smuggling enough marijuana to have bought Miami, then having "pissed it away so fast." Now he's been drunk for over two weeks, and is so broke, he'll have to go fishing. "Fingers" Taylor's favorite verse (according to Jimmy) asserts the preference for younger women . . . who leave . . . then come back again, out of lusty nostalgia.

■   ■   ■

Back at Porter Road in Nashville, if the phone rings, it's Jimmy, at least one last call to Margie.

"Just send me my stool and my rolltop desk, and you keep the rest of it, and I'll see you later."

■   ■   ■

"It was open, new territory," Jimmy told *Rolling Stone*'s Chet Flippo in 1977. "It was a magical place." He told himself at the time, *Oh, I've found the place, this is it.* He was proud to have "met a lot of people who had traveled the Caribbean, smugglers and tourists and whatever, and I loved the history of the islands, the gold trade and the slave trade. There were thriving cities there before America was founded."

Key West's smuggling heritage is venerable, tracing back to its violent beginnings. Environmental authors Mary Durant and Michael Harwood enthused about "Key West: the lure of land's end. Sea, sky, trade winds. A tropical English-Spanish culture steeped in a history of pirates, smugglers, turtlers, revenuers, fishermen, wreckers . . ."

On May 15, 1513, Ponce de León sailed past the rocky islands, having failed to find the fountain of youth at St. Augustine. In 1566 the Spanish governor explored the Keys, searching for a route for his treasure fleet. Around 1700, Indians fought for its possession, incited by the English imperialists, who grabbed the land in 1763, slaughtering Caloosa Indians whose survivors fled to Cuba. An 1829 settler, William A. Whitehead, summed up the history thus far, saying the Keys "were only resorted to by the aborigines of the country, the piratical crews with which the neighboring seas were infested, and fishermen." A battle of 1775 "strewed the island with bones, as it is probable that the conquerors tarried not to commit the bodies of the dead to the ground."

The island was originally named Cayo Hueso ("Island of Bones"), and the British renamed it Key West. It was well-known to the pirates who frequented these waters during the eighteenth century. What archaeologists eventually decided were Indian relics, the locals preferred to revere as "pirate monuments."

Nor had all the pirates ("Brethren of the Coast") abandoned Key West when the United States took it over, in 1819. Commander David Porter attacked all the buccaneer ships he could find, and the Spanish government protested, so he was court-martialed and suspended. He quit, but old-time piracy was effectively ended—replaced, in time, with state-of-the-art smuggling.

Since the most famous post-Hemingway citizen has been Jimmy Buffett from Mobile, ironically, Key West was originally purchased from Spanish owners by Mobilian John W. Simonton in 1822, in Havana.

Fittingly, the island's first settlers—pirates and seamen—had built the first houses, styled after those in their original homes of New England, New Orleans, or the Bahamas. Latter-day frame houses, typically one and a half stories tall, were similar, built securely with joints and pegs to withstand hurricanes. Some older homes have inner trim taken from ships wrecked on adjacent reefs.

Shipwrecking itself was a local blessing. Wreckers became salvage entrepreneurs. Legends say that false beacons and flares were used to lure ships to their destruction. The federal government repeatedly built lighthouses, stifling Key West's "wrecker" industry.

Nearby Indian assaults brought in refugees, so the citizens organized "a land and water patrol" with weapons from Havana, Cuba. Naval ships patrolled, and during the Mexican War, a naval station was installed there. During the Civil War, close to three hundred blockade runners were tried at the Key West court. Cuban refugees flooded Key West in the revolution of 1869. The city was a cigar factory center in the nineteenth century, and strikes in the 1890s led to death threats against Spanish workers used to replace Cuban strikers. In 1898 the sinking of the U.S.S. *Maine* provided Key West with dead and wounded sailors. World War I was exciting as well, with patrolling ships, planes, dirigibles, and observation balloons, trying to halt German attempts at oil-running from Mexico—and Saturday-night dances for American servicemen, many of whom married Key West girls, the music courtesy of Cuba. Like Pascagoula, Key West suffered from postwar cutbacks in government defense spending.

Charitably, Prohibition contributed *its* fair share, according to the Work Projects Administration Key West guide book, with "rum-runners who knew every channel, bayou, and sand bar, made life miserable for government officials, and exciting chases brought to mind filibustering activities of another century."

Key West's financial wreckage in the Thirties placed it under federal New Deal salvage control. Federally subsidized artists covered the walls of cafes and nightclubs with murals, and children were trained to produce craft items for the tourists. Jimmy's Margaritaville store was well foreshadowed by the 1930s shops that sold ashtrays, buttons, buckles, coconut-shell pins, palm-fiber hats, purses, and fish-scale novelties.

■ ■ ■

It was the smuggling sanctity of the island that meant so much to Jimmy. "What did you think of *High Times* singling you out as the smugglers' favorite?" queried interviewer Bob Anderson in 1976. He claimed that

"A Pirate Looks at Forty" was popular in the leading drug-export country, Colombia.

"As long as I don't get arrested, that's fine"—though he feared that if the DEA (Drug Enforcement Administration) read his *High Times* interview, "I'll be put on their list." Jimmy praised the "whole coastal culture . . . anybody who grows up on the ocean is exposed to it." Phil Clark had been a shrimper, and Jimmy mentioned how shrimpers used to run cigarettes to South America, then bring marijuana back. He said it was no "big crime," not till it became big business with Jamaica and its gunboats. Initially, it was just honest fishermen seeking a little more money for their families; it was their "way of life." Anderson felt that even though smugglers made more money than anyone else, they were not perceived as "greed heads," because they were so fondly romanticized. "Absolutely," exclaimed Jimmy, and he hearkened back to "total pirate" Sir Francis Drake, as well as the films of Errol Flynn.

Asked about the best place to shop for marijuana, Jimmy said, "There was some that washed up in Key West that wasn't too bad, even though it was wet." He then condemned the U.S. Coast Guard at Key West for stopping people's boats to check out "that safety equipment shit," then seizing their marijuana and unfurling their own pirate flag every time they made an arrest—"a big marijuana leaf with a skull and crossbones." Then "four days later there'd be some good pot on the street."

Writing about Jimmy in the *Washington Post,* Gordon Chaplin told how in 1976 various Key West officials were indicted on dope and corruption charges (one who was acquitted was later convicted), including Fire Chief Joseph "Bum" Farto, "who later jumped bail" and, according to librarian Tom Hambright, perhaps "went swimming with the fishes." Hambright tells of all the "Bubba busts" in the mid-1980s, with (laughingly) maybe more cops *in* jail than out. Underpaid in their day jobs, they might pick up a thousand dollars a night moonlighting.

Mary Durant and Michael Harwood wrote in 1980 that beneath the city's fetching facade was a "seamy world of heavy trade in contraband (hard drugs, guns, illegal aliens, you name it)," facilitated by the "machinations of secret agents of every persuasion (federal connections, Cuban connections, South American connections, underworld connections)." One of their sources called Key West "spooky" because "*every* one is an agent." A retired policeman told Durant and Harwood that next to drug-running, murder was the biggest crime (his wife deplored "too many shoot-outs"), since there'd been seven unsolved murders in the past two years, with no one trying hard to solve 'em. "They pick up their paychecks and don't give a damn."

In his witty and urbane *Memories of Key West* (1994), reformed English teacher Lee Dodez says many people came to Key West "for the open freedom and the relaxation, and marijuana provided the means." Those police who *weren't* selling drugs looked the other way. "Drugs were common and drug arrests were rare." Gradually, as the price of marijuana rose, heroin and cocaine competed—and the police actually *arrested* people! But "with the heavy use of coke, crack, and heroin in the Eighties, practically anything can still be bought on the streets."

In the *High Times* interview Jimmy said he hoped marijuana would be legalized "because all the lawyers smoke it." He said morality should not be legislated, and he endorsed NORML (National Organization for the Reform of Marijuana Laws), whose lobbyist Keith Stroup he knew personally ("I admire what he's doing"). Jimmy felt that "the only crime-oriented drug is heroin, I think." He opined that cocaine was promoted because it was more expensive than marijuana, yet is so "easy to process." Next to his interview (page 54) was a page-long advertisement for Checkit, a service to help people analyze their cocaine to make sure it was "pure." On page 19 was a ⅓-page colored advertisement for Jimmy Buffett "Coral Reefer Band" T-shirts . . . across from a marijuana equipment advertisement. Jimmy lamented that there wasn't enough marijuana in America anymore: "There's a shortage." Not anymore. By 1994 marijuana was a hit in Tennessee—topping the charts at Number 1 as a "cash crop," and with ten thousand NORML support signatures.

Bob Anderson asked if Jimmy would ever like to retire at age sixty-five—and, perchance, become a senior-citizen rum-runner? He said that his ultimate goal was to head down into the Caribbean when he was sixty-five or seventy, and become a "character in a bar," since at that age "you can't get laid." Jimmy closed the interview by saying he hoped his mother wouldn't read it . . . *but he knew she would.*

For, as David Kronke reported in the *Atlanta Constitution* in 1985, Jimmy "at one time used to smuggle marijuana in off the coast of Florida."

■ ■ ■

"Everyone was saturated with drugs. Jimmy was strictly a tequila man," says Captain Tony Tarracino, owner of Captain Tony's Saloon, off Duval Street. "We became the drug capital of the U.S. without exception"—a bold statement considering Miami's historic heroin heritage. "The local people started mixing grass with horseshit and calling it *mau* [Hawaiian marijuana]. There was a conveyer to dry out grass. Quaaludes were big. . . .

"Of course there were snorters everywhere. People were flying to Jamaica, looking for mushrooms. Acid was pretty big. It destroyed the whole [youth] movement. I think the government dropped the acid on the kids. They fucked up the minds of the great thinkers." And Bob Mayo, of Bobalu's restaurant, adds, "Everyone was on LSD, including the entertainers."

In 1972 the U.S. Air Force supported the mental harassment of an eighteen-year-old girl with LSD; the following year, CIA Director Richard Helms ordered the destruction of the files of his LSD program. Even marijuana had been patriotic, encouraged as "truth serum" by the Office of Strategic Services back in the 1940s—again on nonconsenting victims—by Wall Streeter "Wild Bill" Donovan.

Captain Tony's face became overcast with sadness as he recalled the "nine-hundred-dollar-a-day [coke] habits. So many ODs. So many kids died before they were twenty. They'd find them in their cars. It didn't matter to anyone. . . .

"These were the Love Kids days, the hippies—this was where it was happening. I became the father of the hippies, don't ask me why. I never wore shoes, I was always barefoot behind the bar . . . I sort of became the headquarters, or the place to go if you came to Key West . . . if you were part of the 'rebellion.' Many a night I closed the bar and let the kids sleep on the pool table, on the floor. In the morning I'd come in with ten loaves of bread, and pounds of baloney, containers of coffee."

One day someone brought Captain Tony a shirt to look at—a shirt with a bloody hole in it. It was a murder souvenir from the Kent State campus.

Captain Tony really loved the music. . . .

"I guess Jimmy comes in about that time. These were the crazy days. One of my best friends was Jerry Jeff Walker." Other guests included David Allen Coe and Arlo Guthrie. "Neil Diamond came in one night and put his band up on the stage. There were so many in the music field in those days. I was busy hitting on girls and having a good time."

One night an entertainer was taking a twenty-minute intermission. "Everyone had a guitar, everyone had some originals," remembers Captain Tony.

"Any way I could do a couple of originals on the stage?" asked Jimmy. Captain Tony was "hitting up a blonde at the door," so Jimmy got up and sang for ten or fifteen minutes. Captain Tony thinks he gave Jimmy ten dollars and three Budweiser beers.

"What do you think?" asked Jimmy.

"Get away from originals," commanded the captain to the kid. Why? Because he always told the young entertainers: "Originals are great, but do something people can hum to. 'Cause if you don't, you're dead. Originals don't mean shit. You're trying to give a message, and everybody's trying to give a message."

On August 29, 1994, G. T. Weckerly was performing at Captain Tony's Saloon—following his boss's edict, he wasn't singing an original. He was doing Jimmy's "Last Mango in Paris," and its first line—"I went down to Captain Tony's"—opens up old memories, as Tony Tarracino offers Jimmy a seat by the bar. He alludes to "the last plane out of Saigon" and tells Jimmy, "There is still so much to be done."

■   ■   ■

Captain Tony, the former mayor of Key West (1989–91), is an archetypal Key Westian. He was born in 1916, to Italian puppet-show parents of New Jersey (Manhattan-area puppeteers).

He fled from New Jersey in 1948, evading his gambling debts since he had been betting on horses "after they won." He had eighteen dollars in his pocket as he hitchhiked on a milk truck to Key West. He was awed by the slot machines, blackjack tables, the "women of ill repute," plus so many sailors that the town "looked like it had been spread with cream cheese." He slept in an abandoned truck and finally became a shrimper.

Captain Tony has been typed as a "soldier of fortune, adventurer, armchair philosopher . . . a self-confessed 'dirty old man.'" He used a .38 pistol to calm down his rival fishermen. He made eleven trips to Cuba, three of them after Cuba was designated "off limits"—once the State Department even threatened to toss him in jail, and seize his ship. Yet another version has him running guns at least nineteen times into Cuba in the pre-Castro Batista days, as well as participating in two attempts to overthrow François "Papa Doc" Duvalier of Haiti. Under the menace of machine-gun fire, Captain Tony sank his own boat, then swam in the Caribbean until the U.S. Coast Guard picked him up.

"I worked with mercenaries in Nicaragua," said Captain Tony in our 1994 interview, "and supplied the first shipment of arms that Israel got. I've been to jail in Miami. And the Bay of Pigs—the whole conspiracy was done in my bar."

If someone like Jimmy's grandfather had been in charge of the Bay of Pigs, it might have worked. Instead, the Cubans and the Americans were forced to have separate cooks and separate menus at the huge "secret" metal warehouse in Key West, which everyone knew about. If Jimmy's grandfather had been in charge, why, he would have had them sit down and eat from the same menus!*

"Jimmy became the reality of the world we lost," says Captain Tony. "'Margaritaville' makes them think of the girls they were balling at Woodstock. He came in at a time when the Beatles and Dylan were popular. He came from a world where he was sheltered—Mobile. His audiences turn him on like a guy with a nine-hundred-dollars-a-day cocaine habit. The audience fires him. He'll come out and he knows what they want. The older fans . . . Jimmy keeps them alive."

As for Captain Tony, when he was elected mayor—thanks to Jimmy's

---

* Jimmy's grandfather went to Havana in 1922—and the father of Bay of Pigs leader E. Howard Hunt went there in 1926, with an Army Colt .45 to retrieve some money from his law partner. One of the most colorful Bay of Pigs invaders was a former Vanderbilt University football player from Nashville, William "Rip" Robertson, noted for his loud Hawaiian shirts and straw sombrero. After the invasion fiasco, Nashville lawyer John J. Hooker, Jr., came to Key West to counsel some of Castro's released prisoners.

campaign help—a famous tabloid ran a story, "Hustler Becomes Mayor," and he was falsely reported as having been "a towel boy in a whorehouse. It said they didn't pay me but I could have all the girls." (Which fulfills, at least, his advice to writers: "I tell you, you ought to use humor. I use a lot of humor.")

Thrice-married Captain Tony has over a dozen children himself (and plenty of Catholic confessions), and his saloon ("the Oldest Bar in Florida") has been everything in the past century, from a morgue to a brothel. It was called Sloppy Joe's in the 1930s, a place where Hemingway drank with author Martha Gellhorn, whom he eventually married, dumping his second wife, who'd bought and refurbished his famous house at 907 Whitehead Street. Hemingway wrote numerous short stories in Key West, plus novels such as *To Have and Have Not* (1937), whose pirate Harry Morgan is based on his pal "Sloppy Joe" Russell. (Russell later moved his club abruptly to 201 Duval Street—today's Sloppy Joe's.)

■ ■ ■

"Do you see yourself as a rock 'n' roll Hemingway?" asked New York radio host Jim Ladd on "Inner View" in 1978. Jimmy said he was influenced by Hemingway's writing, "but I don't think we would have gotten along very well, if we had known each other at the time. I don't think the personalities are right."

"Did you ever run into the ghost of Ernest Hemingway down there in Key West?" asked Bonzai of *Mix* magazine in 1986.

"I didn't meet him there, but I looked for him one night in Bimini," said Jimmy. "I stayed in his room at the Complete Angler Hotel and got just drunk enough to hopefully hallucinate and have him walk out of the closet." Sadly, Hemingway's phantom didn't appear, but since Jimmy wrote a short story that night, he feels just maybe "he was there." Jimmy also went to Havana and visited Hemingway's house. He did a documentary and spent some time in the tower he worked in.

In his early, pre-Gellhorn years in Key West, one of Hemingway's friends was an artist named Antonio Gattorno, and they'd go sailing together. Gattorno might bring along a phonograph, play records and sing along, keeping time by beating his fists on the fish box—and he also played a classical guitar. Hemingway himself sang in a "lusty bass," and by 1936 was playing records so much at sea (such as "Stormy Weather") that his guests were covertly tossing them overboard.

■ ■ ■

One of Jimmy's first friends in Key West was struggling novelist Thomas McGuane, who was working on a neo-Hemingway novel, including two played-out Key West fishing guides, which became *Ninety-Two in the Shade* (1973). Its protagonist, Tom Skelton, heads to Key West from a hallucinatory drug scene in Kentucky. Songs like Johnny

Cash's "Orange Blossom Special," Hank Williams's hit "Lovesick Blues," and Charley Pride's "The Easy Part's Over" are part of his new experience. In one bizarre barroom fracas, a Pascagoula childhood memory is cited. Highway A1A provides the novel's continuity, down to the last sentence, anticipating Jimmy's 1974 *A1A* album.

"Key West was a town where you had to pick and choose. It was always a favorite of pirates," wrote McGuane. When Jimmy was playing at the Pier House, McGuane introduced him to the bartender, smuggler Phil Clark. Jimmy began dipping his pen into the "rich alphabet soup that McGuane and his writer friends kept percolating," writing songs about the sort of characters McGuane knew (and was himself writing about). According to Gordon Chaplin, under McGuane's influence Jimmy once sailed out into the Gulf Stream on a sixteen-foot skiff, "out of sight of land . . . and a head full of mescaline." Supposedly, he was going to fish for marlin, "like Hemingway's *Old Man and the Sea*. Sort of."

McGuane, born in 1939, had first come to Key West with his father in the Fifties. He moved there around 1969, with his wife, Portia "Becky" Crockett, and their son. He wrote most of his novel *The Bushwhacked Piano* (1971) in their house at 123–125 Ann Street. The novel exalts the Key West cemetery, with its ground-level crypts entombing victims from the Spanish-bombarded USS *Maine*.

Jimmy stayed in the McGuanes' guest house for a while after he first arrived. *Time* magazine called McGuane a magnet for "a shifting population of the lonely, itinerant, or freaked-out," since he staged hard-drinking parties for friends like painter Russell Chatham, photographer Guy Valdene, poet-novelist Jim Harrison, and Jimmy. He finished *Ninety-Two in the Shade* up at his ranch in Montana, and on his way back to Key West had a car accident from which he emerged unhurt but shaken.

McGuane exemplifies the fact that while "grass" and tourists have been fundamental Key West imports, literature has been its chief export. As he told Jimmy's friend Susan Nadler in *Florida Keys* magazine, "The main thing that brought our gang together was our fanatical interest in writing. Educationally, we came up as the last of the literature-as-religion era." He said that the New Critics still ruled American letters; that if you wanted to be a writer, you were "expected to burn all your possessions and sign on." By contrast, younger writers want to write, become rock 'n' roll stars, make movies, and "charter a plane to Baja." His generation was the last that would settle for nothing but writing—anything else was a lucky luxury, not in the original deal. And Nadler quoted novelist Bill Manville (*Saloon Society*): "I continue to write well here because there is no country club, the golf course is bankrupt, and nobody owns a Mercedes."

■ ■ ■

Bird expert John James Audubon arrived in Key West in 1832, and his "Death of a Pirate" (*Ornithological Biography*) records a sailor's futile attempt at saving the life of a bloodied buccaneer, victim of a gun battle. Mark Twain came in 1867, saying, "If I have got Key West sized up right, they would receive War, Famine, Pestilence and Death without question—call them all by some fancy name, and then rope in the survivors and sell them good cigars and brandies at easy prices and horrible dinners at infamous rates."

Novelist John Dos Passos preceded Hemingway to Key West in 1924. His New York neighbor, poet Hart Crane, wrote a three-verse cycle, "Key West: An Island Sheaf" ("But where is the Captain of this doubloon isle/Without a turnstile? Who but catchword crabs/Patrols the dry groins of the underbrush?") and jumped to his death from a ship coming back from Mexico. Dos Passos said that Key West would be the right place for "Ole Hem . . . to dry out his bones," so Hemingway—tired of wet winters in Paris—followed his advice. (Hemingway: "Nobody believes me when I say I'm a writer. They think I represent big Northern bootleggers or dope peddlers.") Poet Wallace Stevens came and termed it a "summer without end" (collecting a broken jaw from Hemingway as a Key West souvenir, for having trivialized his writing).

Jimmy was enchanted with the New Orleans milieu of Tennessee Williams's play, *A Streetcar named Desire*. Williams first came to Key West in 1941 and later bought a house there, in 1949. Poet Elizabeth Bishop (like Jimmy's grandfather, from Nova Scotia) lived in Key West in the 1940s. Once Truman Capote autographed a woman's navel at the Monster, a Key West discotheque (accompanied by Tennessee Williams), when her drunken boyfriend unzipped his pants and asked for Williams to also autograph . . . or at least "to initial it."

By 1986, Key West claimed to be the home of at least six Pulitzer Prize winners and numerous other book-prize winners—"more than fifty successful authors."

Journalist Susan Nadler wrote in 1986 that Key West had been the home for more successful authors than any town in the world, per capita (population 25,000 in 1995). Patricia Miller, in *Books and Bookmen* that same year, said that for an island one mile long and three miles wide, there were more successful writers than anywhere in America outside Manhattan.

Susan Nadler came from the Jimmy Buffett period, circa 1973–74, selling popcorn next to Captain Tony's. She finished a book, *The Butterfly Convention* (1976), in Key West, a Sixties memoir about spending four and a half months in a Mexican prison for having imported a quantity of hashish (with a "friggin' FBI man telling me that in Mexico you are guilty until proven innocent"). Nadler told Paulie Raymond in *Key West Citizen* that "I never was a very good criminal anyway."

■ ■ ■

Jimmy's chief addiction, however, was Key West's music.

History was on his side. As early as 1881, a visitor had praised its large dance hall, albeit with a "cracked violin and piano." And during the Depression, unemployed musicians formed a Hospitality Band to greet each arriving train and ship.

So Jimmy began soaking up local songwriting themes, which buzzed around Duval Street like the moths that "sometimes obscured the mercury vapor street lights in the August dog days." Drunken Jimmy might make it from the Old Anchor Inn "into the heavy vegetable darkness," and then be lured by the sound of a waltz coming from the "Nautical Wheelers" square-dance club, held upstairs at the Cuban Club, which of course triggered his "Nautical Wheelers" song. He would come there on Friday nights and watch them waltz underneath a large orange-and-white parachute, since it was next door to the Salvation Army where he bought his clothes. In his *Parrot Head Handbook,* Jimmy extols the Key West bars for harboring straights, gays, artists, politicians, and criminals, side by side. After watching the dancers, he would stagger back into Duval Street, where there was unlimited freedom.

■ ■ ■

Jimmy finally moved into an apartment on the second floor of 704 Waddell Avenue, next to Louie's Backyard bar and restaurant. Louie's bartender in 1994, Chris Robinson, came to Key West in February 1972. He says the rent was seventy-five to a hundred dollars a month, and "you could leave your door unlocked."

"He loved to sing the Rolling Stones' 'I Am an Elvis Imitator,'" recalls Robinson, who sentimentally characterizes Key West in the early Seventies as "sleaze with honor."

"You could go swimming naked at noon. I could go catch a lobster at lunch. At least fifty percent of the time, someone was making love on the beach. On every jukebox was 'If You Can't Be with the One You Love, Love the One You're With.'" As for the Chart Room, "It was headquarters for 'Bubba politics.' The mayor, the state's attorney, the sheriff—you could get arrested, bonded, tried, sentenced, everything you wanted—right there! People didn't paint their houses, to avoid taxes."

Authors Mary Durant and Michael Harwood called Key West "an artist's colony, homosexual colony, hippie colony, Cuban colony." Key West commentator Lee Dodez recited a timeless hometown fable: "If you like to screw sheep and you bring a sheep in the front door, no Key Wester will say a word. Try to sneak a sheep through the back door, and you're in big trouble. It is not that the people care what you do;

it's that they have to know about it." Indeed, Key West's literary historian Lynn Mitsuko Kaufelt believes that the town's "lawless tradition" attracts writers, since "contemporary brigands break the law and kill each other over 'Florida snow' (cocaine) and 'square grouper' (bales of marijuana)," and writers are "adventurers of the heart." Since writers often prefer to grow older but not "up," Kaufelt says Key West is where adults can wear "short pants, polo shirts, and sneakers all of the time, and stay home from school, engaging in fantasy."

Even though "everyone here knows everything about everyone, and no one gives a damn," Key West attracts one million tourists a year. It is a dangerous place to visit. Go once, and you will return. The peril is that on your third visit, you may move there permanently.

■ ■ ■

"Actually, very little of my success happened down here," Jimmy told Kathleen J. Hargreaves of the *Key West Citizen* in 1981. "Mostly it happened from working on the road. A lot of people have the misconception that when I came here I stayed in a house in a rented room, and stayed drunk for ten years and became a star. That's absolutely not true. . . . I was quite vigorously on the road, doing concerts. The only way for me to survive was to do concerts."

"People of Texas also rescued me, and kept me alive for a while," Jimmy told the *Texas Connection* TV audience in 1992. From Key West, he would head to Austin, where Jerry Jeff Walker was living. Thanks to "college booking conferences," Jimmy claimed to have played "every junior college in the entire state of Texas"—especially El Centro in downtown Dallas. Texas audiences especially charmed him, with an appreciation that seemed somewhat special over the years, in all of his travels.

"Whenever you were hitchhiking in Texas and you had a guitar case, it wasn't treated as an AK-47—it was treated as something that was admired."

His song "Migration" (1974) refers to his "Caribbean soul I can barely control," with some Texas hidden in his heart. The song alludes to Walker, and singers Willis Alan Ramsey and Michael Martin Murphey, but the real message is implicit in the phrase "we can travel and rhyme. . . ."

For Jimmy now had a home of his own: *the highway.* As the song also admitted, "I got married too early, and it cost me much more than a ring."

The Great Jukebox Holdup (Why Don't We Get Drunk and Sell?)

■

"Titled 'Why Don't We Get Drunk,' the song contains a word (used throughout) not generally acceptable to country programming. . . . Everybody else in country music has been implying it," [B. J.] McElvee said. "Now Buffett comes out and says it." The title strip for jukeboxes put out by the [record] label contains a printed screw on it.

—"Blue Lyric in Country Release Gets Airplay," *Billboard,*
May 19, 1973

That's the last time I play a Buffett record—I'm not going to play any more Jimmy Buffett!

—Cincinnati, Ohio, radio program director to Tom McEntee (ABC-Dunhill Records), 1973

You know, my husband is trying to be a songwriter," Margie had told Capitol Records executive Joe B. Allison in Nashville. Jimmy was still in town at the time, and Margie had become their secretary. She introduced Jimmy to Allison, who had written Jim Reeves's "He'll Have to Go."

"He pitched some stuff to me, but it wasn't anything I could ever use," Allison recalls. "His stuff is so off the wall, it's hard to think of somebody else doing it. He didn't write like everybody else, he was really different. I wasn't all that impressed, to tell you the truth, but as an artist, I thought he was terrific the first time I heard him.

"You get the impression with Buffett, he really doesn't give a damn.

If they like it, fine, if they don't, that's all right, too. He's going to do his thing, he's not going to go with the flow or with the trend. Even the part of the country Jimmy chose to live in [Key West] is a getaway place. That's where you can go and forget all this stuff up here."

Joe Allison had started the country-music department of Liberty Records in Los Angeles in the early Sixties, launched the first radio presentation for the Country Music Association in 1963, and in 1969 won the Academy of Country Music's Jim Reeves Memorial Award.

Jimmy Buffett has since gotten even with Joe Allison.

"I've got one boy who would go to his concert in the middle of the ocean, I think," Allison admits. "My kid saved up twenty-seven dollars one time to buy a ticket to one of his concerts when he didn't have any money."

Soon after turning down Jimmy's songs, Allison remembers, "they divorced about that same time."

Jimmy filed on September 20, 1972, in Key West. Interestingly, the petition says they lived as "husband and wife" until February 1, 1972, and that Jimmy had lived in Florida for at least six months. The final judgment of November 1, 1972, awarded him his divorce—by default, since Margie had filed no response.

■ ■ ■

Gregory "Fingers" Taylor began playing with Jimmy in the early Seventies. "I remember all of us hanging out on the streets of Key West," said Jerry Jeff Walker on *Texas Connection.*

Jimmy remembered summoning Fingers to Key West, where he was rehearsing with other musicians in Tom Corcoran's garage behind a leather shop. Fingers drove down non-stop from Jackson, Mississippi, arriving, Jimmy remembers, in the midst of a hurricane.

"Don't worry, I'll be right back and we'll really get this band together," Jimmy told him—as he was leaving for Miami to play at The Flick.

Fingers said all that Jimmy told him initially was "Look for me on Duval Street"—the mile-long strip of shops, restaurants, and bars.

"So I looked in all the bars on Duval, and at the very last, seediest, *worst* place—Howie's—I found *these* two guys playing pool [Jimmy and Jerry Jeff Walker]. Sort of. They were more or less *lying* on the pool table."

"Boy, I'm glad we lived through all that, and got to write about it," Jimmy said. "There's a lot of luck involved, but it's great. Storytelling is the most essential part of songwriting, to me, and I think that's why we're all here."

Still, Fingers formed his own blues band, Rock City, and played Duval Street for a while before finally joining up with Jimmy.

■ ■ ■

Another Key West friend was Chris Gantry, composer of Glen Campbell's 1968 hit, "Dreams of the Everyday Housewife" (Number 3 on
the country chart, Number 32 on the pop). Gantry knew Jimmy in
Nashville, and Key West was a refuge for both of them. Once Gantry
played a marathon of eleven hours a day, seven days a week, at Louie's
Backyard, next to Jimmy's apartment. (He was married awhile to author
Susan Nadler, who by 1995 was working for singer Lorrie Morgan.)
His album *Chris Gantry "Alive"* (1983) has Tarracino on the cover
wearing a shirt emblazoned "Jesus Is Coming and Boy Is He Pissed!"
Gantry writes Key West short stories, and won the Tennessee Williams
Playwriting Contest in Key West in 1984 (he lives in Nashville today).

Gantry and Jimmy were also Key West comrades of Shelton "Shel"
Silverstein, *Playboy* cartoonist, children's book author, and self-exiled
Nashville songwriter ("A Boy Named Sue" for Johnny Cash). Silverstein's album, *The Great Conch Train Robbery* (1980), mentions
Jimmy in the title song (a Jesse James–style Key West bandit ballad)—
"with Buffett on the jukebox and Hemingway on the wall." The most
notorious song on the album is "Rough on the Living," about how
"Nashville is rough on the living, but she surely speaks well of the
dead"—telling how a fading star is memorialized once he is safely dead,
though when he was still alive his Nashville record producer wouldn't
return his calls.

In the winter of 1972, Jimmy was asked to write some songs for a
1973 television film, *Key West,* starring Stephen Boyd, Woody Strode,
and Sheree North. Boyd played an ex–CIA spy running a boat service
in Florida plagued by "a revenge-seeking maniac." After coming up with
one song about "cruising down the Keys, peace, rest, love and stuff like
that," Jimmy was "pretty juiced," yet they asked him to write the whole
score. They paid him advance money, and since he couldn't read music,
they even wanted to fly him to Los Angeles to work with David Rose.
"When I wouldn't give them the publishing rights, it just fell through,"
he told Al Bianculli of *Zoo World* in 1973. "I didn't care because
everything fell through!"

Jimmy said he worked for three months as a deck hand on the boats,
garnering a bit acting part. "But the producers were fly-by-night 'Mod
Squad' producers and they had such bad luck it wasn't funny." For
instance, they rented helicopters for a hundred dollars a day, but the
cameras wouldn't fit them, so they had to bring other helicopters . . .
into four days of bad weather. They supposedly ran $400,000 over their
one-million-dollar budget. "One scene, they ran a brand-new Porsche
off a bridge and all the cameras missed it."

■   ■   ■

"Steve Goodman was a tremendous influence on Jimmy," says Gerry
Wood. Goodman wrote "The City of New Orleans," a Number 18 hit

for Arlo Guthrie, son of radical folkie Woody Guthrie, in 1972. The railroad song became a country standard, in time.

Goodman had been more or less discovered in Chicago, along with singer-songwriter John Prine, by Kris Kristofferson in 1971. They both eventually got record deals . . . and cult concert followings. Neither ever had a *Billboard* hit, but their songs became live classics, sometimes charting for other artists. Over the years he and Goodman shared Al Bunetta as their manager. Concerning Jimmy, Bunetta says, "He hung out with Stevie once in a while. He was close with Stevie, before my involvement." Goodman and Jimmy would write songs together, Jimmy would stay up in Chicago with Goodman, and sometimes visited Bunetta in New York.

"I was up there watching Jerry Jeff playing at the Quiet Knight in Chicago," recalls Gerry Wood, "and we all ended up at Steve's the next day. Jimmy had this ripple-wine T-shirt. . . ." Jimmy told Chet Flippo that Chicago was the first place outside of the South to welcome him. Late-Fifties star Neil Sedaka was making a comeback at the Quiet Knight, and Jimmy was the opening act. "The crowd wanted oldies, not me. So I went around the corner between sets to a thrift shop and bought a triple-pleated suit and a jar of Dippity-Do, and slicked my hair back and did oldies for an hour. *Then* they liked me." Buffett and Flippo then went over to the Earl of Old Town club, where Goodman and Prine were launched.

Goodman and Prine became bardic role models for the Seventies generation, flaunting post-Dylan poetry in a slightly more country style. Prine eventually moved to Nashville. As for Goodman, as early as 1968 he had leukemia, and at airports would gloomily gripe when he would see the prophetic (to him) TERMINAL sign.

By 1973 Jimmy was back on another record-album cover—not something by the Now Generation, but rather, Steve Goodman's *Somebody Else's Troubles* on Buddha Records. Jimmy is standing between John Prine and Goodman's wife, Jesse. The credits, however, list him as "Marvin Gardens," his songwriter pseudonym for one of his future songs. Perhaps it was to keep him free for his separate record deal; also on the same album, backup singer–pianist "Robert Milkwood Thomas" was really Bob Dylan. (In his days without a band, Jimmy used to introduce imaginary side musicians from the Coral Reefer Band: "Miss Kitty Litter . . . Miss Que Pasa . . . and Mr. Marvin Gardens.")

Goodman and Prine were ahead of Jimmy, showing that maybe you *could* be an original singer-songwriter, with a record deal and a fan following.

On Goodman's album were some striking songs, such as "The Ballad of Penny Evans," about a bitter Vietnam widow who rips up each Army pension check and mails "the damn thing back." Or "The Dutchman" (by Michael Smith), which anticipates Jimmy's "He Went to Paris." Or

Goodman's "Chicken Cordon Bleus," which makes fun of vegetarian dieting and hungers for steak and lobsters—the blueprint for Jimmy's own "Cheeseburger in Paradise."

By 1979 Chet Flippo would be judging Jimmy to be "wittier than John Prine or Steve Goodman, sunnier than Jerry Jeff Walker and harder-edged than the wimps (who know who they are)."

■   ■   ■

Poet Jim Harrison was impressed by Jimmy's intrepid persistence ("a hard peasant streak of practical self-promotion"). In fact, Jimmy even cut a video in Key West in the early 1970s with Rick Trow, long before videos were popular. Elizabeth Willson, in *Florida Trend* in 1991, noted his early business acumen, instilled in part by his *Billboard* music-reporting days. "Ultimately, though, it was the school of hard knocks—survival on the road—that drove home the hardest lessons for Buffett. When he first toured the country, it was just Buffett and a station wagon. He learned to handle his own books, schedule his performances, negotiate contracts. Going on the road to sing rock 'n' roll is akin to going to war or joining the circus, he says."

"The first thing I learned," Jimmy told Willson, "was you find dependable people and let them do the job for you, and not try to run everything yourself."

Such as Don Light up in Nashville. When Jimmy went to Nashville periodically, he taped more songs whenever possible, and Don continued shopping him to different record labels. Jimmy was increasingly visible, as he performed more and more at the Exit/In.

One of his favorite Nashville retreats was Rotier's Restaurant, his cheeseburger source back in his Barnaby "hard-luck days." Founded in 1945, Rotier's still featured its cofounder Evelyn Rotier in 1995. She figured out how to make perfect hamburgers by hand. ("People don't like the machine. We had one and threw it out.") She tells how one night the cook "came in skunk drunk." Some college boys were working, who "were scared of the cook, so they charged people for what they ordered but gave them whatever she cooked."

Jimmy recommends Rotier's in his *Parrot Head Handbook*—pages from which are framed and mounted on the restaurant wall.

■   ■   ■

In 1972 Don Light signed the Glaser Brothers. Tompall, Chuck, and Jim were among Nashville's most visionary entertainers, publishers, and producers. They'd gotten around nineteen rejections of "Gentle on My Mind," written by John Hartford, till finally Glen Campbell from Los Angeles made it a hit in both 1967 and 1968. This song that Nashville was too deaf to hear was still earning Hartford $170,000 a year in the late Seventies, and by 1992 was BMI's *most recorded song* (833 versions).

The Glasers had also broken Tom Paxton's "Last Thing on My Mind" into the country realm.

Their office at 916 19th Avenue South became an "outlaw" headquarters—or, according to Dave Hickey in a 1973 *Country Music* article, a "night-person's lair," with dark walnut paneling, leather furniture, a tiny window, "well barricaded against the outside world." They would "let you in even if you had hair down to your ass," according to outlaw-ologist Michael Bane.

The Glasers were Catholic refugees from Nebraska, and they produced Kinky Friedman and the Texas Jewboys, who had songs like "Ride 'Em Jewboy," "Let Saigons Be Bygones," and "They Ain't Making Jews Like Jesus Anymore." Like Jimmy, Kinky Friedman became a fiction writer in the Eighties, writing mystery novels.

The Glaser studio would be good for Jimmy, if Light could but get him a deal. Tompall Glaser says Jimmy "was pretty disgusted with the fact that Nashville had its eyes closed . . . their idea of what was in and what was out. . . . We were trying to broaden it out, to cuss and discuss. . . . We were all interested in Buffett 'cause we liked his songs, and he didn't sound like Hank Williams. I've always liked him, I really did. I admired him for what he did. I was always sorry he had to leave Nashville to do it, but I understood why. I had to sign *my* contracts outside of Nashville [New York, London]."

Glaser says, "There sure was a lot of drugs going around at that time. There was pills, snorting, and a lot of grass." Glaser thinks it's funny that at MGM there was so much marijuana-smoking that one day country icon Eddy Arnold—with publisher Wesley Rose—came over, then left in bewilderment. Rose telephoned Glaser and asked, "What's that funny smell over there at MGM?" He thought it was a gas leak.

Of Jimmy, Glaser says, "I actually didn't hang out with him. Now, Jimmy smoked grass, and I liked to drink, or do pills, I guess. I had gotten into cocaine a little, by that time, winding down, really. He smoked that heavy grass. I finally just said, 'We're going to have get on the same dope—or quit working together!' " Pause. "I quit all that in 1978. You can put that in there, too. That's probably the reason my outlaw career terminated—I got sick of it."

■　■　■

Jimmy's music was finally appealing to someone with a major record company—producer Don Gant, at ABC-Dunhill. His brother Ronnie remembers, "Don was aware of him. He was going away doing those little college gigs. He used to sit on a stool. Don was turned on by all those songs." Jimmy's booking agent, Don Light, had lunch with him at a restaurant, then took him to his office to hear a Buffett tape. The next day, Gant called back—he wanted to hear the tape again. He came over and brought with him C. Dianne Petty, ABC-Dunhill's music publisher. "Dianne," he said, "I have this act that I really want to sign, but they will never let me sign him, 'cause he's not country unless you get behind it." Petty listened to some Buffett tapes and said they would have to acquire his publishing if Nashville wanted to sell him to Los Angeles.

Petty had been ABC-Dunhill's de facto boss at 1819 Broadway, keeping the fragile Nashville branch open. In her attempt to start a country division, she signed singers Lefty Frizzell and Ferlin Husky to the label.

ABC Records had been founded in 1955 and, in 1966, purchased part of Dunhill Records, whose first hit had been P. F. Sloan's antiwar song, "The Eve of Destruction" (1965), recorded by Barry McGuire. Dunhill featured such youth acts as Steppenwolf, Three Dog Night, and the Mamas and the Papas.

It was also Dianne Petty who had urged ABC to hire Acuff-Rose publishing executive Don Gant. Gant was a graduate of Nashville's East High School (as was Oprah Winfrey) and a compulsive singer, songwriter, and record producer. He had cut songs as a teenager, then joined Acuff-Rose when he was nineteen. He cowrote Roy Orbison's 1967 pop hit, "Cry Softly, Lonely One," and formed Neon Philharmonic with Tupper Sausey, charting "Morning Girl" in 1969 (Number 17 in pop).

Then ABC-Dunhill bought Cartwheel Records and used their office. They signed Cartwheel's acts Billy "Crash" Craddock and David Frizzell and kept the manager, Ron Chancey. Speaking of Don Gant, Chancey says: "Don was high on Buffett. But nobody [else] was high on Buffett, because he wasn't the Nashville kind of artist, and Don, as we know, was hardheaded. If he had something in his mind, he was going to do it or choke . . . and he just kept on and kept on." Singer-songwriter Ed Bruce said Gant was "probably as well-respected as anybody in this town."

"I think Don Gant cut more people than anybody I've known since I've been in this business," says Chancey. Though Gant died in 1987, people still tell him, "Man, I think about Don Gant every day, he was such a powerful influence in my life."

"If there hadn't been a Don Gant, there wouldn't have been a Jimmy Buffett. He believed in him *so* much," adds his brother Ronnie. "Don was a song guy, and that was the thing he was turned on to—and his artistry."

"He expected to sign him as a pop act," recalls Tom McEntee, ABC-Dunhill's record promoter for Jimmy. He says Gant sent the tape to ABC in Los Angeles and they sent it back with a no. Gant sent it again and got no again. "Then finally he sent it to them for a third time and they sent it back and said, 'If you like this guy so much, *you* sign him.' So that's how he came to be signed for the Nashville office."

"He's got some unusual songs," Bob "Robbie" Robison told Gant.

Robison was a record promoter, and future literary agent for songwriting novelists Barry Sadler, Michael Kosser, and Ralph Compton. "One of them is probably one of the most fantastic songs I've ever heard."

"What song was that?"

" 'They Don't Dance Like Carmen No More.' "

"Robbie, *that* song is one of the main reasons I've signed him."

Ironically, Jimmy was now a nominal country act, despite his persistent knocking of the field. "I was always more of a lyricist, so I would play where people were intent on listening to the words," he told *Music Journal* in 1978, "and in honky-tonks they're not. It's Friday night, and they're going to get drunk and dance."

ABC-Dunhill's most creative pop star was Jim Croce, as wild—and as sensitive—as Jimmy, typified by his two contrasting Number 1 pop hits of 1973, "Bad, Bad Leroy Brown" and "Time in a Bottle." Jimmy told Noel Coppage in *Stereo Review* in 1974, "I get a lot of comparisons with Jim Croce . . . we were good friends. He used to visit me down in Key West. Those Eastern slang expressions, he had those down just perfect. . . ."

Tom McEntee says the Nashville ABC office "was a joke for years and years. It was a sagging company. It had a kind of 'Who cares?' image up until the time Buffett got signed." ABC was struggling to build unknown acts when Buffett arrived. "He came into a label that was just on the building side."

As part of the deal, Dianne Petty acquired publishing for some of Jimmy's songs for the album (others would be by Buzz Cason's Let There Be Music). Since so many records are bought by females, it makes common sense to have a woman in charge of the music itself (such as Frances Preston of BMI, or Donna Hilley of Sony-Tree). Petty later ran the SESAC music licensing association, discovering K.T. Oslin, singer-song writer of the unforgettable "Eighties Ladies." Sitting in her SESAC office in 1994, she viewed an early photograph of Jimmy with pride. "You can see, there's an innocent gleam on Jimmy's face in this picture. Because it's like the very first time anybody ever said, 'Yeah, you can write songs.' "

Booking agent Don Light was finally Jimmy's manager. He had approached every possible label. When ABC signed Jimmy, according to Candice Russell, they told him to find a bigger manager, but "I told them that Don knew me before anyone at Creative Management Association or International Famous Agency had heard of Jimmy Buffett."

■ ■ ■

The album was supposed to cost $25,000. Jimmy claims to have said, "Shit, man, I can do it for ten and have fifteen left over to buy a boat." He figured "that's all anybody will ever see of me. I'd sail to Tahiti and open a club for my friends." (Jimmy told Frederick Burger in a 1979 unpublished interview that he hoped to "buy a boat and run a load of pot back from Colombia and be a millionaire! I was still toying with the idea of becoming a smuggler. I still didn't have any faith in the record business.")

The album, *A White Sport Coat and a Pink Crustacean,* produced at Glaser Sound studio, was released in June 1973 with a picture of Jimmy on the cover, sitting in front of a sailing ship toying with some live lobsters, parodying Marty Robbins's 1957 hit, "A White Sport Coat (and a Pink Carnation)."

The first track on Side One was the A-side of the first single, "The Great Filling Station Holdup." As Jimmy told *Zoo World*'s Al Bianculli, it reflected one of his true Key West experiences when a "little urchin was hanging around our beach. A totally crazy, weirded-out chick. She was camping out and I couldn't get rid of her. She had been thrown in jail for going sixty-nine with a guy in front of a Boy Scout jamboree. That's true. She was a flash queen." When the cops nabbed her on a vagrancy charge, she tried to escape . . . and wrecked a police car. She called her father to send down her bail money. Then, since she was only allowed one phone call, she sent a note: "To Jimmy Buffett—wish I was somewhere other than here—need $127 to bail me out." The plot of the actual song is different, of course: The happy-go-*un*lucky lyric sympa-thizes with some good-natured gas-station bandits who use a pellet gun to steal fifteen dollars, a can of oil, some cashew nuts, and a Japanese TV. Then they go sit in a Krystal hamburger shop, till the police nail them—and they earn two years in prison.

"Railroad Lady" (written with Jerry Jeff Walker) extols a sweet rail-road prostitute, one of whose customers bought her a fur coat and a big diamond ring. In three-quarter time, it has a soft, waltzy melody with a honky-tonk, hardwood-floor, dancy feel. Don Gant urged country traditionalist Lefty Frizzell to record it on ABC, and it went to Number 52 in 1974. Frizzell's biographer Daniel Cooper believes he didn't partic-ularly value the song, and why should he have, since a positive love-for-money song doesn't uphold the "Nashville Sound of Morality." Frizzell died the next year, and in 1977 Willie Nelson recorded "Railroad Lady" for his *To Lefty from Willy* eulogy album.

The third song on the album, "He Went to Paris," may be the best—and may be even Buffett's all-time best. The melody is folkie yet catchy, and the Gordon Lightfoot–Joni Mitchell acoustic-style guitar is played by Steve Goodman. The novelistic narrative takes a man to Paris, then to England, where he plays piano and marries an actress. War intervenes and kills their son, then bombs kill his wife and take out one of his eyes. He hops a freighter to the Caribbean, where he drinks beer and writes his memoirs, and tells Jimmy that his life has been both tragic and magic, yet still "a good life, all the way." "That's everybody's dream," Jimmy told Mary Campbell of the Associated Press in 1977: "Get through the whole thing and be contented."

The story came partly from a nightclub "cleanup guy" who would sing songs and tell stories from the Spanish Civil War, reported Richard Harrington in the *Washington Post* in 1989. His name was Eddie Balchowsky—he'd served in the Abraham Lincoln Brigade, against General Franco, and "got his arm shot off." He was a wino, and his war tunes were a nice corollary to Jimmy's granddad's sea songs. When Jimmy was opening for bigger acts at the Quiet Knight in Chicago, Balchowsky would cheer him up after a difficult set. He was a piano player, and a painter, himself.

"Grapefruit—Juicy Fruit" is a Jimmy standard, about the virtues of sin—committed in the drive-in theater, abetted by chewing some gum. It was inspired at Key West's Islander Drive-In (or so he told a Key West audience in 1981). "I used to go to the drive-in a lot," he told a New York City audience in 1977. "When I grew up, nobody got laid at the drive-in. . . . When I grew up, I decided to go back and try that one more time the way I always thought it would be. I committed a little mortal sin out there, for the good of humanity, and wrote this song after I got home."

"Cuban Crime of Passion" was an amusing narrative about Billy Voltaire, a piano player from Miami who, in a fight over a woman in Havana, killed a man, then took his own life. The "knives a-slashin'" made a good newspaper story, journalist Jimmy reflected. The song title was an actual newspaper headline from the *Miami Herald,* and the song derived from stories told by a Key West piano player named Billy Nine-Fingers. The melody is highly singable. Jimmy cowrote it with Tom Corcoran, who told Chet Flippo in 1979 how Jimmy would drop by his Key West home "when he literally didn't have a buck for dinner," so Corcoran and his wife would prepare a spaghetti dinner, and then they'd drink beer and write "a few songs together before things got out of control."

The last cut on Side One is "Why Don't We Get Drunk"—tactfully leaving out of the title the rest of the hook "(and Screw)." The song is credited to "Marvin Gardens," Jimmy's spoofy pseudonym. Again in beer-joint waltz-time, it is a masterpiece parody, sounding like George Jones, David Allen Coe, or Johnny Paycheck, in its demented drunkenness, featuring a convenient waterbed for the couple waiting to enact this song's profound message! Jimmy wrote it during his first years in Nashville, after noticing an Atlanta businessman trying to pick up a whore at the Marriott Hotel at about three in the morning. "I was just really vicious because I could never get anyone to listen to my songs," he told *Zoo World*'s Al Bianculli in 1973. The song was probably encouraged, as well, by Norma Jean's 1964 country hit, "Let's Go All the Way." She was on Porter Wagoner's show for seven years (they were in love), but as Bianculli asked rhetorically, "Can you imagine Porter Wagoner singing Jimmy's underground classic, 'Why Don't We Get Drunk (and Screw),' with Dolly Parton?" It even influenced "Skanky," by Nashville's singer-songwriter Will Jones, on his *Western Fringe* comic-country album (1993).

After "Margaritaville," it's one of Jimmy's most popular sing-along songs. At the close of the "Third Annual Meeting of the Minds" Parrot Head convention in New Orleans (November 3–6, 1994), everyone sang it as the finale of their humanitarian business meeting. At Starwood Amphitheatre, south of Nashville, on July 15, 1994, Jimmy introduced it with his usual attitude: "Let's get a little blue—downright trashy—I always like to think of it as a love song, a song that we know and love. A Nashville-born-and-bred *life* song!"

Side Two opens with his shoplifting anthem, "Peanut Butter Conspiracy," about the days of "hard-luck heroes" working in a nightclub, when he and a friend would steal peanut butter and sardines (and, according to journalist Noel Coppage, "codeine-spiked cough syrup")—another song with a country sound but lyrics not fit for airplay.

The official B-side of the released single was "They Don't Dance Like Carmen No More," one of Jimmy's nostalgic recordings hearkening back to the pre-Elvis Forties. Carmen Miranda (1909–1955) had a convent background, and her father was a fruit dealer—she shared with Jimmy a Catholic kid's ambition to outgrow family discretion and modesty. In the movies, she wore flagrant fruit hats ("bananas and mangoes all piled to the sky") and flashy bracelets. This shimmying sexpot dancer, "the Brazilian Bombshell," was of a Hollywood species that became sadly extinct.

"I Have Found Me a Home" is a gentle Key West tribute, about riding a bicycle and finding warm women who'll rescue him from a cold love. A strong melody lifts "My Lovely Lady," a song about living in anonymity in Key West, avoiding that fame "which brings confusion" when strangers recognize you on the airplane.

The album's last song, "The Death of an Unpopular Poet," was inspired by Walter Cronkite when he announced on television in January 1972 that beatnik poet Kenneth Patchen had died. Patchen wrote free verse, but not in an academic, self-conscious style—he was clear and dynamic. In "Let Us Have Madness," he urges his generation to "follow / The footsteps of this slaughtered age." Jimmy also empathized with Richard Fariña, who first married folksinger Carolyn Hester, and then Joan Baez's sister. Two days after Fariña's 1966 novel, *Been Down So Long It Looks Like Up to Me,* appeared, he died in a motorcycle wreck. He was also a singer-songwriter, who had repeatedly visited Cuba during Castro's revolution.

■ ■ ■

The musicians on *A White Sport Coat and a Pink Crustacean* included pianist Mike Utley, formerly with Jerry Jeff Walker's Dixie Flyers, Sammy Creason on drums, Fingers Taylor on harmonica, and well-respected Nashville fiddler Vassar Clements, as well as several others. Don Gant and Buzz Cason added some back-up vocals. Jimmy named the musicians the Coral Reefers, foreshadowing his eventual band.

Thomas McGuane wrote the liner notes, about "this throwback altar boy of Mobile," with melodies "strewn with forgotten crabtraps, Confederate memories, chemical daydreams, Ipana vulgarity, ukelele madness," placing Jimmy somewhere between "Hank Williams and Xavier Cugat."

■ ■ ■

The single "The Great Filling Station Holdup" was released in May, and went to Number 58 in country music.

A distributor called Don Light, and B.J. McElwee at ABC-Dunhill, and promised to order five thousand copies of "Why Don't We Get Drunk" if they would only make it a single—*for jukeboxes only.* So they pressed a second single, this time with that song as the B-side. "You can still find it on some college jukeboxes," laughs Light. "It was probably in every fraternity house in the country."

No AM radio stations were supposed to have it, not unless they went out and bought it independently. ABC-Dunhill absolutely controlled the shipping and they didn't want *that song* getting airplay. "We didn't want it available for home consumption," says promoter Tom McEntee (who says about eighty-five percent of every single went to the jukeboxes—and with ten to fifteen percent returns, that meant almost *no* singles sold in stores!).

McEntee got an angry phone call from a Cincinnati radio station, ranting about the record. Apparently some local nuns at a convent had heard the "clean" single and had gone and bought it, and by mistake, ended up with the jukebox version, which they accidentally played in a stack of records that was broadcast all over the convent. The righteous nuns called the radio station in fury!

Jimmy's former employer, *Billboard,* announced that FM radio stations were playing it also—that it was being "ordered by the thousands by the one-stops."

Dianne Petty did her part. ABC-Dunhill ordered over a thousand dollars' worth of T-shirts to be shipped with the records, with the words "Why Don't We Get Drunk and . . ." followed by a picture of a wood screw.

She wore hers proudly . . . down on Music Row.

Once in a Lifetime Comes Monday

■

He was not exactly an overnight sensation. His popularity grew like an Alabama live oak: slowly, but strongly. He was big in the port cities like Jacksonville, Savannah, Charleston, Boston, San Diego . . . it was as if his renown leapfrogged out of the South by following the freighter lanes.

—Roy Attaway, "Jimmy Buffett: A Pirate 200 Years Too Late,"
Motor Boating and Sailing (January 1982)

Then I did the record and I went and opened for Andy Pratt at Max's Kansas City [in New York City]," Jimmy told Chet Flippo in 1977, referring to *A White Sport Coat and a Pink Crustacean.* "Since then, it's been full-tilt boogie all the way." Within weeks of the album's issue, ABC got him touring. "He was out of the coffeehouse circuit for good," commented Gordon Chaplin in a 1977 *Washington Post* article.

The show at Max's was in mid-June of 1973, and right before it, Jimmy played at a press conference where *Cash Box* said his "casual approach" covered an "underlying seriousness. . . . He has a fine bagful of tunes."

New Englander Andy Pratt had recently charted "Avenging Annie," but *Billboard*'s Sam Sutherland typed him as a would-be "Super Song-writing Personality" whose live act at Max's was flawed . . . and ultimately upstaged by Jimmy. The Pratt-biased audience of "industry heavies" was at first hostile to Jimmy's "down-home approach," but his backup musicians with washboard (Vaughn Cochran) and harmonica (Fingers Taylor) helped win over the crowd with "his alternately romantic and comic tunes." Pratt had a cult following, but unknown Jimmy knew how to work the adverse crowd, judged Sutherland. Ian Dove in *The New York Times* also slammed Pratt and praised Jimmy. *Variety* liked "They Don't Dance Like Carmen No More"—and Lord Buckley's "God's Own Drunk," which became a Buffett cult crude classic for many years—while Robert Nash of Nashville's *Record World* lauded his "feeling of soft humor and intelligence," claiming that there were "few lyricists around who can match Buffett's warmth [and] sensitivity."

■ ■ ■

Then *A White Sport Coat and a Pink Crustacean* entered the country album charts (Number 43 in *Billboard*; Number 25 in *Cash Box*). *Penthouse* magazine said there wasn't a bad song on the album—that no one but Jimmy would have dared to "deadpan the line 'Honey, why don't we get drunk and screw?'"—and its competitor *Playboy* said it was time to stop aping Dylan, and go for "saltwater and shrimp-boat rock," since Jimmy's "Cuban Crime of Passion" and his Carmen Miranda song displayed "some of the best lyrics around." *Record World* declared him "head and shoulders" above the other singer-songwriters, and "a marvelous talent." Robert Christgau in the *Village Voice* confessed, "My shit detector went crazy," when he noticed McGuane's notes on the album cover, saying Buffett shared his "sexism . . . covert nostalgia, reverse preciousness, and brain-proud know-nothingism"— yet his country-style songs were "classics of sheer hair." Years later, John Swenson of *Rolling Stone* praised two of the album's "crazed hippie anthems."

Yet the album didn't sell enough to suit Jimmy. "Nobody at ABC really understood what I was trying to do," he griped to *Washington Post* reporter Gordon Chaplin in 1977. "They had me typed as a country-western singer because of the old days in Nashville. . . . I didn't get any promotion or ads," he finished.

"We *did* run ads," responds Dianne Petty. "I don't know how many he thought he was going to get. We did a lot of adventurous things . . . we spent thousands of dollars on T-shirts ['Why Don't We Get Drunk and . . .']. We were inventive on the promotions side, for him. *No* record artist I've ever met, unfortunately, seems to feel he got his due from the record company. When in truth, if it hadn't been for those dollars that the record company put into that product, *we might not know who the*

Parrot Heads were!" In fact, ABC issued a pioneer video, advertising the album in ABC-owned theaters—*and* they authorized his first songbook.

Dianne Petty says she loves working with music that is "left of center . . . they were the things I was most excited about. . . . We worked the copyrights, but they were not songs that were easily recorded. We knew that—and that was the beauty of being a self-contained writer-artist. He would have a voice that would be unique because of the songs he wrote. He just expected more things that were not possible, not doable. It certainly wasn't because of lack of effort."

■ ■ ■

On July 7 *Billboard* announced that "Capitol's Joe Allison and Audie Ashworth hosted a farewell party for Margie Buffett before she was transported to the Hollywood Capitol Tower."

In due time, another girl had deeply attracted Jimmy—Sally Jane Slagsvol, from Columbia, South Carolina. Her parents (Thomas and Sally Slagsvol) had wedded in a Catholic church; her father was an insurance executive (her brothers also worked in insurance), and her grandfather was an oil-company executive. Several years younger than Jimmy, she graduated from the A.C. Flora public high school in 1969, then attended the University of South Carolina from 1969 to 1971.

Known as "Miss Jane," she had come to Key West and, according to Chris Robinson, was a boyfriend of Larry "Groovy" Gray, who did lawns and furniture. She spotted Jimmy at the Pier House Bar, then moved in with him. (Jimmy said, "She was a hot tomato.") Candice Russell of the *Miami Herald* noticed them together in 1974, with Jimmy wearing "cutoffs, sneakers, and an old shirt, with a shell hung around his neck." A few years later, Gordon Chaplin of the *Washington Post* noticed that "blonde Jane Slagsvol, whose cameo-perfect Southern debutante face . . . looks best in softly-focused close-ups," was tearing up Polaroid pictures her friends were taking from other angles!

At least her new boyfriend Jimmy had a vehicle to drive her around in—a 1953 green rusted Chevrolet pickup truck. ("I bought it for one hundred dollars. It had 'Monroe County Glass and Mirror Company' stenciled on the driver's door.") At one point Slagsvol moved to Atlanta, worked as a waitress, and attended Georgia State University.

■ ■ ■

Jimmy appeared at the Troubadour in Los Angeles in September, arguably the most famous listening room in the nation. Originally founded in 1957 (at a nearby location) by Doug Weston, it became an esteemed venue for folk and rock acts especially, by the mid-1960s, though Weston says, "I brought acts from all over the country who'd never had exposure—I brought every kind of act into the Troubadour that you could possibly imagine." Typically Weston would feature a regionally known act from New York or Nashville, then give them West Coast charisma—many Troubadour debut acts gained record deals as a result. (Sometimes the record companies would buy time at the Troubadour to flaunt a new act.) Incredibly, the club is still in business.

"It's still the best club in the country," Peter Asher (of the Beatles empire) told Judith Sims of *Rolling Stone* in 1973, while calling the dressing room "a pigsty." The 350-seat club had so extraordinary a sound system that live recordings were made there.

Jimmy was opening for Delaney Bramlett (formerly of Delaney and Bonnie and Friends), and once again *Billboard* declared that Jimmy delivered the stronger show . . . with his imaginary band, rousing humorous rapport with the audience. Writer Bob Kirsch said Jimmy should become the headliner, that he was far superior to most singer-song-writers.

■   ■   ■

Suddenly—sadly—that same month, Jimmy unexpectedly lurched to the top of ABC-Dunhill's artistic, pop-poetic pinnacle. On September 20, 1973, Jim Croce and his guitar player (and four other people) died when their plane crashed on takeoff, in Natchitoches, Louisiana (site of the 1990 film *Steel Magnolias*). "Time in a Bottle" was a posthumous hit in 1973, as other Croce singles and albums continued to chart.

■   ■   ■

"I wrote practically all of that second album when I was lying around out in Montana," Jimmy told *Stereo Review*'s Noel Coppage in 1974.

Back in 1973, Jimmy had stayed with Thomas McGuane and his wife, Betty, at their ranch in Livingston, Montana. They'd bought this Key West alternative home with some movie advance money around 1970, and once again became superhosts to an army of creative folk. At one point, "there were twenty-seven people living and writing at the McGuanes' ranch, including Jimmy Buffett, who was sleeping in the barn and composing songs that turned up on the radio, it seemed, only weeks later," according to Lawrence Wright in *Rolling Stone* in 1985.

Among the many creative folks drawn magnetically to the McGuanes' Livingston mecca were film director Sam Peckinpah, actors Warren Oates and Jeff Bridges, and authors William Hjortsberg, Jim Harrison, and Richard Brautigan. Several of the guests eventually bought their own Livingston houses. On a typical day, Jimmy might sit in the kitchen and play his guitar, accompanied by McGuane on the mandolin, entertaining Brautigan and the Hjortsbergs.

Brautigan, like Gulf Coast Jimmy, was a regional writer (from the Pacific Northwest) *and* a decadent hippie Bohemian—a celebrity novelist whose ribald eccentricity foreshadowed Jimmy's song-storytelling of the Seventies (and his late-Eighties foray into published fiction). Like

Jimmy—and most any important novelist—Brautigan had a strong sense of place. Brautigan's loyalty to his beloved Pacific Northwest parallels Jimmy's own Mississippi-Alabama nostalgia—even as Brautigan's post-beatnik, San Francisco persona resembles Jimmy's hedonistic, New Orleans–Key West image. Brautigan's *Trout Fishing in America* (1967) was hippie Hemingway; his *In Watermelon Sugar* (1968) was about LSD. Like Jimmy, he admired poetry first ("I figured that I couldn't write a novel until I could write a sentence").

When Bonzai asked Jimmy, "Do you have any useful music-business advice?" in *Mix* in 1986, Jimmy said, "As Richard Brautigan once told me, when dealing with record companies, just remember . . . that they're always the enemy!"

As for McGuane, he was getting high on Hollywood hopes, and would soon recruit Jimmy for a movie deal.*

∎ ∎ ∎

In October 1973 Jimmy recorded his next album, *Living and Dying in ¾ Time,* at Woodland Sound Studio in Nashville. Founded in 1967 by Glenn T. Snoddy, Woodland had already cut hits like "Tennessee Birdwalk" (Jack Blanchard and Misty Morgan) and "Snowbird" (Anne Murray), and would eventually cut "The Devil Went Down to Georgia" for Charlie Daniels, as well as many songs for Barbara Mandrell. (Woodland was one of the twenty-one "Best American Recording Studios" in Randal Zalkind's *Contemporary Music Almanac 1980/1981.*) Snoddy himself had engineered songs back in the 1940s for the pioneer Brown Brothers studio, and later cut hits like Johnny Cash's "Ring of Fire" and Marty Robbins's "A White Sport Coat (And a Pink Carnation)."

Snoddy told *Record World* in 1970 that the current generation of entertainers was "telling it like it is." In 1994 he praised Don Gant for not succumbing to the "Nashville Sound" of overdone production. "You're almost forced into supplying all those little goodies by the competition—and if you don't have them, you're kind of considered *backwoodsy.*" Snoddy says that second-rate producers want to have "all the little bells and whistles" on their sessions, but Don Gant "had the simplicity and foresight to sift through all that—his production values were always *so* good. The world lost a real talent when he died."

The first cut on Side One is one of Jimmy's most durable and famous sing-along songs, "Pencil Thin Mustache." It has the Buffett big-band Forties bouncy feel, with a bridge instead of a chorus. The tune is

---

* Jimmy was asked by director Robert Altman to score the film *Nashville* (1975)—then was bypassed; actor Gene Hackman wanted him to write for a Key West movie, and director Arthur Penn wanted him to write for *The Dark Tower*—two more offers probably never fulfilled. (Penn directed *The Missouri Breaks,* scripted by McGuane.)

Sinatra–Tony Bennett style, recalling the days of old black-and-white movies—when Boston Blackie could solve a mystery, thanks to his mustache, and only jazz musicians smoked marijuana. The song praises "a two-toned Ricky Ricardo" jacket, extolling the role played by Desi Arnaz with Lucille Ball. Arnaz was a 1930s Cuban refugee who played conga music in Miami, and was first encouraged in New York by Xavier Cugat.

The second track, "Come Monday," is Jimmy's second-most-successful song. As he told television host David Letterman in 1983, the song "kept me from killing myself" in the Howard Johnson's restaurant at Mount Tamalpais in Marin County, California, where he was "deathly depressed . . . it was awful." Letterman said it maybe reflected "the color of the roof in those places," and Jimmy agreed: "Sure, the size of the rooms and the food next door."

"Great stories!" enthused Letterman.

The sad, bored emotions ("I spent four lonely days in a brown L.A. haze") are those of a tired, mechanical musician grinding out stock love songs in bar lounges, wishing he was home with his woman instead. The jazzy bridge mentions happier times up in Montana . . . no doubt with Jane, up at Tom McGuane's (the album is dedicated to her).

If the lyrics are typically Jimmy's, the melody is soft pop—more like a Tom Jones, Englebert Humperdinck, or Dean Martin *counter*hippie tune. A song written for the stereotypical whiskey rooms of the world.

The next three songs ridicule standard country-and-western themes. "Ringling, Ringling" (with an upbeat melody) decries the dwindling of a fading Montana town; "Brahma Fear" excuses a rodeo rider for preferring whiskey-drinking, airplane-flying, and sailing to riding a brahma steer; and "Brand New Country Star" laughs at the "crossover" syndrome, the singer shedding his rhinestone Nudie suits in exchange for the country-rock "outlaw" image ("a hot Roman candle / From the Texas Panhandle"). This third song might caricature Waylon Jennings—or maybe Willie Nelson, who left Nashville for Texas in 1972 (while failing to return a .38 automatic pistol he borrowed from RCA's vice president, guitarist Chet Atkins). The song's cowriter, Vernon "Austin Church" Arnold, told Jimmy how Ernest Tubb and his band members ate "all these cheeseburgers, day after day after day, out there on the road." (By 1996 Austin Church was performing his "Thanks Ernest Tubb!" tribute out at Nashville's Texas Troubadour Theater.) And a retake of "Livingston's Gone to Texas" (from the "mislaid" Barnaby tape) completes Side One.

The opening song on Side Two, "The Wino and I Know," drags country music down to New Orleans, portraying a Bourbon Street ice-cream peddler who prefers Hank Snow. (Jimmy credits Gordon Lightfoot's influence—that ability to tell a story, whether it's in fashion or not.) "West Nashville Grand Ballroom Gown" is a classic "Athens of the South" satire, about a gal from the best part of town, who no longer attends church (neither does the "Brand New Country Star"), hitchhiking to Cincinnati and writing her mother a vengeful letter ("Fuck all those West Nashville grand ballroom gowns!"). "Saxophones" alludes to the Shipwreck Lounge in Key West while reminiscing about growing up on "gumbo rock" music. "Ballad of Spider John," a lengthy tribute to a robber, was by Willis Alan Ramsey.

And the closing track, "God's Own Drunk," was a comical recitation from Lord Buckley (1906–1960), an iconoclastic white comedian whose "Black Cross" recitation young Bob Dylan liked to perform (about a black man lynched for reading too well). Buffett heard "God's Own Drunk" down in New Orleans and made it a concert standard, whose opening line, "I ain't no drinkin' man," excuses the narrator's imbibing at his brother's moonshine still.

This time, the musicians were termed "the Second Coral Reefer Band"—including, as before, backup singers Don Gant, Buzz Cason . . . and Bergen White.

White had worked on the Barnaby albums, having studied subtle arranging techniques for Bill "the King of Copy Music" Beasley, down at Spar. So he arranged the horns and strings on the album, a "first" for Buffett. At a Christmas party for MCA (and Margaritaville) Records in 1992, Jimmy sang "Come Monday," and White says, "We were laughing about how far back he and I went."

■ ■ ■

Thanks to "God's Own Drunk," Jimmy's inebriated image gained new, vinyl credibility. A few months later, Alvin Cooley said in *Zoo World* that while everyone in Key West loved Jimmy when he was sober (which was seldom), they also loved him when he was drunk . . . which was most of the time.

He told journalist Candice Russell that he loved small clubs like the Troubadour, because "with the big concerts, you don't get the same magic." So, out of professional necessity, he had been forced to get drunk to face thirty thousand "teenyboppers" when he opened for Three Dog Night. At least when he got drunk for the concert, there was "two of me out there."

Alvin Cooley said that in Nashville, people liked to say, "He's crazy— drinks all the time. What does a kid like that know about country music, anyway?"

Sometime, probably in 1973, Jimmy came to Nashville for "a recent award concert," quite possibly the Country Music Week in October. The ABC-Dunhill executives allegedly tried to keep "Gant's own drunk" in his hotel room at the King of the Road Motel (itself a colorful lodging where Jerry Lee Lewis broke a whiskey glass in the face of a fan, according to Merle Haggard in *Zoo World*).

"He gets interesting when he's around nightclubs," Chet Flippo wrote, saying that once, after he'd "been ejected from a joint [King of the Road] and wasn't real sure of where he was," he wanted to climb a tree and "get his bearings." He was in the parking lot with Terry Paul, the bass player for Kris Kristofferson, and/or his own drummer, Sammy Creason (accounts differ).

"I couldn't find my rent-a-car and, blasted out of my mind on tequila, I stepped on the hood of another car to get a better vantage point," he told Judith Sims in *Rolling Stone* in 1975. Alvin Cooley says they were dancing and singing. They wanted to leave the motel for a restaurant— and Jimmy was wearing golf shoes with spikes.

The car was a Cadillac; suddenly its owner appeared and bellowed: *"Hey, what do you guys think you're doing to my car?"*

Jimmy and Sammy Creason finally spotted Jimmy's rental car, dashed over, and locked themselves into it. The Cadillac's owner pursued them and vengefully jumped onto the hood of *their* car.

Creason opened the window to apologize—a big mistake, since the Cadillac owner hit him—even as Creason stabbed him in the fist with a Bic pen, while he grabbed Jimmy "by the hair and started yanking it out" . . . and slugging him, too. Jimmy told Patricia Ward Biederman in the *Atlanta Constitution,* "I can't remember the details, but he basically beat the hell out of me." He even threw a trash can at him. "Oh my God, I don't want to die in Nashville in a rented Gremlin," cried Jimmy. They managed to roll the window back up, then drove off to a restaurant for dinner and later went back to the motel.

"We've been threatened by that *killer maniac*—when we go back we have to *protect* ourselves," Jimmy said to Creason. So he pulled a tire iron out of the car. And, *yes*—in the lobby of the King of the Road stood their enemy, who grabbed Jimmy's tire tool out of his pocket. Other people came to their defense, shoved them into the elevator, then took them to Jimmy's room. "Oh, my God, lock me in," said Jimmy.

But *who* was after them?

Sheriff Buford Pusser, from McNairy County, Tennessee, on the Mississippi River. Pusser had already killed two members of the State Line Mob (prostitution and gambling suppliers)—and his own wife had been murdered. His authorized biography, *Walking Tall,* appeared in 1971, selling over a million and a half copies and triggering three movies.

Sometime later, Jimmy received an eight-by-ten glossy photograph of Pusser, inscribed, "To my favorite sparring partner. Next time I'll kill you," sent not by Pusser . . . but by Don Light.

■　■　■

Other barroom memories dramatize Jimmy's days in this period.

"Hey, those are good songs, they're going to come through eventually," author Don Cusic remembers Jimmy's band saying to him at the then Hall of Fame motel lounge. "He was really frustrated because his songs weren't getting played. He was kind of down in the dumps, drinking beer at the time." Cusic believes A *White Sport Coat and a Pink Crustacean* was an underground cult album at the time, and remembers "Why Don't We Get Drunk" being a jukebox hit.

Jimmy passed out drunk at the Commodore Lounge of the Holiday Inn Vanderbilt, remembered Bill Vaughn, road manager for the Nitty Gritty Dirt Band. He told this to Mark Brewer, who says Jimmy had "his head thrown back and his mouth open." People sitting near him were tossing popcorn in his mouth; every now and then Jimmy would choke and wake up—then pass out again. "Hey, that's Jimmy Buffett," someone said. "*Who?*" questioned the popcorn tossers.

■ ■ ■

In February 1974 *Cash Box* praised Jimmy's "conversational style . . . which has already earned him a considerable concert following," calling his *Living and Dying in ¾ Time* album "an incredible treat." *Record World* predicted that the "catchy, rhythmically fascinating" first single, "Saxophones," would be a hit (so did *Cash Box*)—but it only went to Number 105 in the pop charts. (The B-side, "Ringling, Ringling," was a good country song.) Still, *Cash Box* said that Jimmy's career would "fly high from here on in," claiming his resemblance to Croce was "uncanny." Peter Reilly of *Stereo Review* praised his "detached sass that I find irresistible." But the *Village Voice*'s Robert Christgau said Jimmy was torn between being Arlo Guthrie and being himself—and that the album's best song was "God's Own Drunk."

■ ■ ■

Next . . . back to the Troubadour, opening for Hoyt Axton. Axton was one of the strongest onstage performers, who'd written hits like "Greenback Dollar" (The Kingston Trio) and "Joy to the World" (Three Dog Night), and whose mother, journalist Mae Boren Axton, was a Nashville matriarch. (She'd cowritten "Heartbreak Hotel" for Presley, and encouraged then-unknown Willie Nelson.)

Hoyt Axton—only two months away from his hit "When the Morning Comes"—would close his shows with happy jamsessions, including Jimmy and friends dropping by, like Neil Young. One morning Joni Mitchell called Jimmy and said she "adored" his music, warning him that she might climb onstage with him some night. She didn't—but the last night of the gig, Axton was reportedly ill, so Jimmy filled in with a 1950s medley: "Maybellene," "Who Do You Love?" "Battle of New Orleans," and Del Shannon's "Runaway." Since even without Axton, he had pulled five hundred customers into the Troubadour, one journalist exuded: "Every time Jimmy plays, he makes new friends."

Not including ABC-Dunhill promoter Tom McEntee: "To me, I thought Buffett was a shit—but forgive me." He remembers that some photographers wanted pictures; Axton said okay, but "Buffett made it like it was the biggest pain in the butt in the world. . . . He burnt a lot of bridges with a lot of folks. Pretty bad. There were people who weren't important to him. Record people were not important to him. He thought, acted, and said things onstage that suggested that they were the whores of the industry, and that was his attitude toward them. He didn't care how hard you worked to break his records. He thought it all happened magically, somehow . . . because the world just fell in love with him. He never seemed to accept the fact that it took months of ass-breaking work to get him going. But that is something in the past, and I don't dwell on those things. At the time, I didn't feel I had a strong kinship with him."

∎ ∎ ∎

The next single, "Come Monday," broke in May, going to Number 58 on *Billboard*'s country charts, Number 30 in pop—and Number 4 in "Easy Listening" (*Cash Box:* Number 68 in country; Number 26 in pop). Tom McEntee recalls that station WRKO in Boston was pushing it up the charts when—all of a sudden—Dave Loggins's "Please Come to Boston" intervened, so they dropped "Come Monday," which was too similar. "That radio station prevented, I think, Buffett from having a perhaps Number One record. Then the entire chain would have gone, which meant San Francisco, Los Angeles—you know, they had a number of major-market cities."

Jimmy was in England when "Come Monday" hit. "I went in to buy a pair of shoes and heard it on the radio," he told Judith Sims of *Rolling Stone*. But Great Britain's BBC radio was refusing to keep playing "Come Monday"—since it was a government station, it wouldn't permit a song to include a brand-name product. So Jimmy came back to Nashville and changed the line"I've got my Hush Puppies on" to "I've got my hiking boots on."

When "Come Monday" first hit the charts at Number 91, his old employer *Billboard* ran his picture—and praised ABC-Dunhill's "lengthy and admirable support" of his "eccentric talents," terming him an "easy-going rock satirist . . . charming, kooky in-person entertainer." They called his manager Don Light a "Nashville heavy."

Though Jimmy likes to complain that he has never received any music awards, "Come Monday" won a BMI pop award in 1974, plus a country award in 1975, and eventually a "Two Million Air Award" for its total of two million radio airplays. "I've only written one love song," Jimmy has said of "Come Monday."

∎ ∎ ∎

"Jimmy Buffett bounces onstage like a hobo surfer, healthy enough to do an orange-juice commercial—his spring suntan, straw-colored hair, and shell necklace," exulted Jeff Nightbyrd of *Zoo World* at an Austin show at the Castle Creek Club in May 1974. Nightbyrd noted "an outrageous hulu girl" on top of his swaying acoustic guitar—burned on by a Montana friend.

He was playing new songs, such as the humorous "Door Number Three," written with Steve Goodman up in Chicago ("She's no big deal to most folks, but she's everything to me"). On the second set he performed "Life Is Just a Tire Swing," reminiscing about his Pascagoula days, chasing sparrows "with rubber-tipped arrows," and picking black-berries and eating fried chicken. One line in the song, about falling asleep at the wheel—and being awakened by a Ma Bell telephone pole—was *true!* "Are you ready for this amazing story?" he asked a call-in listener during a 1989 interview on station WLUP-FM in Chicago. He told how, on his way to a college concert in western Illinois with Steve Goodman, he passed a tire swing—and began working on the song. Then, on their way back to Peoria, he *did* fall asleep . . . and woke up in the field next to the tire swing! There he finished writing the song, and soon, the story became a legend around the campus.

At the Castle Creek Club, up sauntered Willis Alan Ramsey, writer of "Ballad of Spider John," who that same year would earn a chapter in Jan Reid's outlaw epic, *The Improbable Rise of Redneck Rock*. "Shit!" Jimmy apologized. "I'm sorry I missed a few words of your song."

Already the crowd was making some requests. "I wanted to finish early and sneak off to the oyster bar before it closed," he told Jeff Nightbyrd, "but hell! I feel like singing all night."

■ ■ ■

Thanks to "Come Monday," Jimmy was finally up and out of the "Nash-ville underground," where *Zoo World* had loyally placed him, alongside numerous fringe folkies like Hoyt Axton, S. David Cohen (David Blue), Steve Goodman, Bob Dylan, Chris Gantry, Michael Martin Murphey, Micky Newbury, Shel Silverstein, Townes Van Zandt, and Music City misfits like Barefoot Jerry (Wayne Moss group), Dick Feller, Dallas Frazier, Tom T. Hall, Linda Hargrove, Waylon Jennings, Kris Kristoffer-son, Johnny Paycheck, Jerry Reed, Johnny Rodriguez, Troy Seals, Billy Joe Shaver, Ray Stevens, Jerry Jeff Walker, Tony Joe White, among many others. "Who's Who in the Nashville Underground" also listed Dan Fogelberg, one of Jimmy's future closest allies, . . . and his backup singer Bergen White, a sort of "white male Dionne Warwick."

The timing was right.

Austin was now termed the "alternative Nashville." Willie Nelson was on the classic black label Atlantic Records. Waylon "Goddamn" Jennings was managed by Neil C. Reshen—a self-proclaimed "New York Jew with a black wife." Coconspirator Tompall Glaser was telling a British reporter, "I'm just sick of the whole damned prostituted mess. . . . If Nashville doesn't rethink its ideas in the near future, it's going to be too late. It'll cease to be Music City, U.S.A." The Grand Ole Opry was abandoning the Ryman Auditorium in favor of Disney-esque Opryland—a symbolic Music City schism. Australian Olivia Newton-John's 1974 CMA awards were outraging traditionalists. ("The CMA does not represent us. There are no entertainers on the board.") And Dolly Parton was now on the highway sans Porter Wagoner.

■ ■ ■

In June 1974, only weeks after "Come Monday" hit, ex-journalist Jimmy took time out to denigrate those television forums that would honor him in the Eighties. "I don't want to do talk shows because they're just dumb," he told Candice Russell. "I'd like to talk to [Dick] Cavett. But sitting on the Johnny Carson show, in between Zsa Zsa [Gabor] and Rodney Dangerfield, is not my idea of a good time."

At least he praised his record company: "ABC has been very, very good to me. I'm not going to leave them. They let me do what I want in terms of album covers and titles. They have no artistic controls on me at all." He also accused two other record companies (not by name) of trying to seduce him into an adulterous divorce. They "offered me a lot more money and offered to finance any legal hassles when I broke my contract." ABC-Dunhill was shocked—and relieved—to learn that Jimmy had refused to get drunk and screw with anybody else.

■ ■ ■

That summer, "he went to Paris" (probably) to help make a French television documentary on tarpon fishing in the Florida Keys—a "sort of miniature view of Key West for all the people in Frogland. . . . I did that because it was a free trip to France."

When he returned, a former ABC Records employee, Corb Donahue, met with him. Donahue once said, "Anything that rises above the mire is a success. Anything that draws attention to itself and continues on without some sort of great preposterous hype involved is a success." He asked Jimmy to consider going on the road—more or less full-time—at least during this current onrush of fame. Unless, of course, Jimmy really *was* the drunken beachbum of his music persona . . . who might have to think about it for a while. But almost immediately, he told Donahue yes—since (as he reflected later in his *Parrot Head Handbook*) success has "a very small aperture," and if you don't jump right through it, you'll have plenty of time (for the rest of your life) to look back at what might have been.

Soon Jimmy was handling more than three hundred club or concert dates a year. In his commitment to the highway, he had more in common with country singers Ernest Tubb or Little Jimmy Dickens than with many of his fellow Woodstock-generation singer-songwriters. The secret of his success—then and ever since—owed much to his Southern workingman doggedness, something his father, his grandfather, and even his uncle Billy (on a sober day) would have recognized.

For all his tropical, pseudo-laziness, juvenile Jimmy had suddenly decided to become an adult . . . with all this new vinyl merchandise, ready to market.

From Montana to Margaritaville

■

He has a genius for friendship. Jimmy's a most charming guy.

—novelist Thomas McGuane to James Neff, *Country Style*
(January 1977)

We're not outlaws or common thieves," he sang, just gamblers with "cards up our sleeves" . . . looking for the whole show, and not just the dance . . . "bouncing around the mountains," drinking and laughing . . . in Montana, home of "white men and red men."

The catchy theme song, which he wrote, opened (as well as closed) the film *Rancho Deluxe*, filmed in 1974 up near Livingston (Jimmy already owned five acres at Deep Creek). Directed by Frank Perry, the film had a script by Thomas McGuane, who'd first shown it to Jimmy back in Key West. Jimmy turns up in a Montana beer joint singing "Livingston Saturday Night," a song he would rerecord years later.

His strong performance is more vehement than that of many a self-conscious rock 'n' roller. McGuane was in the scene, too, playing mandolin.

The movie was a rather existentialist spoof of the Old West, with its two heroes (played by Jeff Bridges and Sam Waterson) paying their rent to their landlady with rustled (*still warm*) dead cattle. Love and/or sex seem as trivial as ol'-time ranching, thanks to inane fornication (and implicit fellatio) scenes. (At one point, four folks are in the same bed!)

Offscreen dialogue was even more dramatic. Actress Elizabeth Ashley "always had a weakness for writers" such as "psychedelic cowboy" McGuane, she said in her *Actress: Postcards from the Road* autobiography. He invited her to chat with him in a parking lot, and they ended up sleeping together. The next morning wife Becky McGuane praised Ashley's adultery debut: "I think it's wonderful. Usually he just screws these dumb cowgirl teenyboppers."

The film was released in 1975, and the critics praised much of its dialogue, cheered by its kooky characterizations. But the whimsical, circular plot didn't sell many tickets. Jimmy was listed as playing "Himself" in the credits, and despite all his musical charisma (especially on the soundtrack album with Vassar Clements on fiddle and Michael Utley on keyboard), the *Miami Herald*'s Candice Russell said in 1974 he was "soured" because of his bit part. "The artistic people are fine; Frank Perry was a real pleasure to work with," Jimmy elaborated to Penelope Ross (*The Music Gig*) in 1976. "But the experiences with the front office were terrible. Unbelievably horrible things went wrong that the producer was responsible for. He made me realize that the people in the music business were weird, but the movies are doubly weird. Now I know how to handle things if it happens again. On *my* terms."

So, when asked to score *92 in the Shade,* based on McGuane's novel, he "turned it down because I'd just done *Rancho Deluxe* and I was upset with the producer. I just wanted nothing to do with movies right then."

Filmed in Key West, *92 in the Shade* starred Peter Fonda—who eventually fell for McGuane's wife, Becky, marrying her one day. But initially, she was drawn to actor Warren Oates, also in the film. Elizabeth Ashley was in the film as well.

Later in California, he took a new girl onto Ashley's bed, so back in Key West, Ashley smashed his head bloody, with a table lamp. Then McGuane found solace in the arms of *92*'s actress Margot Kidder—whom he married (after she had his baby), and divorced, next. (This marital merry-go-round was worthwhile—or at least worth four pages in *People* magazine.)

■ ■ ■

Jimmy's *A1A* album took its title from the U.S. beach highway that extends down to Key West.

In McGuane's novel *The Bushwhacked Piano* (1973), hero Nicholas Payne migrates from Livingston, Montana, to Key West via "A1A heading down through Key Largo, the mainland becoming more and streaked with water and the land breaking from large to small pieces" (after first stopping in a roadhouse where his woman, Ann, plays country jukebox records by Porter Wagoner, Merle Haggard, Jeannie C. Riley, Buck Owens, Tammy Wynette). In 1981 Florida Governor Bob Graham handed Jimmy his own A1A sign "in recognition of Buffett's promotion of the highway."

An A1A map fills the inside of the album, and a coastline photograph (with an A1A sign) covers the back, while the front cover portrait of Jimmy in a chair with a beer fixes forever his image as the slouching, beerful beach idler.

Despite all of Jimmy's anti–country music blathering, the first four tracks on Side One owe much to the "Nashville outlaw sound," albeit with iconoclastic lyrics. "Makin' Music for Money" (by Alex Harvey) is a country-rock diatribe against musical commercialism. "Door Number Three" (written with Steve Goodman) is one more country parody. "Dallas" (by his road lead guitarist, Roger Bartlett) and "Presents to Send You" keep the country wheel turning, as does the John Sebastian number, "Stories We Could Tell You," a tribute to country-music tale-telling (staring at a guitar in a Tennessee museum). But "Life Is Just a Tire Swing" is Gulf Coast, folkie Jimmy (slapping the home folks a little).

Side Two opens with "A Pirate Looks at Forty," enhanced with vibes (xylophone) by Ferrel Morris. "Migration" humorously attacks Key West retirees, living in mobile homes, whose influx was starting to nag Jimmy ("I hate those bastards so much"). "Trying to Reason with Hurricane Season" cites A1A—and anticipates "Margaritaville" with beach boy slothfulness and Bloody Mary slurping (and an excellent melody). "Nautical Wheelers" was the Key West waltz number, echoing the title of his 1973 album, *Living and Dying in ¾ Time*. And "Tin Cup Chalice" is another lazy-sweet Floridian tune, extolling drinking and sunbathing (in their 1975 album, *Vocal Group of the Decade*, the Glasers released the song—along with "The Christian?"—both coproduced with Buzz Cason).

Recorded again at Woodland Sound Studios, *A1A* featured most of the same musicians as previous Buffett albums, including Steve Goodman on acoustic lead guitar, Reggie Young (electric lead guitar), and Doyle Gresham (steel guitar)—called the Third Coral Reefer Band. Stephen Holden in *Rolling Stone* termed Gresham "tasty," and Jimmy a conventional "cosmic cowboy," some of whose songs depicted "vividly the squalor and enervating languor of life between Miami Beach and Key West." The album was "likable, intelligent and unpretentious." William C. Woods in the *Washington Post* said Jimmy had "melded" calypso and country music to form the "Key West Sound" of "pirates, rum-runners, and barkeeps" while retaining his own "psychic" vision—though Don Shewey (*Unicorn Times*) condemned the "unusual number of trite and throwaway cuts."

■ ■ ■

"In 1974, I didn't know how long I was going to be around, so the first time I ever made any money I went out and paid off all my debts, bought my parents a house [in the town of Daphne, on the Mobile Bay] and bought myself a boat," Jimmy told Richard Harrington of the *Washington Post* in 1989. "If it all fell apart tomorrow, I could live on that boat and be happy and nobody could take it away from me. And the boat was my key to adventure—you just run into it."

With his first fat royalty check, Jimmy bought a thirty-three-foot Cheoy Lee ketch, which he named *Euphoria*. He had been performing in Portland, Oregon, at a club by that name—the Euphoria Tavern, sunk down in the city's warehouse district, named after the Holy Modal Rounders song "Euphoria." It was Portland's version of the Troubadour, having featuring shows by Bonnie Raitt, Muddy Waters, Bob Lind, and Tanya Tucker over its financially troubled years. (The club's name came true in 1975, when one of its owners was busted for drug-running; two others had felony records, leading to public dismay!)

■ ■ ■

Some Troubadour customers were shouting for "Why Don't We Get Drunk (and Screw)" that July. "Well," sighed Jimmy to *Rolling Stone*'s Judith Sims, "you put out a song like that, you've got to live with it."

Sims described Jimmy's appearance: "Buffett is short, with wavy blond hair that just hangs there like the Dutch Boy Paints trademark." Musing about his "wasted, drunk-on-his-ass, hard-travelin' image"—and his onstage boasts about his "sodden exploits"—she asked him frankly about his drinking. As they walked around together at the Los Angeles County Art Museum, he explained, "When you're onstage and the energy's going and the sweat's pouring out of you, you can drink a lot and it's all used up. What'll kill you is drinking at the same pace when you're offstage. I try not to have more than one or two drinks between sets."

■ ■ ■

At last, his hometown was voicing Buffett pride. Two articles that summer in the *Mobile Press* credited his local upbringing, while noting that he was going to miss his tenth-anniversary reunion at McGill High due to a concert tour of England. His August appearance on the traditional television show *Your Hit Parade* was praised—thanks to "Come Monday," peanut butter–swiping Jimmy was momentarily soft-radio sweet, more Perry Como–ish than Dylan-esque. *Your Hit Parade* was the descendant of radio's *Lucky Strike Hit Parade,* born in 1935, whose television version (1950–59) was doomed by its stuffy staff-singers' inability (and unwillingness) to sing rock 'n' roll (Nashville's snobby Snooky Lanson would do Elvis's "Hound Dog" as a joke). Resurrected in August 1974, come September the senile show was once more deceased.

By October Jimmy was back at the Troubadour, and despite Jimmy's Nashvilleophobia, Dennis Hunt of the *Los Angeles Times* termed him "country-folk" (in a story headlined "A Little Country Sunshine")—a sort of hippie-hillbilly who created "a cheery, down-home atmosphere. He makes you feel like you're whooping it up in some backwoods barnyard." Hunt praised "Door Number Three" for being a "droll put-down of the witless television show *Let's Make a Deal,*" with host Monty Hall, where contestants would accidentally swap valuable prizes for worthless "zonk" prizes.

Jimmy's repeated returns to the Troubadour reflected owner Doug Weston's nightclub acumen—his contracts typically gave him several "options" to bring an act back if *he* desired. An exploding superstar might bitterly resent those fine-print clauses—"They Hate It, But They Play It," jested a Judith Sims *Rolling Stone* headline, telling how "Sir Doug Weston" let Elton John *buy up* his three options for twenty-five thousand dollars!

In November Jimmy did a two-and-a-half-hour concert at Mobile's Saenger Theater, aided by his sideman Roger Bartlett. Local journalist Mark R. Kent called him "uninhibited, leaving few stones unturned—and fewer expletives deleted." The crowd gave him a standing ovation.

But Jimmy's hard-road traveling *without a band* was taking its toll as he hit a string of dates in November and December, including Vanderbilt University in Nashville, and Southern in Hattiesburg, as well as others in Florida, Texas, and Illinois. *A1A* was out in December, and it went to Number 25 the following spring. (Of its two singles, "A Pirate Looks at Forty" and "Door Number Three," only the latter charted, at Number 88 on the country charts.)

As early as January, Jimmy was back in Austin, hosting a "Texas country" one-hour television show, sponsored by Lone Star beer. Countless other "outlaws" were riding through the series—Jerry Jeff Walker, Sammi Smith, Ray Wylie Hubbard, Doug Kershaw, Steve Fromholz, and, of course, Music Row renegades Waylon and Willie. The ability to *host* a show was one more country-music skill (exemplified by the Grand Ole Opry) that Jimmy seemed to possess, whereas too many "great" pop entertainers only know how to introduce themselves.

Still, the onrush of concerts in early 1975—nineteen in January and

February—further frustrated bandless Jimmy. "I was not too interested in the hassles of keeping a band together," he told British writer Alan Cackett of *Country Music People* in 1976 (who had liked Jimmy from the start—somehow *Down to Earth* had crossed the Atlantic). "That's why on each album it's been the First Coral Reefer Band, then Second and Third. I didn't want to be tied down, but I realize that people who have listened to the albums may miss the punch of the pedal steel, or the throbbing beat of a bass guitar."

Back in Key West, Jimmy began assembling—finally—a full-time Coral Reefer Band, not just one for recording sessions. In April, Don Light publicly named the band: Greg "Fingers" Taylor, harmonica and keyboards; Harry Dailey, bass; Phillip Fajardo, drums; and Roger Bartlett continuing as lead electric guitarist and harmony singer. Road manager was Mike Wheeler; equipment custodian was Pat Manicchia.

Bartlett and Fajardo were from Austin. As Jimmy told Steve Bogner of the *Austin American Statesman* that month, "Before, it was me and one other playing gigs. It was getting too taxing on me, having to play instruments, sing, and rap with the audience all at the same time." Because of his band, he said, his music was changing; now he had more time to write songs: "It's quite a relief to have the band; it's definitely worth the hassle."

To Penelope Ross of *The Music Gig,* he added: "If ever there's a bad situation or a bad crowd, you can lay back on the band and don't have to carry the whole load yourself. It's the only way I could have done it, even though I get criticized for selling out."

This was one of the most pivotal points in Jimmy's career.

The Sixties and Seventies had countless singer-songwriters of astounding talent, many deemed "poetic," with distinctive voices and albums full of artistic songs, usually remembered for one or two immortal hits. Many refused to build bands—others did so reluctantly, flashing themselves onstage as if side musicians were a necessary evil. Many appeared contemptuous of nightclub work, and all too many looked as if they were more at home in studios than on the road. Even some of today's "country" acts don't look like they could work a nightclub if they weren't already famous. Whereas Garth Brooks, like Jimmy, was a lounge act while in college—and Travis Tritt, in 1991, told Thomas Goldsmith of the *Tennessean:*

> I think the concert dollar being what it is, you need to see something at a show that you're not going to see anywhere else. . . . I learned that in clubs, playing little small places. . . . You've got a place that might seat seventy-five people and on a Saturday night you might have twenty-five people. And they're all drunk and they don't care; they'd just as soon be listening to the jukebox. You have to do something to get those people's attention. And that's where the entertaining comes in.

Jimmy had picked up his doctorate in live music, down in New Orleans with his fellow classmates, the Upstairs Alliance. He knew that a nightclub was a tougher gig than a concert hall, but if you wanted to do the latter, you'd better do it as well as the former. Philosophically, the Coral Reefer Band had been born years before . . . in the dives on Bourbon Street.

His Key West photographer pal Tom Corcoran wrote that "it's true that Jimmy Buffett busts his ass on the road. He doesn't want it widely known, but he's both the singer and the boss." He credited road manager Mike Wheeler with performing the "hourly miracles," by greasing the wheels. But Jimmy kept track of everything, from sound equipment arriving by planes to getting lights on the stage. "Wheeler's there to be generally pleasant . . . Buffett tells him when to be an indignant son of a bitch." Jimmy knew that the sooner things were straightened out, the sooner he could squat on his "busted ass. He used to be the Clown Prince of the smuggling set. Now that his ship has come in he gets a little more respect."

■ ■ ■

By now, he had rented a house in New England for vacations, and he told Associated Press correspondent Natt Yancey in March that Nashville—like Atlanta—was too big a city. "Cities are too fast a pace. I've got lots of energy, but I don't want to spend it worrying about traffic or the air I breathe."

With no hot hits from the *A1A* album, the following month he complained to Austin journalist Steve Bogner that "Nashville is getting too routine. It is very closed as far as recording goes. Publishing-wise, no one can just walk in off the street anymore. Of course, I never really had a good time there. I recorded my last two albums there merely out of convenience. When you're there, you're just a member of a mass of people who are trying to make it. The longer you stay, you grow stale, get lazy, and become resentful of other people's successes.

"I like to keep things at a simple level," he continued, praising Austin over Nashville—"It's easier here, friendlier"—while admitting, paradoxically, that it would never become an important recording center ("In a way, that's nice").

ABC-Dunhill had been pushing Jimmy harder ever since Jim Croce died, tightening the schedule for his recording sessions, yet as James Neff reported in 1977 in *Country Style*, he never wanted to be identified as a country musician: "Every time ABC Records would line up an interview with a country-music publication, Buffett would shudder. Not another of those fan-mag hacks [i.e., journalists] asking him about Marvin Gardens (a fictional character Buffett created for an old album)."

His former publicist, Cathy Roszell, said of journalism graduate Buffett: "Jimmy is a private person. He doesn't trust people at first until he really gets to know them."

■ ■ ■

In June, Jimmy and his new band went back to the Troubadour, and *Billboard*'s Bob Kirsch thought he seemed "a bit less inspired" than before, while admitting he "more than pleased the packed house." They moved on to Washington, D.C., playing at the Cellar Door, a prestigious listening club up in old Georgetown (once a British colonial city). He told the audience that many of his songs were written in "the Jimmy Buffett Memorial Hammock"—and the *Washington Post*'s Larry Rohter, reacting to "A Pirate Looks at Forty," said that Jimmy was as good a performer "when he's serious as when he's funny."

That August he opened for the Eagles at the Carolina Coliseum in Columbia, South Carolina. The Eagles were one of the most popular acts of their time; their single "Lyin' Eyes" would go to Number 2 (and Number 8 in country) that October. Jimmy would become one of their closest colleagues before long. They had one of the most aggressive managers in history—Irving Azoff.

"We were all just a bunch of punk kids who were the same age," reminisced Azoff about his first days with the Eagles. "Other than Bernie Leadon, who didn't think it was funny when I crashed into the back of his rental car, everybody thought everything was hysterical."

At some point Azoff, who was five foot three, began looking up at Jimmy, who was taller (but not much taller) than he was.

Also that August Jimmy played Miami, and the *Herald*'s Bill Cosford declared he had a "conch-rock . . . droll Key West–Nashville hybrid sound." Then he and the Reefers played at Ebbetts Field in Denver, where Freddy Bosco of the *Rocky Mountain News* (apparently unaware how much Jimmy loved to hate the country-music industry) compared him to Hank Williams, citing the latter's "Hey, Good Lookin'" as an analogy. If Williams were around in 1975, he would be poking fun at life like Jimmy—yet "Buffett is no dumb bumpkin, much as he affects hick manners." Indeed, "cowboy sociologist" Jimmy was ten times more direct than Hank Williams—asking a woman to get drunk and do something that "will not fit through the censorial funnel of a family newspaper."

At September's Boarding House date in San Francisco, Phillip Elwood of the *Chronicle* praised the "first-rate jazz sound" of the band, lauding Bartlett and Taylor for swapping solos on certain songs. Buffett was a "controlled humorist, unusual among country folk-rock," and his funnier songs recalled Arlo Guthrie's "Alice's Restaurant" or Don McLean's "American Pie," while being "less long-winded and rather more tongue-in-cheek."

■   ■   ■

Again, November was studio month . . . and the new album was *Havaña Daydreamin'*.

The first cut on Side One, "Woman Goin' Crazy on Caroline Street" (written with Steve Goodman), celebrates a wanton Key West gal with a strong melody. "My Head Hurts, My Feet Stink, and I Don't Love Jesus" isn't really sacreligious—it almost makes a statement against being a boozy bum. (Nashville's gospel group, the Oak Ridge Boys, supplied the pious backup singing!) "The Captain and the Kid" ("lost" by Barnaby) was finally rerecorded. Fingers Taylor wrote "Big Rig," an overproduced truck-song parody, and Jesse Winchester wrote the melodious love song "Defying Gravity."

The title song, opening Side Two, sounds like an implicit smuggling tune, with strong images ("Ceilin' fan stirs the air/Cigar smoke did swirl") and a pretty melody leading to the title hook. "Clichés" is a love song about an old woman who plays guitar and a young man who writes. "Some is me and some is the band," he said to *The Music Gig*'s Penelope Ross. "It's just some observations about habits, such as my strong addiction to Pepperidge Farm cookies. "Something So Feminine About the Mandolin," a soft folkie song, was cowritten with "Lady Jane" Slagsvol—prophetically anticipating the birth of a daughter, who would learn the stories and the songs. Jane also collaborated on "Kick It in Second Wind." Steve Goodman wrote "This Hotel Room," a goofy, highly singable number.

■   ■   ■

That December he played at the Texas Music Christmas Celebration (with Rusty Weir and Jerry Jeff Walker), then headed back to Aspen, where he, along with Hunter S. Thompson and actor Jack Nicholson, "spent some time observing winter weather," reported Nashville's rebel-country *Hank* magazine. "That must have been one of the more crazy places for the Christmas season."

■   ■   ■

"Every band must have a tune about a groupie," wrote Yvonne Surette of the *Boston Globe* the next February.

Well-tanned Jimmy and his band were the "perfect prescription" for an audience on a "drizzly" evening as they delivered "Please Take Your Drunken Fifteen-Year-Old Girlfriend Home." Surette called it "a funny, all-too-veracious tale of a 'fifteen-year-old quaalude queen.'" (A youngster close to Jimmy had a drug problem, according to a confidential source.) Jimmy told Penelope Ross in *The Music Gig* that the song reflected his audience changes—besides older folks, now he was drawing "teenyboppers." Once, in a club in Atlanta, there'd been a little girl "just polluted out of her mind." Jimmy began talking to her and realized she "had no other intentions, because I knew she was bad news." Her macho boyfriend came up and said, "I bet you don't know how old this little girl is—but you can get in a lot of trouble." Jimmy thought to himself, *These people are really idiots to be making a scene.* So he immediately wrote a song about it, and "it was real loose. We played it the last night of the gig."

■ ■ ■

Jimmy had a bus now, a Silver Eagle—"done like a boat inside," he told Bob Anderson of *High Times* later that year. "Got a video cassette, big sound system, ice chest full of beer, telephone, CB, bunk-to-bunk intercom—it's just a cruiser. You get in there and it's like being on the moon. Finish up a gig, you load up your stuff, get on, smoke a joint, go to the bathroom, and you're there the next morning." Indeed, the amalgam of color television, tape decks, and velour padding—plus a pretty mural on the outside—inspired Michael Bane in the *Country Rambler* to judge it as "the gaudiest travel bus on the road. . . . Even Porter Wagoner might wince at the extravagance."

That fall Jimmy had it remodeled. "We got a big Pioneer SA amp and Marantz FM tuner and a Nakamichi 550 Dual Tracer cassette," he bragged to *Rolling Stone*'s Abe Peck. The Nakamichi was portable— they used it to record their shows. (Jimmy's shows are renowned for their precise, clear sound, reflecting his obsession with equipment maintenance. Yet there are some "name" Opry acts who are helpless when out on their own, relying on house equipment that muddies their music— unable, apparently, to show up early and do sound checks.)

When Jimmy bought the bus, he was allowed to pick twenty-six marker signs for the front of the bus. To be able to park anywhere they wished, they would install a GOVERNOR'S STAFF sign, or to get good service at a truck stop, he would put up a LORETTA LYNN sign. (Another one, called HAVAÑA, was risky to flaunt in Key West.)

Then there was one titled TEENS FOR CHRIST. One morning they had just picked up some marijuana and had stopped at a gas station, when two well-dressed men began circling their bus. "My friends were freaking out, thinking it was a setup," he told Bob Anderson. "But it was just two Billy Graham miniatures . . . like those people you see on Saturday gospel shows."

"Hey, how're ya doing, brother?" they asked Jimmy.

■ ■ ■

"Buffett went into a star-spawned slump soon after his great single 'Come Monday' spilled over successfully from his consistent FM [radio] base to the Top 40," commented *Billboard* that March. Buffett had lost some "individuality" by progressing from acoustic solo to his ever-burgeoning band image. ("Every time the royalty checks grew larger, he added another band member.") Still, he had "recovered brilliantly and [had] his career back into high gear" at a concert in Atlanta that February—according to his old best friend, journalist Gerry Wood.

He played in Mobile in July, as well as in Houston, Texas, to a crowd of ten thousand. And he played some dates for Presidential candidate Jimmy Carter. "He was getting the rush from Jerry Brown and Frank Church [Senate investigator of the CIA]," Jimmy told *High Times*'s Bob Anderson. Carter knew Jimmy had sold out a concert in Portland, Oregon, and called him from Oregon. "He invited me to go out on the campaign plane, which I did for a day . . . I went out and saw Carter work. I have a good gut feeling about him . . . I thought *I* worked hard. But the strain that man has to work with and the way he does it . . . but he can handle the whole schedule. That was what impressed me the most—his stamina."

"I talked to Jimmy Carter about normalizing relations with Cuba," Jimmy told Michael Bane in the *Country Rambler* the following year. Then he whispered in a "conspiratorial" tone: "I didn't tell him it was because I wanted to go back to Havana." (Prudish Castro had kicked the Mafia gamblers out of Cuba; then, in 1972, some Bay of Pigs alumni held a classified class reunion at Watergate. Still, Jimmy would have made an excellent ambassador to Cuba, then and especially now.)

What would Jimmy Carter have thought about the movie script Jimmy was writing with McGuane? Its plot included a Cuban dope-runner . . . located in the Florida reptile jungle.

After Carter won in 1976, Jimmy was invited to the White House at least twice. First Lady Rosalynn Carter was seen wearing a Jimmy Buffett T-shirt, though no doubt it was not the "Why Don't We Get Drunk" one distributed by his record company.

■ ■ ■

Sometime in the summer of 1976 Jimmy took time out, to sail in the Caribbean. "I'll just sail around the islands and hang out," he told Penelope Ross, "because I'm running out of stories. It's a good place to do it. The only timetable I follow is doing one album a year. That gives me just enough time to come up with ten or eleven good tunes." He just couldn't write songs as easily while touring, but he *did* draw a lot of his ideas from people he met on the road . . . meaning that his songs were about "ninety percent true."

That October, Wayne Robins of *Newsday* said that one way Jimmy wrote songs was to hold a beer in his hand while watching television ("preferably black-and-white"); the other way was to lounge in a hammock in Key West, letting his mind wander as he watched the water.

At New York's Bottom Line, Robins enjoyed listening to Jimmy singing "My Head Hurts, My Feet Stink, and I Don't Love Jesus"—"You may not hear it on the radio soon, but it'll make a mighty nice bumper sticker"—and he rightly noted the effect of his journalism background on the songwriting, making him "an accomplished, unpretentious voyeur." (Indeed, his reportorial training accounts for his songs' precision and specificness.)

Robins called one of Jimmy's new songs an "incisive example of Buffett's self-awareness," although its hook line was rather . . . eccentric:

"*Wasting away again in Margaritaville . . .*"

Changes in Management,
Changes in Matrimony

■

He labels as "street talk" local rumors that he moved his management headquarters to Los Angeles recently in an effort to rid himself of the stigma of being a Nashville-based artist.

—Laura Eipper, *The Tennessean*, September 15, 1977

I was working on it, and I didn't have a title for it—I was sitting in a bar and had a wonderful frozen margarita, one of the best ones I ever had. That's where I said 'Margaritaville'—*that's* the title I need for this tune," explained Jimmy for the *Solid Gold Summer Hits* radio series in 1989. "I had 'wasting away' and I had a fill-in word there . . . I was looking for the hook. After the little bar experience, I plugged it in." He was at a bar down in Austin, reportedly at the end of a 1973 tour.

But the locale of the lyric was, naturally . . . Key West. Jimmy's former home was not what it used to be—nor, according to him, what it should have remained. Frustrated with "the first major weekend in Key West that they had a major influx of tourism," he wrote the song.

"It was when those tourists first hit, and it was like a Memorial Day and nobody was prepared for it. . . . There was a *polyester invasion* of Key West. You talk about the *touristos*—and their Winnebagos—came thronging to town. You see somebody walking down the street in plaid Bermudas and red socks and green shoes, and you have to chuckle. They're not local. And that was the basis of it."

Back in 1980, he'd been lounging in Louie's Backyard in Key West with radio interviewer Robert W. Morgan, drinking the obvious drink.

"I wasn't finding much to write about in Key West . . . I wasn't spending much time there anymore. Things had changed. The funky bars I had hung out in had been torn down and turned into turquoise [gift] shops."

Morgan asked him, "What does 'Margaritaville' represent, what does it mean to *you?*"

"It was a combination of places when I wrote the song. It was basic, pure escapism from the humdrum and dull routine of everyday life. *Everybody* wants to go where it's warm, and I think their image of a vacation is sittin' by the beach with whatever your cold drink is you want then. It's something to do with being by the beach and being away from what would be your normal life."

"The image people have of you is just this party guy. How real is that image?"

"Contrary to popular belief, I'm not on the beach every day with margaritas, I'm on the road doing concerts a hundred days a year. When I'm out there doing it, it takes quite a bit of effort."

And he told Associated Press reporter Mary Campbell, "It's not a debauched song. It's just a very light song, about a person hanging out on the beach, not caring to do anything."

The first stanza reports the tourists' arrival, and the next two verses are indolent, inane, and carefree, like a compressed, slightly saner "Mr. Tambourine Man." While there is almost no plot whatsoever, the subtext (as in "Livingston's Gone to Texas") changes two times. A woman's supposedly to blame for the narrator's meaningless existence, but really it's nobody's fault; then (as millions of listeners know), maybe, it's *his* fault—till finally it's his "own damn fault."

One stanza was never released—which Jimmy often does at concerts— about "old men in tank tops, cruising the gift shops," bored with their three-day vacations and wishing they could lose weight . . . and knowing they can't. They exemplified the "transition period" in Key West—and Jimmy asked himself: *Was I a part of that?* He wanted to justify his own role in Key West.

In her songwriting guide *The Bottom Line Is Money* (1994), Jennifer Ember Pierce praises "Margaritaville" 's use of alliteration, internal rhymes, assonance (vowel and syllable parallels, like *reason* and *season*), and consonance (words ending with the same consonant sound). The lyric is "a mini–motion picture"; and "strummin' my six-string" for guitar playing, and "frozen concoction" for margaritas, show Jimmy's penchant for original phrasing. Pierce compares it to Jim Croce's"Operator," since Jimmy, like Croce, "knew how to make use of all of his knowledge and use all the devices available to him."

Like many—perhaps most—great songs, much of it was accidental and instinctive. Art largely comes from the subconscious. No one in an office on 16th Avenue South could have, or would have, written a song like "Margaritaville"—or "El Paso" by Marty Robbins (written while driving through the night to Texas), to cite a similar example of an enduring song spawned by spontaneous, unplanned originality.

The easygoing melody is typically Buffett, a song anyone can sing—in another place and time, Mel Tormé could have crooned it. Jimmy's voice has a throwaway, jazz recklessness, strictly onstage club quality. The instrumental break in the middle shows more old-time contempt for contemporary-radio rigidity.

■ ■ ■

A short while before Jimmy recorded "Margaritaville," he told a concert audience that he was going to do an interview with *High Times*—"that Commie dope magazine." Everybody cheered.

The magazine's founder, Thomas King Forcade (1945–1978), of Trans High Corporation, had edited Abbie Hoffman's *Steal This Book* (1971)—a handy shoplifting and bomb-making (and bomb-throwing) primer for American youth. (Published by Pirate Editions, it also offered good drug-marketing instructions.)

Jimmy told *High Times* interviewer Bob Anderson that some things in his "everyday lifestyle" he took for granted . . . until other people wanted to know about them. Some people couldn't imagine reading a sixty-page pot periodical, but hell, a lot of folks smoke grass, and Jimmy wouldn't be interviewed by *High Times* if he didn't want to be.

Anderson had heard about a girl taking off her clothes during a Florida concert. Wasn't her striptease inspired by "Why Don't We Get Drunk"? (Actually, it was in South Carolina—and she just removed her blouse and began "shaking her tits around.")

But didn't Jimmy give her a backstage pass?

"Bullshit," he retorted, saying that *never* happened—that journalists should actually *see* things before they write about them, to avoid "sensational muckraking." Too many of them took too much "fuckin' liberty," so if Anderson misquoted him, Jimmy promised "to kick [his] ass."

Anderson brought him back to a more popular subject: dissatisfaction with his record company.

Jimmy claimed he didn't really want to discuss it, while admitting their past disagreements. ABC really didn't understand what he was—indeed, no record company would have—but he condemned them for pigeonholing him as country-rock in the outlaw vein. "I can't be categorized," he emphasized—but it was still ABC's responsibility to figure him out. They had let him down, and now they knew it! "I've got a legitimate bitch," because ABC acted like they'd done everything for him, that without them he would have nothing. "But I don't buy that shit at all. It's a mutual cooperation thing."

He was grateful that ABC was "comin' around"—and while he didn't want all their time, he wanted his fair share ("I know what other artists get"). Asked if he wanted to become a Number One artist, he said, "Shit no." He said he didn't want to range across the country, desperately trying to promote himself into the Top 40—he'd rather concentrate on his fans, and flail an eager audience of twelve thousand up into "a total frenzy." Those artists who spurned their own fans sure weren't going to be around for long! (At a concert in Portland, Oregon, in the mid-Seventies, John Denver told his audience *not* to sing along, that "this is *my* show.")

To *survive*, he said, you'd better care about more than aesthetics, and any artists who claim that they're not at least *partly* in it for the money are liars! But songwriting was still a lot of fun, *if* you knew what you were doing . . . and didn't "prostitute" your talent.

Anderson then politely voiced a paradox: Jimmy didn't want to be a Number One artist, yet was riled with his record company for what it didn't do for him.

Did Jimmy use booze—and/or drugs—to write with?

"It depends," he explained. No, he didn't get high before going onstage, other than just taking a couple of drinks "to take the edge off. Sometimes I wonder how the fuck I do it. . . . I don't get stoned before shows. But afterwards, I get real high. Writing, to me, is a very sporadic thing. It can happen in any state of mind." After his shows, he had to "cool down," since with the adrenaline flowing onstage, it's a "buzz when you get up there. That may be the best high there is."

Jimmy said it was easy to tell which entertainers were stoned—some of whom perform "great" when stoned, "but I just lose it all."

In one column next to the published interview was a Florida advertisement for "Beautiful Hand-Made Sterling Silver Spoons" to help "shovel that snow" into one's nostrils. (In the Seventies, there was no business like "snow" business.) In the same issue an attorney spoke out in favor of legalizing cocaine: "It's not a narcotic, it's not psychologically addictive, it doesn't cause crime."

That same season, Jimmy told James Neff of *Country Style* that he hoped to help President Carter with a White House study of youth and drugs, promising "no scare tactics or bullcrap. The stuff they're doing now is not working." (The previous year, entertainer Gregg Allman had campaigned for Carter—then was threatened with a cocaine indictment, so began naming the names in the giant Atlanta coke cartel.)

■　■　■

In November, Jimmy recorded the album *Changes in Latitudes, Changes in Attitudes*, whose title came true in more ways than one. Producer Don Gant was replaced with Norbert Putnam, a Nashville super bassman, who'd produced albums for Joan Baez, Neil Young, the Flying Burrito Brothers, and Dan Fogelberg. Jimmy and Don Light (and road manager Mike Wheeler) wrangled a stronger deal—retrieving Jimmy's music publishing and glomming the second-highest contract with ABC. "I had just brought 'em to their knees, because I was so pissed at them," Jimmy told Frederick Burger. He had told a girl "not to tell anybody" that he wanted to go on Warner Bros.—naturally, the rumor spread and "I'd go out and call ABC Records the most low-rent motherfuckers in the world, just sons of bitches." Jimmy got a lawyer in Los Angeles to renegotiate his contract ("I didn't fool around with anybody in Nashville").

That same month, *Wanted: The Outlaws* (Waylon Jennings, Willie Nelson, Jessi Colter, Tompall Glaser) became the first country album to go platinum (a million sales)—another rebel coup d'état that Nashville was proud to honor, since it couldn't be stopped. Jennings had already wrested his studio control out of RCA's tight hands after they'd carelessly forgotten to re-sign him (but had let him record)—now he had *them* by the vital organs.

Jimmy, by contrast, had exerted studio power from the start. Without a road band, he and Don Gant were able to pick their pickers, out of which grew, in part, the live-act Coral Reefers—whereas the autocratic "Nashville Sound" mandated the use of chosen session pickers . . . like cotton pickers on a plantation, under the control of the almighty Southern boss man on the front porch of the record company's mansion. Usually the singer's road musicians were banned from the studio. "I've used a couple band members in the past, but the studio cats make them feel inferior," Jimmy admitted to James Neff in *Country Style* in early 1977—but he had never really been in bondage to the "Nashville Sound" of musical sharecropping. "When we stop having fun, it's time to quit," was his studio attitude, remembers electric guitarist Reggie Young, who played on his first three ABC albums (and two later albums in the 1980s).

■　■　■

By now Jimmy wanted to use even more of his pickers. "That's what the whole blow-up was about," he told Frederick Burger in 1979, stressing his parting with Don Gant, whom he felt still had some of the Nashville "formula" attitude. So Jimmy went to Criteria Studios in Miami to record *Changes in Latitudes, Changes in Attitudes*, which he dedicated to the Coral Reefers.

Side One opens with the title tune, dramatizing the hectic turmoil of his career, visiting airports while pining for those slower days when he sailed on the ocean—with the famous hook line, "If we weren't all crazy, we would go insane." The moody "Wonder Why We Ever Go Home" exudes the same feeling (with Fingers Taylor's harmonica playing like a violin). One of the best songs Jimmy ever cut is "Banana Republics" by Steve Goodman (written with Steve Burgh and Jim Rothermel), about shifty Americans hiding out in Central America (fleeing from the IRS, hustling señoritas, etc.). The melody is memorable, and the song sounds like a movie theme. "Lovely Cruise" is a love song by Jonathan Baham (he played it for Jimmy when he "was in a horrible mood, moping back to my hotel room in Nashville"). And "Tampico Trauma" echoes the plot of "Banana Republics" with a negligible melody (though George Hager of the New Orleans *Times-Picayune* called it an "instant rock 'n' roll classic, with its brooding harp and guitar riffs and drunken momentum").

Side Two opens with "Margaritaville"—titled "Wastin' Away Again in Margaritaville" on the lyric sheet inside (dated December 1976), but changed to simply "Margaritaville" on the album label itself (just as Billy Ray Cyrus altered the title of "Don't Tell My Heart" to "Achy-Breaky Heart"). It's followed by "In the Shelter," another recut of one of the missing Barnaby songs. The infectious "Miss You So Badly" (written with Fingers Taylor) has the same plot as "Come Monday" but with a fast beat—he's in a Holiday Inn, listening to Patsy Cline on the jukebox, pining for his girl up in Montana. Jesse Winchester's "Biloxi" also helps the album. "Landfall" echoes the album's overall mood—but with a mundane melody and crossover country-rock production.

Jimmy's deepening commitment to Caribbean imagery was at once separating him from mere country-rock *and* from neo-hippie folkpop. By the mid-Seventies, Jimmy was setting, not following, a musical trend.

■ ■ ■

Changes in Latitudes, Changes in Attitudes was released in February, quickly gaining some mixed reviews.

Earlier, William C. Woods of the *Washington Post* had slammed *Havana Daydreamin'* for its mostly "mediocre . . . stale" writing; now he extolled *Changes in Latitudes, Changes in Attitudes* for its effective "language that explores the union of booze and memory," and said, "Nowhere does the mix work better than on 'Margaritaville,' the song that best unifies real and psychic setting as it offers a notion of growth through love and loss." Woods claimed that three songs by other people constituted the album's "shortcomings." Actually, the best thing a poetic singer-songwriter can do, sometimes, is to cut someone else's song. (Nanci Griffith thinks every album of hers should have at least one song by another writer.)

At first, George Hager of the New Orleans *Times-Picayune* felt the album "sounded like a string of low-tempo, maudlin gibberish," then he reversed himself, deciding that this was Jimmy's best so far: "a brilliant series of songs about drunkenness, the craziness of the music business, drunkenness, the craziness of life, drunkenness, and drunkenness." But he carped about Jimmy's "wasting away" in "abject besottedness" while plastering the inside of his album with pictures of his yacht and his ranch.

Noel Coppage of *Stereo Review* claimed that neo-folksinger Tom Rush's version of "Biloxi" was superior to Jimmy's, and though he wouldn't "give Buffett a gold star" for this "Recording of Special Merit" album, "Margaritaville" was *very* good." And Robin Grayden of Britain's *Melody Maker* said there were no weak tracks on the album—and that Jimmy's "folksy, homespun philosophies" resembled the style of singer-writer John D. Loudermilk.

But Ira Mayer of *Rolling Stone* condemned Jimmy's sense of humor for "slowly evaporating" album after album. Mayer admitted the drinking songs probably worked well at live shows—"One can get away with one-liner songs if the picking and mood are right"—but the songs' impact was reduced by Norbert Putnam's "overwrought production. . . . A few loose country licks would have been more in order than the strings and flutes provided." Jerry Jeff Walker was better than Jimmy—he could "play 'em all under the table any night."

∎ ∎ ∎

That February, Jimmy returned to *two* of his hometowns.

On the twenty-third, he played at the Mobile Municipal Auditorium, telling reporter Diane Freeman, "I don't like hard-core rock 'n' roll or disco or country." His career had been painful . . . but "now it's becoming a lot of fun."

And on the twenty-seventh he played at the Grand Ole Opry House at Nashville's Opryland. The Opry had abandoned its downtown Ryman Auditorium in 1974—to the disenchantment of artists like Tom T. Hall—in favor of a modernistic theme park. Mary Jane Brown of the *Nashville Banner* noted the changes in Jimmy's own songwriting attitudes. Why were some of his songs so sensitive—and others simply so *dirty?* Well, the truth was that sometimes he really felt "sensitive," and other times felt "just plain dirty."

On April 2, "Margaritaville" entered the pop charts, rising to Number 8, as well as Number 13 in Country and Number 1 in Easy Listening. The song won the 1977 BMI pop award, the 1978 country award, and ultimately, the "Three Million Air Award" for its *three million* radio spins.

Coincidentally (?) that month, Barnaby Records dragged the six-year-old *High Cumberland Jubilee* out of the shelter (with a 1976 date) and distributed it through Janus Records. A forgotten photograph by Gerry

Wood formed the cover. Thus "In the Shelter" was available on two albums that April.

"It was a pretty good perspective," Jimmy thought as he sat down and played both albums. "Well, I *have* progressed." As he told Robert W. Morgan, "Still, to this day, when we record I don't leave anything in the can, because it can come back to haunt you."

■ ■ ■

Jimmy had been living on the *Euphoria*—with Jane Slagsvol—jumping from island to island in the Antilles. He was something of a legend in the locality he was leaving—as he told Robert W. Morgan, "I was more recognized on boats than I was ever recognized in the country. Everybody who had a boat had a Buffett tape, way before I had any success"—meaning probably before "Margaritaville."

Indeed, one distinguished dope-runner boasted about sailing "north from Colombia into a fucking storm" with Jimmy's "Tampico Trauma" playing over his loudspeakers: "Jesus, it'll play with your pride and nerves." He would hang on to the wheel, praying to survive—then, when the sea calmed and the sun shone, he began yearning about inspiring an "all-time smuggling movie," while lamenting that he couldn't even brag about smuggling to his family.

"He became a hero in the Caribbean," Tom Corcoran told Chet Flippo about Jimmy, "when he saved two shipwrecked sailors." He and Jimmy were sailing from the Leeward Islands of St. Martin to Anguilla when they saw a bar. They needed to drink some Heineken, so they headed for the shore—when suddenly the temperature fell thirty degrees and an unexpected storm hit them. They ran out of fuel . . . then the wind died, which rarely occurs in the Caribbean, leaving them "dead in the water."

Amazingly, they rescued two victims of the storm, the Vanderpool brothers. The wind was still stymied. Finally they took them ashore, and one of them said, "How can we repay you for your help?" Jimmy answered, "In fact, we need some diesel fuel," so the grateful Vanderpools went and brought some fuel in a pickup truck. Together they celebrated with either some beer or a bottle of rum.

■ ■ ■

Jimmy's ambivalence toward Key West became well known, since the town was becoming "eaten up by commercialism . . . sunbathers and *turistas*." *Time* magazine reported Jimmy saying that he was cruising around other parts of the Caribbean, encountering "incredible characters down there, as migratory and as gypsy-souled as I am." He had even petitioned Cuba for permission to sail into Havana. They refused—still, he hoped they might reconsider.

Already he believed Key West "had changed for the *worse—changes* in attitudes and all." On one of his many returns, he spent his first six hours sailing through the Marquesas Keys, stopping to help two men from Jacksonville whose catamaran needed its mast reerected. (That got Jimmy's "tail sunburned.") The next day at the Full Moon Saloon Jimmy and friends threw a "long-distance party," and the following day he told his landlords that he wasn't going to return their keys after all— "Hell, I didn't want to leave Key West; that damned apartment might tell on me after I was gone anyways."

In the spring of 1977, Jimmy and Jane had taken Hunter S. Thompson's son Juan with them on their boat. Eventually they started subletting their apartment to Thompson, who began advertising his "Gonzo" boat tours in the yellow pages: "Experience the dark underbelly of Key West."*

Thompson was a devout drugophile—and once staged a Key West coke-snorting contest with Tom McGuane (to the horror of McGuane's interim wife, Margot Kidder). Their friend, author Jim Harrison, said Thompson enjoyed listening to the police on a police scanner . . . and that once he turned his boat so quickly, it threw him and his girlfriend overboard—"The boat continued up on this person's lawn. . . . About ten days later something similar happened to Buffett. It went up on the same yard. This is a true story."

■   ■   ■

Jimmy claims that the Florida Keys theme of his albums wasn't planned, it just evolved naturally. "I don't think it's beatin' a dead horse," he said to *Rolling Stone*'s Chet Flippo, "though some people might say, 'Here's another song about the fuckin' Caribbean.' I think it still has that mystique; the stories are *good* ones. It's still the only place to escape to." He was especially proud when a Buffalo, New York, couple approached him at Louie's Backyard and said, "We don't want to bother you, but we just want to thank you." His music had lured them down there—the husband was teaching school and his wife was working in a hospital.

No doubt Jimmy had contributed to the tourist homogenization of Key West. "Now there's more people looking at the way we live than living the way we used to live, and that's sad," he told Richard Harrington of the *Washington Post*. "It was a genuine wild town, and now they come looking for the places we used to hang out, which we wouldn't go to anymore." He said he left Key West when admirers began stealing

---

* In 1979 Hunter S. Thompson filed for divorce—and moved officially to Key West. In 1980 he pleaded that he owed Jimmy $5,000, plus $1,200 to one restaurant and $1,600 to a bar (for perhaps 2,133 draft beers, at 75 cents a beer, according to "very unauthorized biographer" Peter O. Whitmer).

his hammock. "Every place I wanted to live eventually gets discovered," he told Patricia Ward Biederman of the *Atlanta Constitution.*

■ ■ ■

Jimmy was yearning for a larger boat. He had worked on so many when he was younger—people were always buying boats in Florida and floating them to the Caribbean—and he had always frequented boat shows. Thanks to "Margaritaville," he could afford to buy a forty-eight-foot Cheoy Lee clipper. He christened her *Euphoria II,* and sailed her down to the islands. "She was his outlet, his safety valve from his mounting success in the high-pressure music world," wrote Roy Attaway in *Motor Boating & Sailing.* Up in New England, he sailed around Nantucket and Martha's Vineyard.

Actually, Jimmy's latest change in latitude was about thirteen degrees—and his change in longitude was about twenty-six—from Key West to Aspen. "Key West is a great place to be poor in. But it's easier to be a celebrity in Aspen."

■ ■ ■

"At that time he was living in Aspen and working a lot, and had 'Margaritaville,' and the album before that [*Havana Daydreamin'*] had done real well," recollects Don Light. "We were about ready to renegotiate the agreement . . . and he had an attorney named Allen Leonard who had helped convince him that you really couldn't have any Nashville ties and be a major act."

True. By the mid-Seventies, various country stars had failed to reach their deserved heights—from Sammi Smith and Tammy Wynette, to Charlie Rich and Conway Twitty—while those few who had—Jennings, Nelson, Kristofferson, Parton—used non-Southern managers. (Jimmy and Dolly Parton flaunted major side-by-side stories in *Time* magazine that April.)

Jimmy opened for the Eagles at Madison Square Garden in New York in March of 1977. *Variety* said that his "seven-piece Southern boogie group . . . had a tough job" playing a long, forty-minute set for a crowd that only wanted the Eagles.

The Eagles' manager, Irving Azoff, told Chet Flippo that he first met Jimmy "when he was drunk" at the Hotel Jerome in Aspen. He'd just done an anti–nuclear weapons benefit with the Eagles in Sacramento.

"Hey, we need somebody to go out on this Eagles tour. Do you want to go?"

"Yeah, I'd like to go."

At some point Don Light's phone rang.

"He'd been out opening some dates for the Eagles, so it worked out with Azoff's office to the point where he acquired the management agreement," Light recalls.

While Azoff had replaced Light as Jimmy's manager, Light still had some publishing power with Jimmy's songs, so he netted an ultimate reward from Buffett's first ten albums. ("Over the years, it worked well for him, and worked well for ourselves.")

As Tom McEntee reflects, from his ABC days: "Somebody works to develop you for so long, and somebody comes along and says, 'Hey, buddy, come on over here with me.' That's what happened with [Don] Gant. All of a sudden Gant was phased out. All of a sudden Don Light was phased out, and this was all West Coast manipulation. They were always in this political-intrigue kind of thing. Nashville *was* such a close community—they truly owned the streets, you know. . . . If an act, country, was suddenly crossing over, it couldn't stay as a country act. The sharks patrol the water until they see something they want. They wouldn't waste a minute on somebody like a Buffett in the beginning— but once he is developed, they will come in and do their number. . . . The act is wanting to make it big, and there are promises . . . 'I can make your star shine brighter on the horizon.' Well, of course he's going to go to them."

Born December 12, 1947, Azoff was already hustling music gigs for bands in his high-school days in Danville, Illinois. Within a few years, he was promoting *eighty-six acts* in a five-state Midwest milieu, thus becoming, faintly, the rock 'n' roll counterpart of legendary Harry "Hap" Peebles (1919–1993) of Wichita, who booked music from 1931 to the 1990s.

"You make the music, and I'll take care of the business," Azoff had told Dan Fogelberg when they were both attending the University of Illinois. The first time he heard Fogelberg, a brawl erupted in the bar. . . . Soon, Azoff dropped out of college.

After a Lake Geneva, Wisconsin, concert for REO Speedwagon, four hundred policemen, National Guardsmen, and Wisconsin state troopers—with gas masks and rifles—invited Azoff to court: "They enjoined me and I moved to California."

So he went to work for David Geffen's Asylum Records on Sunset Boulevard in Los Angeles; Fogelberg used to hear them shouting in the office. Geffen eventually gave Azoff the Eagles, so he set up his own company, Front Line Management*—"the top management firm in the history of rock"—representing Fogelberg, Boz Scaggs, New Edition, Warren Zevon, Jackson Browne, Stevie Nicks, Heart, Don Henley (an Eagle) . . . and Jimmy.

Azoff's enthusiasm for his acts seems never to have waned—he probably believed in them more than they did themselves, at times. Fighting with record companies became his fondest frolic. "Sure, I lie," he told *Rolling Stone*'s Cameron Crowe, "but it's more like . . . tinting. I've

---

* Yet Azoff's name is not included on the 1974 corporation papers for Front Line.

inherited a lot of dummies' deals. When that happens, you've got to make it right. It's all just negotiating theatrics." Other quotes became enduring epigrams: "So I lied. It's rock 'n' roll rules: I win, you lose"— and especially: "Either I win, or I win!"

Azoff might tear up a contract—scream, intimidate, smash office fixtures—*anything* to score a point on behalf of his clients. For recreation, some of them would drop into his office for the joyful sound of him shouting over the phone. (*"I'll hire and fire people, spring fucking housecleaning. Nobody's safe."*) He might make ninety calls a day (six phone lines), as the sluggish record-company bureaucrats had to endure their nemesis. A typical Azoff victim was some "forty-thousand-dollar-a-year promotion man at the record label who leaves at eleven-thirty for lunch and comes back at three—and doesn't work Fridays. . . . I'm not going to let some fuckhead stand in the way of the record being a success." The Eagles' Don Henley called him "Napoleon with a heart," but wondered why his tiny manager never got physically beaten up by his face-to-face foes. Eagle Glenn Frey said he looked like a "Jewish Dennis the Menace."

Azoff told *Rolling Stone*'s Charles M. Young, "Our motto is 'Pay now, pay more later.' Figure out a fair price, add a third, and that's what we get in our contracts." Nicknamed "Big Shorty," "the Poison Dwarf," and "Swerving Irving," he was "easily one of the most-loathed men in the music business," asserts Frederic Dannen in *Hit Men: Power Brokers and Fast Money Inside the Music Business*. He reports Azoff threatening to hurl a television set out of a hotel window to silence some noisy construction men below.

Certainly Azoff would open some new doors for Jimmy . . . having once kicked a new one into existence in a hotel room, next to Eagle Joe Walsh's room ("There was no adjoining door, so I made one"). When his acts would wreck their own rooms, Azoff would cheer them on, charitably paying off the hotel owners later. He even helped Glenn Frey avoid an Eagles drug-search in the Bahamas ("If you bust him here, he can't play in the U.K., Australia, Japan").

Jimmy told Frederick Burger that Azoff succeeded in retrieving the Eagles' song publishing from Warner Brothers. "Irving said, 'This isn't fucking right, you can't do that—it's unconstitutional.' " Azoff grabbed Jimmy's publishing back for him as well, granting him around $200,000 a year by 1979.

Unlike Irving Azoff, all too few managers have been successful booking agents. "They are rare," wrote former agent-manager Scott Faragher in *Music City Babylon: Inside the World of Country Music,* "and their knowledge is the result of thousands of miles on the road with their artists." But probably no other large-scale manager has earned more loyalty from his clients than Irving Azoff. The animosity that has inflamed so many of his rivals reflects, in part, that basic music-business emotion of *jealousy*. Like the late E. E. "Si" Siman, founder of the 1950s' *Ozark Jubilee*, Azoff himself resembles a latent vaudeville comedian.

■ ■ ■

Jimmy appeared on *Austin City Limits* on PBS-TV on June 6. This public-broadcasting show was in its second year—a thriving, desert music cactus planted by Willie Nelson when he arrived in Austin in 1972. In the beer joints, he'd played those jazz chords outlawed in the Nashville studios ("If a song had more than three chords in it, it wasn't commercial"). Thus his Dripping Springs Reunions became post-Woodstock, hippie-Texas cult concerts—paralleling Jimmy's own live-audience alliance. The charm of *Austin City Limits* itself has always been its commitment to live, authentic performing, devoid of clever camera work ("no tricky zooms, no freezes"), thanks initially to cameraman Paul Bosner. Jerry Jeff Walker, Townes Van Zandt, and Charlie Daniels were featured in 1976; in 1977, Jimmy shared the show with Rusty Weir (others that year: Willie Nelson, Delbert McClinton, Guy Clark, Larry Gatlin). Jimmy would be invited back.

To this day, *Austin City Limits* upholds the classic realism absent in most country-music videos.

■ ■ ■

Like any suddenly successful act, Jimmy was increasingly incommunicado. David Standish, who used to let him stay at his house when he performed in Chicago, was put on hold for three days in New York, till he finally got through to him.

Azoff protected journalist Jimmy from the prying press. James Neff of *Country Style* said in 1977 that Azoff hadn't let anyone interview the Eagles in two years—"Such thinking hasn't hurt them." Similarly, Bob Dylan's manager, Albert Grossman, shrouded Dylan with mystery . . . by making him refuse virtually all interview requests. Dylanologist Bob Spitz says Grossman believed journalists were "nothing more than parasites, either bloodsuckers or sycophants who would take your words and use them to their own advantage." (One television scriptwriter says Jimmy once granted "five minutes" to the Nashville Network—then when the time was up, glanced at his watch, and said, "That's it!")

"It's permissible to lie to the press, but not to your clients," Azoff explained to Charles M. Young of *Rolling Stone*. When other acts lied about selling more tickets—and more records—Azoff dutifully inflated his figures as well. "Be honest? There are more important causes in the world. I didn't write the rules. I just live by them."

Of course the press *was* welcome . . . if it was elite enough. After a monthlong concert tour, Jimmy and Azoff lounged about a hotel room in New York City that August, talking to *The New Yorker*. Jimmy bragged about sneaking into the Oval Office at the White House when

President Carter wasn't there ("A friend of mine works there as a photographer . . . I had my Yankee warmup jacket on"), and returning when he *was* there. Jimmy talked with Vice President Walter Mondale for about fifteen minutes . . . then with Admiral Rickover, who reminded him of his grandfather ("Toward my old age, I think I'd like to be ambassador to Martinique"). *The New Yorker* praised Jimmy's "drooping reddish-blond mustache" and said that while he was almost "never not genial," he was upset because his final concert at Central Park had been rained out.

And *The New Yorker* reporter met Miss Jane, who "is, like Jimmy Buffett, blond and slight, and not very tall." Jane handed the reporter an invitation, which stated: "It will begin at five in the afternoon and last until it is over. In addition to the usual eating, drinking, dancing, and carrying on, we intend sometime during the evening to be married."

■　■　■

Another marriage, another log cabin. From Porter Road, Nashville, to Snowmass, Colorado. "Old Snowmass," as it's called, is secluded and remote. *Not* touristy . . . unlike late-Seventies Key West.

"This is my first piece of land," he told MarLyn of *Colorado Homes and Lifestyles*. "The first thing I saw was the covered bridge taking you across the river to the log house." After buying the house and land for a hundred thousand dollars in 1976, Jimmy eventually had the foundation rebuilt—until the building totaled 1,208 square feet. Though they were already living there, their marriage license placed Jimmy at Snowmass, but Jane at Aspen.

"How does a warm-blooded sailor with the sea in his veins end up buying land in the mountains?" wondered MarLyn. Well, one winter Jimmy did a show at Aspen, then he and Janie rented a purple Victorian house and he tried to learn to ski. Three broken legs later, he switched over to restoring his mountain cabin retreat.

Nearby Aspen had been the largest silver-mining camp in the world in 1893 but had dwindled to a population of six hundred by 1930. Skiing took the place of mining, and by the 1950s, musicians and writers—especially playwrights—made it their habitat. Celebrity residents included actress Jill St. John and singer John Denver, and part-time residents such as actor Jack Nicholson, and Eagles Don Henley and Glenn Frey . . . and, of course, Hunter S. Thompson and Jimmy.* Drug busts have also been frequent, since, according to writer Virginia Hopkins, "the jet set—the fur coat, cocaine, and 'the second home' crowd—

---

* Other residents include ex–Barnaby Records singer Claudine Longet, ex-wife of Andy Williams, who accidentally shot and killed her Aspen boyfriend (his brother was once convicted of owning 850 pounds of marijuana). "Aspen is forgiving," said *Aspen Times* editor Bill Dunaway. "We have a live-and-let-live morality."

decided that Aspen was the place in which to be, and gave the town a reputation for drugs, sex, and life in the fast lane."

The cabin had a humorous reputation, according to Paul Vermilyea, who was its caretaker for three years on Jimmy's behalf. Earlier, it had been a happy haven for cocaine snorting, serving simultaneously as a pornographic-video studio. All thanks to acid rock band charisma, from Jimmy's Snowmass predecessors. "They went fucking bonkers, and thought everybody was out to get 'em," reports Vermilyea, describing bullet holes blasted in the wall. "Everything was done in this goddamned hippie ethic, and everything leaked or the doors didn't close. They even had matchbooks made up for the place called 'Heartbreak Hotel.'"

His brother, Tom Vermilyea, was Jimmy's carpenter. "The way I work with my clients is to get to know them over the years. We call each other and talk about design, and work out an integrated scheme of color, function, and movement." Such as an extended kitchen with plenty of counter space for Jimmy, who likes to cook. Or a mahogany staircase leading up to the house's four bedrooms. Mahogany was everywhere, since it resists sun and water, and only needs to be waxed twice a year. Jimmy and Janie planned to entertain a lot of guests, so their dinner table had to seat fourteen people.

Years later, Janie would say, "Marriage didn't change anything at all. We got married because we knew we wanted to have a baby."

Jimmy's parents were invited to see the Snowmass cabin, says Paul Vermilyea: "He shows his parents around the fucking estate—it was such a gorgeous setting, even when the house was a piece of shit."

Irving Azoff even visited. Jimmy was flashing his .357 magnum revolver, with wad-cutting explosive cartridges. "Azoff was fairly gently raised," testifies Vermilyea. "He never had any fucking experience with a pistol."

"Hey, why don't you blow some of the branches off this cottonwood? It's fun," suggested client Buffett.

A .357 magnum has an exciting kickback (Jimmy and his unauthorized biographer enjoyed the same caliber pistol in the Seventies), which caught Azoff unprepared.

"He was holding it so weenie-like and it fucking hit the hammer right into his goddamned forehead. He almost decapitated himself. At least he held on hard enough, it didn't put a *dent* in there."

Manager Azoff counseled Jimmy: "*Don't ever do that to me again!*"

■　■　■

A week before his wedding, Jimmy played a tent-show date at Snowmass. His opening act was drowned out at times by the rowdy, rude audience . . . talking, walking, ordering drinks. They quieted down for Jimmy—then after "Margaritaville" they exploded with violent applause, whistling and shouting. *Aspen Times* reporter Evaleah Graham noted the Caribbean-Colorado corollary: "a strong subjective similarity between the oceans and the mountains . . . there is the same laid-back, freewheelin', free-loving, salty-language existence here."

The wedding was held August 27 in the Rocky Mountain mining town of Redstone, fifty miles west of Aspen. The town was built by John Cleveland Osgood in 1900, for his coal and steel business, and his inn, The Redstone Castle, was the site of Jimmy's wedding. Renamed the Cleveholm Manor today, it has red sandstone walls that were carved by Austrian and Italian stonecutters; the inside walls are decorated with leather, silk, damask, and velvet; Tiffany chandeliers add to the charm, and a Tudor-style clocktower adorns the mansion outside.

Jimmy and Janie arrived in a horse-drawn carriage, and the Reverend Frank E. Hawey of the United Methodist Center performed the ceremony. One of the three hundred guests was Keith Stroup, marijuana lobbyist of NORML. (His mild product, *grass,* was upstaged at the wedding by the more exciting *coke.*)

Paul Vermilyea attended, finding it "funny watching people gravitate up and down the place—it was cavernous, full of big labyrinths of rooms downstairs, all the fucking wenches trying to beat the door down because there were just a few of us who had some blow [cocaine]. It didn't matter how fucking cool you looked—they had all this goddamned music going on, but everyone was running around trying to find someone who was holding out some blow. You've got rock stars that we would pay anything to wait in line and go see—but nobody was paying any attention to them, ha, ha, ha!"

Indeed, the guests included singers J.D. Souther, Glenn Frey, Joe Walsh, Dan Fogelberg, Emmylou Harris, Bonnie Raitt, and gonzologist Hunter S. Thompson. Jimmy, Souther, and Frey joined in with the local band Starwood. Guests enjoyed twenty-four hours of celebration, supported by three meals served, and, most crucial, three thousand dollars' worth of champagne, complemented by an alternative beverage for the connoisseurs. . . .

Margaritas.

.

Where
Is
Jimmy Buffett?

■

I don't want people to think I just go out and drink, smoke, and lay on the beach every day. Sure, I'm for having good times. But when I see people in everyday walks of life doing it at my shows, I hope the rest of the week they are providing for their families and working hard.

—Jimmy to Russ DeVault, *Atlanta Constitution*,
December 3, 1983

I think the career speaks for itself. The longevity and that kind of stuff. He can make his own rules . . . but he always did. If any of those big boys didn't want to play with him, he'd go and do his own thing. Jimmy doesn't have to worry about working for anybody ever again. If he doesn't like a deal, he can say no for the rest of his life. But he's always sort of had that attitude anyway.

—Tom Corcoran, interview, October 5, 1995

From *FM* to *Urban Cowboy*

■

Songwriter Jimmy Buffett, the patron saint of sun-slick boat decks and of the one-two punch-drunkenness of the hammock's sway and lethal tropical drinks, is stretched out high and dry on a couch in the Watergate Hotel.

—Eve Zibart, *Washington Post*, July 13, 1978

It doesn't seem that his new marriage (his second) is going to make him any less of an independent spirit," commented *People* magazine. He and Janie flew on a Concorde airplane to Paris for a brief honeymoon, but then Jimmy returned home for a Midwestern tour, while Janie stayed in Europe with a girlfriend.

"We have an independent relationship because we're apart a lot of the time," she would tell MarLyn of *Colorado Homes and Lifestyles* a few years later, citing Jimmy's springtime Caribbean commitment to fishing. Which he confirmed to Laura Eipper of the *Tennessean:* "She actually travels more than I do," he said, while extolling their ultimate marriage after six years' cohabitation (not to mention albums he had dedicated to Janie): "I couldn't forsee anybody else coming along who could put up with me, or understand me the way she can, or who I could understand as well." He said theirs was an ideal marriage because she wasn't going to say, "All right, I gotcha, so now get off the road and stay home."

As a follow-up showdate, on September 19, Tom McGuane married Laurie Buffett (they eventually had a daughter named Anne). He and Jimmy had been working on a film tentatively titled *The Mango Opera*.

■　■　■

In October, Jimmy was back in Nashville since the Country Music Association (CMA) had nominated "Margaritaville" for Single of the Year. And *Changes in Latitudes, Changes in Attitudes* had gone to Number 12 in pop, as well as Number 3 in country in *Cash Box*.

"As far as the talk about my hating Nashville—I love this town," he told Laura Eipper . . . while admitting his prior hostility "when I was broke and couldn't get a song cut. But I don't know anyone here who hasn't said things like that when they were down." With some Nashville pals, he'd just gone down to 2206 Elliston Place and performed at One-Eyed Jack's.

The CMA Awards were in October—ABC had calculatingly released the single "Changes in Latitudes, Changes in Attitudes" in September, and it went to Number 37 in pop . . . but up to 24 in country. Still, Jimmy didn't win the CMA award. Nor has he ever received one more nomination, despite his categorical country status (thirteen chart singles) and immense album sales.

At the same time, some other organization nominated him as "Best New Album Artist"—which he thought was funny, since *Changes in Latitudes, Changes in Attitudes* was his *seventh* (including his Barnaby albums).

"Margaritaville" went gold (a million sales), and the album went platinum (a million sales). James Neff of *Country Style* said Jimmy had struck "a commercial formula" with producer Norbert Putnam, and while losing "a few purist fans and the fawning of the rock press [*Rolling Stone*'s review] . . . he gained a million new fans instead."

Jimmy told the Associated Press's Mary Campbell how grateful he was that ABC had advertised this album, forcing the salesmen and promotion men to push it. "I was a victim of no advertising in the past. I'm more than happy to share the success of this album."

■　■　■

Like many of his other songs, "Margaritaville" and "Changes in Latitudes, Changes in Attitudes" sparked their own enduring reactions . . . and bizarre anecdotes.

Sam Malvaney, a student at Louisiana State University in Baton Rouge, remembers going to a local nightclub, the Cahoots, to hear Jimmy. The parking lot was littered with bottlecaps. He stepped on one—and it cut through his turquoise-colored flip-flop shoe, puncturing his heel. Malvaney could hear Jimmy singing "Margaritaville" at the same time, where he "blew out my flip-flop, stepped on a pop-top, / cut my heel, had to cruise on back home." Sam missed the concert. Unlike Jimmy, who doctored *his* injury with doses of frozen margaritas in the song, Malvaney went to a hospital for some stitches ("I wanted to go on in, and I was bleeding so bad I couldn't").

By 1994 Malvaney had moved back to Biloxi from Honolulu, creating advertising jingles to lure people into the gambling casinos without actually mentioning gambling, to foil the Federal Communications Commission (FCC).

As for "Changes in Latitudes, Changes in Attitudes," it resurfaced on *Jane Fonda's Workout Record* (1982), with Fonda herself overdubbing a recitation that became a unique duet. (Though it probably *wasn't* envied by duetters Loretta Lynn and Conway Twitty—or George Jones and Tammy Wynette.) Fonda used Jimmy's song for buttocks exercises— her opening lyric, "Are you ready for buttocks tucks?" is followed by repeated "Squeeze it" vocalizations. The Fonda-Buffett-buttocks duet has two versions—one for beginners and one for "advanced" exercisers. The album went to Number 15.

The same song invokes melancholy memory in the heart of Donna Nelson, of Pascagoula. She once worked at Capitol Records in Los Angeles, along with Margie Buffett, starting in the fall of 1973. Nelson's later husband, Julian Macrae "Mac" Rucker, grew up around Pascagoula and knew Jimmy's cousin Baxter Lumpkin. "My husband loved Jimmy Buffett, and had all of Jimmy's books, and was definitely a Parrot Head. As a matter of fact, I got *sick* of it!" she laughs. "He loved Jimmy as a poet, as a storyteller."

When they married, her husband told her that if he died, she was to have him cremated, and his ashes scattered at sea . . . while playing "Changes in Latitudes, Changes in Attitudes" as his eulogy. He was an entrepreneur, hoping to retire in the Florida Keys—he even began writing a story about the Caribbean. But his financial losses made him terminally depressed, so he sent his wife a suicide note.

On November 3, 1994, he sat in his car in the garage and turned on the engine. Donna Nelson kept her marital vow—chartering a boat, then "after we said the prayer, and spread the ashes, we played 'Changes in Latitudes, Changes in Attitudes' and told Mac *good-bye*. I dropped these four red roses off the boat, one at a time, and these roses circled around our boat. I said, 'Thank you, God, for making this perfect for Mac.' Mac was free at last."

■ ■ ■

That December, Tom Corcoran's "Wastin' Away in Marijuanaville" article in *Crawdaddy* told how the Drug Enforcement Agency had grabbed eighteen tons of pot from Cuban smugglers the previous December. Dope-runners from the Bahamas loved Jimmy's "A Pirate Looks at Forty," each one thinking he wrote the song just for him. Corcoran then explained how, in the zealous smuggling profession, the boats are overseen by airplanes, who forewarn them of any Coast Guard pursuers.

"Smuggling saves wear and tear on the hands. . . . Practice makes perfect. The people who import marijuana are not dummies; efficiency and intelligence pull the odds of failure off the lifelines." But the latest arrested Cubans didn't even have Buffett tapes on their boats—to the sheriff's deputies' surprise—since the "Buffett pirates" were off on some other ocean, looking at age forty "and pissing it all away."

The genial marijuana mythology ignored Colombian statistics, however: three deaths a week in smuggling-related fights, and sometimes dope-clique combats slaying large numbers. At least marijuana was a beneficent United States enterprise—over fourteen billion tax-free dollars bolstering the economy, plus generous employment opportunities for the Drug Enforcement Agency.

■ ■ ■

In the summer of '77, before his wedding, Jimmy had been away on his boat, songwriting—then in Miami, that November, he recorded his next album, *Son of a Son of a Sailor*. He told Jerry Parker of the *Chicago Sun Times* that "I'm singin' a lot better, since I quit doin' a lot of coke. I used to do a whole lot of blowin', but I don't do it anymore. That stuff tears up your throat, and it definitely shows on the new album. It's gonna be big." (Frank Rose of *Rolling Stone* called his album voice "richly languid," and *Playboy* admitted that it had "improved.")

The title song, "Son of a Son of a Sailor," has another grabby, singable melody, and the lyric fulfills one of Nashville songwriter Harlan Howard's admonitions—put in at least one word not in any other song. Jimmy contrasts the thrill of aquatic "adventure" with "a man just released from indenture." He boasts about reading "books about heroes and crooks," and makes his latest smuggling boast: The "son of a gun" has loaded "the last ton / One step ahead of the jailer." As with "Margaritaville" and other lyrics, he changes words in the chorus each time, giving the listener more than songwriters usually bargain for. The song has "familial sadness," according to Walter Dawson of the Memphis *Commercial Appeal*.

The lyrics of "Fool Button" are comical—with Jimmy's ever-constant land vehicle, the rent-a-car—though the melody is negligible; in "The Last Line," written by Keith Sykes, the singer says that he's "given my life for songs that I sing." (Sykes wrote it as his grandfather's clock was ticking back and forth . . . and it won some Memphis airplay right after Elvis died.) Jimmy's live-act favorite, "Livingston's Saturday Night," follows.

The next song, "Cheeseburger in Paradise," became another concert classic, with its ludicrous defense of "carnivorous habits" in defiance of weight-loss vegetarianism. (The way to lose poundage, apparently, is via Jane Fonda calisthenics!) "Did you ever make it to Vegetarian Heaven, or not?" asked radio interviewer Jim Ladd in 1978.

"I did it to lose weight once, and it was never the 'cosmic experience' it seems to be to some people. . . . I went right back to Danish ham and cheeseburgers, right after it was all over."

When he had just bought *Euphoria II,* Jimmy and his captain, Larry Gray, were about to leave Fort Lauderdale, when they sent Tom Corcoran down to pick up a McDonald's bag of burgers. The next morning, Corcoran took a picture of Jimmy and Larry Gray drinking beer and eating their last two Big Macs. Hence the song, written months later, which repudiates the diet of sunflower seeds and carrot juice, prescribing therapeutic cheeseburgers instead.

The song was supposedly written at the Select bar on the island of St. Barthélemy (in the Leeward Islands of the Lesser Antilles), according to Phil Kaufman, a legendary road manager. In his brilliantly bawdy memoir, *Road Mangler Deluxe* (1993), Kaufman says the bar was "a hideout for all the rock 'n' rollers in those days"—and that actress Elizabeth Ashley (McGuane's lover) was "one of the original ladies" in the song. (Ashley's photo in his book is inscribed, "To Phil—Fuck you— Liz"; and she helped hustle book reviews for Kaufman.)

"That is the *stupidest* song I have ever heard," said wife Janie to Jimmy when he played it for her with his guitar.

"You've got to wait till you hear the band."

"Who's going to listen to *that?*"

As Jimmy told Jim Ladd in 1978, "If she doesn't like it, it's a hit."

Besides Steve Goodman's "Chicken Cordon Bleus" (1973) anticipating "Cheeseburger in Paradise," another predecessor was Chris Gantry's "Rock and Roll Health Food Nut" (1975), with lyrics like "Let's make love, but first let's eat some vegetables with rice."

The first song of Side Two, "The Coast of Marseilles," was written by Keith Sykes on Thanksgiving Day, when he was hung over, waiting for his wife to get dinner ready. Jimmy calls it one of his favorite all-time songs—its soft-ballad melody is enhanced by some beautiful Fingers Taylor harping. "Cowboy in the Jungle" has the same infectious quality tune, a parody of the "outlaw" movement—an out-of-place cowboy with "shrimpskin boots" down in South America. "Mañana" is an amusing song about a girl who hates the "goddamn cold" weather up North, and is looking for a captain down around St. Thomas; again, the chorus subtly varies each time, hoping at the end that Anita Bryant records *none* of Jimmy's songs! The last song is Jimmy's slow, touching "African Friend."

Issued in March 1978, *Son of a Son of a Sailor* reaped rich reviews from critics who were increasingly glad that Jimmy couldn't be pigeon-holed. "You can't really categorize Buffett, except, perhaps, to file his albums under *B*—for Buffett and brilliant," wrote Robin Grayden for England's *Melody Maker,* amused that he was scarcely "country" but still charted country. John Rockwell of *The New York Times* termed him "soft rock."

Thus each year the list grew longer of what Jimmy was *not* (i.e., traditional country, progressive country, outlaw country, crossover country, hard rock, etc.). "I don't play loud, and I try to write good lyrics," he told Rockwell that March, up in New York for a concert. *Rolling Stone*'s Frank Rose praised Harvey Thompson's saxophone on "The Last Line," and Jimmy's general Key West milieu in the "raw South Florida bars, where barefoot pot smugglers and Perma-prest businessmen dine at rough-hewn tables coated with an inch of plastic, while multicolored fish parade from one end of the table to the other."

The album went to Number 10—and to Number 6, in country, in *Cash Box.* It was Jimmy's second million-selling album.

■ ■ ■

"I don't have to yell a lot anymore. I haven't destroyed a hotel room in years," Irving Azoff told *Rolling Stone*'s Cameron Crowe on March 26, in his own backyard wedding reception for his marriage to Shelli Cumsky. "I've met the right person and I'm settling down," he said, asking Crowe *not* to tell readers about his shouting over the phone to the record companies. To give him something nicer to write about, Azoff gently shoved a piece of wedding cake into his mother-in-law's face.

But when *Rolling Stone* printed unfavorable words in its Random Notes column, Azoff corrected them over the phone ("You fucked me, asshole! Now make it right!"), despite their two important Buffett stories (by Judith Sims and Chet Flippo), followed by a Flippo cover story of Jimmy in '79 and seven Random Notes mentions in 1978 alone. *Rolling Stone* had also launched *Outside* magazine, with a hunting article by Tom McGuane—and Jimmy's "Antigua Blowout," which earned him another cover picture.

■ ■ ■

Sometime after his recording session, Jimmy went on a three-month *Euphoria II* cruise (the boat contained two five-hundred-pound air conditioners, a room for forty-eight cases of beer, a hardback-book library, a freezer filled with tenderloins, and "a salon which converts into a dance floor").

In February he performed a Miami benefit for old friend (and Key West landlord) John "Jack" Spottswood, Jr., who was campaigning for the U.S. Senate.

When his album came out, Jimmy began touring. That April in Laramie, Wyoming, with palm trees and a backdrop picture of a boat onstage behind him, he said that the last time he was in Wyoming, he had come as a hitchhiker! That same month in Milwaukee, when the audience began shouting requests, he retorted, "Shit, I can't play 'em all at once. What do you think this is, an eight-track machine?" At one point, Jimmy banished his band and played acoustic solo—after introducing his imaginary Coral Reefers (Marvin Gardens, Kitty Litter) from the bad ol' days.

Washington's Birthday, February 22, 1978, was National Condom Day in San Francisco. Jimmy sat on a panel of judges—with Grace Slick, Alice Cooper, and Frank Zappa—while entertainer Barry Melton and his band performed "sex and drug songs while kids danced and smoked dope and winos read anti-VD pamphlets." The stage was decorated with eight-foot-tall red letters spelling "VD" . . . and three hundred condoms inflated with helium. Jimmy and the judges awarded a gold condom to the best entry—a catchy couplet: "From using a condom you will learn / No deposit means no return."

■ ■ ■

Jimmy's own ever-expanding band—including session pickers from *Son of a Son of a Sailor*—now including drummer Kenny Buttrey, who had performed on Nashville albums by Bob Dylan, Joan Baez, and Neil Young. And electric lead guitarist was Tim Krekel.

One night Krekel was playing in Nashville at the Old Time Pickin' Parlor, when Don Light heard him. Chet Atkins wondered if he came from Louisiana, because of how he played; no, he was from Kentucky— and Light wanted him to play for Jimmy. "I'd heard Buffett a little, but never really listened a lot," Krekel told Allen Howie of *Louisville Music News*, "so I got some of his records and realized he was a really fine writer." Then he met Jimmy and Fingers Taylor at a date in his hometown, Louisville, Kentucky. Three weeks later Krekel was flying to Florida, for the Sunsplash Festival in Lakewood. "There's this skinny 'Fingers' character, sitting there about half out of it, listening to this blues stuff." So Fingers challenged Krekel to identify the musician on the record player; he said that it was Freddy King, which impressed Fingers, who was "a real blues nut." Just before midnight, Jimmy dropped by, and soon he was summoning Krekel to Sarasota, Florida, to join the Coral Reefers. They flew around the country by jet plane, Krekel seeing Los Angeles and the West Coast for the first time—and enjoying playing softball with the Eagles.

By the time they got to the studio to cut *Son of a Son of a Sailor*,

Krekel and the band had already mastered the songs, from their months on the road. In 1994 he summed up his year with Jimmy: "In retrospect, it was the nicest gig I ever had in my life. He really took care of everybody. He's real in all his dealings. There ain't anything phony in him at all. I got to play with some of the greatest musicians in the world!"

In the film *FM* (released in April 1978) Krekel played backup as Jimmy once again sang "Livingston Saturday Night," at one point yelling, "Allright, Timmy!" as Krekel whipped into a solo break. (Instrumental breaks are reminiscent of the days of big bands—and of Ernest Tubb, who likewise usually announced his sideman by name.) Jimmy's film performance was for a Save the Whales benefit concert—already, in real life, he'd been booked for a whale-saving concert in Japan in 1977.

∎ ∎ ∎

The eccentric, counterculture movie *FM* starred Martin Mull as a hilarious rock disc jockey—and gave singer Linda Ronstadt a superb live performance (in spite of her pretty voice, she rocked well). Producer Irving Azoff had harried the MCA film company to release it on time, threatening to buy it for $5 million and resell it for $10 million, as well as kicking butts on the telephone to get the soundtrack album issued. "Excuse me, but every time I think of *FM*," he complained to journalist Cameron Crowe, "I gotta piss." Two weeks before the movie was issued, he demanded (unsuccessfully) that his name be yanked from the credits, since he had told MCA "it's not authentic." Azoff felt it was an AM movie.

The album cover's leading photo was of Jimmy—despite all the other name acts: the Eagles, Boz Scaggs, Joe Walsh, James Taylor, Bob Seger, Steely Dan, Tom Petty, Billy Joel, Dan Fogelberg, et al. The movie didn't succeed, but the album went to Number 5. Still, Azoff hammered on MCA Records to ship, ultimately, more than a million copies, almost half of which cruised on back home as "returns," to the ire of MCA's Sam Passamano, Jr. In vain, he'd tried to warn Azoff about the deceptive market ("He was nonstop pressure, calling me every day, hollering"). For years, the dead albums were wastin' away again in MCA's vinyl-mausoleum warehouse.

By now, Front Line Management included Howard Kaufman and Nina Avramides (who are today's Buffett bosses at HK Management). Publicist Larry Solters once reportedly set fire to a Hollywood magazine with some unwelcome writings, then loyally jumped up and down, stomping on it, to soothe Azoff. In *Hits* music magazine, Azoff once courteously posed and smiled for the photographer—while giving the finger to the readers.

∎ ∎ ∎

In May 1978 (just as *FM* was appearing), Jimmy was scheduled to play a "five-thousand-dollar grudge match" softball game at the University of Southern California—for the Eagles, against *Rolling Stone*'s "Gonzo" softball team (including Hunter S. Thompson, Chet Flippo, and Cameron Crowe). Already the Eagles had lost a game against Jimmy's Coral Reefers, 10–9, down in Coconut Grove, Florida. But Eagle Glenn Frey said the journalists ought to spend more time playing ball and "less at the typewriters, so they won't be humiliated"—for the losing team would have to donate five-thousand-dollars to the 1978 UNICEF World Nutrition Program. Alas, Jimmy missed the game, having slid into second base while playing for Doherty's Restaurant at Palm Beach, when "my cleats locked on it and I broke the shit outta my leg." (Emmylou Harris and road manager Phil Kaufman drove by his house and sang "Take Me Out to the Ball Game" to laid-up Jimmy.) With a hip-to-toe cast on his right leg, he appeared on NBC's *Saturday Night Live*.

When the Eagles swaggered onto the ball diamond—without Jimmy—the *Rolling Stone* players shuddered at their sharpened spikes. "Somebody might get hurt," complained editor Jann S. Wenner. "How exciting," laughed Azoff. "Do your writers ever think about that?" The Eagles switched to tennis shoes—yet still won the game—and Azoff wore a sports jersey that asked: "Is Jann Wenner Tragically Hip?" (When *Rolling Stone* ranked Azoff in "The Heavy Hundred," he was quoted: "I'm on this list because I found Jann Wenner his limo driver.")

As for Jimmy, he and the Coral Reefers played against the White House ball team that July. They had no pitcher, so Jimmy attached a shin-guard to his cast and staggered out to the mound. "Under the bill of his cap, his water-blue eyes were steely," observed the *Washington Post*'s Eve Zibart. "Around his neck hung the solid-gold anchor he wears instead of a wedding ring. He talked up the infield, he batted with a pinch runner. The White House stomped them, 26–11." The next day, he told Zibart that "it'll be funny tomorrow. It's not funny yet."

Zibart also learned that he wanted to write a novel . . . and maybe an *autobiography*—"nothing vindictive, just humorous." Jimmy was staying at Washington's exciting Watergate Hotel, two of whose other celebrities—novelist E. Howard Hunt, and future radio star G. Gordon Liddy—had discussed killing one of Zibart's *Washington Post* colleagues, Jack Anderson, with some LSD.

■　■　■

Meanwhile, on AM (not FM!) radio, Jimmy was charting moderately in 1978: "Cheeseburger in Paradise," Number 32; "Livingston Saturday Night," Number 52 (91 in country, his last for six years); and "Mañana," Number 84.

Then in August at the Fabulous Fox in Atlanta (and at the Maurice Gusman Cultural Center in Miami) he recorded a double live album, *You Had to Be There—Jimmy Buffett in Concert* (parallel to Joni Mitchell's 1974 live two-disc *Miles of Aisles*). Introducing "Morris' Nightmare," cowritten with Tim Krekel, he said to the smoking audience, "Hey, that's good shit, I smell it, all right. We'd better start this song before I get hungry." The song is a jovial dancing 'n' rum song that attacks disco (the audience cheers!), making fun of middle-aged tourists. (Krekel also wrote Crystal Gayle's 1984 Number One country song, "Turning Away.")

The album appeared that Christmas—with a picture of Jimmy wearing his cast (his broken leg had allowed him time to write his *Outside* magazine article). He told Mark Childress of the *Birmingham News* that he detested the current fad among pop stars, of sneering at their audiences: "I *started* playin' in bars, and I always was more of an entertainer than a singer or a musician to begin with. So to me, it was the point of audience contact—working *off* of an audience, instead of *to* one."

■ ■ ■

Eve Zibart said Tom McGuane was Jimmy's "common denominator in a Faulkner-esque confusion of relationships," since McGuane's first wife, Becky, had married Peter Fonda. That December, McGuane went down to Cuba with wife Laurie Buffett. They were sailing in the nostalgic path of Jimmy's father, who'd visited Cuba when he was but a year-old kid with his captain dad in 1920, then returned himself in 1966 on the USS *Arlington* "on a shakedown cruise" from Mobile to Guantánamo Bay, where all he'd been able to see was barbed wire across the old naval base. Now, in 1978, McGuane was in a race that Jimmy's mother called "the first sanctioned by the two countries during Castro's rule." McGuane sent her a letter on December 10 telling her that he was "transporting your daughter to a Communist nation"—and that if the journalists grabbed the story, they should be reminded of the family's Cuban tourist heritage.

Certainly the times had changed. . . . Back in 1975, Senator George McGovern had visited Castro—and picked up a souvenir memorandum of twenty-four alleged assassination attempts on Castro. Only nine were acknowledged by the tax-supported Mafia murder librarians (exploding cigars, drugs, etc.). The mob's recruiter, Bay of Pigs general Charles Cabell (former Air Force UFO scholar), was the brother of Earle Cabell, mayor of Dallas on its most famous day—and a future Howard Hughes staffer.

■ ■ ■

That same winter, brother-in-law Tom McGuane's ex-lover, actress Elizabeth Ashley, was out on the road promoting her autobiography with Phil Kaufman, known as the "executive nanny" in the trade. Kaufman recalled them having dinner with Jimmy and Janie at Raoul's restaurant in Soho in New York City. Rolling Stone Mick Jagger was waiting to get in, so on the way out, Kaufman made sure Jagger got his table. They were heading next to a nightclub with the Buffetts, making a hundred-dollar bet as to who would get there first. Kaufman and Ashley, versus Jimmy and Janie, *drag-raced through New York City in their limousines,* all part of Kaufman's literary finesse as a book 'n' author "Road Mangler Deluxe."

■ ■ ■

In April of 1979 in Los Angeles, desperate, angry ABC Records employees began smashing records against the walls of the office. Some three hundred of them had just lost their jobs.

Jimmy's label ABC had been purchased by MCA, even as some record distributors sued MCA and ABC for $1.3 million in damages, for sticking them with unsold records. Back in 1973, John Phillips, singer-songwriter (from the Mamas and the Papas), sued ABC-Dunhill for $9 million—even as Senator James Buckley of New York was investigating "widespread charges" of drugs, payola, and organized crime in the record industry, which he said was "willfully taking advantage of young artists" such as Phillips. At least rockologists Steve Chapple and Reebee Garofalo, in *Rock 'n' Roll is Here to Pay,* said that Jim Croce, who died in 1973, "with ABC's help turns out gold album after gold album from the grave." But in 1975 ABC had lost $28 million, to which the press had "overreacted" with "negative publicity," according to company executives, who claimed their losses had accrued over several years ("We're still weak, but we're in the black"). Plummeting sales incited a $12 million lawsuit by its recent chairman, Jerry Rubinstein, in 1977; he received a settlement. By 1978 ABC had lost so many tens of millions of dollars, it offered itself up for sale, but since its lone bidder was MCA, the asking price had to sink.

In Nashville, songwriter-producer Alex Zanetis had sued ABC in 1973 for having brought them country acts Lefty Frizzell and Ferlin Husky, only to lose his job to Don Gant. Zanetis, too, received a settlement. In 1974 ABC-Dunhill bought Dot Records, which was started in Goodlettsville (north of Nashville) in 1951 by Randy Wood with a thousand dollars. He launched Pat Boone, Jim Lowe, Jimmy Gilmer—then Dot's Seventies boss Jim Foglesong took over ABC in Nashville, with acts like Donna Fargo, Don Williams, Tommy Overstreet, and Roy Clark. Fogelsong was himself "country and northern"—from West Virginia, with a New York college degree in music. He became Nashville's hillbilly sophisticate, a respected gentleman in spite of his ability to read sheet music *and* practice yoga in the office.

"Buffett was totally assumed by the West Coast as a pop artist," says Foglesong—even before he went to MCA, he knew about Jimmy. Buzz Cason had brought him a Buffett tape, and then he played softball with Jimmy—on an music-industry softball team—in a West End park in Nashville.

Besides taking over ABC, MCA also possessed Decca Records, whose misty genealogy hearkened back to a London music-instrument store founded in 1832. The Decca Gramophone Company issued its first record in 1929; its American branch ultimately launched Bing Crosby and country acts Ernest Tubb, Red Foley, Kitty Wells, Brenda Lee, and Loretta Lynn.

Yet MCA, one of the "big six" record companies ("Music Cemetery of America" to its critics), had nose-dived from a $14 million profit in 1978 to a $10 million loss in 1979. The entire industry was suffering from rocketing costs for tape and record manufacture, which drove up retail album prices to $8.98, and still didn't offset the overhead. In 1981, for example, Tom Petty condemned MCA for raising one of his albums to $9.98. He said he didn't need the "extra dollar"—that MCA was "just motivated by greed."

Riding to the rescue of record buyers was that historic civilized art of *counterfeiting*—twenty to forty percent of record returns were now discovered to be fake. At least the U.S. Congress minded *its* own business, keeping its damned nose out of the payola process that helped the hits to happen.

In these desperate, inflated times, Irving Azoff continued to rub sticks together. His genius was his seemingly tireless commitment to jamming this act up against that act, to raise each of their prices. Despite all the drug jokes, one gets the impression that the Eagles and his other entertainers were forced to stay up late and write songs, and/or movie scripts, if they had any free time left. Azoff was the ludicrous antithesis of the good ol' Nashville managers and bookers, who hoped to get their act some country-fair date next summer . . . and take ten percent.

"I've got more money than God," Azoff liked to say. He claimed that the record business had been supplanted by the "music delivery business" (i.e., music videos, cassettes, compact discs, T-shirts). He labeled the black vinyl disc as being "a dinosaur, it's history."

Films were more important, since they created by-product albums as a matter of course. "Colonel" Tom Parker had made a lot of money from calculatedly mediocre Elvis films and soundtrack albums. So what could you do if the films were maybe, uhh, *good?*

He had planned a "high-adventure dope story" film, hopefully starring Jimmy, who would write the songs.

Azoff also wanted to make a TV film titled *A Pirate Looks at Forty*, starring Jimmy and Oakland Raiders quarterback Ken Stabler. Another TV film he proposed was *American Archipelago*, about the true life of David Alderman, falsely arrested and bullied in a drug arrest. Other film ideas included "*Dope Story*," and "*Chess Match*," a "paranoid comedy" about hypnosis, drugs, championship chess-playing, and politics.

In sum, as Dale Pollock assessed in *Variety*, "Thanks to his client

Jimmy's father, James Delaney
Buffett, Jr., worked at Alabama
Dry Dock & Shipbuilding Co. in
Mobile for many years, starting
in 1948. This 1939 photograph
captures the working men's joy
at leaving work at the end
of the shipbuilding day.
*(COURTESY OF UNIVERSITY
OF SOUTHERN ALABAMA)*

In 1940, Ingalls Shipbuilding in Pascagoula, Mississippi, designed the *S.S. Exchequer*, the world's first all-welded ship. Jimmy's father worked at Ingalls, and in 1941 began dating Ingalls's secretary, Mary Loraine Peets, whom he married in 1942. *(COURTESY OF JAMES W. MCINGVALE, DIRECTOR OF COMMUNICATIONS, INGALLS SHIPBUILDING)*

Spring Hill Chapel in Mobile, Alabama, where Jimmy served as an altar boy—and where he married Margaret Washichek on July 19, 1969. *(STEVE ENG)*

The graves of Jimmy's grandparents—James Delaney Buffett (1887–1970, center stone), icon of Jimmy's immortal "The Captain and the Kid" song, and Hilda S. Buffett (1897–1989, right stone)—and their son William Norman Buffett (1924–1991, left stone), Jimmy's uncle Billy, of his song (and short story) "The Pascagoula Run." Machpelah Cemetery, 3000 Machpelah Street, Pascagoula, Mississippi.
(STEVE ENG)

Jimmy and sister Loraine Marie (born 1948) at home in Mobile, Alabama, in November 1949.
(COURTESY OF ADDSCO COLLECTION, UNIVERSITY OF SOUTHERN ALABAMA ARCHIVES)

LEFT: Jimmy's mother, Loraine "Peets" Buffett, at work at Alabama Dry Dock & Shipbuilding Co., circa 1949. *(COURTESY OF ADDSCO COLLECTION, UNIVERSITY OF SOUTHERN ALABAMA ARCHIVES)*

RIGHT: "Aunt Reed" Bass Tyrone, housemother at the Epsilon Nu chapter of Kappa Sigma, University of Southern Mississippi, Hattiesburg, Mississippi, 1959–84. According to her notes, she posed for this fraternity house picture with Jimmy in the late 1960s. Jimmy always has something kind to say about Aunt Reid (in spite of her alcoholic-prohibition policy for the fraternity house). *(COURTESY OF THELMA BASS)*

LEFT: Jimmy's initiation request for the Epsilon Nu chapter of Kappa Sigma, University of Southern Mississippi, Hattiesburg, Mississippi. *(COURTESY OF EPSILON NU CHAPTER OF KAPPA SIGMA)*

Jimmy at the Epsilon Nu chapter of Kappa Sigma, University of Southern Mississippi, Hattiesburg, Mississippi: 1968 (left) and 1969 (right).
(COURTESY OF EPSILON NU CHAPTER OF KAPPA SIGMA)

The Upstairs Alliance band, featuring (left to right) Richard "Rick" Bennett, Bill Kehoe, Bettye Williams, and Jimmy Buffett. From the 1968 *Southerner* annual of the University of Southern Mississippi, Hattiesburg, Mississippi. *(COURTESY OF RONALD D. PHILLIPS, EXECUTIVE DIRECTOR OF U.S.M. ALUMNI ASSOCIATION)*

Site of Product Sound Studio, 1961 Airport Boulevard, Mobile, Alabama. Upstairs on the left was where Milton L. Brown, Travis Turk, John Ed Thompson, and Nick Panioutou ran the studio, which recorded Jimmy's first single in 1969, "Abandoned on Tuesday"/ "Don't Bring Me Candy."
(MEAUREEN MACLAY)

Jimmy's New Orleans apartment in the late 1960s, 616 Ursuline Street (Apt. 305).
(STEVE ENG)

Prolific Mobile songwriter Milton L. Brown, in 1980. Brown cofounded Audio Mobile Records, which issued Jimmy's "Abandoned on Tuesday" single (1969), and he cowrote Jimmy's first Barnaby single, "The Christian?" (1970). He also wrote "Every Which Way but Loose," title song of the 1978 Clint Eastwood film —and Number 1 in country, Number 30 in pop.
(RON WHEELER, COURTESY OF MOBILE PRESS-REGISTER)

Jimmy's business card from his 1969–70 days with *Amusement Business* and *Billboard*.
(COURTESY OF BILL KEHOE)

Jimmy's first published sheet music, for his 1970 Barnaby release, "The Christian?" —which has not been rereleased by MCA or Margaritaville Records.
(COURTESY OF HANSEN HOUSE MUSIC PUBLISHERS)

Jimmy partying in Key West, with novelist Thomas McGuane,
circa 1971–72. *(CHRIS ROBINSON)*

Captain Tony's Saloon, 428 Greene Street, Key West, Florida.
Formerly Sloppy Joe's, it was an Ernest Hemingway hangout (1933–37) and one
of Jimmy's most beloved singing sites in the 1970s. *(STEVE ENG)*

Jimmy's apartment in the 1970s, 704 Waddell Street, Key West, Florida.
(*STEVE ENG*)

Two publicity photographs taken around 1974 that illustrate the various sides of Jimmy.
(*COURTESY OF MCA/BUZZ CASON COLLECTION*)

PROCLAMATION

WHEREAS, Jimmy Buffett has regaled music lovers with his unique style of story telling of his travels and experiences for twenty-five years; and

WHEREAS, Margaritaville has become more than part of his music with the opening of the store in 1985; and

WHEREAS, the move to Duval Street and opening of a cafe in 1987 in conjunction with the store brought Jimmy Buffett fans a means to enjoy his music, taste the food of the Caribbean and take home souvenirs; and

WHEREAS, Margaritaville and Jimmy Buffett have provided support and benefits to many local charities, including the MARC House; and

WHEREAS, the cafe has enjoyed celebrity appearances since its opening with national and local talent; and

WHEREAS, Jimmy Buffett fans who call themselves Parrot Heads will convene in Key West in February to celebrate the Parrot Head lifestyle.

NOW, THEREFORE, I, Dennis J. Wardlow, Mayor of Key West, do hereby proclaim the week of February 15th through February 20th, 1993 as

PARROT HEAD WEEK

in the Florida Keys and Key West and urge all Parrot Heads to sit back, enjoy and appreciate the madness.

WITNESS my hand and seal of the City of Key West, Florida this 19th day of February, 1993.

Dennis J. Wardlow, Mayor

(COURTESY OF MARTY MCATEER)

Handbill (circa 1974) from
the Exit/In at 1108
Elliston Place, Nashville.
(COURTESY OF MIKE RICHARDS,
MUSIC & MORE,
HENDERSONVILLE, TENNESSEE)

EXIT/IN
Nashville's Music Forum

Elliston Place · for reservations call 327-2784

March 12 — March 16

ABC/Dunhill
Recording Artist

JIMMY BUFFETT

Admission
Tues. $2.00
Wed. & Thurs. $3
Fri. & Sat. $3.50

Showtime 8:30 p.m. and 11:00 p.m.
Mellow Time 3:00 — 6:00 p.m.
Live Broadcast · WKDA-FM (103.3)
Midnight Wednesday · Sponsored by **Grand Central**

Jimmy at Nashville's Fan Fair, June 9, 1993, at
the Tennessee State Fairgrounds.
(TIM NAPRESTEK)

Ticket for Jimmy's 1977 concert at his alma mater, the University of Southern Mississippi, Hattiesburg, Mississippi.
(COURTESY OF EPSILON NU CHAPTER OF KAPPA SIGMA)

Jimmy Buffett at Blockbuster Pavilion, Devere, California, October 1994.
(SCOTT RUBY)

Jimmy Buffett at Blockbuster Pavilion, October 1994.
(SCOTT RUBY)

Jimmy with a broken leg being interviewed in Palm Beach, Florida, in May of 1978 by Frederick Burger of *The Miami Herald.* Burger has published stories on Jimmy and Fingers Taylor, and is a longtime Willie Nelson expert.
(JERROLD HOWARD)

RIGHT: Michelle Umstead, who in 1987 tried to encourage Mobile Buffett followers to support his "Save the Salt Ponds" Florida cause. (JAY FERCHAUD, COURTESY OF MOBILE PRESS-REGISTER)

LEFT: Jimmy and Susan Collier at the World's End Restaurant in Nashville, in April of 1984. He had performed some of his songs at a special reception in honor of Buzz Cason, who would handle around sixty of his Coral Reefer Music tunes through Southern Writers' Group USA. Collier has been listening to Jimmy since 1973—and today is an esteemed Music Row publicist whom *Tennessean* reporter Robert K. Oermann nicknamed "Queen of the Coral Reefers" in 1993. She is a lifetime Jimmy collector. (COURTESY OF SUSAN COLLIER; PHOTOGRAPHER UNKNOWN)

RIGHT: Jimmy signing a copy of his novel, *Where Is Joe Merchant?*, for Jason Matson at Davis-Kidd Booksellers, 4007 Hillsboro Road, Nashville, in October 1992. (COURTESY OF BETH GWINN)

New Orleans Margaritaville cafe in historic
Storyville (1104 Decatur St.), adjacent to Margaritaville
store (1 French Market Place), both established in 1992.
(Steve Eng)

Jimmy's Key West home, which has a "Beware of Occupant" metal sign on the gate. *(STEVE ENG)*

Margaritaville store and cafe, 500 Duval Street, Key West, Florida. *(STEVE ENG)*

Jimmy Buffett at
Irving Meadows
Amphitheater,
California, October
1996.
(SCOTT RUBY)

An older and wiser Jimmy along with Mike Utley at the New
Orleans Jazz Festival in 1994. *(COURTESY OF PAUL MARSH)*

roster and lack of label affiliation, Azoff can range across several diskeries to use a variety of talent on celluloid and vinyl."

Pollock cited other titles like *Life in a Coed Animal House* . . . and an eleven-million-dollar forthcoming film titled *Urban Cowboy,* with Jimmy on the soundtrack along with the Eagles, Fogelberg, Boz Scaggs, Bonnie Raitt, Linda Ronstadt, and Johnny Lee, among others. Lee was an unknown country performer, singing in a Houston club, when Azoff asked him, "You want to be in that movie *Urban Cowboy?*"

"I damn sure do."

"Okay, I'm going to make a star out of you, boy."

Lee didn't think much more about it, and went and had a beer. But then one of Azoff's aides helped Lee dig through a box and they found a song titled "Lookin' for Love," which went to Number 5 for Johnny Lee in pop, and Number One in country.

■ ■ ■

By escaping from Nashville into Azoff's L.A. hands, Jimmy was now singing in a film that would boomerang back and change the "Nashville Sound" for good or ill, for several years to come.

Hello, Texas—Hello, St. Barts
(and Montserrat)

■

*Of all the year's country box-office triumphs, the movie that would
come to symbolize the era in country music was* Urban Cowboy.

—Paul Kingsbury, *The Grand Ole Opry History of Country Music:
70 Years of the Songs, the Stars, and the Stories* (1995)

*I name myself "a native" of the West Indies . . . Montserrat, a mountain-
mass, loveliest of the lovely, but touchy! uncertain! dashing into tan-
trums, hurricanes, earthquakes, brooks bubbling-hot, soufrières [sul-
phur-swamps], floods.*

—M. P. Shiel, "About Myself," *The Works of M. P. Shiel*, vol. III (1980)

Jimmy had a song for *Urban Cow-
boy*—"Hello, Texas" (by Brian Collins and Robby Campbell), which
revives his own "hitchhiking to Austin" spirit, claiming to have left some
partying in Chicago, but instead of traveling A1A to Key West, he rides
down Interstate 10 to Texas.

"Country music is the city cowboy's Bible, his literature, his self-help
book, his culture," wrote Aaron Latham in his 1978 *Esquire* article "The
Ballad of the Urban Cowboy: America's Search for True Grit." With
director James Bridges, he wrote the script for *Urban Cowboy*. Since the
pop-music industry was having its worst recent year in 1979 (with worse
to come), having dropped from $112.7 million in profits to $68.4 million,
Gilley's club down in Houston, Texas, was a safe place for Irving Azoff.

Gilley's looked as big as "the MGM Grand Hotel or St. Patrick's Cathedral," according to Latham. Other than its size, though, its cathedral similarity was nil: "Everybody's been with everybody," the leading cowgirl told Latham, informing him "which cowgirls had given venereal disease to which cowboys and vice versa." Latham's new cowpoke subspecies rode pickup trucks rather than horses; worked in petrochemical plants, not corrals; lived in house trailers instead of bunkhouses; and saddled up with the labor unions instead of trail drivers or the Texas Rangers. When Willie Nelson played there, forty-five hundred folks jammed into the club ("An urban cowboy doesn't have to know how to brand or rope, but he must know how to dance," noted Latham).

But right outside of Gilley's, George Jones's fan-club president was *raped,* then beaten to death with a tire iron. So club owner Sherwood Cryer (after passing his lie detector test) installed a punching bag, charging twenty-five cents a slugger, "to give the honky-tonk cowboys something to hit besides one another. . . . At closing time, there is blood on the bag."

Cryer also thought an electric bucking bronco just might "go over in his shit-kicking honky-tonk," and thanks to the movie the following year, it gave Gilley's international renown. Feminists should have approved, since women seemingly could outride the men ("A woman has nothing to lose," sniped the urban cow*boys*).

■ ■ ■

Though Jimmy, according to his song "Migration," has long held "Texas hidden here in my heart," he could still "barely control" his Caribbean soul, as well.

"When Jimmy Buffett isn't onstage, it's a safe bet he's on the water—preferably St. Barts in the French West Indies," wrote Roy Attaway in *Motor Boating and Sailing,* since he "needed a retreat from adoration, and tiny (eight square miles), remote, very-French St. Barthélemy was the one place he could almost be guaranteed surcease (barring the occasional reporter)." Eventually Jimmy became part owner of the Autour du Rocher hotel, on a hillock offering a stunning view of Lorient Bay below.

Back in the winter of 1978, Jimmy had sailed down there, to nearby Antigua, with Janie. He felt that "even the money is pretty," preferring to spend "money decorated with conch shells, palm trees, sailboats, and royalty," than keeping currency featuring the faces of "old men" in his wallet. The big attraction was the Antigua Sailing Week. At the Admiral's Inn, Janie once went through a wrong door, colliding with a waiter, whose trayful of lobster dinners crashed to the floor, with "an incredulous waiter evil-eyeing the apologetic heroine."

But why wasn't he hanging around Hollywood, trying to get a movie deal with Azoff? Mainly because he disliked the recording industry in Los Angeles, as he told Associated Press reporter Peter J. Boyer, while there for a concert. Boyer agreed that "it doesn't care much for him," either.

According to Jimmy, "I don't fit into the mold of what they want: I should live out here. I should have a big car. I should be tickled to death to be on the cover of *People* magazine."

"Hollywood is imitation life. You're supposed to live in a canyon and snort cocaine all the time. It's the best place to work, but I could never live out here."

■   ■   ■

By now Janie was pregnant—and Jimmy was off on a tour in early 1979, oblivious to the abrupt merger now in progress between ABC and MCA.

"Hell, I'll always stay on the road," he said to Boyer. "Some guys get tired of playing their own stuff all the time. Well, hell, that's what the people are out there for. Moan as much as you want, but there's no other way you could live in this lifestyle. I mean, what's two hours of your time?"

His opening act was the Amazing Rhythm Aces, several of whose songs (such as "Third Rate Romance") charted in both country and pop. As a sort of warm-up for *Urban Cowboy,* Jimmy was in Austin in February—and back in Auburn, Alabama, in April. Fingers Taylor did several solos (wearing a white hat with its brim down over his eyes), and Keith Sykes was praised by the *Auburn Plainsman*'s Ford Risley for his strong guitar work. Jimmy termed his Coral Reefers "the maniacs"— then played without them, sitting on a stool with a drink. He closed the show, again by himself, with "Tin Cup Chalice."

On his return visit to Hattiesburg—almost certainly in 1979—Jimmy became entranced with nostalgic, shoplifting déjà vu. He remembered how he used to go and order a charcoal steak at the Winn-Dixie—not a packaged one, but a fresh tenderloin—just to see if he could steal it. His band members knew his song "Peanut Butter Conspiracy" and were aware how he had worn a trench coat and sucked in his stomach in order to shoplift chickens. Jimmy told Robert W. Morgan on his 1980 radio interview that when they came through Hattiesburg at four in the morning, his Coral Reefers wanted to relive the song. "They said we ought to make a pilgrimage to the original Mini-Mart."

So Jimmy checked one out about four blocks away, then exclaimed: "We can't pull a forty-foot bus with a palm tree painted on the side into town at four in the morning, and think people aren't going to see us. And then unload twelve screaming maniacs at the Mini-Mart—and it will all come back to haunt me. And they'll throw us all in jail until I pay 'em back."

As for his band members, Jimmy took them on his *Euphoria II* in between shows. They played pinball, and as Jimmy told *Birmingham News* reporter Mark Childress: "You can ask everybody in there. They'll bitch, and yell, and raise hell about something, but after six months off, when we came back to work, everybody was ready to go."

And the band members were *safe* on the *Euphoria II*. At least when a customs inspector climbed aboard, Jimmy believed he would be pacified by the framed picture hanging over his chair: of Jimmy in the Oval Office, with President Carter and Vice President Mondale.

■   ■   ■

His next major destination was Montserrat—a volcanic island in the British West Indies, the whimsical site for recording his *Volcano* album in early May 1979.

Montserrat ("the saw-toothed mountain") lies twenty-seven miles southwest of Antigua, with mountains rich with green forests, and beaches powdered with black sand from the volcanoes. Irish settlers arrived in 1632—supposedly some rebel captives dumped by Oliver Cromwell.

The combination of slaves and Irish are well symbolized by Montserrat-born novelist M. P. Shiel (1865–1947), who was supposedly descended from Irish kings, but whose mother was part black. Shiel was himself cheerfully a little crazy, thanks to the winds and volcanoes. His father had him crowned "King of Redonda," an uninhabited volcanic isle to the north, in 1880. Though the British annexed Redonda, in London Shiel still claimed to be "King Felipe I." He passed his realm to English poet John Gawsworth ("Juan I"), who made many fellow writers (including Dylan Thomas and Lawrence Durrell) "dukes" of Redonda down in the pub. A latter-day Redondan monarch, Jon Wynne-Tyson ("Juan II"), like Jimmy Buffett, is a novelist and popular defender of animal rights. And he was at Antigua's Admiral's Inn in the spring of 1979, one year after Jimmy.

Wynne-Tyson was heading for Redonda for a regal ceremony with A. Reynolds Morse—who believes that Herman Wouk's novel *Don't Stop the Carnival* (1965) deserves a "Shiel-Redonda Literary Prize" for its imaginary island of Amerigo set in about the same location. Since Jimmy wants to make a musical out of Wouk's novel, he at least deserves to become a duke of Redonda.

Like Margaritaville, Redonda is a comical cult kingdom, popular in books and especially on British TV, radio, and newspaper pages. And Jimmy's hero, Harry Belafonte, starred in a science-fiction film, *The World, the Flesh, and the Devil* (1959), based on Shiel's apocalyptic novel *The Purple Cloud* (1901). Jimmy has already renamed Montserrat "Skull Island" from the film *King Kong*.

■ ■ ■

But how did the *Volcano* album transpire?

"I sort of went back and looked at *A1A*," he told radio interviewer Jim Ladd, " 'cause that's sort of the consensus of opinion overall, from feedback from the road—that's probably everybody's favorite album. I was just trying to dissect it and wondering, 'What the hell is so different about this that everybody likes it? What was I doing?' What I *wasn't* doing was working very much at the time, so I had a lot of time to write." Jimmy worked on the album for about six months.

Then he heard that Beatles producer George Martin, who had set up AIR (Associated Independent Recording) Studios in London, was installing a West Indies branch in Belham Valley, Montserrat. Jimmy went down and saw that it was almost finished. "It looked really nice, it was almost like a working vacation to take the band and the crew down there." He told interviewer Chet Flippo that "I've always wanted to make an album in Paradise."

Lead guitarist Barry Chance remembers that the group America had cut some sessions there first (a folk-rock band of U.S. military sons from Central High School, London), but believes Buffett was the first to do a complete album there. This opened the door for many others, including Stevie Wonder and Elton John (*Too Low for Zero*), whose biographer Philip Norman says, "Artists could work with total concentration in congenial surroundings. AIR-Montserrat became the in-place to record for everyone from Paul McCartney and Eric Clapton to Phil Collins and the Police."

After arriving, one of the first stops for Jimmy and the Coral Reefers was Café Le Capitain ("There are bars and then there are *bars*, and this one's classic"). A "woop-wop" band was playing what Jimmy calls "down-island stuff, more calypso, happy, good-time music" than reggae—a sort of calypso style maranga. The band had a banjo-ukulele player, and someone was playing "a long blow pipe." The "woop-wop" enchantment was intensified by the hovering magical menace of Galway's Soufrière—Montserrat's mist-shrouded volcano—with a rainbow that arced down to the studio.

At times, Jimmy and the Coral Reefers took a break over at St. Barts, which Chet Flippo termed a "smugglers' haven." He was proud that so many of the local dope-runners worshipped Jimmy: "He is *theirs*. . . . Lord, they swear by the man." (His tapes are a necessary instrument for their floating importations.)

Flippo was supposed to meet Jimmy at his beloved bar Le Select in Gustavia, capital of the island—"a real crossroads for smugglers and other exotic charlatans. It's a tawdry, open-air whitewashed-stone joint with outhouses that would make a sewer rat gag. . . . Naked hippie children crawl across the floor," reported Flippo. A customer whispered to him: "Big party last night. Everybody on the island was fucked up. Lots of acid." (Le Select's garden restaurant was named, years later, "Cheeseburger in Paradise.") Jimmy didn't show up—but they met anyway, at L'Entrepont, a harbor bar. Here a "blond, bronze, pigtailed woman" told Jimmy that he really ought to drink "a lotta pineapple juice. It'll make your come taste *sweet!*" Buffett blushed "a pulsating scarlet through his tan."

Jimmy played tape tracks for Flippo off his new album. "Last night we drank twenty-five bottles of champagne in here and never got around to eating. And that was just the beginning. *Lord,* I got to settle down. I got a record to finish," said Jimmy.

"*Horseshit,*" responded Flippo, no doubt upholding the "Let's get drunk and interview" Caribbean credo. He called Jimmy "the perfect composite of a rocking folkie." (A *Rolling Stone* emeritus, Flippo has now followed in the footsteps of Jimmy and Gerry Wood—to Nashville's *Billboard* office in 1995.)

■   ■   ■

Volcano was Jimmy's favorite album in years.

The first song on Side One, "Fins," has a strong, driving sound, with a pop-hook chorus, stating that the girl is menaced by shark fins on her left and on her right. She's heading down to Antigua, then Montserrat, getting "postcards from the road" (the subtitle of Elizabeth Ashley's autobiography). Jimmy wrote the song in a Daytona bar, imagining that the men huddling around some beauty-contest girls were really sharks— land sharks, a species Jimmy says is steadily increasing. Barry Chance wrote the melody; Jimmy wrote the lyrics (also credited are Tom Corcoran and Deborah McColl).

Then follows the title song, "Volcano," where Jimmy says he doesn't know where he's going to go when the volcano blows, so his girl had better love him *now!* He cringes at the lava coming down—and runs off a list of places he *doesn't* want to visit by airplane (Three Mile Island, after the nuclear pollution—"I don't want to see my skin aglow"; Nashville; San Diego). Nor does he want to see the Ayatollah—who would soon be holding U.S. soldiers hostage!

"Volcano" was cowritten with Keith Sykes and bass player Harry Dailey, more or less on the spot. "We actually went to a volcano," says Sykes, "and the steam that was coming out was condensed on these rocks—and that steam was very hot. We went down about a hundred and fifty feet from where it was coming out of the earth." Then they dammed up some rocks and made themselves "a little hot tub, and jumped in and made us a sulphur bath. Then we went back down to the studio and wrote the song. There wasn't even a demo—we just wrote the song and then cut it."

Jimmy says his Montserrat adventures could fill a book—and someday maybe they will!

Years later, in 1985, "Volcano" was challenged by some young drinkers at Montserrat's rum bar-restaurant, Village Place, near Salem. They winked, and told the singer Sting (né Gordon Matthew Sumner, who was also recording at AIR) that the song wasn't written about the actual volcano—but was really about the "Volcano" drinks (four brands of rum, grenadine, pineapple juice, orange juice, Montserrat lime juice) imbibed by Jimmy and singer-songwriter James Taylor over at the now-closed Agouti bar at the town of Plymouth.

The next song, "Treat Her Like a Lady" (written with David Loggins), condemns life on the mainland, including (once again) rent-a-cars, hotels, and California earthquakes. The song sympathizes with whales—"an endangered species," with whom Jimmy identifies since, like so many Sixties entertainer-types facing the 1980s, he feared he was destined for the "elephant burial ground."

■　■　■

James Taylor had flown down to sing on the album (followed by his brothers Hugh and Alex), and Jimmy said that on "Treat Her Like a Lady," Taylor made Jimmy's favorite lines sparkle. Jimmy called the Taylors "the Railing Stains." Outside the AIR studio, James Taylor would sit sipping a piña colada by the swimming pool. Jimmy jested: "Hey, James, did you know you can make records here?"

"I'm still amazed by this," Taylor told Chet Flippo. "Every time I look around I think how this goes against the Puritan ethic with which I was raised. They told me I should have brought a psychoanalyst with me, to deal with this beauty," alluding to the "palm trees and red hibiscus and lavender bougainvillea" decorating the hillside leading up to the volcano.

■　■　■

Another singable number on Side One is "Chanson pour les Petits Enfants," with back-up singers chorusing in French, featuring the luscious soprano of Deborah McColl. *Rolling Stone*'s Don Shewey praised the "Cat Stevens–style instrumentation."

Side Two opens with "Survive" (written with Mike Utley), a Forties-style poppish melody, with lyrics reminiscent of "Come Monday" about surviving till he can see her again (written on the road, with the blues afflicting him like a bad cold). Critic Shewey accused him of trying to "ape Barry Manilow"—probably an unintentional compliment. But Jimmy was proud of the piano-playing and how he had been inspired by Billy Joel's *52nd Street* album. ("*Shit!* I can write a Billy Joel song. . . . Eat your heart out, Billy Joel!" he said to himself.) "Boat Drinks" is another Buffett standard—where Jimmy is going to fly to "Saint Somewhere" ("I gotta go where it's warm"), suffering from "cabin fever," having fired six pistol shots at his freezer! "Dreamsicle" was one more catchy number, telling of Jimmy's flippant philosophy ("I got house pets / Lear jets"), yearning to sail and to smoke grass.

Jimmy wrote the slow, touching story-song "Sending the Old Man Home" in Cedars-Sinai Hospital in California, "Demerol-ed out of my head," with his foot in traction (broken leg number three). He had just finished reading Herman Wouk's *War and Remembrance* (1978), and had watched James Cagney's film *The Gallant Hours* (1960), where Cagney played Admiral Halsey and "looked a lot like my grandfather," he told Chet Flippo in *Look*. So, after leaving the hospital the next day and flying home to Alabama, Jimmy "wrote what sounds like an Irving Berlin, USO, 1945 end-of-the-war song." The government is tearing down the officers' club in Pearl Harbor . . . yet the old banished World War II veteran still dreams about his Navy flying days, *and* his pretty Hawaiian girls. Like "The Captain and the Kid" and "He Went to Paris," it's another profound naval eulogy. (At Montserrat, Jimmy wore around his neck a little gold anchor and a sailing-ship's steering wheel; his aunt Patsy Lumpkin has a tiny wheel and ship's bell on the door of her Pascagoula home.)

On the basis of those sailor songs alone, the Nashville Songwriters' Association International—which has singer and Communist journalist (*Daily Worker*) Woody Guthrie in its Hall of Fame—needs Jimmy Buffett in there as well.

▪ ▪ ▪

Certainly the *Volcano* session had been efficient, thanks to the Montserrat milieu. "There's no distractions for the band," Jimmy had told Flippo. "We've cut eight tracks in eleven days. It's almost like recording camp. Waterskiing at eleven, snorkeling at twelve, swimming at one, and into the studio at three. . . . I think this is the best bleeping album I've ever done."

Jimmy was eating cheeseburgers lubricated with beer, and back in the studio, waiters kept everyone fueled with silver trays full of mango daiquiris and piña coladas. Buffett and James Taylor harmonized for hours, "Sending the Old Man Home," while around twenty others of the gang ate dinner upstairs. Hugh Taylor served pitchers of martinis, "a harbinger of the all-night party to come." After the studio was "drunk dry," two more, unrelated Taylors—James and Fingers—went scouting for more booze, glomming some moonshine.

Chet Flippo woke up in the morning to see James Taylor doing his "Jonestown sprawl" on the ground, singing "Somebody Stole My Hair." He said that he and Fingers were going to go on a world blues tour for people who have money but lack the blues—whereas the two Taylors are "in the opposite camp. We may not have the blues for long, but it's gonna be a fair trade."

But James Taylor's then wife, Carly Simon, complained about his "extravagant lifestyle," saying that while he did drugs, she *hated* drugs—and that he drank and partied constantly, "flying off to St. Martin or St. Barts to go on benders with Jimmy Buffett," instead of staying home with the family.

Jimmy was planning on taking the band on down to St. Barthélemy for more parties. "The way that I've settled into my lifestyle means constant change," he told Flippo.

"Where do you live?" people tended to ask him. It was the "hardest question" he had to answer—"because I'm always moving around. . . . I'll keep goin' till they drop me into the ground."

■　■　■

One spot he liked to visit in the warm weather was good ol' Aspen. This year, there was a really good pretext for partying—and Jimmy didn't intend to miss out.

On June 1, 1979, Janie gave birth to seven-pound Savannah Jane Buffett. "Like any normal parent," he announced a welcoming party for his friends that lasted a mere fifteen hours. "Savannah Jane was born at seven A.M., and I cracked the champagne at seven-thirty," he said, and Jack Nicholson and others came over and stayed till ten that night. Next was the "coming home from the hospital" party—then two more parties, adding up to "really about a week's worth of parties."

■　■　■

But newborn Savannah Jane would have her own effect on her daddy. It was time to dump (not sink) the *Euphoria II*. And build a new, smaller boat, named . . . *Savannah Jane.*

"How much do you live on your boat?" asked radio interviewer Jim Ladd. Jimmy told him how he'd put it up for sale. "It's not that tragic. I wasn't spending enough time to warrant it. I had a great time on that boat and I wrote a lot of great songs. When I built that boat, I went totally *overboard* on the thing."

"What can you have on a boat that's 'overboard'?"

"I put everything on it you can possibly have on it. At that time, I was only thirty, and I was nowhere near ready to retire and sail away—I was enjoying what I was doing for a living, but I wasn't going to the ends of the planet. Which is what I built that damned boat to do—it had everything on it. So there I sit with this beautiful fifty-four-foot catch—it can do anything, it could split the atom!"

Jimmy would come in off the road, with two or three weeks off, and tell his captain and crew: "Oh man, I'm burned out. I'm ready to hit it."

They would mildly agree that they were ready . . . "as soon as that part comes in from Puerto Rico." To Jimmy, ordering a part from Puerto

Rico was like ordering one from Thailand. So, with all these hassles—and so little time for *Euphoria II*—he sold it. Or rather, he sold *her*.

■ ■ ■

In the summer of '79 Jimmy visited Nantucket, where he became enamored of a new nautical lady—a sloop fashioned by the Sanford brothers. They were building modern versions of the original twenty-six-foot *Alerion* built by Nathaniel G. Herreshoff in 1912. Their current model featured African mahogany on the outer-hull layer.

But Jimmy refused to have an engine installed, not wanting "to ruin the aesthetics" of the *Savannah Jane*. Besides the two bunk beds and a galley with a two-burner stove, he had his mandatory bookshelf and a four-speaker stereo, plus a VHF radio.

The actual construction of the boat began that October, but already in September, *Volcano* had been issued, aimed at the Christmas market.

■ ■ ■

Besides a back-cover picture of Jimmy sitting next to the volcano, inside *Volcano* was a lengthy rhymed-and-metered poem, "Mystery South of Us," from Don Blanding's *Floridays* (1940). Like Jimmy's songs, Blanding's verse was rich with vivid imagery ("Florida thrusts like a guiding thumb / To the southern islands of rumba and rum, / To the lands of mystery that lie below, / To the places I know I'm going to go"). Blanding was an artist, and his illustrated poetry books sold widely, in the tens of thousands each year. *Vagabond's House* alone (1928) went through forty-eight editions (150,000 copies). Like Jimmy, Blanding traveled incessantly, exploring live and dead volcano craters in Hawaii, where he lived for a time (as well as in Florida). A fanatical journalist and compulsive lecturer (236 talks in 1956), he wandered the South Seas on a freighter; his hobbies were mountain climbing and gourmet cooking.

Don Blanding (1894–1957) was deemed somewhat "bland" by the stuffy critics (rhyme 'n' meter is academically verboten) but, like Jimmy, was too successful and too sincere to care. (Jimmy needs to start Margaritaville Press, and issue a Blanding *Selected Poems*—or even set some Blanding lyrics to music.)

Volcano was "Buffett's biggest album ever," predicted Irving Azoff. "I'll be surprised if it's not Top Five." It went to Number 14 (Number 10 in pop and Number 8 in country in *Cash Box*), and the three singles charted moderately: "Fins" (Number 35), "Volcano" (Number 66), and "Survive" (Number 77).

Reviewer Shewey felt the album was too light, but for three songs: "Volcano," "Treat Her Like a Lady," and "Chanson pour les Petits Enfants" ("That Buffett manages to tap a child's sense of wonder without going smug, sentimental, or religious, might be the best thing about him"). Shewey otherwise patronized Jimmy's "complacent" beach-lounging persona, yet seemed grateful that at least "he's not an arrogant son of a bitch." Unlike Montserrat's volcano, the album was in no "danger of erupting."

But his old ally Gerry Wood felt that Jimmy had attained "newfound maturity in life," expounding in *Billboard*:

> Here we have an album that once again establishes Buffett as one of the wittiest and most skillful writers of our era. . . . Fortunately, Buffett evades his penchant for making good—not great—rock music and concentrates on making great—not good—pop music. Buffett the writer meets Buffett the performer in a gentle clime washed by turquoise waters and enough rum to create a high tide. . . . In this LP, Buffett is less profane, more profound. Less pedantic, more poetic. And, despite the title, less volcanic, but more valid.

Simultaneous to *Volcano*'s release was the warm-up of the next Presidential campaign. Progressive pop acts like Jimmy were regarded as Democratic Party mainstays—but for which candidates?

"The White House is pursuing Willie Nelson," reported *New York Times* writer Wayne King, but "Jimmy Buffett, the country-rock singer, appears to be deserting President Carter for Senator Edward M. Kennedy." (Kennedy had conducted interviews in 1977 investigating Operation MK-ULTRA, the LSD experiments that had triggered one suicide kept secret.) Jimmy turned over several hundred seats in a Florida concert to Kennedy, for a straw poll to be taken. "When word of the Buffett defection reached the White House," Wayne King said that Chief of Staff Hamilton Jordan and aide Timothy Kraft supposedly called Jimmy and reenlisted him.

"He waffled," griped a Kennedyite.

Carter "probably has too much integrity to be a good President," Jimmy told Patricia Ward Biederman in the *Atlanta Constitution* years later. He complained that Carter employed inept political sidemen ("any good rock 'n' roll road manager and crew would have run a better show"), who wanted stars on the campaign trail to be seen and not heard. They have a "window-dressing attitude" toward celebrities— "They would love to please audiences the way we do." Jimmy said no one cared about his political values, so long as he got his "matching funds . . . they thought all you wanted out of it was your picture made with them." Jimmy had his own agenda—but Carter's boys wouldn't listen: "I wanted possibly to be nominated as a representative to the International Whaling Commission. After all, I see more of America than any politician does until they decide to run for President. I go across the country twice a year and I've done it for twenty years."

Guitarist Barry Chance remembers their softball games with the White House staff on their trips to Washington, D.C. "They were a bunch of cheating motherfuckers, man—every time they'd score one run, they'd count it as four. Jimmy got real pissed off one day—he had three limos pull up, and we left."

■ ■ ■

Hurricane Frederic had struck Mobile, Alabama, causing churches and civic groups to form Area Interfaith Disaster Services—featuring Jimmy at a benefit concert on March 5, 1980.

Jimmy had told Tom Mason of the *Mobile Register* that David Allen Coe had "stole" the melody of "Divers Do It Deeper" from "Changes in Latitudes, Changes in Attitudes," adding, "I would have sued him, but I didn't want to give Coe the pleasure of having his name in the paper." Earlier, Coe had a strong Key West theme album, *Spectrum VII* (1979), with a liner note addressed to record reviewers: "Jimmy Buffett doesn't live in Key West anymore."

Otherwise Jimmy seemed proud that different acts were doing tunes you might call a "Buffett song," which he defined as a "catchy, good song; well written; with something to say in the lyrics. I like to maintain a sense of humor." He thought it funny that the Nitty Gritty Dirt Band's "American Dream" was being mistaken for his. He'd almost recorded it himself, then went for *Volcano*. "It's a pretty good Buffett song [pause]. . . . I can write a Buffett song better than anybody."

And he warned Mason that he wasn't going to change his show—it wasn't go to be a G-rated family performance: "They don't want to see the toned-down model."

Indeed, reviewing the show, Lolo Pendergast of the *Mobile Register* noted his "impetuous craving for the wild, with a barrage of bawdy songs one would find in no hymnal." At least onstage he referred to his days in "Admiral's Corner" at the Admiral Semmes Hotel, and gave credit to his old mentors, Father Victor, now at McGill-Toolen, and songwriter Milton Brown.

But as "Divers Do It Deeper" entered the country charts that month (at Number 86), the critics kept comparing David Allen Coe to Jimmy. Coe retaliated with his *Nothing Sacred* album, on his *very* independent D.A.C. label, advertised as "Not for Sale in Stores" and "not recommended for AIR-PLAY." It was full of touching songs—of a physical sort—nostalgically depicting an orgy in Nashville's Centennial Park, as well as publicizing such unique entertainers as Linda Lovelace, Anita Bryant ("Fuck Aneta Bryant" [sic]) . . . and Jimmy Buffett. "Jimmy Buffett Doesn't Live in Key West Anymore" condemned record reviewers as "motherfuckers who think music is a whore," advising them: "Don't lay all that Key West Jimmy Buffett shit on me." He lamented that Jimmy was no longer a bar-hopper on Duval Street, having moved to Malibu (Janie eventually lived there), while envying his pictures in *Roll-*

ing Stone ("The rich keep getting richer . . ."). Unauthorized pornographer Coe suggested that he and Jimmy get drunk and screw. . . .

A true collector's item (D.A.C. LP-0002), the album has other stirring titles like "Pussy-Whipped Again" and "Cum Stains on the Pillow" (why not "Cum Monday"?).

■ ■ ■

Urban Cowboy was released in June 1980.

John Travolta somehow believably portrayed a Texas oil-refinery worker hanging out at Gilley's, where he meets a honky-tonk honey (Debra Winger) whom he hastily marries. Fortunately, for plot interest, their marriage wastes away at Gilleyville—for a time—as the cinematic blender mixes alcohol, music, and good ol' violence (and vile language) with incessant electric bull–riding. Critics were not wholly awed—Jay Robert Nash and Stanley Ralph Ross called it "dull, vapid and *long*"— but *The New York Times*'s Vincent Canby, after registering his reservations ("overstuffed with nonessential details"), admitted the actors were "splendid" and that the film was a pseudo B-movie of elaborate, self-conscious artistic quality.

Under the zany vulgarity ran the continuity of morality, which in part accounted for *Urban Cowboy*'s immense success. Of all people, Irving Azoff had trail-driven his electric cattle into Nashville. With a soundtrack crammed with music by Bonnie Raitt, Johnny Lee, and so many others (often from Azoff's ranch), the film, according to Country Music Foundation director Bill Ivey, "spread not only country music but cowboy dress, pickup trucks, mechanical bulls, and a slew of other symbols of country living into an urban society long thought immune to the charms of rural culture." Ivey said it triggered talk-show dates for Willie, Loretta, and Dolly, and "generated a spate of dramatic films (some fine, some laughable) that featured these stars." For years, urban-cowboy clones would clog Nashville's corral chute.

Of the eighteen tracks on the soundtrack album, Jimmy's is the first (plus, as usual: Fogelberg, Boz Scaggs, Joe Walsh, the Eagles). The album lived twenty-three weeks in the Top 40, peaking at Number 3.

It was issued by Azoff's independent Full Moon label and Asylum Records—acknowledging Walter Yetnikoff, one of Azoff's sometime allies and frequent rival. David Geffen called Yetkinoff "an absolutely honorable man who keeps his word, which is more than you can say about the Irving Azoffs of this business." Of Yetnikoff, Azoff said, "We have a love-hate relationship. Once we screamed for two hours, then ended up throwing darts for the points on Dan Fogelberg." Yetnikoff himself said that "Irving's problem—and he's not a bad guy—is that it's not a character flaw, it's a genetic defect. Irving lies when it's to his advantage to tell the *truth*. He just can't help it."

Azoff's explanation: "Walter? Dennis the Menace as Attila the Hun."

■ ■ ■

Jimmy's touring persisted as ever. Once, in Raleigh, North Carolina, the sound went out, and after kicking the stage monitor in vain, he resorted to his acoustic guitar, but when the house lights came on, the audience booed, still wanting more of Jimmy. Critics gradually began pining for older, "better" songs, while invariably praising the live shows themselves. For example, "Dreamsicle" was a good song if you had forgotten the better one, "Grapefruit—Juicy Fruit" from 1973, according to Geoffrey Stokes in the *Village Voice* that year. "As Buffett the songwriter has weakened, Buffett the performer has been bolstered by the ever-larger Coral Reefer Band," said Richard Harrington in the *Washington Post* that summer.

"Happy Birthday, America," Jimmy said to his audience on July 4 in Minneapolis. Satellite radio was sending him and his Coral Reefers out live to about fifty cities, from New York to Los Angeles. "How much beer do you think was drunk in America today? . . . I know that the people on the radio can't smell all this good reefer you all are smoking here in Minneapolis [interrupted by deafening applause]. "*I can!* It smells like burning bushes!"

■ ■ ■

In September he headed to Muscle Shoals to cut another album, *Coconut Telegraph,* and also went to Bennett House in Franklin, Tennessee, for some additional recording. The house had been built in 1875, by the owner of the local hardware store (today's Bennett's Corner), and in the early twentieth century became an antique shop, then a men's clothing store. In the 1970s, Norbert Putnam purchased it, and recorded Dan Fogelberg—and Jimmy—in the comfortable studio (with the kitchen, dining room, and parlors turned into professional settings). Amy Grant and Whitney Houston are among the many to record there, and luxurious bedrooms still remain for those rare musical guests/customers who don't need booze, cigarettes, or drugs.

By early November Jimmy was at the Grand Ole Opry house once more.

Save the Manatee ("Slow, Slow, Slow Your Boat")

■

A sight that is getting more and more rare now is that of a manatee, or sea cow—the wonderful mammal lives exclusively in the water, like a fish, and that has furnished the foundation of many a mermaid story by thrusting its head and shoulders out of the ocean near shore, just in time to let a startled crew see it.

> —"Strange Sea Monster," *The* [Ocean Springs, Miss.] *Progress,* February 20, 1904

In the next quarter of a century this creature will become extinct unless specimens are preserved simply to prevent the complete loss of one of our most wonderful sea creatures.

> —"The Vanishing Sea Cow," *The Pascagoula Democrat,* August 20, 1912

At a February 1981 concert at Tallahassee, capital of Florida, Jimmy sang his song "Growing Older but Not Up" from the *Coconut Telegraph* album. The line about seeing himself as an old manatee—heading south into the colder waters, imagining himself steering around a boat that cut scars in his shoulders—especially capitivated someone in the audience:

Governor D. Robert "Bob" Graham. They met backstage and Jimmy told Graham how he sympathized with the manatees, and over the coming months, they talked some more.

"It's a Florida problem with a Florida solution," Jimmy announced at a local news conference in March 1981. He was planning to sell Buffett-and-manatee T-shirts, netting at least two dollars each (having just sold several hundred thousand shirts on tour). He wanted to stick up posters in "dive shops near manatee dive areas" (and near the boat ramps, fuel docks, and marinas, close to where the manatees were most endangered), and to hold benefit concerts, public-service announcements . . . *plus* form a nonprofit committee.

The friendly "sea cows" were being carved up by the whirling propellers of the potential half-million Florida speedboats—since the manatees often floated just beneath the surface of the water, with just their nostrils . above the surface. Sometimes they would get lodged in dam floodgates, or canal locks.

In spite of the U.S. Marine Mammal Protection Act (1972), and the Endangered Species Act (1973)—plus Florida's own Manatee Sanctuary Act (1978)—by 1980 there were *more manatee deaths than births.*

"We've got more boat kills," Jimmy said in a TV interview. "What we're seeing now is an increase in irresponsible boat operators. In this state, you don't have to have a license to drive a boat. . . . We're killing manatees, we're killing each other. . . . In the state of Florida, you can put down your money and buy a 500-horsepower boat and hit the Intracoastal. You've got a thousand people a day moving to Florida, and they're buying boats—you've got more boats than manatees. I think that's the reason why our kill rate is up so much—people running boats without knowing anything about operating boats."

Indeed, some eighty percent of the manatees were "prop"-scarred on their inch-thick skin—in spite of the law restricting boat speeds in crucial locales, with a thousand-dollar maximum penalty and a potential year in jail. (By 1980 there were over half a million speedboats in Florida.) Divers (who *do* do it deeper!) were even banned from playing with manatees underwater! Over a toll-free state telephone line someone could report a "manatee death, injury, or harassment" (still in effect today: 1–800–342–5367). Yet vandals even slew them occasionally.

That May, Jimmy was back at Tallahassee, endorsing a manatee-protection campaign for the Department of Natural Resources. (Governor Bob Graham was simultaneously thanking him for having earlier publicized highway A1A on his album.)

In the fall, retired smuggler Jimmy was out giving manatee lectures as something of a budding political activist ("Rebel with a cause," the *Boston Herald* called him). Two of his concerts raised a total of thirty-five thousand dollars, which he gave to Natural Resources director Elton Gisendanner at a public ceremony in December. Soon, 365 warning signs were made and mounted—to slow down the deadly boats.

Governor Graham anointed him "official guardian" of the manatees. The informal Save the Manatee Committee attracted the Florida Audubon Society, whose tax-exempt status was an immediate enticement. Jimmy became chairman, and said in 1992 that he'd always expected the committee to one day become independent. "I did it because it's something that I wanted to do for the state of Florida, and to do something to make the manatee representative of the preservation of our lifestyle." Repeatedly he went to Tallahassee, promoting state licensing for manatee funding; he filmed television commercials to win funding to support the manatee adoption plan, and, of course, staged fund-raising concerts.

In January 1982 he moved with "some of his staff" into a secluded home in north-central Florida (Fowler's Bluff, ten miles north of Cedar Key). His realtor told the press that he didn't know if Jimmy had been motivated by his manatee-protection cause or not. At least the home was in a hundred-foot wooded lot, overlooking the Suwannee River.

By June the Save the Manatee Committee was working with Sea World in Orlando, considering potential Buffett concerts that fall. On July 15, Jimmy was scheduled to swim underwater and be videotaped with a manatee. (As Albert Falco once told Captain Jacques-Yves Cousteau, "I am the same person, yet I am no longer the same. Under the sea everything is moral.")

■   ■   ■

The manatees had been in the Florida waters for millions of years.

The Floridian subspecies, *Trichechus manatus latirostris,* belongs to the order of Sirenia, a reminder that the ancient legend of "sirens"—singing mermaids—derives from these creatures. (One of the American manatees' Asian cousins, the "dugong," may have been the source of the legend.) Bungling boater Christopher Columbus, who mistook San Salvador for islands near China and Japan, three months later (in 1493) compounded his errors when he "saw three mermaids . . . They were not as beautiful as they are painted though they had something like the human face."

The nineteenth century's predecessor to "Colonel" Tom Parker (and Irving Azoff), P. T. Barnum, loyally engineered a composite mermaid with a monkey's head sewn to a fish's body, unfurling an eighteen-foot banner to help advertise it on its road tour. He claimed "this most-remarkable curiosity" came from a London natural-history museum (which didn't exist).

Manatees are actually distant relatives of the elephant, measuring up to sixteen feet long and weighing thirteen hundred pounds or more. They look like torpedoes, or "an Army duffel bag stuffed with volleyballs," according to *Southern Living;* others call them "sea elephants"; and Florida Indians called the manatee Big Beaver, due to its big flat tail. But they are passive, and won't fight even to defend themselves or their young.

"I shall never forget the scare I got at the first sight of a manatee," said fisherman John Mansfield in *The Progress* (Ocean Springs, Mississippi) in 1904. He was relaxing in the stern of his boat in Florida's Indian River, when suddenly he saw a "sea monster" with a huge, lobsterlike tail. When it started eating grass, he realized it was a manatee—"a veritable cross between a cow and a seal, and a fish and a waterbug."

Manatees themselves tasted good: the early, carnivorous, Spanish Catholics deemed them "fish," so their sailors could chomp down on them on Fridays! The manatees' hides made good whips, to help the Dutch keep their Indian slaves busy developing America. The Indians at least used manatee hides for their canoes.

As early as 1907 Florida passed its first protection law. The *Pascagoula Democrat* remarked in 1912: "The flesh is very delicious and brings a high price, having strong resemblance to the very finest veal. The skeleton is valued at $100."

"They look a bit like Grover Cleveland," reported *Time* magazine in 1980: "Same whiskers, thick wrinkled skin. Hefty too: up to 2,200 pounds of blubbery bulk." But unlike Cleveland, from New Jersey, manatees came from the rivers of West Africa and the Amazon basin, as well as Florida.

Their fatality rate is due in part to their slow conception schedule— maybe one baby after six months, and no twins. Births are only once every five years, and a manatee can live maybe thirty-five years in its small, family group, or herd (of fifteen to twenty animals).

The *Miami Herald* (ca. 1979) said manatees "are friendly and curious and harmless and defenseless. They swim languidly to welcome any creature or thing that enters their watery world. . . . Though manatees are not good for much, they are good."

"It's a struggle we hear about nearly every day," says Melle Brauderick of Ocala, Florida. She grew up in Colorado, a teenaged John Denver, and especially Jimmy Buffett, enthusiast. "Whenever we lose one, we count them as they go. It's pretty emotional around here, at least for Florida residents."

One reason to save them is their usefulness in clearing water plants out of irrigation channels, for the manatees are herbivores, or vegetarians, and in their diet choice, they certainly differ from their "Cheeseburgers in Paradise" savior, Jimmy Buffett. At least in terms of food, the manatees more resemble singer k.d. lang, noted for her "Meat Stinks" campaign against cattle owners. Why, manatees may eat one hundred pounds of plants a day! But, like Jimmy until recently, they *do* have a vestige of a mustache.

■   ■   ■

By 1990 SAVE THE MANATEE license plates were being offered in order to raise money for the Save Our State foundation.

But any political activist must know how to hit the sidewalk—and not blow out his flip-flops—while marching up and down, thrusting a protest sign. Jimmy accomplished this Sixties-style feat in April 1992, waving his fist for *People* magazine (which named him "poet laureate of Florida hedonism"). Around his neck he flashed an "Audubon Is for the Birds" sign, confirming his desire to withdraw the Manatee Committee from the Audubon Society. Consequently, the Audubon Society had changed the locks on the Manatee Committee's Orlando office—and froze its assets ($700,000) and grabbed its mailing list (32,000 members).

Jimmy's longtime administrator, Judith Delaney Valdee, was cast overboard by the bureaucratic captain—"pirate," Jimmy would have said. "I've been calling it a hostile takeover," Jimmy told the *Washington Post*'s William Booth, accusing the Auduboners of coddling big-business "polluters" from the phosphate and fertilizer industries. The "takeover" accusation was deemed "bunk" by Audubon's Florida chapter president, Bernie Yokel, who said corporations became more environmentally aware once they started donating.

But in April of 1992, Jimmy staged a concert and raised $65,000 for his separate committee concept.

The Audubon Society didn't wish to lose the Manatee Committee—they called him a fickle and naive child—so he sued them and eventually escaped their political aquarium. (Irving Azoff was a litigation champion, so plaintiff Jimmy may have learned the "Let's get drunk and sue" credo from Front Line Management.) In his 1992 deposition (taken over the phone), Jimmy insisted that he never made any money from the committee—never even took expenses reimbursement for his traveling. By now the 1985 membership of 3,200 had jumped ten times—to over 30,000 in 1992.

Judith Delaney Valdee, the Audubon-ousted director, is today's executive director of the Save the Manatees Club, of which Jimmy is cochairman (with Dr. Stephen Humphrey). He's turned an old quotation into a Manatee maxim: "*Each species is the spoke in a magic wheel; to lose one is to diminish the whole!*" His fifteen-year commitment (as of 1996) is something of a show-business exception—though Farm Aid (performing since 1985 with Willie Nelson, John Mellencamp, Neil Young) is more of Jimmy's ilk. (Today's nationwide number: 1–800–432–JOIN.)

Meanwhile, Florida is still number one . . . in human boat-caused wrecks, accidents, deaths. As for the manatees themselves—who can only swim fifteen miles an hour—their mortality rate hasn't much changed: 84 dead in 1993, and 120 in 1994.

So, in 1994, Jimmy was once again recording radio public-service announcements for Florida and Georgia.

In September of 1995, an unknown Florida tourist with a SAVE THE MANATEE license plate dashed north through Hillsboro Village in Nashville, past Vanderbilt, then swung east on Broadway, past the Wild Boar Restaurant, original site of Lum's, where Jimmy had signed his paper-napkin deal with Buzz Cason in 1969.

Jimmy Grows Up, as Well as Older

■

America is a land of youth-worshippers . . . we are cheating ourselves,
individually and collectively, out of the rewards of maturity by a puerile
refusal to grow up and behave like adults.

—Dorothy Carnegie, *Don't Grow Old—Grow Up* (1956)

Jimmy Buffett: Growing Up" was
the title of a Peter Reilly article in *Stereo Review* back in 1980. Calling
him "one of the few Free Spirits left amongst us . . . frolicsomely open-
minded and open-hearted as he ever was . . . master of the cheerfully
impudent ogle at the world," Reilly still believed that "Jimmy was reaching the listener in softer places than usual" with tighter, less goofy songs
that were "more humanly appealing."

Since "Volcano" hadn't charted as high as he'd hoped, Jimmy was
now digging deeper into his songwriting and forcibly expanding his ever-
widening concert career. Painful as it sounds, Jimmy gained more than
he lost by falling off the radio airwaves. Though it sounds like sour
grapes, many artists with Top Ten hits aren't prepared for the road, and

sometimes go broke (and/or get divorced), flogging their few big hits, then plunging into oblivion when their singles start missing the charts. Albums are built around hits—or, more recently, are supposed to cause them—and usually stop selling without them.

Except for those rare acts with concert followings. "Buffett's concerts are like visiting an ocean resort after Labor Day," said Mike Joyce of the *Washington Post* in 1981.

As John Swenson summarized in *The New Rolling Stone Record Guide* (1983): "Buffett is a protean figure—part comic, part drunkard, an inconsistent but occasionally great songwriter, leader of an ersatz country-rock group called the Coral Reefer Band." Robert Christgau had praised a number of Buffett albums in his *Rock Albums of the '70s: A Critical Guide,* deciding that he's "certainly more likable than the average professional rakehell—he's complex, he's honest, he takes good care of his sense of humor, and above all he doesn't come on like a hot shit." But he omitted Jimmy completely in his 1980s sequel guidebook.

■ ■ ■

Already Irving Azoff was fighting with MCA, which he claimed owed several million dollars in royalties to Steely Dan's Walter Becker and Donald Fagen, for "material breach of contract." Eventually, Azoff sued MCA—partly out of his frustration over their handling of Jimmy Buffett: "I alleged they were so inept, they didn't legally constitute a record company at all." Frederick Burger of the *Miami Herald* said Jimmy wanted *off* MCA, but was going to give them a last album, titled *My Dog Ate My Homework and Other Great Excuses.* Azoff lost the case, but at least Jimmy wasn't dropped in the early Eighties when the record industry sank deeper and deeper into the mire of moneyless muck.

Acts that had struggled into prominence in the early Seventies were by now making huge demands—which the record companies sometimes met to their own disaster. President Carter's double-digit inflation had, in part, opened the Oval Office door to President Reagan, who cleverly reduced inflation by ballooning the national debt.

As record albums rose in price, home taping fulfilled the American dream of self-reliance, inciting record companies to rally their usual antagonists, publishers and songwriters, to form the Coalition to Save America's Music. The domestic cassette conspiracy followed the sheet-music photocopying scandal—reprint piracy by the Chicago Catholic churches and the University of Texas. While the U.S. Congress pondered the tape trauma, the record companies, in desperation, began closing down pressing plants, warehouses, and their smaller local offices.

In 1981 MTV started its twenty-four-hour-a-day eternal music-video television marathon, further hoisting songs out of their vinyl grooves.

Recording artists now had to pay for their videos from their royalties, which—hopefully—were increased by the videos.

■ ■ ■

Coconut Telegraph arrived in February 1981, and while it only went to Number 30 in pop, the song quality had not abated.

The title number on Side One is a journalistic spoof, mocking sensational news items ("I'm not one to deal in gossip / But was he that big a fool?"). The melody is snappy.

"Incommunicado" (written with Deborah McColl and M. L. Benoit) alludes to novelist John D. MacDonald (1916–1986) and his detective hero, Travis McGee, at Cedar Key near Jimmy's own house. In the novels, McGee lives on a houseboat. (Jimmy sells MacDonald novels in his Margaritaville stores.) But actor John Wayne is the song's real hero, having died in 1979—inspiring Jimmy to drive up Independence Pass over Aspen and stroll over the Continental Divide, awed by the vast expanse below, somehow thinking also of Travis McGee. He remembers heading for Leadville, eating some Mexican food, then composing his song while heading back to Aspen. Jimmy nostalgically honors films like *Red River* and *The Man Who Shot Liberty Valance*.

"It's My Job" by Mac McAnally defends sleeping late and writing songs, jeering at mundane employment ("any manual labor I've done purely by mistake"). It's his job to be "better than the best," stating in no uncertain terms Jimmy's modest goal. McAnally "reminds me of me seven years ago," Jimmy said. (He's a session picker—an artist with many of his own albums—who told the *Tennessean*'s Robert K. Oermann, "All my stuff is left of center of the mainstream.") The song was released as a single before the album, stopping at Number 57 (Jimmy's *last* pop *hit*).

In "Growing Older But Not Up," Jimmy says his "metabolic rate is pleasantly stuck"—that he would rather "die while I'm living than live while I'm dead."

Those three songs are Buffett standards—as are three more from Side Two. Not a bad average for an album minimized by the critics. "The Weather Is Here, Wish You Were Beautiful" manages a new, comical rhyme like Ogden Nash (or Lord Byron in *Don Juan*)—"beautiful," with "the daiquiri's too fruitful." The collaboration with David Loggins, "Island," has a nice Forties sound (preceded by a 1934 Guy Lombardo Number 1 song, "Stars Fell on Alabama"). The last song on the album is the enchanting "Little Miss Magic," a tribute to daughter Savannah Jane; who else would describe a child entranced by a ceiling fan? Jimmy claims (as of 1980), "Your mother's still the only other woman for me." (Once Savannah pointed to a location on the globe and told her daddy she'd once been a Chinese princess. And he feels that a father who doesn't write a song about his daughter deserves to go to hell.)

■　■　■

The daughter-named boat, *Savannah Jane*, was now being kept at Jimmy's additional home at Baie St. Jean in St. Martin. (Janie and Savannah Jane were often there as well.)

Sailboat journalist Ron Attaway remembers having dinner with him at L'Entrepont on St. Barts. He reported that Jimmy had successfully blended his first two loves, music and the sea ("not necessarily in that order"), with his third—food. Attaway documented his dinner: *calalou* (okra soup), fish soup (with French bread and dollops of aioli), curried pork, and freshwater Dominican shrimp—followed by a fluffy mushroom omelette. Jimmy was eating anything he wanted . . . but very little of it. (Dolly Parton would one day endorse a similar diet plan.)

Attaway reported that Jimmy liked shooting birds, doves, quail, ducks, and fishing for speckled trout in Alabama bays. When Attaway was wearing his "Jimmy Buffett—1981—Coconut Telegraph Tour" baseball hat in South Carolina, one of his boatmates told him that Jimmy had been up the road, playing and singing in a club. Two days later a man on the dock spotted his visor and said that Jimmy had been riding a ferryboat to Daufuski, playing and singing.

"That's it," concluded Attaway. "You put Jimmy Buffett on a boat, and that's where he is: home."

■　■　■

Even Aspen was sometimes home. On June 25, 1981, he played Snowmass at possibly his most unusual concert. Around five thousand people showed up as part of the thirteenth annual "deaf camp picnic," as two onstage interpreters conveyed to the non-hearing, through sign language, the immortal messages about a pirate who had pissed away his smuggling profits, expatriated Americans exiled in the Banana Republics—and, of course, a Margaritaville beach lounger. The money-raising was facilitated by vast barbecue and beer sales to the deaf kids, supplying seventy percent of the school's budget for the coming year.

John Denver was the usual lead act—Jimmy and Denver had played the year before—but since Denver was right now "somewhere over China," it was Jimmy's turn as headliner. (Denver was busy distancing himself from his wife.) Back in 1976, Denver had purchased a thousand acres at Snowmass himself to establish his own antinuclear program, Windstar. He and his colleagues felt the wind and the sun were better for mankind than nuclear power.

John Deutschendorf, alias John Denver, was in Denver on June 8, 1982, for a Windstar concert with Judy Collins . . . and Jimmy. It was a "mobilization for peace" benefit, even as other such demonstrations were rocking across the country.

■　■　■

Jimmy's personal life was cleaning up, but it would have been an invasion of privacy to reveal it. His audiences were still addicted to illicit topics. In 1981 in New York City, he sang an unrecorded substitute verse of "Margaritaville"—after breaking his leg and cruising back home, instead of using booze in the blender for his medication, he said, "God, I still feel pain / I wish I had some cocaine / But that's been gone since early this morn." The audience sang along with ecstasy.

But the following year he began to apologize for the changes in his narcotic attitude. "Number One, I'm getting old," Jimmy explained to John C. Van Gieson of the *Tallahassee Sentinel Star*. "I mean, when I was nineteen, twenty years old, I could roar all night and go out and cruise on a fishing boat in the morning. All of a sudden you wake up one day and hangovers last two days and they hurt. I don't particularly like to feel bad like that, but I like to have a good time. I like to enjoy life, but I don't do it to the extent I once did. . . . If I drank as much and took as much dope as everybody thought I did, I'd have been dead a long time." That same year he confessed to the *Miami Herald*'s Frederick Burger: "It hurts too much to drink liquor, but I'm not preaching anything. I want to stay around to spend it [the days and years of life]. I don't want to be a wino or flame out." He said he wanted to settle down and open a fishing camp.

Indeed, for all the booze 'n' drug reverences in his songs (and the marijuana passing freely among his audiences), Jimmy's career seems to have been devoid of the chemical upsets afflicting so many others. Seemingly no "no-show" concert cancellations, nor public conflicts with authorities. His abiding addiction is performing—and chronic writing—with all the resultant self-discipline. He has been sober about his work, from his earliest days in Key West, preferring playing in a club to drinking in one (though doing both was best of all). As he said to Terry Rose for Seattle's KIRO radio in 1992, "You asked about drugs—the greatest narcotic is applause." So the B-side to his beach-bum hit persona has *gradually* become "Why don't we get sober and sing."

Still, Fingers Taylor, who toured briefly with James Taylor in 1980 (and assisted his album *Dad Loves His Work*), while otherwise staying with the Coral Reefers, finally had enough. Enough Coral Reefering. Enough coke. Enough booze.

Someone backstage was always handing out cocaine, which, according to the *Atlanta Constitution*'s Frederick Burger, "kept [Fingers] Taylor soaring and allowed him to drink more." On one early-morning arrival in San Francisco, Fingers jumped onto the baggage-claim conveyor belt "and merrily rode it round and round." In the hotel, he tore down the hallway pictures, then unhitched some small chandeliers, stashing them all in his room. Jimmy didn't appreciate Taylor's vandalism, but Taylor felt "everybody knew this wasn't the real world; it was only rock 'n' roll." Taylor and the Coral Reefers were driven to the shows by a chauffeur, and someone else would "push them onstage, even if they couldn't walk."

Fingers Taylor said: "People were always backstage giving me cocaine. I never had to pay for it. I could spot 'em. But drinking was my favorite thing. Then I'd take a Valium to help me get to sleep." He was the last one to go to bed—others wanted to sleep, but he *needed* partying ("I couldn't get enough"). When Taylor staged a party, "We're talking big-time. Every four or five nights on the road, we'd tie one on."

Yes, his Coral Reefer cavalcade career "was like a ten-year-long party in some respects." But if Taylor wanted to grow older, he would simply have to grow up. "I wanted to keep living. I didn't have any particular aspiration to be the next Hank Williams." Williams, after all, completed his recording tenure with the assistance of chloral hydrate—a time-honored prescription, which painter-poet Dante Gabriel Rossetti also utilized for *his* creative termination in 1882.

In May 1983 Fingers Taylor woke up—for almost the last time, having nearly overdosed with whiskey and sleeping pills. Admitting that he was an alcoholic (how many entertainers—and/or writers—are that honest?), he checked into a hospital detoxification program in his hometown, Jackson, Mississippi. "A lot of musicians think they play better when they're drunk or high. I certainly fell into that syndrome . . . I made a lot of money playing all those years with Buffett. Spent it. You know, it's only rock 'n' roll."

Taylor began playing (and singing) in small clubs with maybe fifty customers, counseling younger alcoholics, and promoting his own album, *Harpoon Man* (1984). At one point, Jimmy got Taylor to provide a musical tape to use onstage in his absence. When his audiences would scream for Fingers, Jimmy would oblige by stepping on a button so that a full-sized cutout picture of Taylor would pop up, synchronized with the taped music.

Inevitably, one day he rejoined Buffettville . . . a grown-up who had now grown older (his 1989 MCA album, *Chest Pains,* was produced by Michael Utley).

■　■　■

Alas, the once-resplendent drug charisma was losing its luster.

In 1980, Nashville lady Charlotte Nugan learned of her husband's supposed suicide in Sydney, Australia—his Nugan Hand bank was an alleged drug-money laundromat, tainted with CIA connections. In November 1980, a naked sixteen-year-old girl was found in the Los Angeles house of a popular entertainer, wasted away in intoxicationville. He was charged with illegal possession of grass, coke, Quaaludes, and contributing to the delinquency of a minor. The following month, singer-songwriter Tim Hardin ("If I Were a Carpenter," "Misty Roses") died of heroin. And in March of 1982, David Crosby (of Crosby, Stills and Nash) was arrested for driving with an illegal pistol, while under the influence of cocaine.

Even President Reagan began meddling with the uncivil rights of Florida tourists stoned on vacation. While drug-running accusations would later animate the Iran-Contra concert, in the spring of 1982 his administration set up roadblocks on Jimmy's immortal A1A, shaking down all cars heading up from the Keys for any drugs or illegal aliens. Traffic was backed up for twenty-three miles—and "tempers and bladders backed up for at least as far," wrote Stuart B. McIver in *Hemingway's Key West* (1993). On April 2, the Key West mayor and his political co-rebels founded the "Conch Republic" in retaliation—by declaring secession from the U.S. (and war along with it!), tossing a loaf of stale Cuban bread in the air to affirm their revolt. Key West tourists today are offered Conch Republic T-shirts, flags, silver coins, passports, etc. Each year there are Conch Republic ceremonies and celebrations— like Margaritaville (or the Kingdom of Redonda), it's one more whimsical Caribbean empire. A political exercise of Southern states' rights (and rites).

Jimmy was even pinned with a ribbon in 1984, appointing him as Conch ambassador to Margaritaville ("Two similar states of mind in which the only real crime is wearing a tie").

■   ■   ■

His *Coconut Telegraph* tour notwithstanding, Jimmy was still spending summertime at Snowmass. "I enjoy the summers here more than anything else," he told interviewer MarLyn. "I'm just not a cold-weather person. Christmas is fine here. I plan to add a writing studio facing the river over there, with a pond and a swimming pool." Then he grinned. "When I finally get it all done, Janie will probably divorce me and I'll end up living in a trailer in Basalt."

Janie added that while Jimmy was off fishing in the Caribbean in the spring, she and daughter Savannah Jane would visit her parents in South Carolina. As for his obsession with cooking: "He works so hard on the road that when he comes home he needs a lot of things to do to stay busy." Jimmy's typical Colorado recreation was softball and tennis— which usually led to four dinner parties a week, with an average of fourteen guests. He called his softball team the Downvalley Doughboys, and since most were middle-aged, "They are chunkers and like to eat."

Jimmy did most of the cooking, such as Jambalaya soup: "a variation of my Mississippi grandmother's recipe." He mixed hot sausage and rice with cracked blue crab, letting it cook for around four hours. He even had fresh seafood flown in from Mobile on Rocky Mountain Airlines—five pounds of fresh crab, ten pounds of shrimp, several flounder—thanks to an old high-school girlfriend now running a business. And Jimmy poured the chocolate icing over a seven-layer Doberge cake (a New Orleans recipe). "It's wonderful to see the expressions on people's faces when you cook them a fresh West Indies salad or a crawfish dish or stone crabs," said Jimmy to John Van Gieson. "I'm a tyrannical cook, though. I won't let anybody in my kitchen. It's like I'm the captain of the ship." A typical dinner welcomed actress Anjelica Huston, who won an Oscar for Best Supporting Actress for *Prizzi's Honor,* with Jack Nicholson. The table was decorated with orchid sprays, and the floor featured a Colombian rug with Picasso's *Three Musicians* woven into it. Jimmy might have played piano for the guests—an electric Yahama, a Christmas gift from Janie one year. (With a recording machine inside it, he could save instant melodies when a songwriting idea hit him.)

The house was strewn with magazines, and MarLyn reported that he was writing a satire for *Inside Sports,* plus a short story for *Esquire.*

Savannah Jane liked to run around the yard in her cowgirl boots and white pinafore, pointing to the strawberry plants and telling MarLyn, "They are the wrong color now, but will be red like the flowers soon and then you can eat them."

Her father was planning to sail to the South Pacific that fall, for musical enchantment: "I know the Caribbean, so now it's off to Tahiti and Bora Bora, through the rat-holes and unknown islands where Somerset Maugham did some of his best writing."

Maugham went to Hawaii in 1916—like Jimmy at Montserrat, visiting a volcano (Kilauea on Hilo island)—and en route to Samoa, met the whore whose real name he immortalized in his unauthorized tale "Miss Thompson" (1921), which became the 1932 movie *Rain,* and eventually *Miss Sadie Thompson* (1953). His novel *The Moon and Sixpence* (1919), about painter Paul Gauguin, who lived in Tahiti, was another success.

■   ■   ■

Jimmy postponed his trip until 1982, heading back to the Bennett House studio in Franklin to record *Somewhere Over China* in October and November of 1981. "He's really broadened himself," photographer friend Tom Corcoran told John Van Gieson, after the album appeared. Jimmy had been reading classic novels by Faulkner over the past few years, and a quote from *Mosquitoes* highlighted the album cover ("The boy that belongs to a secret pirates' gang and who dreams of defending an abstraction with his blood hasn't quite died out before twenty-one"). "He's grown up very nicely," continued Corcoran. "He's expanded his horizons as the opportunities arose"—such as sneaking off to Mexico, not telling even his wife or manager, and sequestering himself in a hotel with no telephone to write the album.

The opening song—"Where's the Party?"—was written with Steve

Goodman and Bill LaBounty, its theme similar to Dolly Parton's "Two Doors Down" (1978). Reviewer Bill Lammers complained that Jimmy's singing didn't convey "the humorous insight his lyrics contain," and the *Nashville Banner*'s Michael Erickson said it was "hardly from the same bottle as 'Margaritaville.'"

A song with a good melody is "I Heard I Was in Town," written with his veteran keyboardist Michael Utley, dedicated to Key West citizens (now and especially then)—no doubt a David Allen Coe riposte. Utley was a graduate of the Dixie Flyers backup band on Jerry Jeff Walker's 1970 album, *Bein' Free* (he'd moved to Miami that year), and has been in Jimmy's grooves since his first ABC album. "It wasn't till 'Margaritaville' that Jimmy wanted a full-time piano player," Utley said in the *Coconut Telegraph* (1995). "It's very exciting—I don't think I could ever completely retire." The song itself was inspired by false rumors about Jimmy's whereabouts—drug agents had spotted him at parties two thousand miles away from where he really was, and he'd been seen in countries where even he had never traveled.

The last song on Side One was the title tune, with enduring music and a sentimental yearning for becoming a modern-day Marco Polo, air-traveling over the Himalayas and Peking—"between fact and fantasy / Still six thousand miles away" from where Jimmy really wanted to be, putting "a little distance / Between causes and effects."

The best song on the flip side is "If I Could Just Get It on Paper," dedicated to William Faulkner, agonizing over Jimmy's prose-writing future—simple words may turn into clever phrases, and chapters into books, "but it's harder than it looks." You can say (sing!) that again. Like Side Two's opening track, "When Salome Plays the Drum," the tune itself is pleasant; at his best, Jimmy knows melodies are more important than lyrics (the most painful of all songwriting truths). The closing number, "On a Slow Boat to China," is one more big-band cover (seven chart versions 1948–49, including Benny Goodman's).

Reviewer Michael Erickson said that for anyone but Jimmy, the album would be "great," but for him it was merely "good," a rather stereotypical comment, as reviewers increasingly began to praise certain cuts on Buffett albums without otherwise rating them terribly high—Jim Knoblauch said it had "a few slip-ups or unrealized goals," yet closed by telling Jimmy, "Keep up the good work," whereas Parke Puterbaugh in *Rolling Stone* wondered how hard Jimmy really *wanted* to work.

■　■　■

Somewhere Over China charted in early '82, peaking at Number 31 with no chart single. But "Key Largo," sung by Bertie Higgins (written with Sonny Limbo), went to Number 8 that same spring, on the obscure Kat Family label (CBS subsidiary).

Higgins, born the same year as Jimmy (1946) in Tarpon Springs, Florida, had been a singer in a Florida band, the Roemans, on ABC Records long before Jimmy (mid-1960s). Their discoverer, Felton Jarvis, produced John Hartford's "Gentle on My Mind." When Higgins's girlfriend moved out, he moaned that "we had it all / Just like Bogie and Bacall" . . . and the song brought her back. If Jimmy were to cut it today, it would chart again.

Higgins's album, *Just Another Day in Paradise,* went to Number 38, with good tunes like "Casablanca" and the title cut. Sweet pop singing, too. Higgins recorded in Atlanta, thanks to Bill Lowery, a famous music publisher with decades of Nashville renown ("Young Love," "Games People Play," "I Never Promised You a Rose Garden," among others). Higgins's follow-up, *Pirates and Poets,* mentions Errol Flynn and Hemingway in the title song.

■ ■ ■

"Despite what they call themselves, the Moral Majority is not the majority in America," Jimmy told John Van Gieson. "The majority of people in America are hardworking and like to get out and have a good time on weekends." He said that his goal onstage for two hours was to make them forget their day jobs and daily troubles. "If my music is a salve or a tonic to them, then I feel great."

In Baton Rouge that March, he sang "Pelican Summer Sun," an unrecorded song he'd written years before on Bourbon Street. He and Deborah McColl sang "Steamer" together. Jim Clinton of the *Baton Rouge State Times* said that "he never takes himself too seriously. His stage presence is commanding but benign. It is terribly difficult to dislike him. At the Assembly Center Thursday night, no one tried."

During his show at Nashville's Municipal Auditorium that April, he repeatedly "took contextually related potshots at religion, organized and otherwise," wrote *Billboard*'s Edward Morris. "In this born-again age, his sniping was downright refreshing."

Also that month, Jimmy visited Liz Ashley in New York, to tape a cameo for *All My Children,* the ABC-TV soap opera. Ashley threw herself into his arms for a picture in *People* ("Ashley Gets Buffetted"). "He's like my baby brother," she reflected. "When one of us is nailed down in a hot gig, generally the other comes running."

■ ■ ■

The Ninth Annual Faulkner and Yoknapatawpha Conference was held on August 4, 1982, at "Ole Miss"—the University of Mississippi at Oxford, Mississippi. Recalled B. C. Hall and C. T. Wood in *Big Muddy: Down the Mississippi Through America's Heartland:* "Among those who had paid their respects in recent months were novelist John Updike, poet James Dickey, Justice Sandra Day O'Connor, playwright Beth Henley, actors Ed Asner and Tommy Lee Jones, film director Calvin Skaggs, and pop icon Jimmy Buffett."

Present, too, were Jimmy's future literary friends, novelists Willie Morris and Barry Hannah.

Hollywood Daydreamin'

■

There's a huge baby-boomer audience out there, and they're being overlooked. They're the people my music is aimed at, and I think that they would go for a film with a good story with characters and humor that remind people of the fun and humor that really meant something to us back in the Sixties.

—Jimmy, *Chicago Tribune*, July 13, 1986

I came to this Faulkner conference because I am Southern and I am originally from Mississippi," Jimmy told the Associated Press. "As a writer, I see a lot of analogies between what I am writing about and what Faulkner wrote about. Faulkner drew most of his themes from the world around him, and that is what I try to do with my songs. Basically everything I write about is drawn from everyday experiences."

Fittingly, Faulkner's favorite book was A. E. Housman's *A Shropshire Lad*—immortal lyric poetry, reminiscent of ancient English balladry, paralleling modern country music's timeless folk origins. A copy rests on the shelf of Faulkner's home in Oxford, Mississippi.

Jimmy was planning a book of his own, *My African Friend and*

Other Stories, whose title tale would be a novella (based on his song), accompanied by short stories, some unedited magazine pieces, maybe even some poems. "It'll just be a small book. This will be a good preliminary thing to do before I hit forty, and try my major work. If it takes off, we'll look for a New York publisher."

An Ole Miss visiting lecturer offered to write the introduction: Willie Morris. Born in Jackson, Mississippi, he had edited *Harper's* magazine when Nixon and Kissinger were slowly withdrawing the U.S. from Vietnam, at the cost of an extra eighteen thousand American boys. Morris wished Kissinger had joined the soldiers himself! He had written a prizewinning memoir, *North Toward Home* (1967), awash with Mississippi Delta nostalgia and wired with New York City excitement, as well as many other books. Morris wanted Jimmy for his own publisher, Yoknapatawpha Press, named after Faulkner's imaginary county. But Jimmy's book wouldn't appear, as had been announced, for Christmas 1983; in December 1983 he was still talking about Morris adding the "finishing touches."

■ ■ ■

Ole Miss even asked Jimmy to become a visiting professor—as did the University of Florida! While he apparently declined these offers, local writer-in-residence Barry Hannah became another friend. Hannah's own fiction was fairly fraught with surrealistic Southern humor and social irony, mixing Civil War flashbacks with Vietnam War tragedy.

Jimmy and Hannah took time to work together on a movie script, *Evening in Margaritaville.* Jimmy sat down at the same table where Faulkner had completed his novel *Absolem Absolem*—owned by Yoknapatawpha Press (one of whose founders was Faulkner's niece)—and finished working on the script. Naturally the title became *Margaritaville.*

By October, Jimmy was saying that former *National Lampoon* editor P.J. O'Rourke was now writing (rewriting?) his screenplay, to be finished in January 1983. The *National Lampoon* had inspired the demented collegiate comedy *Animal House* (1978), starring Jimmy's pal John Belushi.* O'Rourke is a *Rolling Stone* political editor, an iconoclastic humorist, and author of best-selling nonfiction (*Parliament of Whores, Give War a Chance*).

Jimmy hoped that *Margaritaville* could be produced the following summer, set in Key West and Cedar Key. He assumed Universal Pictures would do it, for a mid-1984 release. "It will be a message movie," he told the *Miami Herald*'s Frederick Burger. "Yeah, it's going to have a moral: 'Don't take things too seriously.' Pure escapism.

"I play myself currently as the narrator, looking back ten years at a

---

*Belushi enjoyed punk-rock pioneers the Dead Kennedys' song, "Too Drunk to Fuck," a possible sequel to Jimmy's "Why Don't We Get Drunk."

bar in Margaritaville. It's more like an *Our Town* approach." In other words, Key West circa 1971, but not too autobiographical. "It's going to be more of a thinking movie than *Animal House,* but it's going to be funny." Jimmy aimed to do a few cameos, while using for main actors some soap-opera "recognizable faces" who wouldn't be a "big pocketbook" expense.

"I've been working on it for four years," Jimmy told the *Tennessean's* Sandy Neese in 1983. "It's gonna happen. . . . It's a coconut rock 'n' roll, a tropical musical." He was by now working on a "second draft" of the film.

■　■　■

In November 1983, he was working with ex-Monkee Michael Nesmith, now a television producer. Actor Harrison Ford had introduced them in Aspen the previous year, near Christmastime. Jimmy had gone down to his parents' home in Daphne, Alabama, to work on the script. "The movie isn't going to win an Academy Award," he declared to Lynn Van Matre of the *Orlando Sentinel,* "but it has a good, fun story line." He said he'd borrowed from William Faulkner's Yoknapatawpha County to create his own mythical island with palm trees.

Jimmy planned to walk on at the start of the film and announce, "Nothing you see on the screen in the next ninety minutes is *important.* If you're one of those people who goes to the movies to have your life changed, I'd suggest you get your money back and wait for a foreign film. If you want to have a good time, stay."

"Well, Jimmy," said Nesmith, "however it turns out, in twenty years it'll be just another four o'clock movie on TV."

Film shooting was to start in March of '84—then didn't. It was "back on the front burner," he told the *Tennessean's* Robert K. Oermann in April. "I've revitalized the treatment for it; everyone in Hollywood likes it now." All he needed was somebody to do "the final screenplay."

Yet in June 1984 he said to reporter Eddie Menton that while he wrote the story, Terry Southern was going to do the script. "We've put together a production company and will do the movie ourselves."

■　■　■

On *Nashville Now* (TNN) in October 1984, Jimmy sang the missing stanza of "Margaritaville," about "old men in tank tops." Singer Brenda Lee asked host Ralph Emery, "He's going to make a movie out of that?"

"We're actually going to start it up in April. We're shooting it in the Bahamas. Cast of thousands."

"Who's going to be in the picture?" asked Emery.

"*Me.*" Jimmy then admitted that there would be other familiar faces— no doubt old acquaintances who owed him favors (or vice versa).

The plot?

"It's a story of a little, laid-back island—and condo developers come to the island. And what ensues? *The Battle of Margaritaville!*"

"Is it going to have fistfights?"

"Blender wars. If it doesn't kill me, it should be pretty good."

■ ■ ■

Down in Key West in 1985, he informed local reporter Betty Williams that he had written his film script about this very place. "If you stay in this town long enough, ridiculous things will happen that are fun to write about . . . all the crazy things happen." He called Margaritaville "a microcosm of Key West. It's a place where crazy people hang out and are not afraid to be crazy. . . . I couldn't live in Los Angeles and I don't particularly care to live in New York except for a couple of weeks out of the year."

By now Jimmy was "touching up" his latest draft, for Nesmith to start producing in January of 1986. "Boy, does that make me feel good," he told David Kronke of the *Dallas Times Herald*. "That's seven years for me. Everything seems to be in place to make it happen, to make it a quality piece of work. That's important. Hell, I could've gotten it done five years ago, but to retain some control and to insure it represents what Margaritaville is supposed to be—that's just as important to me."

Jimmy once met a woman who told him, "I'm twenty-one years old and I never read a book and I'm proud of it." So, as he explained to the *Chicago Tribune* in 1986, "Just to show the dumbness of that woman, I took that line and put it in my movie." But thus far, his attempts at wooing Hollywood had failed, despite his belief that there was a market for "a rock 'n' roll comedy" aimed at the post–World War II generation.

"I don't know how film deals are made out there in California. I see movies that are horrible pieces of crap get made all the time. They're in a phase right now of making teenage movies, and they see *Margaritaville* as old hat. . . . I don't mean for this to sound like 'The World According to Jimmy Buffett,' but by going out and playing live shows, I see more of America than most people. If somebody did something with a little bit of intelligence and humor and subtlety, it's not going to be thrown off the air."

Someone had even offered him some independent money to make the film, which he was now considering. The script needed to be rewritten, as a low-budget movie, for some musicians to perform in "who have acting capabilities." He was blocking out time that fall to keep working on it. He told Robert K. Oermann that year how Hollywood said, "Oh, that was in the 1970s." He was thankful that Michael Nesmith thought otherwise.

He expounded the plot for Craig Modderno's 1986 *USA Today* interview: "The film is about two guys who end up on a South Seas island, who have an adventure. It's a rock 'n' roll, Robinson Crusoe–type fantasy." He qualified it by saying that most rock 'n' roll movies put the music ahead of the comedy and the adventure. "This will have all three. I figure twenty-two years onstage has prepared me for most acting roles. I could be a believable character, but I think Macbeth would be too far a stretch for this Key West conch.

"I'm going to shoot *Margaritaville,* though, if we have to do it in video," Jimmy promised Todd Everett of the *Los Angeles Herald Examiner* in July. "I figure we're going to play to seven hundred thousand people this summer, and if there's not a market there for a major motion picture, there's still a very viable audience for a home video."

Meanwhile, he had written, then abandoned, a play written for Broadway. "They said I could sell out eight shows in six days, gross two hundred fifty thousand and probably lose twenty thousand. I said: 'What . . . ?'"

■ ■ ■

Then Michael Nesmith quit the film project when Robin Williams' movie *Club Paradise* appeared in 1986—about tourists visiting a teenaged resort, in a script rated PG due in part to drug jokes. Ex–*Newsweek* editor Terry McDonnell had just started the popular-culture zine *Smart,* so Jimmy helped back his magazine, and the two of them rewrote the *Margaritaville* script. In early 1988, McDonnell compared it to "a modern Hope-Crosby saga set in the Caribbean."

"I've battled for years trying to get a screenplay of *Margaritaville* written," Jimmy said at the Miami Book Fair in 1989. He said "the deal" was more important in Hollywood than the integrity of the screenplay—that they were making it look "like *La Cage aux Folles* meets *Godzilla.* To create a myth is a tricky thing to do—their movie was not what I envisioned *Margaritaville* to be."

His old schoolmate and fellow club musician Rick Bennett helped at one point. "It ended up there was so much money owed on the damned thing that it got dropped. And Jimmy got disillusioned on it real fast. Jimmy's point is: It's fine if it's working, and if you're putting it together and the magic is there. When people start jumping on it before it's even there, it almost foreshadows what's going to happen, you know? Everybody claimed to have a piece of it. It was EMI who had it in L.A.— by the time they gave the bill and charged everything, it just became a nuisance. Some things pass. Some things you can't come to visit again."

Yet in his 1992 book, *The Parrot Head Handbook,* Jimmy said that he was still attempting a film version of "Margaritaville." He said he would mix in all the places he'd visited, and feature a "twelve-volt man," and start a new genre. And in 1994 Gary Graff of the Knight-Ridder news service said the film was still being considered, "like a fish in a box that won't die."

■ ■ ■

Since Margaritaville is a mythical place, perhaps it needs to stay floating in the minds of the Parrot Heads, rather than on the screen. Or maybe Jimmy needs to pay for it all himself—Willie Nelson invested around $2 million to launch his low-budget but credible *Red Headed Stranger* (1987), based on his 1975 recording, and advertising it with Wrangler jeans as a sponsor.

Montserratean M. P. Shiel's novel *The Purple Cloud* attracted Hollywood as early as 1927—twenty-six years after it was published—but its film version appeared twelve years after his 1947 death, in 1959. And alcoholic world-traveler Malcolm Lowry (1909–1957), with a Buffett-like love of landscape and water, spent almost a decade writing his popular novel about Mexico, *Under the Volcano* (1947). Thirty-seven years after it was published, a film was finally made, in 1984—after sixty-six screenplay versions! Two posthumous cinematic achievements.

IF THE PHONE DOESN'T RING, IT'S PROBABLY HOLLYWOOD, headlined the *Chicago Tribune* back in 1986. So why not call television? Johnny Cash struggled for years to get his minor masterpiece, *Murder in Coweta County*, onto CBS-TV in 1983. Jimmy could maybe shovel *Margaritaville* onto HBO cable television, or perhaps the Nashville Network. After a couple of TV runs, there'd be a video out there . . . and most Parrot Heads could wend their way to the tape rental store.

From Tahiti to Nashville

■

I've always had a good Country following. I started out in Nashville, and I couldn't get anybody to listen to what I did down there. It was so closed-doored. Now I think it's the only place to go.

—Jimmy to Jill Warren, *Indianapolis Star,* June 22, 1984

It *is* a long way over there. That's why I like it. I've been in Tahiti for six weeks on two trips this year, and I'm going back in January," Jimmy told the *Miami Herald*'s Frederick Burger in the fall of 1982. He'd been to Hawaii for a concert; then his friend Tom Moffatt took him to Tahiti for another show. Afterward, at Moffatt's house above Cook's Bay, Jimmy gazed down at the view below him, when suddenly the calypso song "One Particular Harbor" rose in his imagination (cowriter: Bobby Holcomb). It exudes wanderlust—"ruled my world from a pay phone"—pining for his younger days in the Caribbean sunshine. . . . One more Buffett concert classic, ignored by radio the following year, when it became the title tune for his next album.

Meanwhile, he *was* getting radio play—drinking Miller beer and advertising it. (*Rolling Stone* called it "Miller time in Margaritaville." Jimmy said, "This is the closest thing I've had to an AM hit in five years.")

At least he had gotten film exposure in 1982—on the soundtrack of *Fast Times at Ridgemont High,* produced by Art Linson and Irving Azoff. Rated R, this ribald high-school comedy wasn't technically available to high-school kids since, among other information, it supplied schoolgirl fellatio instructions in the cafeteria. Starring Sean Penn, it was directed by Azoff's journalist crony Cameron Crowe (based on his 1981 novel of the same title), touting the slogan "Hey dude, let's party." Penn played Jeff Spicoli, subject of Jimmy's song "I Don't Know (Spicoli's Theme)," written with Mike Utley.

■ ■ ■

"We went through a bunch of horseshit," recalls Coral Reefer Barry Chance, concerning a fiasco circa 1982. "We had finished a tour in Miami on probably Saturday night. This got into some real heavy shit, over a period of a few months. We happened to be going home on a day when there was a shuttle launch, where people would come up on their boats to watch. There was a guy who had a yacht chock-full of cocaine. And he ran it aground, and he abandoned the yacht." The Coast Guard seized it, and soon the culprit was testifying to the United States Treasury that Jimmy, Harry Dailey, Fingers Taylor, Deborah McColl, and Barry Chance were all on board when the boat ran aground!

"Apparently he had an album with everybody's name on it," speculates Chance. "He rattled off all these names. Bob Graham was governor of Florida, so Jimmy had to fly us back to court proceedings three or four times—when we're off tour and he's having to foot the bill for expenses—to fly us to Florida to give depositions. At the time the shuttle was launched, I was already home. I had traded my plane ticket for cash and took a bus back to Nashville. So everybody had perfect alibis. But it really put us through a bunch of shit, and the next time we went to Florida, everybody comes up and says, 'Hey, man, you want to do a bump?' and our whole motto was '*We don't do that anymore.*'"

You can say that again, and Jimmy did. "Whoa, I'm stopping this stuff," he decided when he saw *executives* snorting cocaine. Now, in the 1980s, cocaine, AIDS, and nuclear weapons were threats that bothered him. Finally, in 1985, he said, "I don't endorse the use of drugs," to *USA Today.* "I have outlived all my dangerous vices," he told the same paper's Craig Modderno the following year. "Getting older means you clean up your act. I can't do things as long as I used to. I'd rather spend time with my daughter than go out and get high. I try to stay away from that kind of lifestyle that could have killed me in the past."

■ ■ ■

"The six-inch, dull-colored dusky sparrow, with yellow stripes on its wings and white flecks on its breast," was the excuse for Jimmy's Miami concert on March 20, 1983. "An unlikely coalition"—of Walt Disney Productions, the Audubon Society, and Jimmy—joined forces to try and save a dying species of sparrow. Highways and the human population explosion were wiping out the birds—there were now only five male survivors left. With no females to be found, despite eight years of swamp searches, it was time to breed them ("back-crossing") with a female Gulf Coast sparrow. Then offspring would be further inbred to create a species that was ninety-five percent correct!

Another, hitherto endangered species, MCA Records ("Music Cemetery of America"?), was now receiving protection from Front Line Management. Retired plaintiff Irving Azoff, in 1983, was named president of the company he had sued. Like most major labels, MCA had a prestigious litigation heritage.

In the midst of $6 million in losses in 1979 (causing them to dismantle their A&D staff), they were sued by Ron Alexenburg for $2 million—for closing down Infinity Records. On the positive side, they got a court injunction to halt Olivia Newton-John from escaping to some other label. Then, in 1981, British rocker Elton John sued *them* for breach of contract, so MCA obligingly sued *him* (and David Geffen) for sneaking some of his songs over to Geffen Records. Blues matriarch Ella Fitzgerald also sued them that year, trying retroactively to void her 1951 Decca contract because of their purported accounting incompetence. When MCA allegedly hurt the sale of a Steely Dan album by selling it high, at $9.98, Irving Azoff told *Billboard* in 1981 that it was (naturally) over his "screaming objections."

■ ■ ■

"I decided to come back since I'm staying on the [MCA] label," Jimmy informed *Tennessean*'s Sandy Neese in 1983. "I think Irving will make a big difference. He's a dedicated man. And country music's the only thing that's making money for MCA. I've done eleven albums and been through five regimes at the label. Nobody knew what to do with me. They'd fight me on what singles to release, and I got no tour support. I've survived for fifteen years in this business, and I thought I should be listened to." (The next year, he quipped to the *Tennessean*'s Robert K. Oermann: "I feel like the Filipino cook on the ship who sees the captains come and go. I've been through 'em all, you know?")

Jimmy was in town for Fan Fair, meeting Buzz Cason and Brenda Lee at an MCA showcase (in 1988, Brenda Lee would sue MCA for $20 million). Then, going onstage as a substitute for Loretta Lynn, he did

"Margaritaville"—and the response reminded Sandy Neese that he had some real Nashville followers. Jimmy thought the country audience wasn't much different from his own followers (seventy-five percent of them were much younger than Jimmy!).

That same week, Azoff held a party for MCA acts and their managers at the Stock-Yard restaurant, which in 1985 was taken over by Tree music-publishing magnate Buddy Killen. (For some reason, Killen opposed cocaine being left as a tip for his waiters. In his memoir, he names Jimmy and Fogelberg among his welcomed guests.)

"The country division has been supporting the company," confirmed Azoff to *Variety,* "and as far as I'm concerned, we're going to operate with no budget ceiling [in Nashville]." Yet he ridiculed RCA for signing Kenny Rogers for a $15 to $20 million deal. Later that year at a concert, Jimmy disparaged "Islands in the Stream"—Kenny Rogers's and Dolly Parton's Number 1 country (and Number 1 pop) hit, as if no one could write better ocean tunes than he could. The song (written by the Bee Gees) borrowed its title from a Hemingway novel.

Azoff had purged most of the MCA staff, but said that Jim Foglesong "is expected to remain with the company."

"Irving is brilliant," comments Fogelsong, who as an ABC executive had visited ABC in Los Angeles when Azoff was managing Jimmy. "He does what he thinks he has to do. Just hearing the shouting match going on in the offices and just profanity flying everywhere," with Azoff threatening, "I'll take him off the label. I don't care. Contract or no." Later Fogelsong saw *Azoff* leaving, with one of the ABC executives sighing, "Whew, that guy is *tough!*"

Other MCA country acts included Don Williams, Lee Greenwood, Ray Stevens, Loretta Lynn, Reba McEntire, George Strait, Razzy Bailey, the Oak Ridge Boys, and Barbara Mandrell. "She's one of my favorites," Jimmy said of Mandrell, "and if you believe that, I have some swamp land in Florida for sale." (In 1986 Mandrell sued MCA for allegedly withholding $1.2 million in royalties.)

Bruce Hinton was now MCA's Nashville general manager. He'd started almost two decades earlier as an eighty-five-dollar-a-week Warner Brothers warehouse worker. He became a promotion man for Warner/Reprise Records in Los Angeles, then for Columbia Records in New York, then Amos Records in L.A.—followed by his own independent promotional agency. He moved to Nashville in 1984. "From around 1968 to the early seventies, Hollywood was what Nashville is now in terms of lifestyle," he told *Billboard's* Gerry Wood. "All the studios were within four or five blocks. . . . It was a little village. That's long since gone in Hollywood, but thankfully that tight-knit musical community idea is in full bloom here." (Hinton is currently a vice president on the board of directors of the Country Music Association.)

■ ■ ■

Jimmy was touring less, according to Barry Chance, who left the Coral Reefers in 1983. "Jimmy was always so appreciative of his crowds. He knew that the people we played for were the people that put him where he was. And he never lost contact with that." As for the critics' chronic complaint that Jimmy's songs are too similar, Chance says, "I don't agree with the 'repetitiveness' [stigma]. Man, I couldn't hold it against a guy that was writing for his fans."

Fondly, Chance remembers how Jimmy named him "the curse of Hertz Rent-a-Car" since Harry Dailey, the bassman, Fingers, and Chance "got real drunk in Sacramento one night, and we just tore the shit out of this rent-a-car. Just tore the insides out of it, and everything, for some reason—I guess because we *could*. Then we turned the rent-a-car in, and we claimed that somebody had vandalized it and we had had coats stolen out of it. They settled for it." Pause. "One time, right after I pulled this bit, the crew [the Coral Reefers] took a rent-a-car and painted up the driver's side of the car like Richard Petty's race car. Just on the left side. It was always—*constantly*—some kind of horseshit like that, y'know. But it was all laughed off and absorbed, somewhere, through the accountants. Occasionally we *would* have to pay for it. Fingers and I tossed a TV out into the Webb Pierce [guitar-shaped] swimming pool at the Spence Manor [hotel] and it cost us $740." (Earlier, Pierce had flaunted a guitar-shaped pool behind his home, as a tourist attraction, for selling records and tapes—till neighbor Ray Stevens stopped him, for having violated residential zoning with a commercial enterprise. "Music City, U.S.A." does not include the suburbs.)

"One night we were in Tuscaloosa, Alabama, playing a show," Chance remembers. The Reefers were staying in a newly remodeled motel, and after the show, Chance was partying in his room with some Nashville pals. "I had this old gal with me that was drunk—passed out on the bed, all her clothes on, the lights are on, and she's *out*." His friends had to leave; about thirty minutes later when he returned and stuck his key in the door, he learned that the lights were out.

"Well, I thought she'd come to and turned the lights off." So he took off his clothes and climbed into bed to snuggle up close to her. But instead of her, it was some *man!*

"What the fuck are you trying to do?" growled the fellow as Chance snapped on the light.

"It was Buffett. I had gone to the wrong room, but my key fit that door. Thank God it was somebody I knew, because he could have blowed my brains out! Here I go crawling into bed with Buffett with no clothes on—he wakes up real startled, and that scared the shit out of me."

Chance even remembers that "there were some times when Irving [Azoff] and Jimmy were at each other's throats. One time in Oklahoma

City, we're in a motel room, and there's seven or eight of us, and we're getting drunk, and getting wild and everything. Me and Jimmy, we go pour beer in the TV, and Jimmy pulls a real fine picture off the wall, and takes it out of the frame, and turns it over and puts it back in the frame. It's nothing but like cardboard. And he took a Magic Marker and he wrote on it, 'Please send the bill for this to Irving Azoff, Front Line Management.' He was doing everything he could to piss Irving off. Because Irving had pissed *him* off.

"We were in Irving's office one day—Fingers, myself, and Harry [Dailey] and Deborah [McColl], with Jimmy—and we're talking to Irving about our pension. Irving had to take a call, and here we are, a bunch of hillbillies, making a thousand to fifteen hundred a week. Here's little Irving sitting behind his desk, going, 'Yeah, yeah—forty-four mill? Yeah, we can handle that. No problem.' *Click.* He hung up. And we just kind of looked at each other—'*forty-four million, no problem, we can handle that*'—and we then realized we were in a *powerful* office."

Chance regards his Coral Reefer days as unsurpassable. But Jimmy broke up the band, temporarily, around 1983, in order to work on his *Margaritaville* script, so Chance moved to the Nashville Network for a couple of years, playing with such esteemed guitarists as Fred Newell, as well as at Buddy Killen's Stock-Yard restaurant.

As for touring on the road, "It is like war," Jimmy said to Craig Modderno of *USA Today,* recommending that twenty years on the road be compared to Vietnam or Korea. "Most of my peers who have been on the road are either dead or broke."

Barry Chance would have agreed with that: After leaving Jimmy, he was on his last day of touring with Elvis imitator Jimmy "Orion" Ellis. There on the highway, he was but eighteen inches away from drummer R. E. Hardaway when a drunk driver smashed into Hardaway, carrying him over a hundred and thirty yards, legs cut off, face removed, blood and brains all over. Chance was at the funeral with Porter Wagoner (Hardaway was an ex-Wagonmaster).

■ ■ ■

"God's Own Drunk," by Lord Buckley, had appeared on the albums *Living and Dying in ¾ Time* and *You Had to Be There.*

Son Richard F. Buckley, Jr., sued Jimmy in August for $11 million in "copyright infringement." Though Buckley received royalties regularly, he was offended by additional "instances of profanity, or words and phrases of immoral content and bad taste," plus the "drug-culture references" which gave a "false impression" of Lord Buckley. Jimmy's onstage humor was "false, malicious, oppressive, defamatory," et cetera *and* et cetera.

Buckley's attorney supplied a verbatim transcript of the 1962 version (recorded by Jimmy in 1973) next to a transcript of the 1978 live version, with more updated lyrics—"bad-ass ... son-a-bitches ... GOD-DAMN ... scared the shit out of me"—which otherwise upheld Lord Buckley's humorous, alcoholic integrity posthumously.

In 1981 Richard Buckley, Jr., had heard both album versions and signed an agreement with MCA, reaping at least fifty thousand dollars. Unfortunately—for Parrot Head journalists—it never went to court. It would have been a good, live, "You had to be there" interview concert.

In 1985 the lawsuit was dismissed. Since, back in 1973, the recitation had gotten onto an album with lyrics like "Why don't we get drunk and screw," and "Fuck all those west Nashville grand ballroom gowns," Buckley Jr. had long since been "put on notice" as to what to expect.

The defense rested.

But Jimmy didn't. During the case, he had a girl walk onstage displaying the enemy attorney's phone number, while urging his audience to call 'em up ("Let them know what you think of them harassing me"). Other times, he would perform "Lawyer and Asshole," a song dedicated to attorney *and* client—whom he invited to "kiss my ass" since the client's father, Lord Buckley, was turning over in his grave.

■ ■ ■

One Particular Harbour came out in 1983—and didn't make the Top 40. Yet Jimmy spent around a year and a half, off and on, putting it together. ("It was the first album where I didn't go into it as a project and stay right with it till everything was done . . . we meticulously sat and listened to tracks. Before, we never had the support of the record company like we do now.") As ever, some of the songs are "album cuts," while others, including the Tahitian-inspired title tune, have permanent charm.

"Stars on the Water," the opening cut on Side One, is one more concert classic, written by the gifted Nashville singer-songwriter Rodney Crowell, then husband of Rosanne Cash. It alludes to Mobile (Jimmy wishes he'd written it). "California Promises," by Steve Goodman, has an exceptionally pretty melody. Goodman came into the California studio almost by accident, and played the song for Jimmy, according to Goodman's manager, Al Bunetta: "He loved it so much he cut it, then and there." (Goodman died of leukemia in 1984.) Backup singing was by Rita Coolidge (Kris Kristofferson's ex-wife), and a guitar solo by jazzist Earl Klugh.

"Honey Do" (written with Mike Utley), on Side Two, is another 1940s quality pop number, with Mills Brothers–style backup vocals. "We Are the People Our Parents Warned Us About" is one more sing-along, bragging about dodging Vietnam via college, "too dumb or too smart" to be a priest or a Navy officer. Jimmy confesses to getting a guitar and playing "acid rock" in a bar. Once again, songwriter Jimmy changes his hook—to "Where are the flashbacks they all warned us would come?" (He brags about playing afternoon golf!) And "Twelve Volt Man" has a misty melody, and extols an anonymous man down in

Mexico, whom Michael Nesmith discovered (with a Buffett album collection—modestly, not mentioned in the song) singing and playing tapes on a weird battery system. Jimmy wrote it on Yucatan's peninsula, Isla Mujeres. As for "Brown Eyed Girl," it had already been a hit twice (Van Morrison, El Chicano). And he wrote the sentimental-sad "Distantly in Love" on the Huahine beach in the Pacific, having missed his fifth wedding anniversary with Janie, at the opening of her play back in Colorado.

Jimmy told Rex Rutkoski of *Music City News* that the album was intended to "mend fences" since "I was fighting the record company so much—they never worked my last album, *Somewhere Over China*. I was the first one to ever let the Oak Ridge Boys sing on a pop record," recalling "My Head Hurts, My Feet Stink, and I Don't Love Jesus." He said they won't admit being on the record since "they were gospel, then."

■ ■ ■

Jimmy and Buzz Cason were toasting their new business merger that April in Nashville, at the World's End Restaurant at 1711 Church Street, with margaritas, naturally. Buzz's Southern Writers Group U.S.A. had just taken over about sixty Buffett songs from Coral Reefer Music. Jimmy just had to get up and sing a little for the audience (including the Oak Ridge Boys' William Lee Golden, as well as Rodney Crowell . . . with Buzz singing backup, of course).

Jimmy bad-mouthed bad ol' Nashville to reporter Robert K. Oermann. "This town was controlled by a few families. It was not as open as it is now. . . . I'm burying the hatchet, and buying a new Weed-eater. . . . It looks like a lot of cards are falling into place here now, and I want to be in the middle of the deck." He said he hoped "He Went to Paris" would become a hit for someone. Oermann agreed that it "and other Buffett masterpieces could be and might be."

■ ■ ■

That June, Jimmy was recording his next album, *Riddles in the Sand*.

His producer was Jimmy Bowen, whom Azoff had just made Nashville's MCA president. MCA was now fifth of the six companies in Nashville. Bowen would eventually get the label up to Number One. (Tony Brown and Mike Utley would help in the producing.)

"Nashville is such a small town . . . in Los Angeles, entertainment-business people do business from ten to five-thirty. There are few watering holes there where people meet at the end of the day," Bowen told Robert K. Oermann. "Basically they fan out into a city of eight or nine million people after work.

"They don't sleep together, they don't eat together, they don't share each other's traumas and good times like we do here. Here we're a 'city' of five thousand people inside a city of half a million. The entertainment industry is incredibly close. We live with each other. We do our recreations together. There are absolutely no secrets."

Bowen was born in New Mexico in 1937. His daddy was a police chief. He sang an unexpected rock hit on Roulette Records in 1957, "I'm Stickin' with You." Invited to the Grand Ole Opry, Bowen had to restrict his drummer to only playing a snare drum with a brush, hidden behind a curtain. By 1964 he was a producer who coaxed has-been Dean Martin into wasting four hours on a session, instead of one (Bowen had spent twice as long on *his* 1957 hit). The result: "Everybody Loves Somebody" went to Number One, selling fifty thousand copies in one day. Another time, Frank Sinatra, a 1950s rock 'n' roll hater, was cutting a Ray Charles quality blues number, "That's Life," for Bowen. Angry when asked to try it again, Sinatra under friction gave the song its excitement, sneering the closing line, "Myyyyy, myyyyy!" then stormed away. "That's Life" went to Number 4—and "Strangers in the Night," also produced by Bowen that same year (1966), went to Number 1.

Too old for progressive rock, Bowen moved to Arkansas in 1976, commuting to Nashville in a car with a broken muffler, while studying country music firsthand, back in Eureka Springs. Finally he moved to Nashville (1977), cutting sessions at the "outlaw" Glaser Brothers' studio. Hits by Hank Williams, Jr., Mel Tillis, and countless others, made him a maverick mentor as he bounced from company to company, upsetting the sluggish Music Row clique by demanding expensive, digital recordings. At MCA (for the second time), he seemed proud to be so busy he didn't even have an office, preferring the studio. (Studios tended to serve as his second—and sometimes first—home, as his first several wives could testify.)

More than any single person, Bowen booted country music into larger markets, raising album budgets from the $15,000 to $25,000 range to $125,000 at the least.

By the time Buffett and Bowen partied at MCA with *Riddles in the Sand,* Nashville was struggling ahead in spite of the overall record business' "three-year slide" (1979–81). By 1982 country music continued to inch ahead slightly, in what was otherwise "the worst year of setbacks" in the larger record industry, according to Carter Moody of *Music Row* magazine. Studios were improving, as they desperately diversified, doing lots of commercial "jingles." Yet the only new act since 1981 to go gold had been the Judds.

Supposedly Azoff dropped forty-one acts at MCA, so, thanks to conflict of sincere interest, Jimmy was in the front line of five survivors. Jim Fogelsong remembers the hectic early Eighties: "I do remember two specific albums—that almost ninety percent of the ones shipped, were returned. One was shipped five hundred thousand, the other shipped a million." Foglesong left in March of 1984, replaced by Bowen. "Irving was very, very, very fair to me in my severance. I was not fired. In fact, they offered me a better deal than what I had." Foglesong moved to Capitol without missing a day. (Something of a music statesman, he now teaches at Vanderbilt's Blair School of Music.)

■ ■ ■

Jimmy claimed to Jill Warren of the *Indianapolis Star* that "an American music renaissance" was coming out of Nashville, while qualifying his position: "It's not like I went down there in a cowboy suit and rode around on a horse." To Holly Gleason of *Country Song Roundup* he said that people aren't "educated enough to realize what's going on musically in Nashville." If they saw that a record was cut there, they would think, 'Oh, my God, he's gonna put on a suit and sing like Porter Wagoner.'" Jimmy had encouraged the Nitty Gritty Dirt Band to move to Nashville and get with Norbert Putnam. "About a year later, I figured I should take my own advice."

Yes, he and Nashville had "kissed and made up," he told Robert K. Oermann. "My records have been played on country radio, but it honestly wasn't what I was listening to. Lately, I *have* been listening to it, and I've found it's what I like to listen to." He defended the music's sound, the versatility, with "more room to fluctuate musically than in any other form of music." He claimed rock and pop were simply "formulated" these days. At least he could still be acoustic—he believed *he* hadn't changed, but Nashville had. For instance, drumming used to just be "rim tapping, but now they go all-out and really pound away."

■ ■ ■

Despite having boasted about the time taken on *One Particular Harbour,* Jimmy told Michael McCall of the *Nashville Banner,* "We basically came here to do four tracks, and we ended up doing a whole album in six days. The proof of the pudding, I guess, is that I love listening to that record still. *Riddles in the Sand* was "preproduced" in Los Angeles, Jimmy said. "For an album today, it did set a record. We weren't in a rush, it just happened that way." (For some reason, Jimmy Bowen believed that time was money—he and Glen Campbell used to write and produce five songs a week back in 1961.)

"When you're not Michael Jackson, or a boy wearing a dress, it's hard to get on the radio," Jimmy told Mark Schwed of United Press International. Schwed joked that "old rock stars never die. They just become country singers." Jimmy admitted his beach-bum dope image might have kept him off the radio in years past.

Nineteen eighty-four wasn't the best year. Still, *Riddles in the Sand* at least went to Number 87 in *Billboard*—but it hit Number 58 in *Cash Box* (and Number 23 in *Cash Box* for country), and while none of the singles charted in pop, three did in country, extending into 1985.

Including the opener for Side One, "Who's the Blonde Stranger?"

written with Mike Utley, Will Jennings, and guitar player Josh Leo. Once more, an unforgettable melody—but with strong, story-song lyrics. Husband and wife are each off with a blonde (or blond) alternative marriage act. The song was Texas-inspired, where Jimmy had seen horses down by the beach (cowriter Jennings was his "Texas prof"). In fact, it prompted the "Gulf and Western" album cover: Jimmy on the beach, dressed like an aquatic, not urban, cowboy, his horse with a life preserver on the saddle . . . country "crossover," from desert to gulf. It went to Number 37.

The next cut, "When the Wild Life Betrays Me," cowritten, like most of the songs on the album, with Utley and Jennings, went to Number 42. "We wanted to write a good honky-tonk, beer-drinking, late-night closin' song," Jimmy told Sergeant Dick Fellows on an Air Force *Country Music Time* radio interview. With dance-hall, waltz-time rhythm, its melody resembles Dan Fogelberg's "High Country Snows," the title song of his own album the following year.

"Ragtop Day" (also written with Utley and Jennings) was a stock rocker about Friday-night good times, and would have made "an ideal beer commercial," said *Country Rhythm*'s Gary Kenton. Another, unusual song by the writing trio, "Come to the Moon," is an ostensible space-traveling odyssey—actually, an invitation to a lover to come along. Jimmy sings with his alternative voice, the soft lounge voice, mastered in Holiday Inns (rock critics to the contrary, if you can't croon, you can't survive in a hard-liquor bar)—one of Jimmy's best songs, words *and* tune.

But the other chart record was the pretty "Bigger than the Both of Us" (by Rhonda Coullet)—it went to Number 58 in country. As usual, most of the album's melodies competed with the lyrics in quality (such as the last cut on the album, "La Vie Dansante," which became a video), though in some of the album's choruses, he doesn't have enough solo lines . . . maybe too much *choral* reefering.

Side One of the album was aimed at country radio. "Some disc jockeys are so goddamned lazy, that they don't want to flip a record, so you gotta make it easy for them," he told Larry Rhodes in *Country News*. To justify the Caribbean flip side, he claimed rather lamely that "to me, country and Caribbean music go together real well. . . . You know what they listen to in Tahiti? Ferlin Husky and Ernest Tubb. I have a plumber in St. Barts who can speak maybe two or three words in English—and he's got the largest collection of country singles I've ever seen."

■ ■ ■

"Who's the Blonde Stranger?" had finally charted the following March, and the next month (April 2), Jimmy was appearing on Ralph Emery's *Nashville Now* TV program . . . as *guest host*.

"Ralph is in the islands, and I'm in Nashville," he announced. "I hope Ralph's having a good time in the Caribbean."

On the show was Dan Fogelberg, songwriter John D. Loudermilk—and a six-foot-tall, blonde female entertainer. She had recently appeared in the "Who's the Blonde Stranger?" video, in fact. Back in 1973, in an Austin club, she had originally approached Jimmy and asked him to dance with her. "No, man, you're too tall," he responded. But they became friends.

So who's was the blond friend? Marshall Chapman. A Nashville Vanderbilt University graduate (1971), Chapman majored in French "so I could be sure of never getting a job." Small-club dates followed, and major record deals and the usual ups-and-downs. Anyone who can write songs for Olivia Newton-John, Ronnie Milsap, Emmylou Harris, and Tanya Tucker has a talent that won't go away.

With her funky blues band, Marshall Chapman remains one of Nashville's most respected acts.

Floridays Bidness (T-shirts and Salt Ponds)

■

The only "break" anyone can afford to rely upon is a self-made "break."
These come through the application of persistance. The starting point
is definiteness of purpose.

—Napoleon Hill, *Think and Grow Rich* (1937)

For the future, Jimmy might be advised to get an honest job and get
out of the fun rut.

—Fred Bayles, Associated Press, October 3, 1986

I'd better look at some other ave-
nues if I want to keep this lifestyle I've grown accustomed to, Jimmy
said to himself back in 1981. He was irked that people were walking
the streets of Key West, wearing airbrushed Jimmy Buffett T-shirts.
That's about when he started seeking a beer sponsor—and contemplating
issuing some clothes of his own, thinking, *I'm sure going to live by the*
beach when my music career's over, do some fishing and open up a
restaurant.

"I was getting so commercially ripped off in Key West by bad imita-
tions of me, or bad T-shirts or bad singers, and I was catching a lot of
grief for it," he said to *Florida Trend*'s Elizabeth Willson, in her 1991
article "Making Millions in Margaritaville," "because people thought *I*

was ripping everybody off. They thought I had all this Margaritaville this-and-that."

At first he believed that "maybe I'll just open a big club somewhere in Florida and run junkets to me," as he said to Russ DeVault of the *Atlanta Constitution* in 1983. "I can stay on the beach and play four nights a week in my own showroom."

But half a year later he was griping that he was unable to franchise a Margaritaville club in Florida because he couldn't get the trademark rights—too many clubs around the country were already using the name, such as Chi-Chi's Mexican-restaurant chain.

Well, at least down in Mobile, friend Dan Sweet opened up JB's Margaritaville club in 1984—with a licensing agreement insuring a Jimmy gig once a year for the next three years (sounding like Doug Weston's Troubadour contract in L.A.). Jimmy mused about arranging other deals with clubs in Key West, Houston, Texas, and the Virgin Islands.

■　■　■

Back when he landed in Key West in 1971, Jimmy had met a nineteen-year-old girl named Donna, who was making salads next door at Louie's Backyard. She'd come to Key West that same year, via a Greyhound bus from South Carolina. Called Donna Kay "Sunshine" Smith by the 1980s, she told Paul Lomartire of the *Miami News* in 1988 how they "got high and ate coconuts. Whoever went fishing that day came in and brought the fish in, and we lived communally and ate communally."

In the early 1970s Jimmy played a date in Columbia, South Carolina, Sunshine's hometown. She was there for a visit . . . and constituted one-third of the audience in the bar. Her mother fed Jimmy and gave him a place to sleep. He told Sunshine he'd never forget her hospitality.

Around 1983, when he felt his record sales slipping, Jimmy said, "I'd better diversify—so I'll go into business." Sunshine told Lomartire that Jimmy is a "big daddy" who feels obligated to protect some of his long-term allies, such as Steve "Hobbit" Humphrey, his road manager, whom he feared would be out of a job after the band breakup. "Let's start a T-shirt company and you can run it. That way, you can still have a job and take care of your family." Bobby Liberman, later road manager (1988), confirmed Sunshine's testimony to Jimmy's loyalty: "He's a very generous guy. I've got a house in Key West to show for my trouble."

Ironically, Jimmy's uncle (probably Billy Buffett) offered him a tropical T-shirt in 1955—and he refused to wear it! By 1975 he personally owned fifty-seven tropical shirts. . . . His uncle was now claiming credit.

Hobbit had started working for Jimmy as a guitar tuner, and he likes to remember when three members of the road crew jumped onstage wearing bear costumes, then chomped down on Jimmy's sunglasses. Their encore was to hurl potatoes, tomatoes, and heads of lettuce across the stage at him. Such firsthand business experience made Hobbit a natural for the T-shirt enterprise.

Artist Michael La Tona sold Hobbit a box of T-shirts he had designed—and Hobbit showed them to Jimmy, backstage at a Fort Myers concert. Hobbit said he should have his songs illustrated on the shirts, so La Tona produced a "Margaritaville" shirt, followed by "Cheeseburger in Paradise," and "Son of a Son of a Sailor." Hobbit worked frantically to make the business succeed, claiming he couldn't even watch television, there were so damned many T-shirts stacked up in his living room! He turned his garage into the Caribbean Soul T-shirt warehouse, with his daughter functioning as his mail-order assistant, licking stamps for the packages ("but I did let her break every half-hour for a sip of ice-cold water").

By now Jimmy was back in Key West much of the time, in spite of his Nashville foray—and David Allen Coe's obsolete "Jimmy Buffett Doesn't Live in Key West Anymore"—*without Jane*. On March 12, 1984, she formally disclaimed her ownership of their Snowmass property, then in August of the next year, moved with daughter Savannah Jane up to Grandview, New York.

In 1985, promoting *Last Mango in Paris* on the *Tonight Show*, Jimmy told Johnny Carson he'd just had a *date* in New York . . . with wife Janie.

"Wasn't that nice," offered Carson.

"It's nice to date your wife," Jimmy confirmed.

"How long you been married now?"

"I was married about twelve years [actually they were married in 1977], but I haven't lived with my wife for six years. She wanted some space—she lives in Malibu and I live in Key West."

"That's a lot of space," noted Carson.

Jimmy laughed, stirring some audience guffaws.

"That will stretch out a marriage considerably," judged Carson.

"Heh, heh . . . there's theories that you know about marriage in the Eighties. So we date occasionally, and you don't get into fights. I got over forty—I got a little spoiled in a two-room house where they try to move stuff in and you don't want it there. And there's nothing like giving half your income up to make you inspired to write more songs."

"You'd like to have this both ways," said Carson. "You'd like to have a marriage over *here*"—gesturing to the right—"and maybe just a—"

Jimmy interrupted just in time, comparing his marriage to the man on the *Ed Sullivan Show* who used to spin plates on his hands. He began demonstrating this in effect, then chortled: "After tonight, it's probably all going to go to hell."

"I know. I've never heard of a marriage therapist suggesting it's like balancing plates." Pause. "So, Malibu and Key West?"

"Malibu and Key West," echoed Jimmy. "It's *space*."

Carson dropped his head with an involuntary laugh.

The following year Jimmy told Craig Modderno of *USA Today* that it was tough for anyone to be a road musician's spouse. He called Janie "a good woman" who had nicely raised daughter Savannah Jane. "I see them both often. I'm too old to date anymore, and I'm no longer wild. When I first got on the road, I was a Catholic altar boy gone crazy. Now I'm thinking more in terms of family and being a good parent."

Jimmy told Gulfport, Mississippi, interviewer Marcia Hill of WLOX-TV in 1989 that commitment to his *career* was overwhelming. "I had problems committing myself to marriages, and other relationships, and *family* and all. Because I didn't realize that I was committed to my work more than anything else. I tried to do other things along with it, and they were the ones that eventually suffered—because I *never* lost my commitment to my music or my art."

"Is family *important* to you?" asked Hill.

"It's important, but I live by myself. I see my family—my wife and I are now separated, and have been for eight years [contradicting the 1985 testimony to Johnny Carson]. My daughter lives with her in California. We see each other, we have a very nice relationship, but she only does what she wants to do and needs to do. You're dealing with an erratic personality, when you marry an artist," he said, laughing. "Don't make any qualms about that. We're a basically crazy people. And it takes that kind of craziness and commitment to be successful. And there's a price for that."

■ ■ ■

At least Jimmy had traded Aspen back for Key West, where maybe there could be some business fun: "I felt like, if I have become this entity here, why don't we do it and make an effort to do it right?"

One day he called Sunshine, to complain about how the ceiling in his shabby apartment had just fallen in on his bed.

"Jimmy, why are you living in that dump? You're a millionaire. You can live anyplace you want to."

Meanwhile, Sunshine had hit bottom herself around 1984—with two sons and zero husband, about to lose her house through foreclosure, as she told Paul Lomartire. "Get the kids off the street," Jimmy advised. "Let's open the Margaritaville store. If it makes money, fine—if it doesn't, that's okay, you just get your life together, get the bank off your back. The main thing is to have fun."

Of course, a beach-lazy Buffett could have rented out his name—splurged the front money—then dissociated himself from the Margaritaville investors when they went broke. But unlike many music colleagues, he possesses dollars-and-cents common sense.

So Jimmy, Sunshine—and Stephen H. Humphrey—joined hands financially in December of 1984, and set up the shop at Number 4

Land's End Village in Key West. Official opening was January 28, 1985, with Key West Mayor Richard Heyman cutting the ribbon—looking "ready to christen the new venture with a bottle of tequila."

On the first day, the store was drained of its basic stock, selling seven hundred dollars' worth of T-shirts. Jimmy's publicity proclaimed it "a cheerfully shabby place, with its weathered front porch, well-used rocking chair, and lobster-trap display cases." Besides "Caribbean Soul" T-shirts, there were cookbooks, jewelry, nautical maps. The store opening event was a two-day First Annual Margaritaville Film Festival, showing old and new Buffett videos. On the countertop were the *Coconut Telegraph* newsletters.

Thirty-five-year-old Sharon Lehmann arrived from St. Louis and took over the newborn mail-order operation, for five dollars an hour. Her husband then followed, to help run the newsletter.

But the walk-in customers kept asking, "If this is Margaritaville, where are the cheeseburgers and margaritas?" So Sunshine opened a food window on the street, backed by a margarita blender, a griddle, and a deep fryer.

Then the shop lost its lease, so Jimmy recruited Kevin Boucher, previously JP's rock club proprietor in New York City, and the business expanded, via $250,000 in renovation plus a $25,000 sound system. Now it was at 500 Duval Street—a shop next to a Margaritaville Cafe featuring entertainment. Jimmy's attorneys had warned against it, but he borrowed the quarter-million dollars anyway, and sunk in fifty thousand dollars of his own cash.

Jimmy even felt his customers would be "hot for fossils," so began bringing them in and placing them on the shelves. "The fossils are going to be in a sculpture garden in Jimmy's yard," said Sunshine dryly. "We try to appease him when he wants to put things in the store like fossils." (Parrot Heads are not paleontologists, apparently.)

Sales in the store itself climbed from $940,000 in 1986 to $2.1 million in 1990. That December, it sold $50,000 worth of merchandise—some local shops take a year to sell that much. In 1994 it was offering a "Parrot Head Prophylactic—Why Don't We get Drunk and . . . SAFELY" with other printed advice: "Stick one on and stick around."

The cafe featured balconies, wooden ceiling fans, and a ceramic tile-covered bar, and its pink-, red-, and turquoise-colored chairs had the effect of a garden of tropical flowers, according to bartender George "Lime Wedge" Murphy. Buffett fans were encouraged to mail in photographs for potential decor display, preferably those that were "socially embarrassing." By 1990 it was serving two thousand cheeseburgers a month, plus its large menu of seafood and ribs, grossing sales of over $3 million a year. "To have the luxury of a name like Jimmy's is something I've never had before, and it's wonderful," said Boucher.

Entertainers like the Neville Brothers would occasionally appear.

Sound man J. L. Jamison said that while most of the time his boss Jimmy was easygoing, when he wanted him to do some "rotten" job, Jimmy would bribe him with some food. Doorman Pat Molloy claimed to have taken hundreds of hours of training, and therefore knew how to deal with a seventeen-year-old redhead who swaggered up shaking her hips, or a drunk New York tourist who knows Jimmy is close by and offers fifty dollars to find him. Molloy recommends substituting a Buffett impostor, dressed up in cheap Hawaiian clothes, who can talk with a nasal twang so that you can pocket the fifty-dollar Buffett finder's fee. He also says you must *never* let a customer leave who is drunker than you—it simply proves you aren't doing your doorman job!

■ ■ ■

"He usually introduces me as the woman who runs his life," Sunshine told Paul Lomartire. Soon after the store opened, she spotted a girl, Gina Knight, who'd just landed on a Trimaran sailboat en route to some vague destination. Her captain had disappeared—she was stranded. "Sunshine assessed her as possessing Margaritaville ambience. Someone was on vacation, so she hired Gina for a couple of weeks. Six years later she was still working at the store ("It's been a hell of a vacation, thanks to whoever you are"). Another employee, Amy Tepe, came down for the summer in 1986, stating, "It's been a five-year summer and I don't think it's ending soon!" One bank girl, Linda Price, helped draw loans for Margaritaville. Catholic schoolteacher Anna Marie Lepschat also worked at the store, proud that her second-graders knew Jimmy's song "Jolly Mon Sing." One cafe hostess, Jackie Schofield, attended the program at the Salvador Dali museum in St. Petersburg (instigated by A. Reynolds Morse, biographer of Montserrat's Redonda "King," M. P. Shiel). Many other similar employees support the store—riding to work on their bicycles.

Jimmy had already been "King of Krewe of Clones" in the parades held from 1981 to 1984 in the week before Mardi Gras. He craved purchasing the Storyville Jazz Hall, but the club was under financial and legal stress, and Jimmy's offer in 1990 fell through. Then, on August 5, 1992, the Margaritaville store (and cafe) opened at 1 French Market Place in New Orleans, in the old Hibernia bank building, with a marble floor and overhead chandeliers. Sunshine did her best to tout Parrot Head souvenirs in this new location.

One of its tastiest products is Al Rose's historical tribute, *Storyville, New Orleans: Being an Authentic, Illustrated Account of the Notorious Red-Light District* (1974). Packed with scholarly photographs of naked whores, it features documented dialogue ("She'd take hold of your prick and then milk it to see if you had the clap"—and "I been fucking f'om befo' I kin remembuh! Shit, yes! Wit' my ol' man, Wit' my brothas, wit' d' kids in da street. I done it fo' pennies, I done it fo' nothin'," testifies a Crescent City carnal queen, in an authorized interview).

The New Orleans store was opened by Kevin Boucher, who moved there from Key West. One of the Key West bartenders, upset over the move, went to New Orleans to see Jimmy's performance. He lit up a joint of marijuana—and was summarily fired.

But will there be more stores? "I don't want them every mile in America," Jimmy told Vernon Silver of *The New York Times*. "I don't need the money, so I don't want a cash cow out there." Jimmy believes he got a D in a college marketing class, "but I remember supply and demand."

Silver confirmed Jimmy's astuteness, since "New Orleans, after all, is a time-tested place where people have been known to waste away with a frosty drink."

■ ■ ■

Sunshine Smith terms herself "the Jimmy Buffett interpreter because he's a very private person. He doesn't like to do interviews—he doesn't like to meet new people because everyone wants to be his best buddy because of who he is." Yet she encouraged Pat Jordan to give him a cover story for *Southern Living* in 1988. She had him call Los Angeles, where he "got a not-very-pleasant woman who barked at me over the phone that I should identify myself more clearly"—she was sick of "kooky requests" from fans who wanted to locate Jimmy and go to his doorstep with "a six-pack of Coors and a few loosely rolled joints."

Jordan made it to Key West, spending an hour with Jimmy in his "comfortably cluttered house, the house of a bachelor." He judged him to be "short, stocky"—and watched Sunshine serve him a cheeseburger and French fries. (As of 1994, the beach house with its stucco outer wall still bore a metal plaque warning, BEWARE OF THE OCCUPANT.)

Jimmy told Jordan he was "a great performer," and yet "a mediocre singer and writer." He compared himself to Frank Sinatra—whom he saw at a concert for older ladies. ("They didn't give a shit that he was flat. They just reminisced and went away feeling good.")

Jordan found some Key Westers miffed by Jimmy's distance—damning him as "Jimmy Stuffit"—though jealousy is sure proof of an artist's success. Jordan's analysis of his concerts was profound: "No one really comes to a Jimmy Buffett concert to hear *him* sing. His fans come to hear themselves. *They* are the concert. Jimmy's just the vehicle for them."

■ ■ ■

In February 1985, Jimmy started the *Coconut Telegraph* newsletter—a bimonthly with a circulation of nine thousand by 1986 (with subscribers in the U.S.A., Canada, Australia, Israel, Taiwan, England, Germany). It's still in print after a decade, and while its size has increased (with reprint articles, interviews, and feature stories on Utley, Fingers Taylor, Marshall Chapman, as well as manatee manifestos), Jimmy has wisely never expanded it into a newsstand periodical, with a flashy cover, a new title, and expensive design and layout. It's also crammed full of mail-order products, tour schedules, record and book notices. Circulation today is over fifty thousand (call 1-800-COCOTEL). Jimmy says it's strictly for "non-inquiring minds"—and *Billboard*'s Gerry Wood called it "the Buffett bible for his fans, and the Margaritaville store is their mecca."

Advertisements (in 1995) offer a $13.50 Margaritaville metal bucket for keeping drinks on ice, a $6.50 coffee cup, a $19.95 parrot cap with a stuffed cloth parrot's head on top, numerous $14.95 T-shirts, and selected books for sale—books Jimmy likes to read, not just write.

With one exception.

The Jimmy Buffett Scrapbook by Mark Humphrey, with art design by Harris Lewine (1993), he icily advertises as "an unauthorized biography by unauthorized authors that we are unauthorized to authorize." While not "involved" in its writing, he admits that his followers need it—so he "unauthorizedly" offers it for sale.

"Buffett was not happy this book was being done," Humphrey told authorized interviewer Rick Bird of the Scripps Howard News Service. "He put the word out to his friends, 'Don't talk. Don't cooperate.' Since the book's come out, he's selling it in his stores. So I guess it's now approved." Bird confirmed that Jimmy "gives interviews sparingly these days, usually when it's necessary to sell a record or his book."

Humphrey told Carol Cain of the *Mobile Press Register,* "He wants to control his image and didn't want things to come out that weren't his product." Cain added that many Mobilians believe Jimmy resents Mobile "because he rarely grants interviews to local media."

■   ■   ■

The store operation was a good alternative to sagging pop-radio airplay.

The *Last Mango in Paris* didn't make the album Top 40—though, once again, it scored high in country: Number 7 in *Cash Box*. None of the singles made the Top 40 in pop, but *three* charted in country.

The hilarious "Gypsies in the Palace" (written with Glenn Frey and Will Jennings) went to Number 56. It jokes about some wild friends who frolic at an entertainer's home while he's away, taking off their clothes, forming a conga line, drinking wine, trying to avoid stepping on broken glass—exploiting his resources, shooting the lock off his closet to sample his precious possessions. (Once when he returned to Colorado, Jimmy noticed his car had been driven into the creek by his caretaking home-watchers. They said they didn't know where it was.) One of Jimmy's best recordings.

"If the Phone Doesn't Ring It's Me" (written with Jennings and Utley) is a nice early-Fifties quality pop tune—Number 16 in country—which Rosemary Clooney (or Jo Stafford) would have liked. Latter-day counterpart Crystal Gayle recorded it (she likes melodies more than you're supposed to).

"Please Bypass This Heart" (written with Jennings and Utley) went to Number 50 in country. Other worthy album tracks were "Frank and Lola" (written with Steve Goodman), a Lucy and Ricky Ricardo nostalgic-sounding song, and "The Perfect Partner," by Marshall Chapman.

Backup singers included Glenn Frey, Marshall Chapman, Wendy Waldman, Mel Tillis's daughter Pam Tillis, and of all people, Roy Orbison. Actor Harrison Ford cracked a whip on "Desperation Samba." Produced by Jimmy Bowen, again with Michael Utley and Tony Brown.

That same year *Songs You Know by Heart—Jimmy Buffett's Greatest Hit(s)* appeared, songs from 1973 to 1979. The title itself is embarrassing: Which 1990s country acts have many—in some instances, *any?*—songs that their listeners "know by heart"? Buffett discologist William Ruhlmann notes in *Goldmine* that it scraped onto the charts at Number 100—but is now his best-selling album (double platinum), ranking *fifth* in Billboard's "year-end ranking for 1993."

In 1986 the *Coconut Telegraph* was offering a *Live by the Bay* video—filmed at Marine Stadium in Miami in 1985, with Jimmy promising "no fucking health food" before singing "Cheeseburger in Paradise." He alluded to his Coconut Grove beginnings, and praised his Coral Reefers, including keyboardist Mike Utley ("sporting his nice set of pajamas—I wouldn't wear that shit in public," Jimmy said of Utley's attire, while admitting he had "the right build"), steel drummer Robert Greenidge from Trinidad, conga drummer Sam Clayton (from Delaney and Bonnie, and Little Feat), and Josh Leo (whose singer-songwriter album *Rockin' on 6th* appeared in 1983).

Looking at his audience with binoculars, he said, "We're making a Parrot Head film so you can take this shit home with you." He asked if there were any dope dealers out there—or any DEA officers—then recommended that if so, they *ought to get together!* In "Why Don't We Get Drunk" Jimmy asked, "Why don't we get stoned and screw?" Before singing "The Coconut Telegraph," he expressed fear that some of the people would become victims of the song—by waking up in the morning, not knowing whom they were with, or maybe ending up swimming in the bay by the crack of dawn. And in "A Pirate Looks at Forty" he pleaded, out of lament to the late Phil Clark, "Don't anybody drown out there."

Indeed, at a Mud Island concert in the Mississippi River outside Memphis in 1986 occurred a macabre prophecy fulfillment. Unseen by Jimmy, a helicopter was swooping throughout the show—accompanied by blue-light police boats cruising the solemn waters. Against the advice of security officers, a man carrying a beer can had gone wading in the river. The next morning he was found drowned. Maybe forty-two years old. As reporter Rheta Grimsley Johnson judged: "Buffett is the twelve-year-old kid still alive in our forty-year-old bodies. . . . Jimmy was singing of sharks, ragtops and African parakeets when the man drowned."

"I've gotten letters from people blaming me for their kids getting killed, and I've written back," he said to the *Los Angeles Times*' Robert Hilburn. "I understand their grief, but I feel I bring a hell of a lot more joy than pain to people." His followers were normal 364 days a year, then one day "we come to town and some of them get blasted, but that may help them get through the other 364." He began adding lines to "Why Don't We Get Drunk?" advising his listeners to utilize (1) designated drivers and (2) condoms. (At a Chapel Hill concert in 1988, in the midst of "Why Don't We Get Drunk" a woman handed Jimmy a bag of condoms and he began tossing them into the crowd with "safe sex" admonitions—soon, some inflated condoms were floating above the audience.) He began preaching drunk-driving warnings before his concerts, urging people to use "tipsy taxis." At least a large number of taxis began showing up before the shows.

The Parrot Heads themselves had been so nicknamed in the early Eighties at Cincinnati's Riverbend Music Center by Timothy B. Schmidt, a former Eagles guitarist. "These aren't Deadheads," he exclaimed, distinguishing them from followers of the Grateful Dead, "they're Parrot Heads." Their costumes and goofy headgear were spontaneous, their own damned fault! And the climate was appropriate—the best Buffett fans often live up North, imagining they are in Key West instead of Ohio, New York, or other cold spots of similar latitudes.

■　■　■

To confirm his changes in altitudes from Aspen to Key West, the *Floridays* album also appeared in 1986. It credits Don Blanding, author of a book of the same title, and is one of his best-produced albums (by Mike Utley).

On Side One, "Creola" is one of Jimmy's prettiest melodies (written with Ralph MacDonald and William Salter), and best-recorded vocals (seven minutes' worth!). "Nobody Speaks to the Captain No More" echoes "Sending the Old Man Home," once more lamenting a hero whom life has passed by, but is still folkie-nostalgic.

The title song on Side Two recalls how his parents tolerated his "crazy ways," which were "just a phase" anticipating "better days." Another memorable melody is "It All Falls Down" (by Matt Betton), claiming that his life is an "open book . . . by James Joyce and Agatha Christie." The song sounds autobiographical, with Jimmy bragging that he never passed his SATs (Scholastic Aptitude Tests). "No Plane on Sunday" (written with Mike Utley) and "When the Coast Is Clear" (written with Mac McAnally) are two more pleasant-sounding cuts; and "You'll Never

Work in Dis Bidness Again" (written with Utley, Vince Melamed, Josh Leo, Willie Weeks, and Matt Betton) peevishly attacks show business—to make it in Hollywood, you don't need talent, just an aggressive attitude (not to mention *any* other script but *Margaritaville*).

No country chart singles from this album. (Nor any for the next seven years!)

■ ■ ■

On October 27, 1986, Jimmy appeared at Del Rio's club at 500 Duval Street (formerly Lazy Afternoon, and today's Margaritaville address), to a standing-room-only crowd. Why? To save 407 acres of the "salt ponds" (ponds, marshes, uplands) around the Key West International Airport. The show was backed by Sunshine and Patti Lancaster. He reminisced about his early days there at the Island Drive-In Theater, the Boat Bar, and Howie's Lounge. He honored a large aviation group from the VF-45 division of the Naval Air Station, but also urged his audience to go to the city commission meeting, to save the small amount of undeveloped land. Joan Borel of the Audubon Society rose and spoke for preserving the salt ponds.

Then Jimmy started performing, backed by the Full Sail Band, who'd flown in for the concert. He asked, "When we get through saving the Salt Ponds, will I be the only endangered species left down here?"

Next evening, at a meeting of the City Commission, he compared the Salt Ponds crisis to his Save the Manatee cause, calling his presentation "one of the greatest exercises in democracy since seventh-grade physics."

Then the Florida Land Acquisition Selection Committee voted 5–1 to allow him to raise $1 million through a concert to help the state buy the 407-acre Salt Ponds. The tract had been used for over one hundred years for salt production. Jimmy offered his concert *if* the city and state would pay up the rest of the $3.5 million cost for the Salt Ponds—he would probably raise $1 million—otherwise, condominiums were threatened to be built. ("I believe anybody who builds a condo should have to live next to the elevator for a year.")

The land was owned by two dozen developers—including one who wanted to throw up a thousand houses.

Jimmy had now formed "Friends of Florida," initially raising four thousand dollars. The following year, twenty-four-year-old Michele Umstead, a college business manager in Mobile, was gaining publicity for one of Jimmy's concerts, trying to raise funds for the Salt Ponds. She and her husband had gone to Key West and seen for themselves the need. ("I'd like for Buffett to have support from his hometown.")

"If we as humans want to assume the role of landlords, then we have to take care of all the tenants," became Jimmy's axiom.

The condominiums couldn't be stopped, however—a sixteen-year battle with a condo developer had failed in court, since he had bought his land before the protection laws were imposed. But Jimmy's Friends of Florida at least helped save the rest of the Salt Ponds. The FOF helped Key West grab some grants to preserve ten acres "containing the island's last remaining hardwood hammock," which became Little Hamaca City Park.

Over half the Salt Ponds area was preserved—and environmental historians Katharine and Joe Roach were surprised that the flippant folkie of "Peanut Butter Conspiracy" and "Cheeseburger in Paradise" renown would have committed himself to the ongoing fight. They thanked his FOF for having provided "a home for birds and other wildlife in the island city."

A Pirate Looks at MCA
(Some People Claim That There's a
Mobster to Blame)

■

Morris Levy and twenty others have been indicted by a federal grand jury in Newark, New Jersey, on extortion charges involving the sale of out-of-print MCA records. Country discs from the Nashville MCA office are reportedly among the old records involved. . . . Senator Albert Gore, Jr., is the head of a congressional group that is investigating alleged payola and organized crime in the pop music business.

—*The Tennessean*, September 26, 1986

If singer Jimmy Buffett, who is signed to MCA Records, wants to make an expensive new video, the decision would be resolved by his management, Front Line, and his record label, MCA, which are both under the same ownership," reported the *Los Angeles Times* in a May 1986 story, "MCA in the Front Line of a New Controversy." Irving Azoff claimed you'd have to have "a very narrow view" of the industry to think the people weren't working hard for each artist, whose record deals were controlled by lawyers, anyway. "So when Jimmy Buffett's contract at MCA comes to an end, his attorney will call the shots about whether he stays here, not me or anyone else." Indeed, Mike Gormley praised Azoff's company for handling one of his acts: "MCA has busted its butt for Oingo Boingo. . . ."

Azoff's Front Line Management had just been purchased by Azoff's MCA Records. On paper at least, the president was Howard Kaufman (Jimmy's HK Management manager today), and Azoff the mere secretary. They were changing their name to MCA/FLM Corporation—to become one more of at least twenty-eight other MCA corporations, including MCA Radio Network, MCA Discovision, and MCA Events.

Already MCA *events* were becoming exciting news stories in Los Angeles. Azoff also sold MCA his other two companies: Full Moon Records and Facilities Merchandising (T-shirts, souvenirs). Total purchase price for the three companies: $24.7 million (with Azoff taking about $15 million in MCA stock for himself). "Front Line was not as big a moneymaker as it once was," judged *L.A. Times* business reporter William Knoedelseder in *Stiffed: A True Story of MCA, the Music Business and the Mafia* (1993). "The acquisition surprised and angered many in the record business." Industry analysts thought his combined companies were worth more like three or five million dollars. Azoff was probably being gifted with extra cash, "minimizing his tax bite."

Back in 1962, the Kennedy administration had invoked antitrust laws to force MCA to drop MCA Artists—now "MCA is again representing talent which it also employs," wrote Dan E. Moldea in *Ronald Reagan, MCA, and the Mob* (1986), citing Jimmy and Dan Fogelberg (Full Moon) with Front Line.

Nashville MCA executive Jim Foglesong, on the other hand, saw this not as conflict of interest, but quite the opposite. Taking Front Line (and the two other companies) out of Azoff's hands prevented problems ("MCA had the reputation as being the toughest company in the business"), according to Fogelsong, who cites MCA's subsidiary Universal Pictures as similarly being "the most honorable," due to its profound contracts that avoided conflicts of interest.

"There's a conflict-of-interest committee at MCA, Inc., that has carefully dealt with all Jimmy Buffett matters here," Azoff told Michael Goldberg of *Rolling Stone* that year. "Any financial deals with Buffett always went to that committee, and they will continue to."

MCA had sought clearance from the Justice Department, to avoid antitrust restrictions barring them from *booking* clients. (The Justice Department accepted the naïve theory that artists' managers don't do booking.) Record-company rivals sniped, as always: "It's shocking. They'll be dealing out of self-interest" (David Geffen, Geffen Records), and "Somebody is going to get the short end of it. If not, it would be the first time in history going back to Plato" (Bob Krasnow, Elektra Records). Azoff called his denigrators "small-minded" and "crybabies."

Another manager and record-company president, Danny Goldberg, said of Azoff's supporters: "From their point of view, they now know everything he does serves the interests of MCA."

Jimmy probably got less interest and push, out of Azoff's honest need to never show favoritism. At least with conflicts of interest, one never exactly walks the line. But considering the body count of dead and dying Eighties acts, Jimmy was lucky . . . to even survive.

Meanwhile, MCA itself rose up against the odds, vindicating Azoff's presidency. By now he was getting Glenn Frey and Waylon Jennings roles in the show *Miami Vice* (NBC-TV), resulting in songs like "Smuggler's Blues," written by Frey (with J. Tempchin), on an Azoff-instigated *Miami Vice* album (1985), which spent *eleven weeks* at Number One. "I wrote scripts for *Miami Vice* and *Amazing Stories* that I would have starred in," Jimmy said wistfully in 1986. "They may still use them." (Probably not.)

Burgeoning MCA could now afford $750,000 to provide Azoff with his "Taj Mahal" office suite, replete with a private shower and gold-plated fixtures, a huge conference table hewn of stone, and a mirrored bar.

"What Irving and I thought would take us five years to accomplish, we've achieved in just two years," boasted Myron Roth, Azoff's assistant in 1985. MCA was now fourth among the top six companies on *Billboard*'s pop charts—with seventeen albums scoring that January, fifteen of them Azoff-signed acts. "We were forced to beg, borrow, and steal because we had nothing to release," Azoff told the *Los Angeles Times*. Recalling his old days as a manager, he used to draw a line and say, "Everyone on this side I'll kill for and everyone on the other side is the enemy," admitting that since he went from bossing sixteen employees to six hundred, "I've toned down somewhat . . . my past abrasive style."

■ ■ ■

Azoff well summed up the Eighties when he said, "The real problem with the record business is that a gold record [sales of five hundred thousand copies] doesn't necessarily mean the record was profitable."

Yes, *Billboard* reflected airplay of singles, not sales, since vinyl 45s were fast becoming antique collector's items, unavailable in all but the biggest stores. So-called "hits" were now the means, not the end, to profit—hopefully, listeners would buy their favorite song on an album (and swallow the other nine cuts) for around ten dollars. Compact discs were replacing vinyl albums, too.

So did how one get airplay? In the good ol' days, a Rolex watch and/or a "date" with a shady lady might impel a disc jockey to give a record an extra spin. One of the conveniences of good ol' vinyl albums was the cardboard cover—which could also nicely protect crisp hundred-dollar bills and plastic-bagged cocaine for "playlist" consideration. At least in those relatively brighter times, the disc jockeys chose the music and were allowed to talk about it on the air. But with "program directors" issuing mandatory playlists, the audacious celebrity disc jockeys became a virtually extinct species. Their successors, rarely even permitted to announce a singer's name, played what was in *Billboard*—and *Billboard* would say that it simply charted what the stations were playing. When asked where these "hits" came from, the radio stations and *Billboard* would point their fingers at each other. Like when the policeman asks people in the wrecked car: "Which one of you was driving?" and they answer, "None of us was drivin', officer—we was all in the backseat."

In 1973 the country charts lurched forward, with thirty-five Number Ones, after twenty-six the year before. By 1983 there were fifty—in the fifty-two weeks that constitute a year. The stations were artificially instituting a new Number One each week, which in the short run was one-derful. Every record company wants as many Number Ones (and awards!) as possible, but album *sales* didn't necessarily equal airplay "hit" excitement, as the accountants could account for.

Robert K. Oermann said in 1987 in *The Tennessean* that "Buffett hasn't had a major hit since 'Margaritaville' ten years ago: If his audiences routinely respond the way they did last night [June 4 Starwood concert], that indicates there's something wrong with the contemporary radio and record business."

Nashville business veteran Ruth White (Reed Records) remembers that in the mid-Eighties, concert promoters often didn't know the artists' names but they knew the songs. "The bookers say, 'We book the song—everything's the song.' If you don't believe it, just watch how fast they fall when the song doesn't happen." Recalling how Hank Snow went twenty-one weeks at Number One with "I'm Moving On," she says today, "It's like the kiss of death when you get to Number One . . . you go *whoppo!* It shouldn't be like that," but the radio stations think "they got to move 'em fast."

■　■　■

Which is where the "hit men" came into play. *Airplay.*

While Jimmy was selling white T-shirts, MCA began trying to sell record promotion—probably not of *his* songs—through a colorful independent expert named Joe Isgro. Actually, Isgro's favorite shirt color was *black* ("I've been accused of being in the Mafia because I wear a black shirt"). Isgro kept a box of forty or fifty photographs of dead Viet Cong he had supposedly killed. "Un-fucking-believable. Guys with their faces shot off. It would make your skin crawl," somebody confided to payola-ologist Frederic Dannen, author of *Hit Men: Power Brokers and Fast Money Inside the Music Business*. "Joey comes out of the limo looking like someone from *Miami Vice,*" observed a record-company executive.

Isgro ran a rhythm and blues label out of MCA—and ran a restaurant where Los Angeles policemen enjoyed eating and watching. Isgro knew how to carry a hundred thousand dollars in his pockets, and employed bodyguards who might say, "I'd love to kick the shit out of somebody today." Proud of his automobile, Isgro griped, "Fucking sad state of affairs in this country that I should be afraid to drive a Rolls. I've been a renegade all my goddamned life. I'll be fucked if I'm going to sell that car."

He represented several record companies simultaneously, claiming a mild annual income of $10 million. His Mafia pals—such as Gambino star Joe Armone—enticed journalists and federal investigators, but nothing criminal was ever proven. Frustrated Senator Al Gore complained about the "conspiracy of silence" amid the record companies in his failed Congressional payola inquiry. Gore said he lacked witnesses "in some cases, because of threats of being physically hurt."

Isgro was, after all, a flamboyant if not final solution to the playlist problem.

For some reason, Azoff didn't like him, and since airplay was costing more money than could be gleaned from record sales, he slammed his small, firm foot on the promotions brake. "The New Payola," on the *NBC Nightly News* (February 24, 1986), provided him inspiration, televising real, live Gambino mobster acts at the record companies' Hall of Fame banquet on January 23 (wasting away again in Mafiosaville?). Azoff's Front Line front man, Larry Solters—by now an MCA-er—threw himself in front of one cameraman to protect Azoff from being filmed. He reportedly tackled him, but in our *BookPage* book-review interview in 1991 he explained, "It was more of a running block. *He* moved to the left. *I* moved to the left."

Within days, MCA—and all the other major companies—decided to drop Isgro and friends. "Let me tell you who the organized criminals in this fucking country are. It's the fucking press . . . rotten no-good cocksuckers," Isgro said. He sued the record companies for price-fixing (where but in America could "hit men" cancellation be deemed monopoly tyranny?), but was then distracted by his own indictment, from which he was acquitted. Modestly he moved from unemployment to producing a movie about Teamster immortal Jimmy Hoffa!

Isgro and Azoff certainly agreed on one thing—the vileness of the vulgar press. Those fuckin' First Amendment farts! "It's very 'in' right now to look for negative things at this record company, which has been the victim of a media witch-hunt led by the *L.A. Times,*" griped Azoff in May 1986. Soon, *People Weekly* (November 17) invaded Azoff's antisocial privacy, by exposing his birthday gift to Michael Lippman, who managed singer Melissa Manchester. Azoff and wife Shelli had packaged a boa constrictor, carried by "Hollywood animal handler" Jim Picciolo over to Lippman's party. Picciolo felt he had been unjustly used when he learned that the greeting card said, "Happy Birthday, Michael. Now you have two of them. Love, Shelli and Irving." Lippman exploded—since it was meant to insult his wife. Besides, he had his own "morbid fear of snakes."

■ ■ ■

Meanwhile, old Buffett albums were floating along in the "cutout" ocean of sinking vinyl and tape. "Cutouts" are records no longer regularly retailed, but sold out the back by the thousands, at sometimes only a dime apiece wholesale, to reach the discount bins. Cutouts are the equivalent of "remaindered" books—with reduced (or zero) royalties for singers, songwriters, and music publishers.

Other MCA cutout "stars on the water" were Conway Twitty, Loretta Lynn, Barbara Mandrell, Tom Petty, and Azoff's Steely Dan, among many. At least they were all on the list of MCA records offered to John Gervasoni of Scorpio Music. But he claimed he never received them.

Gervasoni had been preceded by John LaMonte, another frustrated cutout patron. LaMonte had proudly counterfeited *Introducing the Beatles,* a moribund first album reissued apparently legally—and once bought some dumped Beatles albums, reissuing them in plain new covers for huge profit. Counterfeiting is an art form—a beginner can reproduce the record itself, but it takes taste and skill to duplicate the colored cover correctly. Some unschooled counterfeiters can't even get the spelling right.

"The only good thing about counterfeiting was that you knew you had a hit when they counterfeited," laughs Jim Foglesong. "Because they didn't counterfeit any of the dogs. That's true—they didn't mess with any of the other products, they wanted something they could sell. It's sort of like the other cliché we have in the business: You know you are starting to achieve success when somebody sues you."

Jimmy Buffett records were being counterfeited, along with those by Tom Petty and the Who. MCA unsuccessfully sued Scorpio Music for this, though their boss, John Gervasoni, felt cheated of cutouts that had been ordered but never received. "In all my years in the music business, I've never seen more blatantly obvious counterfeit product," railed Azoff, as Buffett cassettes—and those of other MCA Platinum Plus artists (Elton John, Olivia Newton-John, Steely Dan, Neil Diamond)—surfaced.

Question: Would Buffett, Mandrell, Newton-John, Petty, et al., have been informed had the dump-out of their *good* records occurred? If the phone hadn't rung, it would have been cutouts of still-catalogued, royalty-due albums.

■   ■   ■

Irving Azoff was named "Man of the Year—City of Hope" in Los Angeles in 1983—and Humanitarian of the Year for the T.J. Martell Foundation in 1987 (leukemia and cancer research).

"I'm having fun," Azoff ("MCA's abrasive wizard") told *Newsweek* in 1988, defending his belligerent style. "When it stops being fun, I'll stop doing it." ("Irving Azoff loves to be hated," was the article's lead sentence.) He denied rumors that he would resign due to MCA's "inadvertent association with an organized-crime figure," claiming a seventy-five percent company sales increase. But a few months later he was saying, "If you're going to allow a tree to grow, you have to prune it sometimes," justifying his 1988 staff cutbacks.

By 1989, however, he had shoved MCA up from its 1983 $8 million pretax loss to $60 million in net gain out of $661 million in revenue, thanks in part to having bought Detroit's Motown Records. Yet he quit MCA that year, frustrated by its refusal to expand and purchase Polygram, starting his own Giant Records instead (accurately reflecting his ambitious imagination, not his physical stature). On the way out, he lamented all the dramatic legal (and illegal) moments: "It was a witchhunt beyond my wildest dreams. The fact that it could happen is another reason not to hold a corporate job."

But for the journalists of the *Los Angeles Times*, Azoff happily sipped coffee—and cut up his MCA company credit card. Just in time. MCA's stock dropped almost two points on November 20, the day after *60 Minutes* (CBS-TV) showed the story "Hollywood and the Mob," exposing MCA Home Video president Gene Giaquinto—whom MCA had fired once they found the videos were being packaged by an East Coast company with Mafia ties. MCA issued a statement attacking the prosecutors, while refusing to be interviewed on television. Their attorney refused to return phone calls to CBS, *Billboard* reported.

In 1990 *Hit Men* author Frederic Dannen said in a *Country Music People* interview that one of the Gambino crime-family members was claiming that they now controlled two top country-music acts. (He thought it might be an exaggerated publicity boast.)

Captain Jimmy Buffett at Pascagoula

■

Of all the fabricks, a ship is the most excellent, requiring more art in building, rigging, sayling, trimming, defending, and mooring, with such a number of severall termes and names in continual motion, not understood of any landsman, as none would think of, but some few that know them.

—Captain John Smith, in Frank Shay's *A Sailor's Treasury* (1951)

Who would ever hope to get close enough to Jimmy Buffett at a sold-out concert (often, the only kind) to actually thrust a package into his hand? Yet Melody Bradley, the marketing director of the Jackson County Port Authority, did just that. At the Mississippi Coliseum at Biloxi, Mississippi, in late August 1987, she attempted to turn the singer-songwriter of "The Captain and the Kid" himself into a captain!

An honorary captain, that is ... of a 110-year-old cargo ship, the *Governor Stone*, named for a former Mississippi governor.

The ship was built in 1877 by Charles A. Greiner, probably at a shipyard founded by Miguel Leon Pol, a Spanish immigrant, back in 1850. Entrepreneur Nathan Dorlan bought the *Governor Stone* in

1880—and his legendary background certainly would have startled Jimmy Buffett, an admirer of pirate Jean Lafitte. Dorland had supposedly killed one of Lafitte's men, named Spud Thompson, many years before. (Lafitte's men had staged a drunken party, in order to rob local citizens—and steal their boats—so Dorland challenged Thompson to a duel, and beat him dead with his bare fists!) The *Governor Stone* had its own grim past—the hurricane of September 1906 had killed at least two of its crew members. The ship was abandoned and left grounded amid some trees. Years later it was sold, and the bodies of the crewmen were discovered inside.

Often it was used to ship oysters and beer—now it was going to become a floating monument to the Pascagoula, Mississippi, "shipbuilding saga." Melody Bradley was impressed that Jimmy's grandfather had spent his career sailing in and out of Pascagoula, and that his shipbuilding father had been born there, as had Jimmy.

So this birthplace captaincy for Jimmy was, frankly, overdue.

He called Melody Bradley back. "At first I thought it was a joke. No one expects to answer the phone and hear Jimmy Buffett on the other end. He was totally enthusiastic and had obviously read every word in the packet."

Then she received his letter pledging "his wholehearted support," in partial tribute to the Buffett family's sailing ship heritage at Pascagoula. He recommended a "project manager" who would know best how to preserve such a precious and priceless historic schooner.

■ ■ ■

Jimmy was nominating his father, James Delaney Buffett, Jr., to supervise the maintenance of the ship when it arrived. Since his dad had worked at the Ingalls shipyard in Pascagoula—and had managed government contracts for the Alabama Dry Dock in Mobile—the Port Authority accepted him (aided by port captains Robert Payne and Joe Frederic).

"Jimmy was just bubbling over about bringing the *Governor Stone* back to Pascagoula, when he called me," his father added. "He told me to see that she is rigged the way a schooner should be."

The boat's former owner, John Curry, of Tarpon Springs, Florida, claimed it was "the oldest American cargo vessel still afloat." He was tired of maintaining the sixty-three-foot ship—so he gave it to Pascagoula. It arrived from Florida on Sunday, August 30, and was anchored at River Park during the Flagship Festival on Labor Day. The new Buffett-oriented ship was illuminated by fireworks at ten P.M.

The ship's transfer to Pascagoula had been championed by Economic Development Director Linda Rosa. "Jimmy's endorsement of this project is deeply appreciated," she exulted. "It lends a level of credibility and commitment with long-term implications both for the schooner and for Jackson County."

On Sunday, September 13, Jimmy landed at the Jackson County airport in his own plane. He was back from New Orleans, having given a concert for seven thousand people—and had just seen Pope John Paul II.

"It's a good cause . . . it's essential to keep your traditional roots and values," he said to the (Pascagoula) *Mississippi Press,* and suggested that it would be a "great idea" to use the boat to train Sea Scouts. He had been one, but "we didn't have a boat then—it would have been better if we'd had a boat." He said that some of his sailing friends might be able to help out in the refitting of the schooner, since he was personally connected with sailing twelve-meter boats in the America's Cup competition. To help in the fund-raising, he autographed posters of the ship. "You've got to start locally. You can sell crew memberships and apply for state and federal restoration grants. A cause like this is not controversial and has no downsides."

Then he flew his plane over the *Governor Stone,* "wigwagging his wings in salute," heading back to Key West. But the composer of "The Captain and the Kid"—always a kid himself—was now a captain, too.

■   ■   ■

But by 1990 the ship had been acquired by the Appalachicola Maritime Institute (of Appalachicola, in northwest Florida). Their goal for restoration? To use it as a "sail trainer" for disadvantaged young people, and as a means to interest the public in the history of sailing. Pascagoula descendants of the ship's early owners cheered on the effort.

Well, Jimmy Buffett had told 'em so, back in 1987.

"Jolly Mon Sing"

■

This folk-rock country-western singer-songwriter sailor with a Carib-bean soul has turned the other side of forty and found a new place for his creative energies—a book for children.

—"The Talented Jolly Mon," *Sail* magazine (August 1988)

For years, Jimmy had been saying that while he yearned to write something besides songs, his music career had always "gotten in the way"—by 1987 all twenty-three years of it! Such remarks had been impressing Bonnie Ingber, an editor at Harcourt Brace Jovanovich. With good reason. Her husband, Joe Ingber, was one of Jimmy's colleagues (studio picker, songwriter, producer).

Joe introduced Bonnie to Jimmy, and she became "very interested in the concept of songwriters providing the text for picture books because often lyrics are to a poem or simple story. . . . He tells tales."

Jimmy was already working on a book—a children's book. Initially, he'd just wanted to jot down a story his daughter, Savannah Jane, had been telling out loud. As he had sung in "Little Miss Magic" (written for *Coconut Telegraph*), sometimes he caught her dreaming and wondered just "where that little mind meanders." Now, when he'd seen her sitting at his computer, pretending to type, he knew she needed help. Together they transcribed, then revised, her story. ("Savannah Jane . . . is a bit difficult to work with. I wonder where she got that from.") The tale derived, too, from "Jolly Mon Sing" written on board his boat *The Magic,* as Marshall Chapman remembers, for the *Last Mango in Paris* album (1985).

So Bonnie Ingber signed Jimmy to a two-book deal.

■   ■   ■

But why should an entertainer write a children's book? Well, some of them certainly do—such as neo-folksingers Tom ("Last Thing on My Mind") Paxton, Shel Silverstein (Jimmy's Key West friend), and country singers Louise Mandrell and Ricky Van Shelton. Dolly Parton has even turned her own favorite song, "Coat of Many Colors," into a children's book.

Creativity in general demands a certain childlike playfulness (a fact ignored by all too many artistic theorists, "creative" writing teachers, and hyperserious literary scholars). Children themselves are not always endearing in their acts of creativity—from finger-painting indelible pictures on their bedroom walls, to creating a mess in the kitchen when they try to cook something.

As Jimmy wrote in his first adult book (*Tales from Margaritaville*) two years later, "Ever since I was a child, I have had a recurring dream of visiting an island."

■   ■   ■

The text of *The Jolly Mon* is less than two thousand words, a reminder of why so many would-be writers think writing a children's book is a fast path to some easy money. But as with songwriting, there's nothing more deceptively simple than writing a commercially successful children's book.

The protagonist, nicknamed "the Jolly Mon," lives on the Caribbean island of Bananaland, entertaining the fishermen ("He could sing more fish out of the ocean than anyone"). His persona is enhanced by a magical guitar that surfaces miraculously (floating in Snapper Bay!), its neck inlaid with conch pearls, decorated with a dolphin emblem and starry little diamonds. Beneath the dolphin are inscribed some verses proclaiming the guitar's commitment to "songs of the sea; no lesson for learning, just play upon me," adding that the constellation of Orion will protect the guitar player, so the Jolly Mon won't need any guitar lessons—the guitar will teach him how to play!

Now his act is really together. Residents of the idyllic island, with their banana-and-fish-diet formula for bliss, can also enjoy good music, dished up for dessert! This picking, singing celebrity can fulfill everyone's appetite for music. (If Savannah drew her plot inspiration from her father's professional life, illustrator Lambert Davis blatantly patterned his illustration of the Jolly Mon after a portrait of the late reggae legend Bob Marley.)

But life on the road for any traveling entertainer has more bumps and potholes than expected. The Jolly Mon's tour route is nautical—island to island, from Pumpkin Island and Parrot Key, to Mango Bay—in his ship called the *Orion*. (According to *Sail* magazine, Davis's illustration of the boat was patterned after "Buffett's own twenty-six-foot Nat Her-reshoff–designed Alerion sloop, *Savannah Jane*.") The Jolly Mon, according to *Publishers Weekly*, "is a rather passive mythic character"—so makes good pirate-bait. The pirate profession, at least in this book, is woman-liberated, the leader of the band of male buccaneers is a lady named One-Eyed Rosy. She has an eye for vandalism, and orders her crew to smash the Jolly Mon's guitar. But she fails, since the guitar is magical, and pirate proof!

So her next-best alternative is to simply try and drown the Jolly Mon. He tries to save his life by playing a song, but the pirate queen is not easily deterred. They wrap the Jolly Mon in chains and sink him. Yes, to paraphrase Tom T. Hall's judgment of where guitar-playing can lead the hopeful musician (in the song "The Year Clayton Delaney Died"): "There ain't no money in it, it will lead you to an early *watery* grave."

Well, children's books aren't likely to have morbid, macabre endings, so expectedly, the Jolly Mon's career (along with his guitar) resurfaces once more.

The Mon's rescuer is a dolphin named Albion. And an outdated Freudian literary critic might say that the pirates represent country-music radio (or even MCA!)—and that the dolphin-savior is no less than Harcourt, Brace, Jovanovich itself, giving Jimmy bookstore circulation in lieu of airplay! (In the introduction, Jimmy hearkens to the classical poet Arion, supposedly saved by a dolphin from some pirates, in the Mediterranean off Italy, circa 625 B.C.)

■ ■ ■

Fittingly, the Harcourt, Brace, Jovanovich children's division is based in San Diego, and the book's illustrator, Lambert Davis, lived in nearby La Jolla. Davis himself was conveniently born on an island—Oahu, in Hawaii—and was an honors graduate from the Art Center College of Design in Pasadena. His hobbies were surfing and swimming, and he spent productive moments chatting with Jimmy and Savannah Jane. "I had to do a lot of research down at the beach," Davis told Terri

K. Benson of the Macon *Telegraph and News*, "swimming and soaking up the sun so I could give the book an accurate, lighthearted atmosphere."

His brilliantly colored acrylic illustrations drew consistent praise. Jan Walker of the *Orlando Sentinal* felt that his "soft style" captured "the mood and even the unique light of the Caribbean," and *Publishers Weekly* praised his "blend of realism with fantasy and sensitive use of color."

■ ■ ■

The last page of the book presents "Jolly Mon Sing" (in sheet-music form).* In April 1990 a promotional cassette was issued, with Jimmy reading the book aloud, and Savannah reading lyrics and some dialogue (both with "spunk and sensitivity," according to *South Florida Parenting*). They also sang together briefly, with Mike Utley leading the backup band. Beverly Bixler Fischer in the *School Library Journal* decided that the tape was "a good introduction to a musical style that may be unfamiliar to many children." At the close of the tape, Jimmy reads the book's preface.

Father-daughter duets have their faint antecedents—from country acts such as Red Foley and daughter Betty ("A Satisfied Mind"), George and Lorrie Morgan ("I'm Completely Satisfied with You"), and the Kendalls, to pop's "The Voice" Sinatra accompanied by Nancy.

■ ■ ■

Reviews of *The Jolly Mon* were fairly generous. Adults could enjoy the book, too, several critics said—though a few rated Davis's art stronger than the text (such as *Kirkus*, which termed the plot "undistinguished" while admitting the Jolly Mon was a "stylish and sympathetic hero, pictured in Davis's splashily brilliant acrylics as a handsome, dreadlocked young man").

Few commented on the prose style. As a songwriter, Buffett has an ear for language,since all lyric writers have something in common with poets: They believe every word counts. And that without *rhythm*, words lack impact—an insight lacking in many "serious" authors. For example, the magical dolphin Albion "leaped out of the sea and did not come down. He flew up into the night, and his shadow passed in front of the silver moon that hung over Snapper Bay."

■ ■ ■

When the Jolly Mon began his island-entertainer's tour, his enthusiasts in Bananaland outfitted him for his voyage with gifts, and food, and especially "books to read as he made his way through the islands."

---

* As "Jolly Mon," it appears on the 1990 *Feeding Frenzy* live album.

On May 5, 1988, Jimmy and Savannah Jane appeared on the *Today Show*—then, for an encore, showed up at the American Booksellers' Convention in Anaheim, California. Jimmy's new tour for MCA started May 29 at Anaheim . . . even as MCA released his next album, *Hot Water,* in June.

The End of the Eighties
("Homemade Music")

■

It's either here or Opryland.

—Jimmy, onstage at Starwood Amphitheatre, Nashville, July 11,
1989

At a Chapel Hill, North Carolina, concert, Jimmy said his album was tentatively titled *Stranger Than Fishing.* (His tour was nicknamed "A Parrot Looks at Forty.") He told the audience that "My Barracuda" had been inspired by a homeless couple who were camping out below the bridge near his house in Key West. He was rowing his skiff, and they looked like they wanted to jump in his boat, till he told them, "If you don't do that, I will make you famous." They were two former circus performers, and the song is a poignant portrait of their strained marriage ("She don't know if he loves her or not").

Critic Michael Hetzer said the concert was "a predictable, warmed-over rehash of Buffett's predictable, warmed-over music. But so what?"

282 ■   *Jimmy Buffett*

He quoted Jimmy: "I've never won an award for my music. But this is enough." Hetzer, however, noted his latest inclination was more toward rock 'n' roll, citing John Denver's "somewhat frantic . . . uncomfortable" appearance with an electric guitar, while concluding that Jimmy was simply too relaxed and modest to fall on his rock face.

In Milwaukee he would joke about how he had liked the Texas scene before "it became hip to be an outlaw," having retreated from the Willie Nelson–Waylon Jennings milieu "when groups of Hell's Angels start showing up at concerts."

He returned to Starwood Amphitheatre southeast of Nashville. On-stage also was Steve Cropper, a guitarist graduate of the famous blues instrumental band Booker T. and the MG's. Cropper begin to see analogies between his beloved Memphis recording capital and Nashville ("It's going to take teamwork, to try to break down the barriers, and the idea that Nashville is here with a giant fence around it").

Backup singer Rita Coolidge was there (born in Nashville in 1944; her 1971 *Nice Feelin'* album included future Buffett players Mike Utley and Sammy Creason). So was Marshall Chapman—helping Jimmy sing their cowritten "Smart Woman (in a Real Short Skirt)," from the *Hot Water* album, now released.

Clark Parsons of the *Nashville Banner* praised his concert sell-out event even though "radio has forgotten him," echoing the *Tennessean*'s Thomas Goldsmith, who said he drew "huge crowds throughout the country without major radio airplay or record sales in recent years."

"This song is about the trials and tribulations of not getting on radio," Jimmy said, introducing "Homemade Music" to the audience. "That's okay, 'cause we can sell out Starwood [fifteen thousand tickets], but I still believe 'Homemade Music' should be on the radio."

It was the album's opening cut, bragging that he "ain't no video king" since homemade music "ain't on the radio / Where did all the good songs go?" Where indeed? Former Tree Music president Buddy Killen complains that "there aren't as many great 'standards' written nowadays." Killen also bemoans the industry's new top-heavy bureaucracy, where "only the lawyers seem to win." Indeed, Jimmy's "Homemade Music" lyric deplores the omnipresence of lawyers and managers—and jeers at the evolution of records, from vinyl to tape cassettes to compact discs. He even sneers at the Japanese, presumably for their manufacturing everything—anticipating, also, their impending purchase of music companies.

Nashville's Tree Music publishing company, started without an office in 1951 (Buddy Killen kept the song tapes on the seat of his car), was sold to Japanese-owned CBS Records in 1989 for $40 million. Then Jimmy's own label, MCA—with its entire conglomerate, films and all—was sold to Matsushita Electric Industrial, the universe's largest consumer-electronics manufacturer, for $6.59 billion in 1990 (the "largest purchase ever of a U.S. company by a Japanese firm"). Was "the Athens of the South" becoming the Tokyo of the South"? Then the German Bertselman (BMG Music) bought out RCA (but kept the image of dog Nipper with his nose in the gramophone), colonizing at least fifteen Nashville song publishers in the invasion of Music City, International.

■　■　■

A soft, subtle song was "Pre-You," written with Ralph MacDonald and William Salter, whose unusual title coins a perhaps new term for new lovers—a former lover was "pre-you," and she can swim away while the current couple stays on the beach. (Jimmy heard the "pre-you" phrase in a San Diego hotel, when a sailor recounted the anecdote.)

Also for the album, Jimmy and Michael Utley wrote "Prince of Tides," based on the 1986 Pat Conroy novel of the same title. The novel dramatized a ravaged Southern husband flirting with a New York Jewish psychiatrist—who was also counseling his sister, named Savannah, for her suicide attempt, still haunted by murders in her family. At least, like Jimmy's daughter Savannah, she wanted to write books. "That's What Living Is to Me" claimed another literary inspiration—from the phrase "Be good and you'll be lonesome," from Mark Twain's *Following the Equator: A Journey Around the World* (1897).

■　■　■

"Homemade Music" was a single, and *Goldmine*'s William Ruhlmann notes that it failed to chart, though its successor, "Bring Back the Magic," went to Number 24 in Adult Contemporary, thanks to (as usual) an endearing, enduring melody. The album itself went to Number 46.

The following year *Nashville Banner*'s Michael McCall complained that Jimmy's last five albums hadn't gotten much airplay ("Radio's closed minds frustrate Buffett"), though each of them had "at least a couple of songs as catchy, witty and wise as Buffett's best-known hits. So why don't they get played?" McCall lauded the growth of Jimmy's sell-out concert ticket sales—from 8,000 (1986) to 10,000 (1987), to 15,500 (1988)—wondering why "local radio stations refuse to play his new songs (or hardly any new songs by anyone not named Madonna, Tiffany, Bon Jovi or Rod Stewart) . . . the stations play the same microscopic selection of old Buffett songs. Again. And again and again and again. 'Margaritaville,' 'Come Monday,' and 'Pencil Thin Mustache' get as much airplay these days as they did when they were hits ten to fifteen years ago."

Yet McCall felt Jimmy's newer albums were somewhat desperate, lusting for airplay by "settling for a shallow sentiment or cheap joke." He urged people to call stations and beg for Buffett—and if they retort, "It's not on our playlist," tell 'em the station's no longer on your playlist; if they say, "That song doesn't suit our format," tell 'em the station no longer suits your taste. He condemned radio for not playing different artists and new artists, and in summation of his article said: "If they refuse, turn them off."

■ ■ ■

In the meantime, fiction-writing was pressing harder and harder on Jimmy's mind. After all, if he could do a children's book, why not follow up with one for adults . . . which would sell better!

By mid-1988 he was admitting to carrying around copies of *The Elements of Style* by William Strunk, Jr., and E. B. White, and *Hemingway on Writing,* everywhere he went. Strunk and White especially stressed the concept of *style*—not the self-conscious, pretentious "literary" style, but that which comes from within. "The singer enjoys his good times, but he's as fond of books as he is of parties," Lynn Van Matre had written in the *Chicago Tribune,* "and it bothers him that people seem to read less and less these days."

"I have volumes of experiments," he would tell the *Washington Post*'s Richard Harrington. "I always kept journals, on the road and on my boat. And not just navigational logs, because the boat was my big adventure *and* my insurance policy . . . I started writing longhand journals of the people I'd meet. I have cedar chests full of stuff."

"I never considered myself 'a songwriter.' I've always just thought of myself as a writer," he explained to Garland Reeves of his hometown *Mobile Press Register.* "I've written for magazines and newspapers and this was just a logical progression. I feel comfortable writing prose. I've been threatening to write a book for a while. And when you roar past forty, suddenly you're looking back instead of ahead. So I thought, 'I'd better get these down before I forget them.'"

As he expounded to television interviewer Larry King that same year (1989): "I've been fortunate enough to travel all around the world, and also fortunate enough to keep my eyes open and write my thoughts in what I call my 'eternal journal.' I put it all together and out it comes."

As he had sung in "If I Could Just Get It on Paper" (dedicated to William Faulkner), if only he could tell himself *half* of the stories he knew (most of them funny), he might straighten out "the half-truths and lies" by just getting his pen on paper. The song was about songwriting . . . but if the song fits, write it in a book.

He had talked to editor Bonnie Ingber about doing a novel (she handled adult books, too), then realized it would be easier to muster up some short stories and essays around the themes of his music. "What if we did a record and book that could sort of feed off each other?" he asked. Ingber "went wild and set a deadline and there I was."

As songwriter of "He Went to Paris" and "The Captain and the Kid," he had at least two decades' momentum in musical yarn-spinning. He told radio interviewer Linda Wortheimer in 1989 that sometimes when he'd written a song about a dramatic character, he felt, "Well, that would make a good *short* story." Claiming to be an alumnus of "the Great Folk Scare of the Sixties," when singers were troubadours, he added, "I've spent half my life in probably 'twenty-five words or less' routines, so to expand short stories was, in a way, easier, because instead of having to get *one* good line, you had a couple of paragraphs to work with, to give a better description of how you felt."

Country fiddler Charlie Daniels had written a short-story collection, *The Devil Went Down to Georgia* (1985); so had singer-songwriter Tom T. Hall: *The Acts of Life* (1986). Decades earlier, actor Robert Mitchum had written short stories for magazines, as had country songwriter Jim Anglin, brother of Jack Anglin (of Johnnie and Jack, Kitty Wells's backup group), selling stories to *The New Yorker* (with "rough-assed language") and *The Atlantic Monthly* (about a New Orleans madam). Like Buffett, Anglin idolized Faulkner, and knew him slightly (they used to eat together).

■ ■ ■

During his 1988 summer tour, Jimmy was drafting his short-story collection, tentatively titled *My African Friend and Other Stories,* named after one of his songs. Still yearning for his *Margaritaville* movie, however (he'd even written a three-act play with that title), he switched the title to *Tales from Margaritaville: Fictional Facts and Factual Fictions.*

At least "in a book, you're in control of your characters, your story, and you can do what you want," he said somewhat ruefully to Richard Harrington, while still hoping, whimsically, that his film would someday be shot in Key West.

Paul Lomartire in the *Palm Beach Post* commented later that Jimmy "doesn't understand why everyone assumes he's sailing uncharted seas" when he was writing books.

"I didn't have much training writing prose other than what I like to read—and I like to listen and digest stories that flow," Jimmy said, citing his heroes E. B. White (the *New Yorker* humorist) and John D. MacDonald. But it was hard to emulate them, "because I'd have good characters, I'd have good stories . . . but it's like an album. You've got two or three great cuts and then they call the rest of it 'filler.' I didn't want to have filler stories that didn't go anywhere." Novelist friends Thomas McGuane, Jim Harrison, and Carl Hiaasen were his immediate inspiration. He always thought he was "good enough to be on their turf, but nobody else did."

Initially, he had only three short stories completed—and "boxes of notes, bits and pieces," with a looming deadline. So he struggled through February, March, and April of 1989.

"If I Could Just Get It on Paper" (Tales from Margaritaville)

■

Yes, life is a beach, especially with Buffett presiding in his hermetically sealed lifeguard tower somewhere above the sands and over the rainbow.

—Gerry Wood, *Billboard* (September 9, 1989)

Couple of years ago I worked a lot more—three hundred days a year, a quart of whiskey, cocaine till it came out my ears. That's all in the past," Jimmy said to Doug Adrianson of the *Atlanta Herald* in October 1989. He was bragging about his successful tour that summer, while complaining, "I'm tired of beating my head against trying to get on Top Forty radio." Two weeks later he told Paul Lomartire of the *Palm Beach Post* that he was sick of his record company's lack of promotion "and other differences."

Once again he rattled off an advance promise of a theatrical project—*Rules of the Road,* an intended Broadway musical about a traveling rock band, produced by Rocco Landesman (*Big River,* with country singer-songwriter Roger Miller; and *Into the Woods*), and written by

Larry L. King (*Best Little Whorehouse in Texas*). Eagle Glenn Frey (also an actor) was helping him in yet another show seemingly never mentioned again.

At least his book appeared that year. Originally he snubbed his own promotional obligations ("Nooo. I do not do book tours," he told Kayh Hogan Trocheck of *The Atlanta Journal/The Atlanta Constitution* "Weekend" edition. "You might see me on the [Johnny] Carson show or the *Today Show*, but that's it.")

He even threatened to stop touring, implying that maybe he should stay home writing.

But soon after publication he began book-touring, saying he had "dents in my fingers" from signing books in Los Angeles. "It's been crazy today. . . . They sold every copy in the store, three hundred of 'em."

■ ■ ■

In "Walkabout," the introduction to *Tales*, Jimmy jokes about the need "to be alone and free from distractions," in order to be able to write. *Bullshit!* he admits, yet in order to make the most of his theory, when he travels he takes along not only fishing equipment and music, but books. Off he headed to the island of Bora Bora, succumbing to tropical fever, where the beautiful lady at the pharmacy made his momentary sore throat "worthwhile." He ricocheted through an Australian concert tour. ("Walkabout" is an Australian aborigine theory, that every now and then a person must start walking and dreaming to recover lost mental equilibrium.) Then he returned to America, inspired by books— like Bruce Chatwin's *The Songlines,* and Ansle Roberts's *Echoes of the Dreamtime*—but it was Joseph Campbell's *The Power of Myth* that inspired him to get busy and write his own.

His opening essay, "Where is Margaritaville?" relives his Pascagoula childhood fantasies of pirating and island-questing (the *search* for the island is the real adventure). Next comes a series of six short stories, five of them with song versions on the *Off to See the Lizard* album.

The first tale (and longest in the book), "Take Another Road," invokes the film *Rancho Deluxe*. Central character Tully Mars, a Wyoming cowboy, was supposedly a stand-in during the film. Tully Mars is a thinly veiled Buffett, always dreaming of some fanciful island. He has a confrontation with one Thelma Barston, a tribute to the fact that plastic surgeons can "make mountains out of molehills."

Tully leaves Wyoming and begins logging a diary of his wanderings. His first entry depicts the Custer battlefield at Little Bighorn, Montana. One of the park rangers is a Tennessean—Tully is of Tennessee stock— and he alludes to Captain Benteen, Custer's ally.

Tully hits Hannibal, Missouri, next—he's a Mark Twain zealot, of course, carrying one of Buffett's favorite companion books with him,

Twain's *Following the Equator*. The humor heats up when a girl, Donna Kay, accuses him of wanting to marry a lusty blonde with a love of horses, plenty of money, *and* a sense of total obedience!

Tully bounces further south . . . past Elvis's Graceland (grave land), and into New Orleans, for a trysting reunion with his fleeting lover, Donna Kay. She leaves a note pinned to him saying that despite being a white boy, he danced well. He misses her still. In Alabama, his Wyoming sensibility marvels at seeing a mural painted on the roof of a barn portraying a bunch of mermaids observing a cowboy who was riding a large bucking "shrimp."

Jimmy told Linda Wortheimer, "That is my favorite story—that is the last story that I wrote . . . it's a journey particularly through a lot of my childhood . . . he gets to the coast of Alabama and he takes off on a boat."

Jimmy told journalist Garland Reeves that Tully was "a man of honor. He promises to take his horse to the ocean and he does it." Jimmy was in Wyoming, at actor Harrison Ford's ranch, when the idea of Tully's character first occurred to him: "We were out riding one day, and there was this pink trailer with plastic flamingos all around it."

"Off to See the Lizard" follows two sisters, Aurora and Boring Alice Porter, around their hometown of Heat Wave, Alabama, on Snake Bite Key. (Blacks and whites get along on this tiny island, since they have no choice—no room for separation.) The girls are predestined to promote a football team. Ann tells their new coach, seafaring hero Romeo Fleming, not to "fuck with fate." Romeo, coincidentally, is a beach-boy fiction writer. Already he has turned a harrowing shipwreck experience into a best-selling book—and now he has to flog the flagging Lizards team into action. Rain drenches the playing field, until the black and white players are so covered with mud, they are indistinguishable.

And they win.

Their victory party sounds like the aftermath of a Buffett concert—team members jitterbugging on the cafe tables, downing cheeseburgers, and guzzling beer and spewing it on one another.

Originally, Jimmy had wanted to have the two girls run a restaurant, with Boring Alice desiring "to date a man from outer space who came to the Florida Keys to fly-fish." Somehow he changed the plot. "I felt a close kinship to these two characters," he told Linda Wortheimer. "They reminded me of some sisters I had met before." Jimmy said he had been a big Godzilla fan ("and I still am"), but also had been inspired by an expedition off the Gulf Coast that had been prowling about looking for sea monsters. So he stuffed this combination of ingredients into his imagination, then "baked it for thirty days, and out came 'Off to See the Lizard.' "

As Wortheimer noted, the girls in the story are singing the chorus of the song "Off to See the Lizard." But Jimmy told Garland Reeves that he didn't want the short story "to be just a stretched-out version of the song. It started out in left field and stayed there."

The tale "Boomerang Love" also occurs in Snake Bite Key, hometown of heroine Angel Beech. Angel (like Jimmy—and his wives) is from a Catholic family. Her father had been mayor of Heat Wave, and her mother was killed by Hurricane Blanche in 1953. Her father tells her later that he was grateful he never had a son. . . . Since the world wouldn't want someone else like him. Sons and wives can blow away like the wind, never to return, he adds, but your daughter always remains . . . your daughter.

Now another hurricane was threatening the town, and Angel was still living in fantasies, imagining that her mother was a mermaid and her father was hanging the moon, and her first boyfriend was a wandering gypsy, since he had left by sailboat for Tahiti!

"The Swamp Creature Let One In" is a rambunctious golf-course farce, long on pungent dialogue between aptly named players "Lard Ass" Huckle and "Balls" Rawls. They drink while they play. Balls grumbles at the end of the "goddamn" game, calling his partner an "asshole." They repair to the country club, and the bartender regales them with a tale of Reverend Sonny Boy, the preacher of "the Snake Bite Church of the Righteous Serpent." The narrative is as rowdy as "God's Own Drunk," the Lord Buckley recitation Jimmy liked to perform (till he was sued). Reverend Sonny bites a snake in the middle of its head and leaves it for dead, but back on the golf course, it makes a humorous comeback, playing a role in settling the golf-game rivalry once and for all.

The protagonist of "The Pascagoula Run" is a teenager who longs to travel beyond Pascagoula. The *National Geographic* is his inspiration. He's named James Delaney, after Jimmy's father (and grandfather). The character's uncle Billy may have "circled the globe like a satellite and had the scars and tattoos to prove it"—but he's probably modeled after Jimmy's own wild uncle Billy. He utters what might be Jimmy's own credo, that ships preceded airplanes and they will survive when all of the world's airplanes tumble from the sky. And he offers some inspiring advice: Stay with Uncle Billy and acquire more girls than Frank Sinatra obtained. He warns Jimmy Delaney about the risks of "Catholic guilt" on his odyssey through adolescence toward adulthood. Uncle Billy (whom his mother says never grew up) warns him, however, not to enjoy too much recreation. There's always a price to pay.

"I Wish Lunch Could Last Forever" is an impressionistic, emotional odyssey of a girl named Isabella. She shifts from Martinique to New Orleans, gently abandoning her sea-captain lover. His replacement, Slade Patterson, calls New Orleans a haven for esoteric types, where meals are mixed with "mud and blood." Patterson is a musician who heads for New York with pages of music and a head full of visions. He gets a record deal, and Isabella ends up in Paris (where he always wanted to go). Somewhat like the song "Margaritaville," the surface plot is Buffett cuisine, but the subtext is evanescent, nostalgic love, concluded with an understated ending.

While Linda Wortheimer termed tales (and songs) like "Boomerang Love" "romantic," she called "I Wish Lunch Could Last Forever" much "stranger, more amazing." Jimmy told her how some characters in Faulkner's novel *Mosquitoes* enjoyed having lengthy lunches at Galatoire's restaurant in New Orleans. "When I was growing up, Galatoire's—like the St. Louis Cathedral in New Orleans—was one of those places that not many tourists went, but it was a *shrine* of a sort. It's sort of a tradition to go there, and I have *had* some lunches that lasted forever in there!"

"You Can't Take It with You" purports to be set in Margaritaville, where a rich family's black-sheep son lives, drawing a monthly check on the condition that he will *never* return home. When his family cuts him off, he becomes (what else?) a bartender. He hoped to commit suicide, by drowning, but when the "fucking" phone company called to cut off his service, he lost his temper—and found himself wanting to live since the "goddamn" phone company had rescued him. A happy, Margaritaville ending!

The last of the ostensible short stories is "Are You Ready for Freddy?" Jimmy himself is a character, heading back to Margaritaville from Nashville (where he's just cut a record), via Key West. But he's enchanted with the chance to meet Freddy and the Fishsticks, his favorite rock band, on Parrothead Records. (Jimmy and some of his band occasionally play in bars under this alias.) Freddy is an "improved" caricature of real-life Buffett—with two Grammys to his credit, and Hattiesburg college memories.

Freddy communicates some road wisdom, calling one cranky guitar player an "asshole" who will always remain that way, while he himself is more wedded to his career than to any lady.

Freddy reminisces about his halcyon drug-dealing days—he spent his honeymoon in jail, and by the end of his first tour, he was divorced. Narrator Buffett continues to ask Freddy for advice, which Freddy frankly terms worthless. Such as saying that it's foolish to be serious about your career.

As Jimmy told the *Nashville Banner*, "I'm in there as basically a young Jimmy Buffett who drives him to Key West and gets to ask him all the questions everybody always asks me."

■ ■ ■

The rest of the book is Buffett autobiography: anecdotal sketches.

"Hooked in the Heart" relives the filming of Hemingway's *The Old Man and the Sea*— in a dream sequence, with Jimmy waking up with his copy of the novel open across his chest as crickets began chirping musically in the night. (Jimmy actually met Gregorio Fuentes, the real-life inspiration for Hemingway's novel.)

"Life in the Food Chain" underscores the need to have plentiful provisions on one's boat—reliving the story of his father almost starving to death aboard the old sailing ship *Chickamulla,* in the company of *his* father, sea captain James Delaney Buffett.

"A Gift for the Buccaneer" is a travelogue—Jimmy, wife Jane, and daughter Savannah heading to the Yucatán. Jimmy remembers his boyhood adulation of Gulf Coast pirate Jean Lafitte as they make a spooky trip to some pirate's grave in the jungle.

And "Sometimes I Feel Like a Rudderless Child" is a Caribbean memoir commemorating bartender Joe Giovinno, who taught Jimmy how to sail—and Jimmy taught him how to take music with him when he sailed. He and Joe had sprinkled gossip and intrigue over the beaches as they voyaged, Jimmy reflected wistfully, on learning of Joe's death in Honduras in 1987.

■ ■ ■

The *Margaritaville* collection was a fitting debut for Jimmy as an adult author. The stories are not traumatic, hard-hitting episodes with dramatic endings on the one hand. But they aren't inconclusive and ambiguous, either. Like Jimmy's songs, they have a subtle semblance of form (beginning, middle, and end) and, despite their generally raucous humor, hit lightly with understated impact.

The tales aren't written to be "hits." Rather, they're like good cuts on a good album, such as *Off to See the Lizard.* As *Tennessean* music columnist Thomas Goldsmith quipped, "In show-and-book business this is called cross-promotion."

■ ■ ■

Naturally, Jimmy sold out his summer Starwood Amphitheatre concert. Then on October 21, 1989, he was a guest speaker at the *Tennessean's* twenty-first annual Book and Author Dinner at the Stouffer Nashville Hotel. The host was *Tennessean* (and *USA Today*) editor John Seigenthaler. Jimmy gave a witty presentation, then signed books afterward (including mine). Well, if you can't get a Country Music Association award show, how 'bout a Nashville book-banquet gig?

One of Nashville's steel-guitar players, Howard White, had written his own picaresque odyssey, *Every Highway out of Nashville* (with Ruth White). A road veteran who had traveled with Don Gibson, Cowboy Copas, Hawkshaw Hawkins, Jean Shepard, and Hank Snow, White read *Tales from Margaritaville* with a sense of empathy: "I thought after I read that that he would have enjoyed a trip with us, having a few drinks with us, and listening and laughing and all . . . he would have been *one of us* on the road."

■ ■ ■

By December Jimmy was in Washington, D.C., at Crown Books on K Street, signing over nine hundred copies of his book in less than two hours. "If the nuns at school saw me signing like this, they'd hit me on the knuckles with a ruler," he joked.

Yet according to *Publishers Weekly,* Jimmy's book "caused more than its share of holiday blues." An early survey had predicted it would sell well—indeed, it outsold his records, until the publisher's "inventory came up empty." "We certainly could have sold a lot more of it," sighed Kevin Demko. Though the book was hardcover, his store—Paperback Booksmith in Plainfield, New Jersey—ran out of it in early November and received no more until mid-December, when "the demand had pretty much peaked." Harcourt Brace Jovanovich is partly based in San Diego—yet Tom Stoup of Blue Door Bookstore *in* San Diego said, "I guess the publisher didn't print enough because we were never able to get it!"

Well, the first printing of *Tales from Margaritaville* was "only" 45,000. By October the following year there were 300,000 in print—and it had been on the *New York Times* bestseller list for seven months. Jimmy was back on the charts, at least. A trade paperback followed, then a mass-market paperback (both from Fawcett Books).

Reviews were favorable, if sometimes qualified. Thomas L. Kirkpatrick in the *Library Journal* praised the "laid-back style reminiscent of the oral tradition" while still preferring Jimmy's music to his prose; *People* joked that Buffett fans would enjoy it, but others should "keep the tequila, lime, and ice handy to give his prose more kick"; and Janet Kaye in *The New York Times* praised his "lighthearted endorsement of adventure," saying that readers, upon finishing the book, "will be tempted to get out their maps."

By now Jimmy was getting the next best thing to radio airplay: book-shelf permanence. By 1995 *Tales from Margaritaville* was in over *one thousand* library locations.

Stars Fell on Tennessee
(Margaritaville Records)

■

We are delighted the Old Town has found such an owner as Jimmy Buffett. It shows the continuing attraction that our county and its history has for those from all walks of life.

—Mary Evins, executive director, Williamson County Heritage
Foundation, to Bob Holladay, *The Williamson Leader*
(Franklin, Tennessee), March 21, 1991

The same year the book was published, Jimmy campaigned for Captain Tony Tarracino down in Key West, for the mayoral election. Seventy-three-year-old Tony had lost four times before. Now, thanks to Jimmy, he won by thirty-two votes. He had been inspired by Ronald Reagan: "I only got one hearing aid, and I think he's got two. I still make babies, and I'm sure he gave that up years ago." The captain and his kids represented approximately *five decades of procreation* (Catholic Tony wondered if he shouldn't have been a Mormon).

"The greatest thing in Key West is election," he said. "It's like squirrels coming out of hibernation. For two months, they're out running around, then after it's over they go right back to their hole and take their acorns with them."

He was defeated in 1991 in a runoff—"We may have lost our mayor but we got our captain back," acknowledged local citizen "Roy Boy." At least Tarracino has been awed over the years by "Last Mango in Paris," stunned when he first heard the record. ("I almost cried. . . . It shocked me, it was so personal. Everything, it was there just the way I said it.")

∎ ∎ ∎

So, if Jimmy could win an election for someone, and write a book that stayed on the *New York Times* bestseller list for twenty-seven weeks (the song "Margaritaville" was only in the Top Ten for three weeks!), why couldn't *Off to See the Lizard* sell? According to Steve Greenberg of Lafayette, Indiana's, *Journal and Courier*, Jimmy felt it was his "favorite album and had all the elements to be a smash. It wasn't."

"There was an album that had, to me, everything," Jimmy said. "It had enough freshness, great songs, a great producer [Elliot Scheiner]. . . . It's a durable and lasting record. It had enough modernization that the record company should've gotten into it . . . it didn't happen, they went about it the wrong way."

Jimmy claimed four or five songs could have been hits. Steve Persall in the *St. Petersburg Times* praised the opening track, "Carnival World" (written with Roger Guth and Jay Oliver), since its "bouncy melody and clever chorus make this his best shot at the singles chart for the first time since 1981."

Yet Persall, like countless critics of Jimmy's Eighties albums, thought most of it was not strong enough, carping about "upbeat tempos and cute wordplay. . . . Too often, though, he takes the easy, familiar way out. . . . His sense of escapism has become too familiar; a vacation spot visited twice too often. When Buffett acts his age and tries to inform, rather than impress, his music can be touching and amusing, like a James Taylor of the tides. . . . [The album] may be a handy addition for the wanna-be beachcomber." (*Nineteen* years since the first Buffett–James Taylor analogies! Jimmy has *never* learned to write and sing for album reviewers!)

Well, the title tune has an infectious melody, as does "Boomerang Love," and especially "Changing Channels" (written with Mac Mc-Anally), with idyllic, eternal-poetic lyrics. Good music is apparently bad news in someone's office.

Paul Lomartire of the *Palm Beach Post* said Jimmy was "at odds with his record company over his perceived lack of promotion and other differences," and wouldn't be recording in 1990. MCA had probably failed to coordinate *Off to See the Lizard* with Harcourt Brace's *Tales from Margaritaville,* blind (deaf?) to the identical song titles and chapter titles.

What more could Jimmy have done for a record company than write a book—free of charge—to go with an album? Did anyone at MCA *read* the correlated chapters, or make any phone calls to radio stations . . . and maybe mail some books along with albums to the disc jockeys?

As the turbulent triangle (Azoff-Geffen-Yetnikoff) could have attested, music marketing success requires working together like allied troops in the Normandy invasion. Jimmy, who would rather sing, write, read—anything but process business—was frustrated that he had to become his own General Eisenhower if he wanted to move his troops to victory.

But what had been his *own* availability for promotion? "Buffett's reluctance to submit to interviews is odd," wrote Steve Persall in 1991, "considering the fact that he was once a freelance journalist himself." Jay Orr echoed this in the *Nashville Banner:* "He refused interview requests as the date for his Nashville show [August 9, 1991] approached."

■ ■ ■

His next album was an inevitable sequel to the sluggish last one—a composite of 1990 live concerts—*Feeding Frenzy* (1991). With a new song by Mac McAnally, "The City," another hit-that-should've-been (with a grabby melody) condemning urban excesses ("how they keep us in debt / by the trends that they set / in the city"). He gave a political speech to the audience as well, recommending sending the executives from the failed savings-and-loan associations over to Iraq ("That'll solve *two* problems right there"). And instead of building just one B-1 bomber that "doesn't work," he wanted to divert funds into five-dollar bills, and fly it to Russia and drop the money on the Russian people. A week later the U.S. could fly to Russia and drop *mail-order catalogs* on the people—and win them over to capitalism! (But would the *Coconut Telegraph* sell in Moscow?)

Then followed a loving "Why Don't We Get Drunk"—with the audience howling the happy hook line so they could be on the record!

■ ■ ■

Jimmy wanted to go to Castro's Cuba and gather "news" for his forthcoming novel, but he couldn't, so he wrote two letters in 1990 to the Department of the Treasury challenging their "medieval" travel restrictions—as well as the American bureaucracy's ignorance of other nations' interests and needs, and their inability to communicate with people as they really are. He said Cubans would prefer the American way of life if they were free to talk with us. Too late. The damage was done almost thirty years ago by Ivy League intelligence operatives like C. Tracy Barnes, who lied to Adlai Stevenson—making him tell the United Nations that the U.S. had had *nothing* to do with the Bay of Pigs (the "most humiliating moment" of Stevenson's career).

At seven in the morning on January 29, 1991, four Cuban refugees landed at Jimmy's Key West home along the waterfront, in an eighteen-foot boat. They'd left Havana around six o'clock the previous evening: a medical doctor and a professional diver, with both their wives. Jimmy's father was sitting sipping coffee when he saw the couples looking weary and damp (they'd spent twelve hours on the water). So he went in and roused his son, who noted they did have food and water, but no particular charts or maps—but at least a compass. The women tried to make themselves more "presentable" while Jimmy called the Coast Guard.

"Just another day in Margaritaville," said Miami Coast Guard Lieutenant Jeff Karonis, upon learning that Jimmy gave them "refreshments" and some music tapes—then turned them over to the Immigration and Naturalization Service. Dozens of Cubans were pouring into the Keys each month. The refugee camp is but a few blocks from his home.

The *Coconut Telegraph* quoted J.D. Buffett as saying that his Spanish was as bad as their English, and concluded that he already knew his son's lifestyle might result in some unusual event.

The following year the *Telegraph* acknowledged that Fidel Castro's initial overthrow of Batista was maybe "honorable" (but was it honorable to exile *our* Mafia?)—yet there were simply too many Cubans drifting to the beaches of Florida, especially at Jimmy's homeplace, suggesting something was wrong. Then followed an editorial (from John J. Young's Key West newsletter *InCUBAtor*) endorsing investments in Cuba. Hopefully one day there'll be a Margaritaville shop 'n' club in Havana and a *Cuba-nut Telegraph* newsletter.

■　■　■

Jimmy sometimes jokes that he's had one and a half hits. He's charted that many divorces.

Back on December 22, 1988, in Key West he filed for his latest Key West divorce—a rather un-merry Christmas present to Janie, as well as a morbid birthday gift to himself. "We [had] stayed in touch and were good friends but not lovers," he told Anne Trebbe of *USA Today*.

One day he was in Bora Bora, and asked himself, "What the hell am I doing here? I've come all this way to this magical place, and I'm not here with anybody!" He was fishing, and wrote a melancholy song . . . "but there was something missing."

Someone, actually.

Janie.

So on July 11, 1989, he withdrew his divorce action. "My wife and I had been separated for almost seven years. We were reconciled and I was still touring. And writing a book. It was a pretty big menu," he told Mary Campbell of the Associated Press. "If it hadn't been for Janie,

I'd have quit and been a bachelor and gone to live in the woods with my dogs," he told Anne Trebbe. She had "done a lot of work on herself, and dragged me kicking and screaming to therapy."

"Performance had been my life. Family and friends came second," he told Mary Campbell. "My therapist said, 'Performance is *part* of your life, not your *whole* life!' I said, 'Dang!' You're lucky if you live long enough to realize that."

To Robert Hilburn of the *Los Angeles Times* he admitted that his career had always came first: "Everything was about Jimmy's job, what Jimmy wants. Everything else was secondary." He might suddenly decide that he had to go to Tahiti to research something—or go cut an album—and *everyone* had damned well better stay out of his way. Finally he realized "I was about to lose the woman I really loved and who was my soul mate . . . I finally had a heart-to-heart with myself." He admitted that he didn't know what marriage really was, and "never really gave it a shot." If he didn't give it one last honest try, "there would be a real hole in me." All the success possible wouldn't fill his psyche's void.

Jimmy, despite his shunning interviews much of the time, was certainly more maritally candid than many other of his celebrity colleagues. (Space limitations prohibit listing *their* names.)

■ ■ ■

One bonus from marriage renewal was another daddy-daughter collaboration: *Trouble Dolls* (1991). "Some songwriters, like Jimmy, are just natural storytellers," said Harcourt Brace Jovanovich editor Barbara Fish to *The New York Times*.

The protagonist of the story, Lizzy Rhinehart, looks similar to Savannah Jane in the illustrations by Lambert Davis (Savannah day dreamin'?). She is trying to hunt down her lost father, an environmentalist who's crashed his plane down in the Everglades. (Jimmy had gotten a pilot's license and a Lake Aircraft Renegade seaplane back in 1988, so the drawing of the plane in the book was identical to his own aircraft.)

In the story, Lizzy boards her own sailboat, *Parakeet*, and some magical dolls from Guatemala help her find her missing father. (She has no mother—hers died years ago.)

"This is a perfect summertime book," said Michael Carlton in *Southern Living*. While Shirley Wilton in *School Library Journal* chided the complex plot, she concluded that youngsters who liked the Everglades—and maybe liked Jimmy and Savannah Jane—"will enjoy the story for the make-believe adventure that it is."

But as time passed, it became *less* make-believe than either author could have imagined.

In 1991 Jimmy showed an *"Air Margaritaville"* film onstage at the Riverbend concert site in Cincinnati. In a vintage 1940s airplane, he and his crew provided music as he flew on autopilot. "Enjoy yourself," exuded reporter Cliff Radel. "Have a safe trip back to reality." In Boston that summer he arrived "high above [the] stage in the cockpit of the 'Margaritaville Clipper,' a mock-rendering of a Caribbean prop plane." He shouted, "We're coming in over the Cape Cod Canal."

Ah, but airborne Jimmy was on borrowed time. . . .

■   ■   ■

"Buffett plans to return to Nashville with wife Jane and daughter Savannah Jane. Buffett hasn't lived in Music City since fleeing the town in the early Seventies," reported Gerry Wood in *Billboard* in December 1990 (appropriately, down in Key West himself!). "Jimmy is constantly on the go, so it cannot be said any one house is his main home," said one of his Key West representatives a few months later (indeed, the Georgia Music Hall of Fame nominated him in 1990 on the thin pretext of a farm he owned near Thomasville in south Georgia). "But I do know that his wife has been in the [Nashville] area looking at the schools." Jimmy explained that he didn't want to live in Malibu, where Janie had been in reclusion, and *she* didn't like Key West (anymore)—so "Nashville was sort of a compromise."

In April of 1991 he and Janie bought Old Town, an historic house in Williamson County, southwest of Nashville. It cost around $700,000, and they spent much more rehabilitating it. Built in the 1840–50s by slave labor for the Tom Brown family, the exquisite mansion on the Harpeth River is famous for its Great Temple Mound, nearly a millennium old. Some of its Indian graves had carvings that resemble the idols of India or China.

Outside is a limestone bridge built in 1801 by the federal government, developing the Natchez Trace as a trail for travelers from Natchez to Nashville (from Nashville, the initial trip to Natchez was usually down the Mississippi). (The Trace ends a few blocks from Jimmy's 1969 Chesterfield Avenue apartment.)

Old Town is not a known haunted house—but perhaps it should be. While playing with a slave girl, the Browns' three-year-old daughter fell off the back porch and broke her spine. After her death at age sixteen, a white-sheeted ghoul tried to rob her grave but her father repulsed him with a shotgun. One of her brothers died of illness in his room—legend says that his dogs knew he was dying, howling mournfully outside his window. Tom Brown supposedly hid raw gold under the house, and when a slave spotted him, soon both his gold and the slave disappeared! (During the Civil War, Tom Brown did time in prison in Nashville for refusing the Union loyalty oath.) As recently as January 1969, a loyal servant named Anna Bell lost consciousness in the kitchen at Old Town and died of a stroke.

Jimmy and Janie restored everything possible, adding library bookcases and bathrooms, a screened porch, and a new stone wall outside.

"Because of the Buffetts' interest in history as well as cooking," informed their later realtor, "a vegetable garden resembling an historic kitchen garden was laid out in a sunny spot." They even disassembled a two-hundred-year-old guest house in Alabama and moved it up to Old Town.

Out back was an ancient smokehouse (for Tennessee country hams), which they turned into a supermodern music and video theater. ("If you want to see a John Wayne movie, enter 'John Wayne' [on the computer] and it will give you scheduling for all John Wayne movies showing on cable in the United States," according to Fridrich and Clark Realty.)

Jimmy and Janie wrote up a detailed description of all their renovations, and in 1992 won the Williamson County Heritage Foundation Architectural Award.

■ ■ ■

On Halloween of 1991, Jimmy incorporated Margaritaville Records in Tennessee with three Atlanta business backers. It would be "independent" (i.e., funded by Jimmy and investors), but still under the MCA umbrella for distribution and (theoretically) airplay. (If Priscilla Presley had brought Elvis out of hiding, and they had started Graceland Records, *he* would have gotten scant airplay unless she had a major-label connection.)

Margaritaville's eventual vice president was Robert Mercer, born in 1944 in England. A statistician, Mercer worked for General Foods, then landed at EMI Records in London ("foresaking snap and crackle for pop"). He was handed a Sex Pistols demonstration tape in 1976, and remembers, "It just sounded fuckin' awful to me, and I said *no way.*" But the A&R folks insisted, "Listen, the Pistols may be a piece of shit musically, but it's what happening in the streets of London. These are the forerunners of the whole punk movement. . . . Besides which, what do you know? You're over thirty!"

By 1980 Mercer was working with EMI Films (as "Creative Vice President"), and eventually as an independent manager (Paul McCartney) and advocate of Pink Floyd's performance of *The Wall* at the site of the Berlin Wall in Germany.

Jimmy and Mercer were friends in the 1970s, having "kept in touch through mutual friends" according to the *Coconut Telegraph.* (Yes, they had folks in common!)

Mercer was in Nashville in 1990. In the same article announcing Jimmy and Janie's plans to move to the once-hated Music City, it was announced that Mercer was looking for record-industry employment. His wife's name was also cited, by diligent Gerry Wood, as being (Who's the blonde stranger?) *Margie Buffett Mercer.* She likely met him through their mutual company, EMI (which used to be Capitol), since they married in London, September 9, 1978. Buying a house outside of Nashville with him, she had at least raised her standard of living since *her* last

Music City, U.S.A, matrimonial session. From Capitol to EMI to MCA-Margaritaville, Margie had boomeranged (like Buzz Cason) from Nashville to L.A. to London, then back again. Her second marriage license called her a "marketing director" (EMI?), but she was not a Margaritaville staffer.

■ ■ ■

Jimmy needed to sign acts to his new label, and issue something of his own, but first—*get his damned novel done!* "The short-story book was successful. I couldn't leave it there," he told Mary Campbell of the Associated Press. "I didn't try to write *War and Peace*. I tried to write something you could take to the beach. I wanted it to read easy."

As poetic troubadour Donovan had said in 1969, "The trend in pop today is the equivalent of the trend in literature in my dad's time. Songs today take the place of the renegade novelists of two generations ago, simply because no one has time to read books anymore." Twenty years later, Jimmy had broken Donovan's rule. Could he do it again?

At first he titled his novel *The Black Bean Experience*. ("It's not going to be a great American novel. It's a minor American novel with a few major flaws . . . a story of caviar theft, overweight and murder.") But finally it became *Where Is Joe Merchant? A Novel Tale*.

"I think it's human nature to love romantic tales and exotic places," he said to *The New York Times*'s Thomas Clavin. "I sure did. . . . My goal was to write about what I knew and was told—an escapist adventure, that book people would bring to the beach."

Editor Bonnie Ingber agreed. She wasn't really surprised at the triumph of *Tales from Margaritaville*: "Jimmy is by no means an overnight success. He's been working at getting an audience over twenty-odd years of touring and recording. Remember, he has platinum and gold albums. That's a lot of people out there."

Yes—platinum is $2 million in sales, gold is $1 million. Notwithstanding radio indifference (most of the time), by 1990 *Changes in Latitudes, Changes in Attitudes* (1977) and *Son of a Son of a Sailor* (1978) had gone platinum; the live *You Had to Be There* (1978) and *Volcano* (1979) had gone gold. And of course, *Songs You Know by Heart—Jimmy Buffett's Greatest Hit(s)* (1985) would soon become double platinum. ("Shame on you if you don't already own every LP this man's made," cheered Robert K. Oermann when it first came out.)

Though the concert ticket buyers were potential book buyers, the arduous demands of his touring competed, somewhat, with his commitment to the novel. "My intention, being the good Catholic schoolboy that I am, was to write every day on the road. It just didn't work out that way," Jimmy told Beth Levine in *Publishers Weekly*. At least on the road he could absorb the images of people and places: "This turned out to give great substance to my characters. It was like putting gravy on a good piece of meat." For instance, in a South Carolina town he spotted a "human cannonball" in a traveling carnival—a man whose background he engrafted onto one of his characters.

Jimmy had been planning a 120-page book he could write in about a year, but the manuscript just grew. "There were times I said I really don't need this shit. . . . I'll go back to rock 'n' roll," he told Ann Trebbe in *USA Today*. "I learned a tremendous amount about discipline. I would spend a day or two writing a song," he explained to Thomas Clavin, "but writing a novel, I was at it every day for three years, whether I was home or on the road. I couldn't abandon my characters, even for a little while, and the story kept growing." One of his "subliminal" influences was 1930s and 1940s movies with their exotic settings, and man-woman conflicts that didn't resolve themselves "until the last reel."

In some ways, perhaps, his own nuptial estrangement owed its recovery to *Where Is Joe Merchant?*

On April 1, 1992, Janie delivered Sarah Delaney Buffett at the Centennial Medical Center over in west Nashville. "It was totally unexpected. If you had told me two years ago that I'd be livin' in Nashville," he said to Robert K. Oermann, "back with my wife and havin' a baby, I'd have told you you were crazy."

And the novel, still in the writer's womb, was born four months later.

34

Where Is Joe Merchant?
At Number 1, That's Where . . .

■

The freaky brew of characters and scenes Jimmy Buffett sets down in this whimsical Caribbean fantasy seems distilled from recording-session outtakes.

Pirates, con artists, drifters, hangers-on, lost loves, mercenaries and other colorful Joes swirl like debris caught in the Bermuda Triangle. It's fun stuff, leavened with singles-bar theology and warmed-up Zen.

—Bill Bell, *Miami Herald*, September 20, 1992

The secret to many authors' success is having a literary agent. But Jimmy didn't want one.

On his own, he hit up Harcourt Brace Jovanovich for a six-figure advance—pocketing the percentage an agent would have kept. "It doesn't take much to add up numbers, does it? You'd have to be a dummy not to see that if twenty percent of the people who buy half a million of my record albums buy a book, that's a substantial sale," he told Beth Levine. "If you are selling 400,000 albums and playing to 700,000 to a million people a year, you ought to be able to sell 100,000," he told Robert Hilburn, while confessing a little surprise that *Tales from Margaritaville* had sold 400,000.

Still, as *Publishers Weekly* noted, Harcourt Brace was scarcely in healthy financial shape. Editor Bonnie Ingber conceded that "our stock situation is somewhat precarious. [But] our trade division has been doing very well. We just had our best year in seventeen years."

That was in 1990. The print run of *Where Is Joe Merchant?* was originally announced as 200,000 copies. It finally appeared in August 1992, switching Jimmy from his concert tour to his book tour.

■   ■   ■

But who is (was?) Joe Merchant?

A missing rock 'n' roll star—reportedly dead, but just maybe alive . . . hiding out in Communist Cuba. The pursuer? Frank Bama, a compulsive pilot whose plane was his "insurance policy against what I feared most: a boring life." Bama's father had been a Charles Lindbergh protégé, who died in aerial combat in World War II.

Bama heads to Cuba with Key Westian Rudy Breno, whose cover story is that they are doing a Hemingway documentary. But the Cubans think they may be covert invaders, so they knock out Breno and he retreats to Key West. The rather frenetic plot has many Buffettesque elements, from a tire swing to condemnation of condominiums. Joe Merchant's sister, Trevor Kane, shows up. And Charles Fabian, reminiscent of smuggler Phil Clark, works for fanatical anti-Communist Colonel Cairo, and with shootings and tabloid journalism, the plot maintains bizarre momentum.

■   ■   ■

The success of *Where Is Joe Merchant?* was only in part due to Jimmy's name and the prior success of his *Tales* volume. Both factors combined could still not have carried the novel to Number 1 on the *New York Times* bestseller list, let alone held it there awhile. (As Gene Lyons remarked, unlike *Tales from Margaritaville*, "Buffett's novel is no sunshiny cruise on the Gulf Stream.")

Jimmy, thankfully, lacks literary pretense. Unlike so many "serious" novelists, he isn't looking over his shoulder, worried about the critics— nor is he staring at his own navel, obsessed with some personal literary theory. He probably knows something too few aspiring Great American Novelists know—that an author must first entertain the reader, before unloading his ideas or plumbing deep emotions. Yet many elitist critics shun the hedonistic, pleasure-rending qualities of fiction with almost Puritanic diffidence. Whereas Jimmy Buffett acts, on paper, more or less as he does onstage—with zany zest. He doesn't confuse seriousness with *solemnity!* As he told Mary Campbell of the Associated Press, "I'll read something serious, but then I have to read something not serious."

Though he admitted having to peek into Shakespeare for inspiration: "Richard III is the best villain there ever was. I didn't know how to write about bad guys. I found myself going back to the classics to look for clues."

■ ■ ■

Novels are often read in bed, and short chapters make for easier, faster reading.

Where Is Joe Merchant? has seventy-six chapters (in only 382 pages), and unlike so many contemporary novels, they are divided into sections, with comical chapter titles (e.g., "Who's Eating Who?"; "I'd Rather Watch Paint Dry"; "The Snakes Are Talking"; etc.). This layout gives an epic, nineteenth-century feeling (and look) to the book, reminiscent of the time when novelists such as Dickens might write one chapter at a time, in serial sequence, for a magazine. Such a lively, flowing format gives a short-story feeling to each chapter, and to Gene Lyons, the chapter titles "sound like the song list for a new album."

Lucretias Hartberg of the *Tennessean* expanded upon this point:

> For Parrotheads (you know who you are), one of the most appealing features of the book is Buffett's use of his favorite verses, expressions, and song titles. . . . The troubadour of bars and beaches, boats and planes, has woven all those elements together in a tapestry of intrigue, suspense, and cunning.

Some of the critics winced at the novel's zany complexity—Mark Caro of the *Los Angeles Tribune* thought it was "more of a diverting flight than a lasting journey," and the *Boston Globe*'s Steve Moore said lightly that Jimmy shouldn't quit his night job of live, arena entertaining. But Robin Cuzzort of the *Nashville Banner* praised his ability to weave such a zigzaggy plot enlivened by so many bizarre characters. Richard E. Nicholls of *The New York Times* said, "There's a gentle charm to his portrait of loners and outlaws hustling to make one last score. Even the thugs are more inept than lethal."

By now Jimmy had an agent—to negotiate his *next* book—who told him, "The best thing about my writing is that I don't write like anyone else."

■ ■ ■

On the final lap of his 1992 tour, people in the audience began holding up copies of the novel. "That was great," exulted Jimmy. "I'm a big advocate of reading. So I'm happy that this book has people turning pages." Like his once girlfriend from Mobile, Shirlene "Cissy" Terrell: "I was really impressed with his book I read. It was kind of a crazy book, but it was real good, it was written very well. You're not quite sure where he's going with it for a while there. And I'm sure some parts of it are about his own life." (Adds Jimmy: "I don't have to make most of this up.")

Robert Hilburn of the *Los Angeles Times* compared Jimmy and Jane's reunion to the novel—"the hero realizing his adventurous lifestyle alone isn't enough and that he needs a relationship. Pretty autobiographical?" Answered Jimmy: "There's a definite parallel." And he told Mary Campbell of the Associated Press that while Frank Bama wasn't *him*, they liked the same singers: James Taylor and Van Morrison.

"Once I got the lead character and his girlfriend going, it was a matter of connecting old haunts and stories and changing a few names." Looking back at his "wild years," he decided that this had been "research"— and he was glad that he didn't have to invent very much. He wanted the book to be "a very strong character book," pitting good against evil, "a quirky, not-so-normal" story.

At least regarding book reviewers, author Jimmy had grown up, as well as older. Back in 1976 he had told Bob Anderson of *High Times* that as an entertainer, sometimes he wondered "how the fuck" he did it, since a typical audience of "fourteen thousand crazies" would instantly let him know whether they liked him or not. Whereas a *novelist* was at the mercy of "thirteen fucking critics in New York that run your life. They can make you slash your wrists in the bathroom, depending on what they say about you in *The New York Times*'s Sunday Book Review section." Jimmy said that you might spend a year writing a book, then "wait a month for ten people to decide whether it's good or bad."

■   ■   ■

The Associated Press on August 21, 1992, reported him flying into Portland, Oregon, by seaplane, and landing on the Willamette River. Then he headed for a local bookstore to sign some *Joe Merchant* copies, and that night performed at Portland's Civic Stadium.

Then on October 14 he was down in Jackson, Mississippi, signing books at the fittingly titled Lemuria bookstore. (Lemuria is a "lost" continent in the Pacific, discovered—at least in book form—by occult author James Churchward.) More than three hundred Parrot Heads showed up . . . and were offered chances to adopt seventy-five parrots by Laurie Brown of the Jackson Zoo. Jimmy adopted a blue-and-gold macaw named Tootie (but otherwise wouldn't give any interviews, rather idiosyncratic, considering parrots' talkative nature.) But all sorts of folks gratefully got his autograph. Such as the activities director of a local retirement center, China Donnell, who offered her professional diagnosis: "He's probably going to be so tired, he may just be able to sign 'J.B.' His writing is pretty abstract in his book and he is strange and wild." She was sipping a margarita as she talked. And she could define Margaritaville: "It's after you've got a buzz, and you're feeling good and you're wishing you were somewhere exotic . . . with someone else."

Patton Hawkins, a twenty-one-year-old National Guardsman, elaborated: "You want to leave your house, sell your car, your kids, and go rent a boat and disappear." He had been a Buffett follower since he was twelve, and was eager for Jimmy to sign his book, "because I want to ask him what *his* favorite places to go in the islands are—and where he stays there—because I'm going."

One of the signees, Jane McDonald, owned more than a Jimmy Buffett book. She owned his 1964 Falcon convertible, and when she showed him a copy of the car's title, he broke out laughing. He couldn't *believe* the car had made it to New Orleans, since it had lacked a floorboard, a top, and "was just a rusted frame." It had cost Jane a hundred and fifty dollars, and she came primed with a number of car questions for Jimmy . . . then got so excited, she forgot them all. The car had an Air Margaritaville sticker on the driver's door, a green lizard on the dashboard, and a red bag hanging on the shift lever—"all put there by Jimmy Buffett." Supposedly, Key West Margaritaville secretary Cindy Thompson had bought it from Jimmy and sold it to former band member Don Krus, who drove it to New Orleans. Jane took a night job, "just to get the car restored. Two years later I have finally completed it, and it's a beauty."

By closing time at the Lemuria store, *one thousand* autographed copies had been signed.

Avon Books issued an international mass-market paperback the following June and a standard mass-market paperback in August. A vacationer in Martha's Vineyard, President Bill Clinton, went out and bought a copy.

As for his next book, he told Robert Hilburn it might be a short-story collection: "In some ways, I did the novel just to prove to myself I could do it. But I really love short stories [with] recurring characters. The way a certain character will reappear in Larry McMurtry's work."

■　■　■

But, like most fiction writers, Jimmy has Hollywood stars in his eyes, if not in his computer. Writing a *Joe Merchant* movie script was a hoped-for interruption. If his friends in the movie industry didn't follow up the opportunity, then "I'm going to stand on the Nevada border, toss the book into California, and have Hollywood throw me a suitcase full of money. And then I'm going fishing."

Invasion of the Parrot Heads

■

One of the prerequisites of forming a Buffett club is you'd better be prepared to work your butt off.

—Gordon Pike, cofounder of Parrot Heads, Jackson, Mississippi;
interview, November 13, 1994

W"ho *are* these people?" asked Charlie Chase of TNN's *Crook and Chase* in November 1993. "Have you gone out to meet 'em?" He wondered just *who* Jimmy's "Parrot Head" followers really were.

"They're scary, Charlie, they're scary."

"Are these doctors and lawyers doing this, or what?"

"A lot of brain surgeons—a lot of people who work in emergency rooms—like my music."

He cited the film *The Doctor* (1991), where they were singing "one of my songs which we can't do on television."

"Yeah, we know which one," confirmed Lorianne Crook.

Jimmy said his fans were like Mardi Gras: You could either be a bank president or a United Parcel Service truck driver.

Lorianne Crook held up Jimmy's Margaritaville boxed set—*Boats Beaches Bars & Ballads*—containing four compact discs. "This has gone platinum already, hasn't it?"

"Actually . . . today it went to four hundred thousand."

Jimmy learned that it was MCA's best-selling boxed set ("Hell, it's the eighth-selling boxed set in history"). By common industry standards, the boxed set was embarrassing. It had too many songs—seventy-two, with around eighteen per disc; and *The Parrot Head Handbook* inside wasn't a once-over-lightly pamphlet printed in cramped, hard-to-read fine print. It was a square-backed sixty-four-page guidebook, written by Jimmy with every single song annotated as to why, where, and how it was composed (as in a classic poetry book). *Billboard* called the book "priceless."

"Lots of pictures of you in skimpy bathing suits, too, on your boat," noted Lorianne Crook, calling out, "*Girls!*"

"They're old pictures. That's when I had hair and everything. . . ."

Besides dozens of old album cuts, remixed, there were several new releases as well, such as "Everlasting Moon" (written with Matt Betton), an environmental fantasy (moving the moon to a better place) that America's leading science-fiction poet, Bruce Boston, would like. "Domino College" (written with Dan Fogelberg) extols real-life education in the Caribbean ("Make your parents hate you," etc.). "Elvis Imitators" (by Steve Goodman and Michael Smith) is a tribute to the King-in-hiding.

Now, there are artists as famous as Jimmy whose retrospective boxed sets offer as few songs, and as little information, as possible. Underground Nashville gossip says that Richard Weize's Bear Family Records in Hamburg, Germany, usually does a better job on legendary country acts than the Music Row conglomerates.

■　■　■

But there was more to do in 1992 than run a summer tour, promote a boxed set ("I don't give a shit about gettin' on the radio," he told Keith Spera of *Offbeat*. "All I need to do is make sure the stuff is in the store") and sign copies of a best-selling novel. He had to recruit some new acts for Margaritaville. But he wasn't going to imitate the Beatles' Apple Records and sign everyone he personally liked and lose millions as quickly as possible ("Riches Back to Rags"). Indeed, Bob Mercer must have known *that* story, from EMI, himself! Nor did Jimmy aim to change music history, like Sun Records (Memphis) or Monument Records (Nashville), and create countless famous acts like Elvis, Jerry Lee Lewis, and Johnny Cash (Sun), to Roy Orbison (Sun *and* Monument) and Ray Stevens (Monument)—and go out of business, for famous reasons.

So where *had* he found the acts to record? *Bourbon Street.* "I learned to be a performer on those streets. There's a lot more to it than making a video," he told Keith Spera of New Orleans's *Offbeat* magazine, who admitted Jimmy had been "press-shy in recent years." Jimmy compared himself to Ricky Ricardo, who'd drop by a club—and he said he sought groups who didn't ultimately depend upon their records as much as on concert tours.

Yet if you tell an executive that you didn't need a hit, "they'll tell you you're full of shit . . . the music business is so covered with bullshit and hype." He said his relationship with MCA was "sort of like Beirut. . . . Right now we're in a temporary cease-fire," and he condemned the L.A. headquarters while admitting, "I'm in a peace treaty, and I do most of my work out of Nashville." He *did* give MCA credit for the boxed set ("They did an incredible job with the marketing aspect").

"I just really got intrigued with the idea of the kind of talent he might bring to the label," said MCA's Bruce Hinton, "talent that would not necessarily find its way in normal day-to-day business through our own label." Mercer added, "MCA advances us an overhead from which we run this. And they pay for our artists' recording costs. . . . But there's a huge overlap there. As soon as we find an artist that we want to sign, we start to involve MCA."

New Orleans Jazz Fest director Quint Davis pointed Jimmy toward two groups in local clubs: Evangeline and the Iguanas. "With me as a record-company president, they get somebody who was a lawyer in New York," said Jimmy, reinforcing his street-singing background.

■ ■ ■

After ten years of warming up, Dolly Parton, Linda Ronstadt, and Emmylou Harris recorded their *Trio* album in 1987, selling millions. Thus they inspired Rhonda Lohmeyer, Kathleen Steiffel, and Sharon Leger, who formed Evangeline in 1988, named after Longfellow's poem about the Nova Scotian "Acadian" migration to Louisiana.

Steiffel grew up in Bay St. Louis, Mississippi, and attended two of Jimmy's colleges (Pearl River and Southern). After Evangeline's breakup in 1990 ("You get burnt out on Bourbon Street, and we weren't making any money"), she spent a year and a half in Nashville at songwriters' showcases.

By 1991 Evangeline had reassembled (Steiffel rejoined them), playing in La Strata on Bourbon Street, when Jimmy saw them and signed them. (They had won first prize at the Jazz Search contest.) Their first Margaritaville album, *Evangeline,* was recorded at his Shrimp Boat Studio in Key West in February 1992. He sang along on their version of Nanci Griffith's "Gulf Coast Highway." The album sold fifty thousand copies and spawned a dramatic video, "Bayou Boy" (by Rhonda Lohmeyer).

The group now had singer-pianist Beth McKee and instrumentalist Nancy Buchan (fiddle, mandolin). They opened for Wynonna, formerly of the Judds (whose sweet harmonies theirs resembled), as well as for Jimmy on his 1992 tour. "He was a pleasure to work with," affirms Buchan, "very professional—he's had a lot of guys who've worked with him for many years, so obviously he treats 'em right. He's got a great grasp of what works commercially."

Their second album, *French Quarter Moon* (1993), included a Fifties-style rock song, "Let's Go Spend Your Money Honey" (by Kelly Willis and Kostas), which became a video with a comic cameo appearance by Jimmy.

In 1994 they appeared at Nashville's Summer Lights festival, but broke up for the second time. Hopefully, one day there'll be a Caribbean-Cajun theater at Opryland for acts like theirs.

■   ■   ■

Quint Davis also took Jimmy to the Maple Leaf Club on Oak Street to watch the Iguanas.

"It wasn't them as much as watching the audience react to them," Jimmy said. Already they'd won local jazz awards.

The band has been onstage with Bruce Springsteen, Los Lobos, and the Texas Tornados, and they utilize that neglected instrument, the accordion. "The climate is our secret weapon," says saxophonist Derek Huston. "We play those sleazy medium and slow tempos—it's hot down here and you don't want to wear anybody out." Their album, *The Iguanas,* complemented their 1993 tour with Jimmy, during which they appeared for over a million people. Their next one, *Nuevo Boogaloo* (1994), also featured "road-tested" songs, and was followed by *Super Ball* (1996).

■   ■   ■

Other Margaritaville products include Todd Snider's *Songs for the Daily Planet* (1994), a sort of Nineties hippie album ("My generation should be proud," etc.), with Dylanesque harmonica-playing. Snider says that while Jimmy "promotes the idea of personal freedom through the ocean, I like the idea of freedom along the highway and through the underground." One of his favorites is Woody "Hard Traveling" Guthrie. (Snider's 1996 album is *Step Right Up*.)

"We're not a country label, we're not a rock 'n' roll label," Jimmy affirmed. "We're Margaritaville Records and we're as undefinable as me."

One anthology, *Margaritaville Cafe—Late Night Menu* (1993), offered twenty songs, by everyone from Fingers Taylor and Michael Utley and Robert Greenidge, to groups like the Survivors, and Little Nickie and the Sticks. Among Jimmy's cuts was "Another Saturday

Night," an old Sam Cooke hit that somehow went to Number 74 in country music for Jimmy (there was no apparent follow-up).

Another one was "Reggae Accident," by Lucus P. Gravell, about a fellow who has a car wreck, leaves his wife, and heads for Jamaica. Gravell pitched it to Jimmy's engineer, Dave Reynolds, at a Garden State Arts Center concert in New Jersey. He told Reynolds, "Every time I play this song, somebody comes up to me and says, 'That's a Buffett song.' If that just happened once or twice—if it was just my good friends—I wouldn't be here." (Gravell had read Reynolds's name in the album notes on *Feeding Frenzy,* so his song-pitching gall should inspire other desperate writers.) Six months later they called him back and said, "Jimmy's going to cut your song." Gravell wrote it in 1982, but had pitched it before—he wanted it for Steve Goodman, but Goodman died of leukemia in 1984.

Its successor, *Late Night Gumbo* (1995), has Jimmy singing two old favorite standards, "Sea Cruise" (1959) and "Goodnight, Irene" (1950).

■ ■ ■

More of Jimmy's own albums came out.

Before the Beach (1993) reissues the two Barnaby albums, inexcusably *without* "The Christian?" (some sort of publishing retrieval problem, surmises Buzz Cason).

Fruitcakes (1994) was the first studio album in five years, and went to Number 5 in pop. "Everybody's Got a Cousin in Miami" (written with Michael Tschudin) commemorates the Floridian "pirate and pioneer" while honoring a fictitious "cousin" who works out of a pay phone, an "international investor." Apparently, it also extols the Cuban refugees whom Jimmy welcomed to his Key West home. The album's title song (written with Amy Lee) is fairly incredible, praising diverse religion and irreligion (paganism versus Catholicism, and "the WASP and the Jew"). "Six String Music" (written with G. E. Smith) is another homemade music gibe at TV videos—a strong country cut (with Dobro) that manages to visit Africa, and the best song on the album, according to Mark S. Krzos, who felt Jimmy's "pained" voice hadn't sounded so good since "A Pirate Looks at Forty." His "Love in the Library" (written with Mac McAnally), another instant cult classic, recalls the library in Mobile (not far from the Admiral Semmes Hotel) and the value of books between young lovers. "Quietly Making Noise" (written with Michael Tschudin) notes that Oscar Wilde died in Paris (where Jimmy has retained an apartment).

Another album, *Barometer Soup* (1995), offers songs mostly cowritten with Russ Kunkel, Jay Oliver, and Peter Mayer. The title song is good, and "Barefoot Children," with another strong melody, is one of his best ever. "Bank of Bad Habits" asserts that while he's "no St. Ignatius," neither is he a "barfly." Mark Twain's *Following the Equator* triggered

"Remittance Man," and "Diamond as Big as the Ritz" is a tribute to an F. Scott Fitzgerald short story. "Jimmy Dreams" (no cowriter) extols his happy fantasies. "Don't Chu-Know" is another sing-along (Jimmy is one of the "recycled history machines"—"indecision may or may not be my problem"). A pretty listenable album.

And *Banana Wind* (1996) inflicts more outrageous lyrics, such as "Cultural Infidel" ("Someone's got to raise hell, I guess it could me"), as well as a touching tribute to his father, "False Echoes," in which he nostalgically relives days in Cuba.

■ ■ ■

Over the years, Jimmy has persistently aided various charities.

"I'm of the mind that you give something back," he said to Steve Garbarino of the New Orleans *Times Picayune,* in 1988, "and make an example for other people, so they won't be so greedy and apathetic." He had been rending annual performances for New Orleans Artists Against Hunger and Homelessness, since "unlike many of the massive rock 'n' roll benefits," he knew where the money was going—not for mere "concert expenses." Other participating acts the previous three years had been Linda Ronstadt, the Neville Brothers, Allen Toussaint, and Rita Coolidge—raising $114,000 thus far.

That same year he advertised the cause of the Greenpeace organization, which was trying to save dolphins from the tuna industry, which was killing tens of thousands every year. The *Coconut Telegraph* reported that 110,000 had recently been slain in the Eastern Tropical Pacific, and they urged support of the Marine Mammal Protection Act. The magazine also lamented the dolphin and whale "strandings" on the beaches of Florida—advertising a "Whale Friend" program and the Dolphin Research Center.

"A Boxful of Africa" was a short Jimmy essay that appeared in *Heaven Is Under Our Feet: A Book for Walden Woods* (1991), edited by former Eagle Don Henley and distinguished rock author Dave Marsh. Jimmy compared the naturalness of Africa (where he'd taken Savannah Jane in 1989) to the relative environmental harmony of his Georgia habitat. The book (crammed full of famous contributors, from James A. Michener, Arlo Guthrie, and the Reverend Jesse Jackson, to Jimmy Carter, Robert Redford, and Kurt Vonnegut) became a bestseller.

In April of 1992, Jimmy led a benefit at the W. O. Smith Nashville Community Music School (with Mac McAnally and Josh Leo). Smith (1917–1991) had been a blues sideman for entertainers like Duke Ellington and Dizzy Gillespie, then a Nashville music teacher at Tennessee State University. MCA's Bruce Hinton and producer Tony Brown recruited Jimmy to raise money for low-income children. "I hope you have fun and enjoy the show," Jimmy announced in print, "because we are not going to give you your money back. We've got music lessons to pay for." The show was acoustic, and quieter than a Parrot Head concert, raising nearly sixty thousand dollars for the school.

W. O. Smith had written his autobiography just in time—the manuscript was published posthumously by Nashville's Rutledge Hill Press, with stories about Fats Waller drinking a quart of whiskey during a two-hour rehearsal. The school is in the Edgehill community, where black harmonica player DeFord Bailey lived till his death in 1982. (The Opry's first "star," Bailey is overdue in the Country Music Hall of Fame.)

(Other acts had staged W. O. Smith benefits in the past: rhythm and blues band Booker T. and the MGs, and country stars Chet Atkins, Kathy Mattea, Lyle Lovett, and Mark O'Connor.)

In 1995 twelve W. O. Smith students (ages ten to seventeen) contributed to *The Parakeet Album* on Margaritaville Records. Jimmy didn't sing on the album—it belonged to the kids—one of whom, Charli James, aged ten, said, "It'll be a good thing to put on my résumé. 'At age ten, I did an album for Jimmy Buffett.'" One sixteen-year-old girl, Lisa Rutledge, admitted, "I'm used to singing in a group, where if I make a mistake, nobody picks it up." But on "Off to See the Lizard," she made errors that were caught and corrected. Margaritaville Records even paid to send ten of the students to New York City, to perform with Jimmy on the *Today Show*. "Jimmy is going to be in a Santa suit," said W. O. Smith director Jonah Rabinowitz to the *Nashville Banner*'s Beth Stein, "then they'll sing 'Jingle Bells' during the credits."

"Many songwriters refer to their songs as their babies," summarized the *Tennessean*'s Tom Roland, "and some of Jimmy Buffett's material is experiencing a second childhood."

Another impulsive charitable event happened in 1993, in the birthplace of the Parrot Heads, Cincinnati. Connie Musser had bought tickets to four of his five shows—then, a few days before the concert (June 29, 1993), a swimming accident paralyzed her from the neck down. Jimmy did one of the concerts for her, giving her, among other gifts, an autographed beach ball and a three-thousand-dollar machine to help her turn on lights and dial a telephone. She went through physical therapy and some of the paralysis abated. ("I have felt so helpless until now. But there are eleven months before the next Jimmy Buffett concert. I'll be there on my feet in the front row.")

By 1994 he was down in Tampa playing acoustic solo for Democratic gubernatorial candidate Lawton Chiles. Some of the audience was recruited by George "Just George" Cain, "club historian" of the Tampa Bay Parrot Heads in Paradise.

"One of the great environmentalists of this country . . . a great Floridian . . . and he's a fantastic entertainer, the wonderful Jimmy Buffett," exclaimed Sandy Freedman, mayor of Tampa, over the microphone.

"Seriously, if I've done anything in the last ten or fifteen years, besides have a good time and live here," said Jimmy, "it's been to give something back to this state that has been very kind to me and to my family." He said he was trying to "instill responsibility that our natural resources are treasures that we have to cherish because that's why we all came here to live in the first place. And the thought of oil wells offshore, or no Everglades cleanup, or a dirty Florida bay, or a dirty Tampa bay, doesn't fit into Jimmy Buffett's Florida!" He bragged that at least they had forced all the politicians in Florida to offer *some* kind of environmental policy. He then condemned the opposition's lieutenant-governor candidate, who didn't even "want us to wiggle below our waist."

He launched into singing "Fruitcakes," and before he did "Come Monday," he told the audience that when it was a hit "half of you people weren't even alive." He permitted ex-Governor Bob Graham to sing along and clap ("Not bad rhythm for a white guy"). Jimmy promised to go down to Key West the next day and vote.

Opponent Jeb Bush—son of George Bush—had recommended that Jimmy get out of politics and stick with his music. Jimmy said Jeb Bush should get out of politics and go back to condominium development.

George Cain instigated autograph-signing, and Jimmy began signing them on Cain's back. "What about *me?*" asked Cain at one point. "Have I got time for this?" retorted Jimmy—then with his pen initialed Cain's T-shirt. Someone tried to buy Jimmy's hat for one hundred dollars—unsuccessfully. ("I don't need the hundred bucks but I like my hat. I ain't got too much hair left.")

Jimmy had even sent a form letter out to twenty-five thousand voters warning that all the environmental work was "in danger of wasting away. . . . There simply is no choice. Your children will thank you. As the song says, 'How can you tell how it used to be when there is nothing left to see?' "

Lawton Chiles won.

▪   ▪   ▪

The Tampa Bay Parrot Head club is reportedly the nation's largest with six hundred members. But what *are* Parrot Heads? Concert reviewers are charmed by their loony spectacle—"sporting gaudy print shirts, Parrot Head hats, stuffed sharks and plastic flamingos perched on their shoulders," observed the *Cincinnati Enquirer*'s Cliff Radel. They drew their name from the Deadheads, the followers of Jerry Garcia's Grateful Dead; that band had been an even bigger concert act, usually Number 1 in ticket sales. Like Jimmy, the Grateful Dead had only one Top Ten hit (avoiding studio album sessions even more religiously).

But Garcia died of a heart attack in 1995, subsequent to his decades of drug abuse (and recent treatment). And LSD pope Timothy Leary said reverently that the Deadheads were "the finest and largest disorganized religion in the world," before he himself died in 1996.

■ ■ ■

Alas, Jimmy's Parrot Heads don't measure up, don't earn that sort of attention.

Jimmy won't even grant his name or support to the more than seventy groups around the country *unless* they agree to around four benevolent projects each year. (For example, the Tampa group has adopted a manatee; they help out at the local zoo, and assist a lady with a seabird sanctuary for injured seabirds; they do shoreline and river cleanup, and have adopted one of the six-mile causeways to the beach for maintenance.)

Scott Nickerson started the first Parrot Head club in Atlanta in early 1989. Then the idea caught fire and spread across the nation (with groups in Canada and Australia). No group can be closer than fifty miles to another one. Yet there are some members who "relate to the atmosphere and the type of activity created by these clubs, that aren't necessarily Buffett fans," admits Nickerson. "It's just like what they say about Jimmy's concerts: It's not necessarily the music itself, but it's the whole environment or aura." Nickerson runs his musical act, AlA, and is the liaison between Parrot Heads and the Margaritaville store enterprise.

The Atlanta group created the "underwater monopoly contest," raising seventy thousand dollars for the Muscular Dystrophy Foundation. Jimmy wrote his own letter to the Metro Parrot Head Club in Wainscott, New York (run by Marie and Joe Lombardi), thanking them for "doing such a fine job with the road cleanup." He apologized for not dropping by and seeing them, since "between my teenager, three-year-old daughter, and infant son [alluding to his adopted son, Cameron Marley Buffett] pulling on my legs, it's hard to break away from them when I'm not touring."

Gordon Pike started the club in Jackson, Mississippi, with a tiny blurb in the newspaper. "We got about sixty-five to seventy people signed up the very first night we had this thing." Then a local radio station gave them one advertisement per month. "We got a call from a radio station in Hattiesburg wondering what the hell we were doing, 'cause Buffett went to school down there. We have a fairly equal amount between married and single, male and female—air-traffic controllers to lawyers. I don't know if we have a doctor in there or not, but we have professional people. We have bartenders, we have everybody."

Including Josh Sharpe, who joined the club in October 1994. A week later he had a car wreck, and according to Pike, "put himself in a wheelchair for the rest of his life." Pike made some calls to Margaritaville in Key West, but unexpectedly, Fingers Taylor "went up and saw the guy, which was real good," and left him a rare *Chest Pains* album.

Pike continues: "You'd better be prepared to do a whole lot of social stuff. I'd rather have thirty really good members than two hundred 'pay the eighteen bucks, never see them again' members. . . . My thing is, you know what happens when you put a Deadhead and a Parrot Head together? You get a dead parrot, you know!"

"Basically each of the Parrot Head clubs probably target the different charities," says Ron Allred, founder of the Lone Star Parrot Head Club of Watauga, Texas. His group supports radio station KLIF's "Klif Kids" Christmas charity for poor children (thirty thousand dollars in donations in 1995), and the Oklahoma Casualty Recovery and the Riding Unlimited program, which gets autistic children on horseback to coordinate their motor skills.

Allred mentions that Dallas Parrot Heads—and numerous others across the country—are doing Ronald McDonald House benefits, where children with cancer or other life-threatening illnesses have their parents come to dinner at McDonald's restaurants. Parrot Heads bring the cooked meals.

Other groups include the Midwest Tropical Appreciation Society (Flint, Michigan), which runs canned-food drives for a local soup kitchen all year long, gathering money for 2,674 cans in August 1995. The Metro Parrot Heads (New York, New Jersey, Connecticut) rally to clean up their portion of Route 114, plus Seabright Beach in New Jersey; they've handled the New York Cares program, "turning empty lots into community gardens, painting an enormous mural in the Bronx, and cleaning up regional and state parks," and are involved in the Long Island Festival of Trees (for United Cerebral Palsy) and the March of Dimes.

At the fifth annual "Back at the Ranch" concert in August 1994, the Metro Parrot Heads watched Jimmy appear with Paul Simon, who originated this benefit show to assist Long Island charities. It raised over a hundred thousand dollars. "Jimmy worked the audience, signed autographs, and talked with us for a while during intermission," says Metro newsletter editor Lon Ormanian. "What a regular guy. No crowds, no bodyguards, security, or even roadies. He was tuning his own guitar and setting up the microphones, much like the early days."

When Scott Nickerson noted clubs being formed in Beaumont, Texas, New York City, Orlando, New Orleans, and Detroit, he led the First Annual Parrot Head Convention in New Orleans in 1992. A year later seventeen more groups were formed. By 1994 the third annual "Meeting of the Minds," as it was now called, representing more than fifty groups, was held in November, organized by Pam Garges of Dallas, Texas. "Jimmy doesn't even want to step in and become an integral part," says Nickerson, underscoring the independence and self-reliance of all the groups. "He had nothing to do with the forming any of these groups." Nickerson consults with Margaritaville's store operation, and Jimmy's management, to assure compliance (the convention is held at the Margaritaville restaurant), for instance. But the work is up to him and the Parrot Heads.

On November 5, 1994, the mayor of New Orleans proclaimed Parrot Head Week, and representative Jeanne Natham told the audience at the Margaritaville cafe, "I hope you come back every single year for the rest of your lives!"

Conclusion (A Parrot Looks at Fifty)

■

It's an exciting thing for me. I'm able to last this long, and not be a dinosaur, but be a viable act bringing in new fans every year.

—Jimmy to Gary Graff, *Country Song Roundup* (February 1996)

How'd you get up here?" David Letterman asked Jimmy on May 23, 1994.

He said he'd flown his seaplane up from Florida to New York. "It took me four days. The moving van beat me here."

His seaplane was "an old one with engines on top. I have been flying about seven years and just take my time and come up the coast."

"Is it safe? Are you checked out? Do you have any idea what you're doing?" asked Letterman.

The audience laughed hard.

"Yeah, I know—insurance rates are high on musicians. And TV performers."

"Did you ever have any trouble in the plane?"

"Yes."

"*I* would be scared silly to fly myself *anywhere!*"

"You're supposed to be able to react immediately to things. . . ."

"Do you do that?"

"Most of the time. I'm still here. It's a lot of fun."

David laughed, asking Jimmy for details. He said he flew at "seven hundred feet all the way." (Huge audience laughter.) "I never went above seven hundred feet—you can't see the restaurants." Jimmy said someone in a restaurant, exclaimed, "Boy, you look like that guy in that Jimmy Buffett book."

Dismayed, David Letterman declared that his office was five hundred feet high!

But Jimmy exuded, "It's an inspiring trip. That's where I get a lot of my stuff from—it's just being in the plane and looking down."

"It must be very satisfying for you."

"It *is!*"

Letterman had joked about seaplanes having *pontoons*. . . .

Jimmy mentioned that his tour would be starting on Long Island. He owned a house there. He also rented a house in Nantucket, Massachusetts.

∎ ∎ ∎

On August 25, 1994 he and a friend "who asked not to be identified" were fishing in Madaket Harbor at Nantucket. Jimmy decided to leave in his nine-seat, twin-engine airplane (Grumman G-44 Widgeon) at three P.M. "We got done fishing and drained the water out of the pontoons so he could take off. I guess maybe we didn't get it all. About three seconds after he went up, the plane just dipped and he went right in." He was about thirty feet in the air when the plane dove into a wave.

Jimmy noticed something was wrong—but it was out of control. The pontoons in his plane must have filled up with water, speculated Nantucket Fire Chief Bruce Watts: "It must have had a crack or a hole or a break in it somewhere. When Mr. Buffett took off, there was just enough wind to tip the plane and send it back in."

Jimmy started swimming and a boat happened by, and picked him up and hauled him ashore. He was taken by ambulance to Nantucket Cottage Hospital. Police Chief Randy Norris said, "He has some bumps and bruises, but he seems to be just fine." Emergency-room nurse Donna Fleming said, "He walked out with his friends."

He headed to his home on Long Island. His plane was upside down in the water when a man in a sailboat went past. Finally it was pulled from the four feet of water and shipped to New Bedford.

There had been a St. Christopher's medal in the plane. "It's ironic. He wanted that St. Christopher's medal when he was in trouble," observes his aunt Patsy Lumpkin—she remembers that Jimmy went back and got it out of the plane. ("Somebody was looking after me—either St. Christopher or God)."*

Nine days later he wrote a letter to this writer for inclusion in this book. The following spring the James Taylor song "Mexico" (from *Barometer Soup*) reminded him that "I had a brush with death" in Nantucket—and "Jimmy Dreams" upheld his commitment to lovable flying.

■ ■ ■

Jimmy sold his Old Town house to singer-songwriter Kim Carnes in 1994, whose duet with Kenny Rogers, "Don't Fall in Love with a Dreamer," went to Number 3 in country in 1980. (Her "Bette Davis Eyes"—cowritten with Jackie DeShannon—spent nine weeks at Number One in pop in 1981.)

Jimmy and Janie now owned a home in West Palm Beach.

■ ■ ■

The day before his plane crash, on August 24, 1994, he had made the front page of *USA Today,* headlined JIMMY BUFFETT IS BROADWAY-BOUND. He and novelist Herman Wouk were working on a musical version of Wouk's Caribbean novel, *Don't Stop the Carnival.* Ever-hopeful Jimmy (theater . . . film) said he was ninety percent certain that the musical would occur. "We're going to stick with the story and not sell it with overproduction. . . . I don't want to be the central character, but maybe I could write myself a *convenient* part."

At least he appeared, briefly, in the 1995 film *Cobb,* about baseball immortal Try Cobb. Jimmy played a heckler whom star Tommy Lee Jones personally attacks.

■ ■ ■

By now Jimmy was a friend of billionaire Warren Buffett, who said, "He calls me from time to time, but I should be calling him." Warren was named "Uncle Warren" by Jimmy ever since they had met in New York, united by Jimmy's own bottle of hamburger sauce.

Warren Buffett was born in 1930 in Omaha, Nebraska, and since his father had been a Republican congressman, he grew up around Washington, D.C. (His John Birch Society dad always opposed inflation, and urged friends to buy jewelry and gold as a safeguard.) He delivered newspapers, and set up pinball machines in the barbershops. By age

---

* Singers killed in small-plane crashes include Buddy Holly, Ritchie Valens, and the Big Bopper (1959); Patsy Cline, Cowboy Copas, and Hawkshaw Hawkins (1963); Jim Reeves (1964); Jim Croce (1973); plus eight members of Reba McEntire's band (1991).

twenty he had saved $9,800, and with his master's degree in business (from Columbia University), there was no stopping him.

Warren Buffett was frugal and unimpressed with Wall Street trends and fashions, sticking to common-sense investments and living cheaply in Nebraska. But he liked mass media, so bought into the *Washington Post* and the *Boston Globe,* and by the 1980s was purchasing cable TV. By 1995 he had ten billion dollars, a live-in girlfriend, and a friendly wife living in California with whom he still shared business. One of the world's ten richest people according to *Forbes* magazine, he said in 1989, "We've never succeeded in making a good deal with a bad person." (Listen up, record-album cutout marketeers!)

The Omaha Buffetts originally came from Long Island (like so many Buffetts after the American Revolution). But his sister Doris had traced their family's genealogy back to Nova Scotia, so he and Jimmy presumed they were distant kin—"from Omaha to Margaritaville," joked *Forbes.*

■ ■ ■

And *Forbes* was impressed that Jimmy was selling so many compact discs, concert tickets, books, T-shirts, plus food and gift-shop gimmicks. "Maybe there's a certain amount of cheesiness to the whole thing," Jimmy acknowledged, "but it's Economics 101—like it or not, these things sell."

Already he had left Harcourt Brace Jovanovich, securing a $3 million advance for a Random House book of fiction. (Ex-Evangeline singer Kathleen Steiffel has seen him doing research down in Bay St. Louis for that next title.) And he has been moving Margaritaville Records out from under MCA, over to Island Records, which used to record the late Bob Marley. This might amuse Nashville author Scott (*Music City Babylon*) Faragher, who once tried—unsuccessfully—to reel Marley-esque reggae music in from Jamaica, and land it in his Nashville booking agency.

■ ■ ■

No longer on the *New York Times*'s Top Ten bestseller chart, Jimmy was back in the "Top 40" in 1994—as Number 35 in *Forbes* magazine's hit list of "big-money entertainers." He was behind one Nashville act, Garth Brooks (Number 11), as well as Nashville-educated Oprah Winfrey (Number 2), but was at least ahead of Billy Ray Cyrus (Number 37). Jimmy's success was charted from $12 million sales in 1993, and $14,000 in 1994. The next year he was Number 36, having sold $12 million in 1995. (Though *Forbes* failed to account for Jimmy's refusal "to pay the mini-mart back" for the shoplifted peanut butter.)

Jimmy Buffett's career has just begun.

■ ■ ■

Somewhere in the Gulf Stream south of Pascagoula sails the ship of Captain James Delaney Buffett. With one hand on the starboard rail, he's waving back at his grandson.

And at Norfolk Island, some of the Buffett descendants keep to themselves a legend that never dies. Pirate Jean Lafitte had been missing for several years when John Buffett arrived at Pitcairn Island in 1825. The pirate who was with him had supposedly reformed and was seeking salvation. But they do not dismiss the morbid story of Lafitte's rivalry with Buffett over a Welsh woman immigrant. In their lovers'-triangle fiasco, Lafitte's percussion pistol fortunately jammed . . . and Buffett's lead ball missed Lafitte.

He left Pitcairn in 1831, with his wanton woman. He learned in direct fashion that she was pregnant from her abandoned lover, according to one confidential version. (Other gossip has Lafitte himself as the father.) Miraculously, the baby was born at sea and survived. Supposedly, they made it to Rose Blanche, Canada, in 1833, north of Glace Bay, Nova Scotia.

John Buffett was still alive in 1887, and his letter concerning someone's birth that year remains in private hands. But the rest of the story has been through several film-script drafts—though the Pitcairn cult enthusiasts refuse all interviews on the topic.

As Jimmy Buffett himself remarked in his "Barefoot Children" lyric, "Fiction over fact always has my vote."

Discography

■

I've got all the Buffett albums—I'm going to die with more toys than you've got. But every time I think I've got everything of Jimmy's, then someone will pop up and say "Do you have this?" And of course you can't get it off them, they don't want to get rid of it.

—Buffett collector Mike Richards, manager of Music and More, Hendersonville, Tennessee, March 12, 1996

All songs are written by Jimmy Buffett unless otherwise noted. Chart positions: *Billboard*, except for CB (*Cash Box*). "Platinum" = 1 million sales, "Gold" = 500,000 sales—though a double album has to only sell half as many, and a four-disc boxed set has to only sell one-quarter as many, to gain the same rating.

SINGLES (45 r.p.m.)

In some instances, promotional copies have been located with only one song—possibly other versions with a B-side also exist. All chart positions are for the A-side, unless indicated in square brackets [ ].

ca. 1969
"Abandoned on Tuesday"/   Audio Mobile
   "Don't Bring Me   JET-500
   Candy"

1970
"The Christian?" (w/   Barnaby
   Milton Brown)/   ZS7-2013
   "Richard Frost"

"He Ain't Free" ["Ellis   Barnaby
   Dee"] (w/Buzz Cason)/   ZS7-2019

"There's Nothing Soft
About Hard Times"

"Captain America"/ "Truckstop Salvation"	Barnaby ZS7-2023	

1973

"The Great Filling Station Holdup"/"Why Don't We Get Drunk" [by "Marvin Gardens," Buffett pseudonym]	ABC-Dunhill D-4348	#58 (country) #65 (country, *CB*)
"The Great Filling Station Holdup"/ "They Don't Dance Like Carmen No More"	ABC-Dunhill D-4353	
"Grapefruit—Juicy Fruit"/ "I Have Found Me a Home"	ABC-Dunhill D-4359	
"He Went to Paris"/ "Peanut Butter Conspiracy"	ABC ABC-11399	

1974

"Saxophones"/ "Ringling, Ringling"	ABC-Dunhill D-4378	#105 (pop)
"Come Monday"/ "The Wino and I Know"	ABC-Dunhill D-4385	#30 (pop) #4 (Easy Listening) #58 (country) #26 (pop, *CB*) #68 (country, *CB*)

1975

"Pencil Thin Mustache"/ "Brand New Country Star"	ABC-Dunhill 15011	#101 (pop) #44 (Easy Listening)
"A Pirate Looks at Forty"/ "Presents to Send You"	ABC-Dunhill 15029	#101 (pop) #97 (pop, *CB*)
"Door Number Three" (w/ Steve Goodman)/ "Dallas" (by Roger Bartlett)	ABC ABC-12113	#102 (pop) #88 (country) #79 (country, *CB*)
"Havana Daydreamin' "/ "Big Rig" (by Gregory Taylor)	ABC ABC-12143	

1976

"The Captain and the Kid"/"Clichés"	ABC ABC-12175	

"Something So Feminine About a Mandolin" (w/ Jane Slagsvol)/ "Woman Goin' Crazy on Caroline Street" (w/ S. Goodman)	ABC ABC-12200	

1977

"Margaritaville"/"Miss You So Badly" (w/ G. Taylor)	ABC AB-12254	#8 (pop) #1 (Easy Listening) #13 (country) #7 (pop, *CB*) #10 (country, *CB*)
"Changes in Latitudes, Changes in Attitudes"/ "Landfall"	ABC AB-12305	#37 (pop) #11 (Easy Listening) #24 (country) #34 (pop, *CB*) #27 (country, *CB*)

1978

"Cheeseburger in Paradise"/ "African Friend"	ABC ABC-12358	#32 (pop) #29 (pop, *CB*)
"Livingston Saturday Night"/ "Cowboy in the Jungle"	ABC ABC-12391	#52 (pop) #91 (country) #73 (pop, *CB*) #84 (country, *CB*)
"Mañana"/ "Coast of Marseilles" (by Keith Sykes)	ABC 84ABC-12428	#84 (pop)

1979

"Fins" (w/ Deborah McColl, Barry Chance, Tom Corcoran)/ "Dreamsicle"	MCA MCA-41109	#35 (pop) #42 (Easy Listening) #25 (pop, *CB*)
"Volcano"/"Stranded on a Sandbar"	MCA MCA-41161	#66 (pop) #43 (Easy Listening) #61 (pop, *CB*)

1980

"Survive"/ "Boat Drinks"	MCA MCA-41199	#77 (pop) #71 (pop, *CB*)
"Hello Texas" (by Brian Collins, Robby Campbell) [both sides]	Full Moon/Asylum Records DP-90002	

1981

"It's My Job" (by Mac McAnally)/ "Little Miss Magic"	MCA MCA-51061	#57 (pop) #32 (Adult Contemporary) #62 (pop, *CB*)

"Stars Fell on Alabama" (by Mitchell Parish, Frank Perkins) "Growing Older But Not Up"	MCA MCA-51105	
"Elvis Imitators" (by Steve Goodman and John Prine*) [both sides] recorded by "Freddy and the Fishsticks" [Buffett pseudonym] featuring the Jordanaires	MCA MCA-51224	
"It's Midnight and I'm Not Famous Yet" (w/ S. Goodman)/ "When Salome Plays the Drum"	MCA MCA-52013	
"If I Could Just Get It on Paper"/ "Where's the Party" (w/ S. Goodman, Bill LaBounty)	MCA MCA-52050	

1982
"I Don't Know (Spicol's Theme)"	[single] MCA FM 7-69890	

1983
"Brown Eyed Girl" (by Van Morrison) [both sides]	MCA MCA-52333	#13 (Adult Contemporary)
"One Particular Harbour" (w/ Bobby Holcomb)/ "Distantly In Love"	MCA MCA-52298	#22 (Adult Contemporary)

1984
"When the Wild Life Betrays Me" (w/ M. Utley, W. Jennings)/ "Ragtop Day" (w/ M. Utley, W. Jennings)	MCA MCA-52438	#42 (country) #55 (country, CB)
"Bigger Than The Both of Us" (by Rhonda Coullet)/ "Come to the Moon" (w/ M. Utley, W. Jennings)	MCA MCA-53499	#58 (country)

* Coedited by Goodman w/ Michael Smith in *Boats Beaches Bars & Ballads* boxed set (1992).

"Brown Eyed Girl" [both sides]   MCA S45-1161

1985

"Who's the Blonde Stranger?" (w/ M. Utley, W. Jennings, Josh Leo)/ "She's Going Out of My Mind" (by M. McAnally)   MCA MCA-52550   #37 (country)

"Gypsies in the Palace" (w/ Glenn Frey, Will Jennings)/ "Jolly Mon Sing" (w/ W. Jennings, M. Utley)   MCA MCA-52607   #56 (country)

"If the Phone Doesn't Ring, It's Me" (w/ W. Jennings, M. Utley)/ "Frank and Lola"   MCA MCA-52664   #16 (country) / #37 (Adult Contemporary) / #22 (pop, *CB*)

1986

"Please Bypass This Heart" (w/ W. Jennings, M. Utley)/ "Beyond the End" (w/ Marshall Chapman, W. Jennings)   MCA MCA-52752   #50 (country) / #61 (country, *CB*)

"I Love the Now" (w/ Carrie Fisher)[both sides]   MCA MCA-52849

"Creola" (w/ R. McDonald, W. Salter)[both sides]   MCA MCA-52932

1987

"Take It Back" (w/ Mark Betton)/ "Floridays"   MCA MCA-53035

1988

"Homemade Music" (w/ M. Utley, Russell Kunkel)/ L'Air de La Louisiane" (by Jesse Winchester)   MCA MCA-53360

"Bring Back the Magic"   MCA MCA-53396   #24 (Adult Contemporary)

"Take Another Road" (w/ Roger Guth)/ "Off to See the Lizard" (w/ Jay Oliver)   MCA MCA-53675   #18 (Adult Contemporary)

1989

"Take Another Road" [compact disc promotional product]	MCA MCA-1787	#18 (Adult Contemporary)

"Carnival World" [compact disc promotional product]	MCA MCA-18045

1990

"Jamaica Farewell" (by Irving Burgie)	MCA MCA-N/A

1993

"Another Saturday Night" (by Sam Cooke)/ "Souvenirs" (by Vince Melamed, Danny O'Keefe)	MCA-Margaritaville MCAS7-54680	#74 (country) #29 (Adult Contemporary) ["Souvenirs"] #29 (Adult Contemporary)

"Another Saturday Night" [compact disc promotional product]	MCA-Margaritaville MCA-54680

1995

"Sea Cruise" (by Huey Smith) [with other sample recordings by the Iguanas, Rockin' Dopsie Jr., and Bluerunners]	Margaritaville Margaritaville 5006 [promo compact disc single from *Margaritaville Cafe Late Night Gumbo* album]

"Bank of Bad Habits" (w/ R. Kunkel, J. Oliver, Roger Guth, Peer Meyer)	MCA-Margaritaville MCA-3515 [promo compact disc single]

[single reissues]

"Come Monday"/ "Saxophones"	ABC-Dunhill "goldies 45" D-2687

"The Great Filling Station Holdup"/ "Why Don't We Get Drunk"	MCA MCA-2619

"Come Monday"/ "Saxophones"	MCA D-2687

"Margaritaville"/ "Changes in Latitudes, Changes in Attitudes"	MCA P-2792

"Margaritaville"/ "Come Monday"	MCA MCA-53568

"Why Don't We Get Drunk"/"The Great Filling Station Holdup"	Collectibles COL-90013

ALBUMS

All albums 33 1/3 r.p.m. vinyl unless otherwise noted. The MCA vinyl reissues of ABC albums tend to economize, and not fully reprint double covers and other artistic touches. Later compact disc reissues do not include notes, lyrics and other material as inserts, even from MCA vinyl versions. Original albums are more than mere "collector's items."

[September 1970] *DOWN TO EARTH*. Barnaby, Z-30093. *Side One:* "The Christian?" (w/ Milton Brown); "Ellis Dee" (w/ Buzz Cason); "The Missionary"; "A Mile High in Denver"; "The Captain and the Kid"; *Side Two:* "Captain America"; "Ain't He a Genius"; "Turnabout"; "There's Nothing Soft About Hard Times"; "I Can't Be Your Hero Today"; "Truckstop Salvation." Produced by Travis Turk. Recorded at Spar Studio, Nashville.

[June 1973] *A WHITE SPORT COAT AND A PINK CRUSTACEAN*. ABC-Dunhill, DS-50150. *Side One:* "The Great Filling Station Holdup"; "Railroad Lady" (w/ Jerry Jeff Walker); "He Went to Paris"; "Grapefruit—Juicy Fruit"; "Cuban Crime of Passion" (w/ Tom Corcoran); "Why Don't We Get Drunk" (by Marvin Gardens [Jimmy Buffett]); *Side Two:* "Peanut Butter Conspiracy"; "They Don't Dance Like Carmen No More"; "I Have Found Me a Home"; "My Lovely Lady"; "Death of an Unpopular Poet." Produced by Don Gant. Liner notes by Tom McGuane. Song lyrics on the back cover. Recorded at Glaser Sound Studio, Nashville. (#43, country; #25, country, *CB*.) MCA reissues: MCA-37026; cassette: MCAC-1589; CD: MCAD-31090.

[February 1974] *LIVING AND DYING IN ¾TIME*. ABC-Dunhill, DSD-50132. *Side One:* "Pencil Thin Mustache; "Come Monday"; "Ringling, Ringling"; "Brahma Fear"; "Brand New Country Star" (w/ Vernon Arnold); "Livingston's Gone to Texas"; *Side Two:* "The Wino and I Know"; "West Nashville Grand Ballroom Gown"; "Saxophones"; "Ballad of Spider John" (by Willis Alan Ramsey); "God's Own Drunk" (by Lord Buckley). Produced by Don Gant. Recorded at Woodland Sound Studios, Nashville. Double-shaped cover with inside painting reproduction. (#176, pop; #150, pop, *CB*.) MCA reissues: MCA-37025; cassette: MCAC-1588; CD: MCAD-31059; two-album cassette: *Living And Dying In ¾Time* and *A White Sport Coat And A Pink Crustacean*, MCAC2-6927.

[December 1974] *A 1 A*. ABC-Dunhill, DSD-50183. *Side One:* "Makin' Music for Money" (by Alex Harvey); "Door Number Three" (w/ Steve Goodman); "Dallas" (by Roger Bartlett); "Presents to Send You"; "Stories We Could Tell" (by John B. Sebastian); "Life Is Just a Tire Swing"; *Side Two:* "A Pirate Looks at Forty"; "Migration"; "Trying to Reason with Hurricane Season"; "Nautical Wheelers"; "Tin Cup Chalice." Produced by Don Gant. Recorded at Woodland Sound Studios, Nashville. Double-shaped cover with inside photographs, liner notes by Buffett with Highway A1A map. (#25, pop; #62, pop *CB* [1977: #174, pop, *CB*]) MCA reissues: MCA-37027; cassette: MCAC-1590; CD: MCAD-1590.

[July 1975] *RANCHO DELUXE*. Liberty Records [Capitol Records], LT-466. [All songs written by Buffett including instrumentals; all but one vocals by Buffett.] *Side One:* "Rancho Deluxe"; "Ridin' in Style" [instrum.]; "Left Me with a Nail to Drive" (vocal by Roger Bartlett); "Cattle Truckin'" [instrum.]; "Countin' the Cows Ev'ry Day"; "The Wrangler" [instrum.]; "Rancho Deluxe"; *Side Two:* "Livingston Saturday Night"; "Some Gothic Ranch Action" [instrum.]; "Wonder Why You Ever Go Home"; "Fifteen Gears" [instrum.]; "Can't Remember When I Slept Last"; "Rancho Deluxe" [instrum.].

[August 1975] *KICK IT IN SECOND WIND*. ABC Records, ABCD-914. [Acetate demonstration album, never released in this version; predecessor of *HAVAÑA DAY-DREAMIN'*, with same serial number.] *Side One:* "Kick It in Second Wind" (w/ Jane Slagsvol); "My Head Hurts, My Feet Stink and I Don't Love Jesus"; "The Captain and the Kid"; "Big Rig" (by Gregory Taylor); "Please Take Your Girlfriend Home"; *Side Two:* "Woman Goin' Crazy on Caroline Street" (w/ Shel Silverstein, S. Goodman)*; "Something So Feminine About a Mandolin" (w/ J. Slagsvol); "Train to Dixie" (by K. Sykes); "Wonder Why You Ever Go Home"; "This Hotel Room" (S. Goodman).

[February 1976] *HAVAÑA DAYDREAMIN'*. ABC Records, ABCD-914. *Side One:* "Woman Goin' Crazy on Caroline Street" (w/ S. Goodman); "My Head Hurts, My Feet Stink and I Don't Love Jesus"; "The Captain and the Kid"; "Big Rig" (by Gregory Taylor); "Defying Gravity" (by Jesse Winchester); *Side Two:* "Havaña Daydreamin' "; Clichés": "Something So Feminine About a Mandolin (w/ Jane Slagsvol); "Kick It in Second Wind" (w/ J. Slagsvol); "This Hotel Room" (by S. Goodman); Produced by Don Gant. Recorded at Youngun Sound, Murfreesboro, Tenn., and Creative Workshop, Berry Hill [Nashville], Tenn. Liner notes by Buffett. (#65, pop; #54, pop, *CB*) MCA reissue: MCA-37023; cassette: MCAC-1586; CD: MCAD-31093.

[ca. 1976] *THE UNCOVERED JIMMY BUFFETT*. Let There Be Music "not for sale—demonstration record" [issued by Buzz Cason's publishing company]. *Side One:* "The Great Filling Station Holdup"; "The Hang-Out Gang" (w/ B. Cason); "Bend a Little" (w/ B. Cason); "Peanut Butter Conspiracy"; "Ace"; "Livingston's Gone to Texas"; "Railroad Lady"; "England" (w/ B. Cason); "The Captain and the Kid"; *Side Two:* "Tin Cup Chalice"; "Why Don't We Get Drunk"; "Death Valley Lives"; "Mile High in Denver"; "Rockefeller Square" (w/ B. Cason); "Truckstop Salvation"; "My Lovely Lady"; "God Don't Own a Car" (w/ B. Cason); "In the Shelter."

[February 1977] *CHANGES IN LATITUDES, CHANGES IN ATTITUDES*. ABC Records, AB-990. *Side One:* "Changes in Latitudes, Changes in Attitudes"; "Wonder Why We Ever Go Home"; "Banana Republics" (by S. Goodman, Steve Burgh, Jim Rothermel); "Tampico Trauma"; "Lovely Cruise" (by Jonathan Baham); *Side Two:* "Margaritaville"; "In the Shelter"; "Biloxi" (by J. Winchester); "Landfall." Produced by Norbert Putnam. Recorded at Criteria Studios, Miami, and Quadrophonic Sound Studio, Nashville. Inside disc sleeve contains lyrics printed on both sides. (#12, pop; #2, country; #14, pop, *CB*; #3, country, *CB*) [Platinum] MCA reissue: MCA-37150; cassette: MCAC-1652; CD: MCAD-31070; CD: "MasterDisc Line" series, MCAD-10951; two-album cassette: *Changes in Latitudes, Changes in Attitudes* and *Havana Daydreamin'*, MCAC2-6908.

[April 1977] *HIGH CUMBERLAND JUBILEE*. Barnaby Records, BR-6014. *Side One:* "Ace"; "Rockefeller Square"; "Bend a Little"; "In the Shelter"; "Death Valley Lives"; "Livingston's Gone to Texas"; *Side Two:* "England"; "Travelin' Clean" (w/ Lanny Fiel); "The Hang-Out Gang"; "God Don't Own a Car"; "High Cumberland Jubilee/ Comin' Down Slow" (w/ B. Cason). Produced by Travis Turk. Recorded at Creative Workshop, Berry Hill [Nashville], Tennessee.

[March 1978] *SON OF A SON OF A SAILOR*. ABC Records, AA-1046. *Side One:* "Son of a Son of a Sailor"; "Fool Button"; "The Last Line" (by Keith Sykes);

_____

* Silverstein is not credited on the *Havaña Daydreamin'* version (1976).

"Livingston Saturday Night"; "Cheeseburger in Paradise"; *Side Two:* "Coast of Marseilles" (by K. Sykes); "Cowboy in the Jungle"; "Mañana"; "African Friend." Produced by Norbert Putnam. Uncredited liner notes by Buffett. (# 10, pop; #6, country; #9, pop, *CB*; #6, country, *CB*) [Platinum] MCA reissue: MCA-37024; cassette: MCAC-37024 [also: MCAC-1587]; CD: MCAD-31091; two-album cassette: *Son of a Son of a Sailor* and *Coconut Telegraph*, MCAC2-6917.

[November 1978] *"YOU HAD TO BE THERE"—JIMMY BUFFETT IN CONCERT.* ABC Records, AK-1008/2. *Side One:* "Son of a Son of a Sailor"; "Pencil Thin Mustache"; "Wonder Why We Ever Go Home"; "Landfall"; "Miss You So Badly"; *Side Two:* "Havaña Daydreamin' "; "Margaritaville"; "Changes in Latitudes, Changes in Attitudes"; "Come Monday"; "Perrier Blues"; *Side Three:* "Grapefruit—Juicy Fruit"; "God's Own Drunk"; "He Went to Paris"; "The Captain and the Kid"; *Side Four:* "Why Don't We Get Drunk and Screw"; "A Pirate Looks at Forty"; "Tampico Trauma"; "Morris' Nightmare" (w/ Tim Krekel); "Dixie Diner" (by Larry Raspberry, G. Taylor, Carol Ferrante, Eugene ("Rocky") Berretta, and Bill Marshall). Several songs are interspersed with Buffett speaking. Produced by Norbert Putnam. Recorded at the Fabulous Fox in Atlanta, and Maurice Gusman Cultural Center, Miami. Liner notes by Buffett. Inside disc sleeves contain photos. (#72, pop; #29, country; #38, pop, *CB*; #35, country, *CB*.) [Gold] MCA reissue: MCA2-6005; cassette: MCAC2-6005; CD: MCAD2-6005.

[1978] *SPECIAL JIMMY BUFFETT SAMPLER RECORDED LIVE "YOU HAD TO BE THERE."* ABC Records, SPDJ-43. [Disc jockey album.] *Side One:* "Son of a Son of a Sailor"; "Pencil Thin Mustache"; "Margaritaville"; "Come Monday"; "Dixie Diner"; *Side Two:* [Same content].

[September 1979] *VOLCANO.* MCA Records, MCA-5102. *Side One:* "Fins" (w/ Deborah McColl, Barry Chance, T. Corcoran); "Volcano" (w/ K. Sykes, Harry Dailey); "Treat Her Like a Lady" (w/ David Loggins); "Stranded on a Sandbar"; "Chanson Pour Les Petits Enfants"; *Side Two:* "Survive" (w/ Michael Utley); "Lady I Can't Explain"; "Boat Drinks"; "Dreamsicle"; "Sending the Old Man Home." Produced by Norbert Putnam. Recorded at Air Studios, Montserrat (additional recording: Quadrafonic Studios, Nashville, and Sunset Sound Studios, Los Angeles. Liner notes by Don Blanding ("Mystery South of Us"). Inside disc sleeve contains song lyrics. (#14, pop; #13, country; #10, pop, *CB*; #8, country, *CB*) [Gold] Cassette: MCAC-1657; CD: MCAD-1657.

[February 1979] *BEFORE THE SALT.* Barnaby, 2BR 6019. Reissue of *Down to Earth* and *High Cumberland Jubilee* with one additional song. *Side One:* "The Christian?"; "Ellis Dee"; [new album release] "Richard Frost"; "The Missionary"; "A Mile High in Denver"; "The Captain and the Kid"; *Side Two:* "Captain America"; "Ain't He a Genius"; "Turnabout"; "There's Nothin' Soft About Hard Times"; "I Can't Be Your Hero Today"; "Truckstop Salvation"; *Side Three:* "Ace"; "Rockefeller Square"; "Bend a Little"; "In the Shelter"; "Death Valley Lives"; "Livingston's Gone to Texas"; *Side Four:* "England"; "Travelin' Clean"; "The Hang-Out Gang"; "God Don't Own a Car"; "High Cumberland Jubilee/Comin' Down Slow."

[February 1981] *COCONUT TELEGRAPH.* MCA Records, MCA-5169. *Side One:* "Coconut Telegraph"; "Incommunicado" (w/ D. McColl, Mary L. Benoit); "It's My Job" (by Mac McAnally); "Growing Older but Not Up"; "The Good Fight" (w/ J. D. Souther); *Side Two:* "The Weather Is Here, Wish You Were Beautiful"; "Stars Fell on Alabama" (by Mitchell Parish, Frank Perkins); "Island" (w/ D. Loggins); "Little Miss Magic." Produced by Norbert Putnam. Recorded at Muscle Shoals Sound Studio, Sheffield, Alabama (additional recording: Quadrophonic Studios, Nashville; Bennett House, Franklin, Tennessee; A&R Studios, New York City). Inside disc sleeve contains song lyrics. (#30, pop; #29, pop, *CB*; #37, country, *CB*) Cassette: MCAC-1664; CD: MCAD-31092.

[1981] *JIMMY BUFFETT*. Excelsior Records, XMP-6021. *Side One:* "The Christian?"; "Turnabout"; "Richard Frost"; "The Missionary"; "A Mile High in Denver"; "The Captain and the Kid"; *Side Two:* "Captain America"; "Ain't He a Genius"; "Ellis Dee (He Ain't Free)"; "There's Nothing Soft About Hard Times"; "I Can't Be Your Hero Today"; "Truckstop Salvation."

[January 1982] *SOMEWHERE OVER CHINA*. MCA Records, MCA-5285. *Side One:* "Where's the Party?" (w/ Bill LaBounty, S. Goodman); "It's Midnight and I'm Not Famous Yet" (w/ S. Goodman); "I Heard I Was in Town" (w/ M. Utley); "Somewhere over China"; *Side Two:* "When Salome Plays the Drum"; "Lip Service" (w/ M. Utley); "If I Could Just Get It on Paper"; "Steamer" (by John Scott Sherrill); "On A Slow Boat to China" (by Frank Loesser). Produced by Norbert Putnam. Recorded at the Bennett House, Franklin, Tennessee. Inside disc sleeve contains song lyrics. (#31, pop; #27, pop, *CB*.) Cassette: MCAC-1481; CD: MCAD-31168.

[September 1983] *ONE PARTICULAR HARBOUR*. MCA Records, MCA-25061. *Side One:* "Stars on the Water" (by Rodney Crowell); "I Used to Have Money One Time" (w/ M. Utley); "Livin' It Up" (w/ Josh Leo, J. D. Souther); "California Promises" (S. Goodman); "One Particular Harbour" (w/ Bobby Holcomb); *Side Two:* "Why You Wanna Hurt My Heart" (by Arthur Neville); "Honey Do" (w/ M. Utley); "We Are the People Our Parents Warned Us About"; "Twelve Volt Man"; "Brown Eyed Girl" (by Van Morrison); "Distantly in Love." Produced by Jimmy Buffett and Michael Utley; arranged by Utley. (#59, pop; #35, country; #64, pop, *CB*.) Cassette: MCAC-25061; CD: MCAD-31094.

[September 1984] *RIDDLES IN THE SAND*. MCA Records, MCA-5512. *Side One:* "Who's the Blonde Stranger?" (w/ M. Utley, W. Jennings, J. Leo); "When the Wild Life Betrays Me" (w/ M. Utley, W. Jennings); "Ragtop Day" (w/ M. Utley, W. Jennings); "She's Going Out of My Mind" (by M. McAnally); "Bigger than the Both of Us" (by Rhonda Coullet); *Side Two:* [all songs by Buffett, Utley, Jennings] "Knees of My Heart"; "Come to the Moon"; "Love in Decline"; "Burn That Bridge"; "La Vie Dansante." Produced by Jimmy Bowen (for Lynwood Productions), Michael Utley, and Tony Brown. Liner notes by Jim Harrison. Inside disc sleeve contains song lyrics. (#87, pop; #18, country; #58, pop, *CB*; #23, country, *CB*.) Cassette: MCAC-5512 [also: MCAC-25075]; CD: MCAD-31095; two-album CD: *Riddles in the Sand* and *One Particular Harbour*, MCAD-5923.

[June 1985] *LAST MANGO IN PARIS*. MCA Records, MCA-5600. *Side One:* "Everybody's on the Run" (w/ Marshall Chapman, W. Jennings, M. Utley); "Frank and Lola" (w/ S. Goodman); "The Perfect Partner" (by M. Chapman); "Please Bypass This Heart" (w/ W. Jennings, M. Utley); "Gypsies in the Palace" (w/ Glenn Frey, W. Jennings); *Side Two:* "Desperation Samba (Halloween in Tijuana)" (w/ W. Jennings, Timothy B. Schmit); "If the Phone Doesn't Ring, It's Me" (w/ W. Jennings, M. Utley); "Last Mango in Paris" (w/ M. Chapman, W. Jennings, M. Utley); "Jolly Mon Sing" (w/ W. Jennings, M. Utley); "Beyond the End" (w/ M. Chapman, W. Jennings). Produced by Jimmy Bowen (for Lynwood Productions), Michael Utley and Tony Brown. Recorded at Sound Stage Studios. Inside disc sleeve contains song lyrics. (#53, pop; #7, country; #55, pop, *CB*; #7, country, *CB*.) Cassette: MCAC-25077; CD: MCAD-31157.

[November 1985] *SONGS YOU KNOW BY HEART—JIMMY BUFFETT'S GREATEST HIT(S)*. MCA Records, MCA-5633. [re-releases.] *Side One:* "Cheeseburger in Paradise"; "He Went to Paris"; "Fins"; "Son of a Son of a Sailor"; "A Pirate Looks at Forty"; "Margaritaville"; *Side Two:* "Come Monday"; "Changes in Latitudes, Changes in Attitudes"; "Why Don't We Get Drunk"; "Pencil Thin Mustache"; "Grapefruit—Juicy Fruit"; "Boat Drinks"; "Volcano." Liner notes by Thomas McGuane. (#100, pop; #27, country; #140, pop, *CB*; #35, country, CB; #23, compact disc, *CB*.) Cassette: MCAC-5633; CD: MCAD-5633; CD: "24-karat gold Ultimate MasterDisc Series"MCAD-11169.

[July 1986] *FLORIDAYS*. MCA Records, MCA-5730. *Side One:* "I Love the Now" (w/ Carrie Fisher); "Creola" (w/ Ralph MacDonald, William Salter); "First Look"; "Meet Me in Memphis" (w/ M. Utley); "Nobody Speaks to the Captain No More"; *Side Two:* "Floridays"; "If It All Falls Down" (by Matt Betton); "No Plane on Sunday" (w/ M. Utley); "When the Coast Is Clear" (w/ M. McAnally); "You'll Never Work in Dis Bidness Again" (w/ M. Utley, Vince Melamed, J. Leo, Willie Weeks, M. Betton). Executive producer: Jimmy Buffett. Produced by Michael Utley. Recorded at New River Studios, Ft. Lauderdale, Fla.; Ardent Recording Studios, Memphis; Village Recorders, West Los Angeles. Inside disc sleeve contains song lyrics. (#66, pop; #29, country; #80, pop, *CB*.) Cassette: MCAC-5730; CD: MCAD-5730.

[July 1988] *HOT WATER*. MCA Records, MCA-42093. *Side One:* "Homemade Music" (w/ M. Utley, Russell Kunkel); "Baby's Gone Shoppin' "; "Bring Back the Magic" (w/ W. Jennings); "My Barracuda" (w/ M. Utley, R. Kunkel, Steve Cropper); "L'Air de la Louisiane" (by J. Winchester); "Prince of Tides" (w/ M. Utley); *Side Two:* "Pre-You" (w/ Ralph MacDonald, W. Salter); "King of Somewhere Hot" (w/ R. MacDonald, W. Salter, R. Greenidge); "Great Heart" (by Johnny Clegg); "Smart Woman (in a Real Short Skirt)" (w/ M. Chapman); "That's What Living Is to Me." Produced by Michael Utley and Russell Kunkel (and Ralph MacDonald: tracks 1, 2, and 5 on Side Two). Recorded at Shrimp Boat Sound, Key West; New River Studios, Ft. Lauderdale; Criteria Studios, Miami; Rosebud Studios, The Hit Factory, and Clinton Sound, New York City; Coral Sound Studios, Port of Spain, Trinidad; Artisan Recorder Mobile Truck Marine Stadium, Key Biscayne/Wicker Field, Key West; and The Complex, Los Angeles. (#46, pop; #18, compact disc; #45, pop, *CB*) Cassette: MCAC-42093; CD: MCAD-42093.

[June 1989] *OFF TO SEE THE LIZARD*. MCA Records, MCA-6314. *Side One:* "Carnival World" (w/ Roger Guth, Jay Oliver); "That's My Story and I'm Stickin' to It" (w/ J. Oliver); "Take Another Road" (w/ R. Guth, J. Oliver); "Why the Things We Do" (w/ R. Guth, J. Oliver); "Gravity Storm" (w/ J. Oliver); "Off to See the Lizard" (w/ J. Oliver); *Side Two:* "Boomerang Love"; "Strange Bird" (w/ J. Oliver); "I Wish Lunch Could Last Forever" (w/ J. Oliver); "The Pascagoula Run" (w/ J. Oliver); "Mermaid in the Night" (by J. Oliver, R. Guth); "Changing Channels" (w/ M. McAnally). Executive producer Jimmy Buffett. Produced by Elliot Scheiner. Recorded at The Hit Factory, New York City, and Shrimp Boat Sound, Key West. (#57, pop; #16, compact disc; #68, pop, *CB*) Cassette: MCAC-6314; CD: MCAD-6314.

[November 1990] *FEEDING FRENZY: JIMMY BUFFETT LIVE*. MCA Records, MCAD-10022 [compact disc]. "You'll Never Work in Dis Bidness Again"; "The

City" (by M. McAnally); "Last Mango in Paris"; "Come Monday"; "Today's Message" [recitation]; "A Love Song (From a Different Point of View)" ["Why Don't We Get Drunk"]; "One Particular Harbour"; "Honey Do" (w/ M. Utley); "Cheeseburger in Paradise"; "A Pirate Looks at Forty"; "Jolly Mon [Sing]"; "Gypsies in the Palace"; "Fins"; "Margaritaville"; "Jamaica Farewell" (by Irving Burgie); "Volcano." Produced by Michael Utley and Elliot Scheiner. Recorded at Lakewood Amphitheatre, Atlanta; and Riverbend Amphitheatre, Cincinnati. Liner notes by Jimmy Buffett. (#68, pop; #66, pop, *CB*) Cassette: MCAC-10022.

[May 1992] *BOATS BEACHES BARS & BALLADS*. Margaritaville, MCAD4-10613 [boxed set of compact discs]. All reissues unless otherwise noted. *Disc One:* "Son of a Son of a Sailor"; "Havaña Daydreamin' "; "Mañana"; "Treat Her Like a Lady"; "Steamer"; "Jolly Mon Sing"; "Nautical Wheelers"; [new] "Take It Back" (w/ M. Betton) [produced by Michael Utley, arranged by Matt Betton]; "On a Slow Boat to China"; "Changes in Latitudes, Changes in Attitudes"; [new] "Love and Luck" (w/ J. Beroard, J. C. Naimro) [produced by M. Utley, R. Kunkel]; "The Captain and the Kid"; "Tryin' to Reason with Hurricane Season"; "Boat Drinks"; "One Particular Harbor"; "A Pirate Looks at Forty"; "Lovely Cruise"; *Disc Two:* "Margaritaville"; "Grapefruit—Juicy Fruit"; "Ragtop Day"; "Frank and Lola"; "Tin Cup Chalice"; "Knees of My Heart"; [new] "Money Back Guarantee" (w/ M. Utley, Will Jennings) [produced by Buffett and M. Utley]; "When the Coast Is Clear"; "Biloxi"; "Distantly in Love"; "Coconut Telegraph"; "Stars on the Water"; "Who's the Blonde Stranger?"; "I Have Found Me a Home"; [first release on a Buffett record] "Christmas in the Caribbean" (w/ M. Utley, W. Jennings, J. Leo) [produced by Tony Brown]; "Volcano"; "Brown Eyed Girl"; "Cheeseburger in Paradise"; *Disc Three:* "Fins"; "The Weather Is Here, Wish You Were Beautiful"; "Tampico Trauma"; "Livingston Saturday Night"; "First Look"; "The Wino and I Know"; "The Great Filling Station Holdup"; "Why Don't We Get Drunk"; [new] "Elvis Imitators" (by S. Goodman and Michael Smith) [produced by Norbert Putnam]; "Pencil Thin Mustache"; "Kick It in Second Wind"; "Desperation Samba (Halloween in Tijuana)"; "When Salome Plays the Drum"; "They Don't Dance Like Carmen No More"; "The Pascagoula Run"; "Sending the Old Man Home"; [new] "Domino College" (w/ Dan Fogelberg) [produced by Michael Utley]; *Disc Four:* "Come Monday"; "Defying Gravity"; "Survive"; "Incommunicado"; "I Heard I Was in Town"; "Ballad of Spider John"; "Little Miss Magic"; "California Promises"; "If the Phone Doesn't Ring, It's Me"; "African Friend"; [new] "Everlasting Moon" (w/ M. Betton) [produced by M. Utley and Elliot Scheiner]; "Pre-You"; "Middle of the Night"; "Coast of Marseilles"; "Island"; "He Went to Paris"; "Stars Fell on Alabama"; "Changing Channels"; "Twelve Volt Man." (#68, pop; #87, *CB*). With *The Parrot Head Handbook*, a 63-page guide written by Buffett, including career retrospective and annotations of all the songs. (#68, pop; #87, pop, *CB*) Cassette: MCAC4-10613.

[1993] *A PIRATE'S TREASURE—20 JIMMY BUFFETT GEMS*. MCA Records [Australia], MCAD-31213 [compact disc]. Re-releases. "Son of a Son of a Sailor"; "Margaritaville"; "Grapefruit—Juicy Fruit"; "A Pirate Looks at Forty"; "Come Monday"; "Pencil Thin Mustache"; "Changes in Latitudes, Changes in Attitudes"; "Nautical Wheelers"; "Coast of Marseilles"; "Jolly Mon Sing"; "He Went to Paris"; "Mañana"; "Little Miss Magic"; "African Friend"; "Volcano"; "On a Slow Boat to China"; "Stars Fell on Alabama"; "Livingston Saturday Night"; "One Particular Harbour"; "Why Don't We Get Drunk." Liner notes by W. & J. Riner.

[June 1993] *BEFORE THE BEACH.* Margaritaville, MCAD-10823 [compact disc]. Re-releases. "Ellis Dee"; "The Missionary"; "A Mile High in Denver"; "The Captain and the Kid"; "Captain America"; "Turnabout"; "There's Nothin' Soft About Hard Times"; "I Can't Be Your Hero Today"; "Truckstop Salvation"; "Ace"; "Rockefeller Square"; "Bend a Little"; "In the Shelter"; "Death Valley Lives"; "Livingston's Gone to Texas"; "England"; "Travelin' Clean"; "The Hang-Out Gang"; "God Don't Own a Car"; "High Cumberland Jubilee"; "Cumberland High Dilemma" (w/ B. Cason). Liner notes by J. Buffett, with inserted song lyrics. (#169, pop) Cassette: MCAC-10823.

[May 1994] *FRUITCAKES.* Margaritaville, MCAD-11043 [compact disc]. "Everybody's Got a Cousin in Miami" (w/ Michael Tschudin); "Fruitcakes" (w/ Amy Lee); "Lone Palm"; "Six String Music" (w/ George E. Smith); "Uncle John's Band" (by Jerry Garcia, Robert Hunter); "Love in the Library" (w/ M. McAnally); "Quietly Making Noise" (w/ M. Tschudin); "Frenchman for the Night" (w/ R. Guth); "Sunny Afternoon" (by Ray Davies); "Vampires, Mummies and the Holy Ghost" (w/ R. Guth, Peter Mayer, Jim Mayer); "She's Got You" (by Hank Cochran); "Delaney Talks to Statues" (w/ M. McAnally, Amy Lee); "Apocalypso" (by M. Betton). (#5, pop; #6, CB) Cassette: MCAC-11043.

[1994] *JIMMY BUFFETT: ALL THE GREAT HITS.* Prism Leisure Corp. [United Kingdom], PLATCD-4903. Re-releases. "Margaritaville"; "Fins"; "Come Monday"; "Volcano"; "Changes in Latitudes, Changes in Attitudes"; "Cheeseburger in Paradise"; "Son of a Son of a Sailor"; "Stars Fell on Alabama"; "Miss You So Badly"; "Why Don't We Get Drunk"; "A Pirate Looks at Forty"; "He Went to Paris"; "Grapefruit—Juicy Fruit"; "Pencil Thin Mustache"; "Boat Drinks"; "Chanson pour les Petits Enfants"; "Banana Republics"; "Last Mango in Paris." Liner notes by Roger Dopson.

[August 1995] *BAROMETER SOUP.* Margaritaville, MCAD-11247 [compact disc]. Except for "Jimmy Dreams," written by Buffett, and "Mexico" by James Taylor, all songs are by Buffett, Russ Kunkel, Jay Oliver, Roger Guth, and Peter Mayer. "Barometer Soup"; "Barefoot Children"; "Bank of Bad Habits"; "Remittance Man"; "Diamond as Big as the Ritz"; "Blue Heaven Rendezvous"; "Jimmy Dreams"; "Lage Nom Ai"; "Don't Chu-Know"; "Ballad of Skip Wiley"; "The Night I Painted the Sky"; "Mexico." Liner notes by Jimmy Buffett. Produced by Russell Kunkel at Shrimp Boat Sound, Key West, Florida. Cassette: MCAC-11247.

[c. 1995] *COCKTAILS AT SUNRISE.* Flood Recordings OSA [Czechoslovakia], FLD-1006/7 [compact disc]. *Disk One:* "The Wino and I Know"; "Pencil Thin Mustache"; "They Don't Dance Like Carmen No More"; "Trying to Reason with Hurricane Season"; "Fuji Wuji Song" ["Saxophones"]; "Door Number Three"; "Livingston's Gone to Texas"; "Railroad Lady"; "Dallas"; "A Pirate Looks at Forty"; "Everybody's Got a Cousin Miami"; "Come Monday"; "Landfall"; "Volcano"; *Disk Two:* "Cheeseburger in Paradise"; "Sunny Afternoon"; "In the Shelter"; "Why Don't We Get Drunk"; instrumental [Coral Reefer Band]; "Grapefruit-Juicy Fruit"; "Island"; "Son of a Son of a Sailor"; "Cheeseburger in Paradise"; "The Pascaagoula Run"; "Livingston Saturday Night"; "Fins"; "Margaritaville"; "Brown Eyed Girl"; "Defying Gravity." *Disk One:* tracks 1–10—live performance, San Francisco, 1973; tracks 11–14—live performance, New York City, 1994. *Disk Two:* live performance, New York City, 1994.

[June 1996] *BANANA WIND.* Margaritaville, MCAD-11451 [compact disc]. "Only Time Will Tell," and "Jamaica Mistaica" (both w/ R. Kunkel, R. Guth, P.

Mayer, J. Mayer); "School Roy Heart" (w/ M. Betton); "Banana Wind" (w/ Kunkel, Guth, Mayer, Mayer) [instrumental]; "Holiday" (w/ Ralph MacDonald, Bill Eaton, William Salter); "Bob Robert's Society Band" (w/ A. Lee); "Overkill," "Desdemona's Building a Rocket Ship," "Mental Floss," and "Cultural Infidel" (w/ Kunkel, Guth, Mayer, Mayer); "Happily Ever After (Now and Then)" (w/ Dave Loggins); "False Echoes (Havana 1921)." Liner notes by novelist Joseph Conrad ("Lion Hearted"), and Buffett. Produced by R. Kunkel at Shrimp Boat Sound, Key West, Florida. Cassette: MCAC-11451.

[June 1996] *GREAT AMERICAN SUMMER FUN WITH JIMMY BUFFETT* ("Limited Edition"). MCA, MCD-36031 [compact disc]. "Come Monday"; "Changes in Latitudes, Changes in Attitudes"; "Cheeseburger in Paradise"; "One Particular Harbour"; "Bank of Bad Habits"; "Fruitcakes"; "Brown Eyed Girl." Cassette: MSC-36031.

[October 1996] *CHRISTMAS ISLAND*. Margaritaville, MCAD-11489 [compact disc]. "Christmas Island" (by Lyle Moraine); "Jingle Bells" (traditional); "A Sailor's Christmas" (w/ R. Guth); "Happy Xmas (War Is Over)" (by John Lennon, Yoko Ono); "Up on the House Top" (traditional); "Mele Kalikimaka" (Alex Anderson); "Run Rudolph Run" (by Mavin Brodie, Johnny Marks); "Ho Ho Ho and a Bottle of Rhum" (w/ R. Guth, P. Mayer, R. Kunkel); "I'll Be Home for Christmas" (by Kim Gannon, Walter Kent, Buck Ram); "Merry Christmas, Alabama (Never Far from Home)" (w/ M. Betton). Produced by M. Utley and R. Kunkel. Liner notes by Jimmy Buffett. Cassette: MCAC-11489.

MISCELLANEOUS VOCAL RECORDINGS

ca. 1969

"Poopi-Do" (by Milton Brown)/"Bluebird of Happiness" (by Milton Brown) [Sun and the Tan Band, with J. Buffett on background vocals]	[single] SMAR-T 1008

1970

Come Together, The Now Generation [Jimmy on the cover, probably on some backup vocals]	Spar 4806

Hits Are Our Business, The Now Generation [Jimmy on the cover, probably on some backup vocals]	Spar 4807

1977

"Margaritaville," *The Hot Ones*	K-tel [Canada] CSPS-1328

1978

"Livingston Saturday Night," *"FM": The Original Movie Soundtrack*	MCA MCA2-12000

1979

"The Greeks Don't Want No Freaks" (by Don Henley and Glenn Frey), *The Long Run,* The Eagles (with The Monstertones, featuring J. Buffett, background vocals) [produced by Bill Szymczyk]	Elektra/Asylum AS-52181

1980

"Hello Texas" (by Brian Collins, Robby	Full Moon/Asylum Records

Campbell), *Urban Cowboy Original Motion Picture Soundtrack*	DP-90002
"Hello Texas"/ The Eagles: "Lyin' Eyes"	[single] Full Moon/Asylum E-47073
"Survive" (w/ Michael Utley), *Coast to Coast: Music from the Motion Picture Soundtrack*	Full Moon FM-3490

1982

"Changes in Latitudes, Changes in Attitudes," *Jane Fonda's Workout Record*	Columbia CX2-38054
"I Don't Know (Spicol's Theme)" (w/ Michael Utley), *Fast Times at Ridgemont High*	Full Moon/Asylum Records 4–60158 [soundtrack album]
"Partytown" (by Jack Tempchin), *No Fun Aloud,* Glenn Frey [with J. Buffett background vocals as "Freddy Buffett"]	Elektra E4–60129

1985

"Ragtop Day," *The Slugger's Wife*	MCA MCA-5578 [film soundtrack]
"Who's the Blonde Stranger?"; "When the Wild Life Betrays Me"; "Come to the Moon" [B side: Jeannie C. Riley]	U.S. Air Force "Country Music Time" Disc 6 [for program No. 955]
"Christmas in the Caribbean" (w/ Michael Utley, Will Jennings, Marshall Chapman, D. Haig), *Tennessee Christmas* [produced by Tony Brown]	MCA MCA-5620
"Christmas In the Caribbean"	MCA S45-17046 [promotional single with four album songs]

1989

Interview, re: composition of "Margaritaville," *"Solid Gold Summer Hits"* [Radio station promotion album for the weekend of May 26–29.]	United Stations Radio Networks

1990

"Boomerang Love," *Always*	MCA MCA-8036 [soundtrack of 1989 film]
The Jolly Mon [J. Buffett and Savannah Jane Buffett reading from their book, *The Jolly Mon*. With music by Michael Utley.]	Harcourt Brace Jovanovich Children's Books Divison [cassette]

"Who Stole My Monkey?" (by Zachary Richards,   A & M Records
Leon Medica, Craig Lege), *Women in the*   75021–5302
Room, Zachary Richards (with J. Buffett   [compact disc]
background vocals)

1993

"Another Saturday Night" (by Sam Cooke)   Margaritaville
[produced by Russell Kunkel and Michael   MCAD-10824
Utley]; "Reggae Accident" (by Lucas P. Gravell)   [compact disc]
[produced by M. Utley], *Margaritaville Cafe*   MCAC-10824
Late Night Menu. Includes "Some White People   [cassette]
Can Dance" sung by Greg "Fingers" Taylor
(by J. Buffett, M. Utley, Tim Krekel). Liner notes
by J. Buffett.

"Another Saturday Night"; "Gypsies in the   MCA
Palace" (w/ Glenn Frey, W. Jennings); on *The*   MCA3P-2771
Untamed [disc 3] of *The Legacy, the True and*   [3 promotional compact
the Untamed   discs]

"Stars Fell on Alabama" (by Mitchell Parish,   Epic Soundtrax
Frank Perkins), *More Songs for Sleepless*   EK-57682 [compact disc]
Nights [various artists album]   ET-57682 [cassette]

"Stars on the Water" (by Rodney Crowell), *The*   MCA-GRP
Firm: Original Motion Picture Soundtrack   MCD-2007
   [compact disc]

"Gulf Coast Highway" (by Nanci Griffith, James   MCA Margaritaville
Hooker, Danny Flowers) [J. Buffett singing   MCAD-10582
duet with Evangeline], *Evangeline,* Evangeline   [compact disc]
[produced by Justin Neibank]

1994

"Fruitcakes" (w/ Amy Lee), *An MCA Nashville*   MCA
Sampler: 1994. Volume One: Untamed And   MCA3P-3015
True   [compact disc]

"Mr. Spaceman" (by James [Roger]McGuinn)   Jim Henson Records
[Sung by J. Buffett, Dave Goetz (The Great   BMG-KIDZ
Gonzo), Steve Whitmire (Rizzo the Rat)],   [compact disc]
Kermit unpigged [produced by Robert Kraft
and John Boylan]

"Mack the Knife"(by Kurt Weill, Marc Blitzstein)   Capitol
[sung by Frank Sinatra, J. Buffett], *Duets II,*   CDP-7243–8–28103–22
Frank Sinatra [produced by Phil Ramone, Hank   [compact disc]
Cattaneo]

1995

"Sea Cruise" (by Huey Smith); "Goodnight,   Margaritaville
Irene" (by Huddie Ledbetter, John Lomax),   162–535–012–2
Margaritaville Cafe New Orleans Late Night
Gumbo [produced by M. Utley and Greg
"Fingers" Taylor].

Video Appearances (Retail)

■

Dates listed are those of the films themselves. Not included are videos of films otherwise represented by soundtrack albums.

1985
"Turning Around" (w/Michael Utley, Will Jennings), *Summer Rental*

Paramount
VHS-1785
[soundtrack video]

Jimmy Buffett Live by the Bay: "Gypsies in the Palace"; "Door Number Three"; "Grapefruit—Juicy Fruit"; "We Are the People Our Parents Warned Us About"; "Stars on the Water"; "The Coconut Telegraph"; "Come Monday"; "Ragtop Day"; "Who's the Blonde Stranger?"; "Volcano"; "One Particular Harbor"; "If the Phone Doesn't Ring, It's Me"; "Why Don't We Get Drunk"; "Cheeseburger in Paradise"; "Last Mango in Paris"; A Pirate Looks at Forty"; "Margaritaville."

MCA Universal
80332

"Don't Bug Me" (w/ M. Utley, Jay Oliver, *Arachnophobia*

Hollywood Pictures Home Video
VHS-1080
[soundtrack video]

1991
"Why Don't We Get Drunk," *The Doctor*

Touchstone Home Video
VHS-1257
[soundtrack video]

1994
"Let's Go Spend Your Money Honey," *Country*

Warner Music

Video Monthly February 1994 [visual appearance only with Evangeline vocal group]	VHS-0294C
"Fruitcakes" (w/Amy Lee), *Rock Video Monthly Summer 1994*	Warner Music SU94P

ALBUMS OF BUFFETT SONGS

1990

You Sing the Hits of Jimmy Buffett. [Instrumental tracks to sing along with; sample vocals by Bob Lewellyn.] "Margaritaville; "Changes in Latitudes, Changes in Attitudes"; "Come Monday"; "Cheeseburger in Paradise"; "Why Don't We Get Drunk."	Pocket Songs PS-464 [cassette]

1992

Sing the Hits of Jimmy Buffett. [Instrumental tracks to sing along with.] "Margaritaville"; "Changes in Attitudes, Changes in Latitudes"; "Livingston Saturday Night"; "Come Monday"; "Cheeseburger in Paradise"; "Son of a Son of a Sailor"; "Volcano"; "Why Don't We Get Drunk." [Produced by Dan Becherer.]	The Singing Machine (Karaoke Kassette) M-867 [cassette]

1995

The Parakeet Album: Songs of Jimmy Buffett. W. O. Smith Music School Singers [Nashville]. "Christmas in the Caribbean"; "Volcano"; "La Vie Dansante"; "Jolly Mon Sing"; "Little Miss Magic; "Cheeseburger in Paradise"; "Off to See the Lizard"; Chanson pour les Petits Enfants"; "Come to the Moon"; "Delaney Talks to Statues."	Margaritaville Records/ Island Records 162-531 000-2 [compact disc] 162-531 000-4 [cassette]

References

■

BOOKS, ETC.

Alexander, Lamar. *Steps Along the Way: A Governor's Scrapbook*. Nashville: Thomas Nelson, 1986.

Amburn, Ellis. *Pearl: The Obsessions and Passions of Janis Joplin*. New York: Warner Books, 1992.

Asbury, Herbert. "The Terror of the Gulf." In *The French Quarter: An Informal History of the New Orleans Underworld*. New York: Knopf, 1936.

Ashley, Elizabeth, with Ross Firestone. *Actress: Postcards from the Road*. New York: M. Evans, 1978.

Boardman, Barrington. *Flappers, Bootleggers, "Typhoid Mary" & The Bomb: An Anecdotal History of the United States from 1923–1945*. New York: Harper & Row, 1989.

Bononia Docet "Bologna Teaches." N.p.: Kappa Sigma, 1992.

Bowman, Dicy Villar. *The Suarez Family 1798–1980*. [Pensacola, Fla.]: privately published, 1980.

Bromberg, Craig. *The Wicked Ways of Malcolm McLaren*. New York: Harper & Row, 1989.

Buffett, Jimmy. "A Boxful of Africa." In *Heaven Is Under Our Feet: A Book for Walden Books*, edited by Don Henley and Dave Marsh. Stamford, Conn.: Longmeadow Press, 1992. Reprint. New York: Berkley Books, 1992.

———. "A Few Thoughts About the Show." In *The Master Series to Benefit the W. O. Smith Nashville Community Music School, April 22, 1992* [brochure].

———. "Information Form for 'Epsilon Nu's,' " Jimmy Buffett scrapbook, Epsilon Nu, University of Southern Mississippi, Hattiesburg.

———. Letter, September 9, 1994.

———. Letter (published) to Friends of Florida, October 10, 1994.

———. "My Fatal Mistake," Manuscript, 1964. Mary McKay collection.

———. *The Parrot Head Handbook (Boats Beaches Bars & Ballads)*. Margaritaville Records, MCAD4-10613 [1992].

———. Songbooks: *Best of Buffett* [VF0987] (New York: Warner Bros., 1982). *Changes in Latitudes, Changes in Attitudes* [VF0517] (New York: Warner Bros.,

1977). *Coconut Telegraph* [VF0863] (New York: Warner Bros., 1981). *The Jimmy Buffett Songbook* (New York: The Big 3 Music Corp., 1974). *Son of a Son of a Sailor* [VF0587] (New York: Warner Bros., 1978). *The Songs of Jimmy Buffett* [PO248SMX] (Miami: CPP/Belwin, 1978). *Songs You Know by Heart— Jimmy Buffett's Greatest Hit(s)* [PO723SMX] (Miami: CCP/Belwin, 1986).

———. *Tales from Margaritaville: Fictional Facts and Factual Fictions.* San Diego: Harcourt Brace Jovanovich, 1989. Reprint. New York: Fawcett Columbine, 1990. Reprint. New York: Fawcett Crest, 1993.

———. *Where Is Joe Merchant? A Novel Tale.* New York: Harcourt Brace Jovanovich, 1992. Reprint. New York: Avon Books, 1993.

Buffett, Jimmy, and Savannah Jane Buffett. *The Jolly Mon.* San Diego: Harcourt Brace & Co., 1988. Re-released with *The Jolly Mon* vocal cassette as *Jimmy Buffett & Savannah Jane Buffett Read The Jolly Mon.* New York: Harcourt Brace Jovanovich, 1989.

———. *Trouble Dolls.* San Diego: Harcourt Brace Jovanovich, 1991.

Carroll, E. Jean. *Hunter: The Strange and Savage Life of Hunter S. Thompson.* New York: Dutton, 1993.

Clark, Peter. *Hell and Paradise: The Norfolk-Bounty Pitcairn Saga.* New York: Viking Penguin, 1986.

Clark, W. M. "Antiquities of Tennessee." *Annual Report of the Board of Regents of the Smithsonian Institution.* Washington, D.C.: Govt. Printing Office, 1878.

Committee to Investigate Assassinations. "General Charles T. Cabell," "Carlos Marcello," "John Rosselli." *Coincidence or Conspiracy?*, compiled by Michael Ewing. New York: Zebra Books, 1977.

Cousteau, Jacques-Yves, with James Dugan. *The Living Sea.* New York: Harper & Row, 1963.

Davis, John H. *Mafia Kingfish: Carlos Marcello and the Assassination of John F. Kennedy.* New York: McGraw-Hill, 1989.

Dening, Greg. *Mr. Bligh's Bad Language.* Cambridge: Cambridge University Press, 1992.

Denisoff, R. Serge. *Tarnished Gold: The Record Industry Revisited.* New Brunswick, N.J.: Transaction Books, 1986.

Denver, John. *Take Me Home: An Autobiography.* New York: Harmony Books, 1994.

Draper, Robert. *Rolling Stone Magazine: The Uncensored History.* New York: Doubleday, 1990.

Dunaway, David King. *How Can I Keep from Singing? Pete Seeger.* New York: McGraw-Hill, 1981.

Durant, Mary, and Michael Harwood. *On the Road with John James Audubon.* New York: Dodd, Mead, 1980.

Escott, Colin, with George Merritt and William MacEwen. *Hank Williams: The Biography.* New York: Little, Brown, 1994.

Galens, David M. "Buffett, Jimmy, 1946–." In *Contemporary Authors: A Bio-Bibliographical Guide,* edited by Donna Olendorf. Vol. 141. Detroit: Gale Research, 1994.

———. "Buffett, Jimmy, 1946–." In *Something About the Author: Facts and Pictures About Authors and Illustrators of Books for Young People,* edited by Diane Telgen. Vol. 76. Detroit: Gale Research, 1994.

Goodpasture, Henry. *Memoirs of Henry Goodpasture.* N.p.: privately published, 1979.

———. *Old Town.* [Franklin, Tenn.]: privately published, 1950.

Grose, Peter. *Gentleman Spy: The Life of Allen Dulles.* Boston: Houghton Mifflin, Richard Todd Books, 1994.

Hale, Rosalind P. "Development of the Integrated Catholic School in Mobile, Alabama." Typescript. May 27, 1987. "Private Schools (Catholic)" vertical file, Local History and Genealogy Room, Mobile Public Library, Mobile, Ala.

Hamilton, Virginia Van der Veer. *Alabama: A History,* States and the Nation Series. New York: W. W. Norton, 1977.

Hearin, Emily Staples. *Let the Good Times Roll! Mobile, Mother of Mystics.* [Mobile]: privately published, 1991.

Hemingway, Leicester. *My Brother, Ernest Hemingway.* Cleveland: World Publishing, 1962.

Higginbotham, Jay. *Mobile: City by the Bay.* Mobile: Mobile Chamber of Commerce, 1968.

———. *Pascagoula: Singing River City.* Mobile: Gill Press, 1967.

Hinckle, Warren, and William M. Turner. *The Fish Is Red: The Story of the Secret War Against Castro.* New York: Harper & Row, 1981.

The History of Jackson County Mississippi. Pascagoula, Miss.: Jackson County Genealogical Society, 1989.

History of Louisiana. Vol. I. Typescript excerpt, "Singing River." Vertical file, Genealogy & Local History Dept., Jackson County Public Library. Pascagoula, Miss.

Humphrey, Mark, with Harris Lewine. *The Jimmy Buffett Scrapbook.* New York: Carol Publishing, 1993.

Hunt, [E.] Howard. *Give Us This Day.* New Rochelle, N.Y.: Arlington House, 1973.

Hurst, Jack. *Nashville's Grand Ole Opry.* New York: Henry N. Abrams, 1975.

Ivey, Bill. "The Bottom Line: Business Practices That Shaped Country Music." In *Country: The Music and the Musicians,* edited by Paul Kingsbury and Alan Alexrod. New York: Abbeville Press, 1988.

"Jimmy Buffett." MCA Records biography broadside. June 1986.

"Jimmy Buffett." *Williamson County Celebrates the Written Word.* Franklin, Tenn.: Williamson County Arts Council, 1993.

Johnson, Haynes, with Manuel Artime et al. *The Bay of Pigs: The Leaders' Story of Brigade 2506.* New York: W. W. Norton, 1964.

Kane, Harnett P. *Queen New Orleans: City by the River.* New York: William Morrow, 1949.

Katz, Ephraim. "Miranda, Carmen." *The Film Encyclopedia.* New York: Harper & Row, 1979.

Kaufelt, Lynn Mitsuko. "Thomas McGuane—Hotcakesland." In *Key West Writers and Their Houses.* Sarasota: Pineapple Press, and Fort Lauderdale: Omnigraphics, 1986.

Kennedy, Robert Allen. "A History and Survey of Community Music in Mobile, Alabama." Ph.D. diss., Florida State University, June 1960.

Kilpatrick, Andrew. *Of Permanent Value: The Story of Warren Buffett.* Birmingham: AKPE Financial Center, 1994.

The Kingston Trio. New York: Random House, 1960.

Kinser, Samuel. *Carnival American Style: Mardi Gras at New Orleans and Mobile.* Chicago: University of Chicago Press, 1990.

Kuntsler, William M., with Sheila Isenberg. *My Life as a Radical Lawyer.* New York: Birch Lane Press, 1994.

Kwitny, Jonathan. *The Crimes of Patriots: A True Tale of Dope, Dirty Money, and the CIA.* New York: W. W. Norton, 1987.

Laing, Dave. *Buddy Holly.* New York: Collier Books, 1971.

Leary, Timothy. *Flashbacks: An Autobiography*. Los Angeles: J. D. Tarcher [Houghton Mifflin], 1983.

Lee, Johnny, with Randy Wyles. *Lookin' for Love*. Austin: Diamond Books, 1989.

Lee, Martin A., and Bruce Shlain. *Acid Dreams: The Complete Social History of LSD: The CIA, the Sixties, and Beyond*. Rev. ed. New York: Grove Weidenfeld, 1992.

Liddy. G. Gordon. *Will: The Autobiography of G. Gordon Liddy*. Enlarged ed. New York: St. Martin's Paperbacks, 1991.

Lingeman, Richard R. *Don't You Know There's a War On? The American Home Front, 1941–1945*. 1970. Reprint. New York: G. P. Putnam's, Capricorn Books, 1976.

Lisagor, Nancy, and Frank Lipsius. *A Law Unto Itself: The Untold Story of the Law Firm Sullivan & Cromwell*. New York: Morrow, 1988.

McCoy, Alfred W. *Politics of Heroin: CIA Complicity in the Global Drug Trade*. Rev. ed. Chicago: Lawrence Hill Books, 1991.

"McGuane, Thomas." In *Current Biography Yearbook 1987*, edited by Charles Moritz. New York: H. W. Wilson, 1987.

McIver, Stuart B. "Conch Republic." In *Hemingway's Key West*. Sarasota, Fla.: Pineapple Press, 1993.

Mackaness, George. *The Life of Vice-Admiral William Bligh, R.N., F.R.S.* New York: Farrar & Rinehart, 1936.

Maclay, Maureen. "Alabama's Gulf Coast: History and Culture." In *Memoramobilia: Alabama Gulf Coast Potpourri*, edited by Elizabeth T. Coffman and Mary S. Palmer. Mobile: M and B Press, 1993.

Marill, Alvin H. "Key West." In *Movies Made for Television: The Telefeature and The Mini-Series, 1964–1986*. New York: New York Zoetrope, Baseline Books, 1987.

Marks, J. *Rock and Other Four-Letter Words: Music of the Electric Generation*. New York: Bantam Books, 1969.

Mather, Frederic Gregory. *Refugees of 1776 from Long Island to Connecticut*. 1913. Reprint. Baltimore Genealogical Publishing Co., 1972.

Michener, James A. "Ernest Hemingway." In *Literary Reflections*. 1993. Reprint. New York: Tom Doherty Associates, Forge Books, 1994.

———. *The World Is My Home: A Memoir*. New York: Random House, 1992.

Mitgang, Herbert. *Dangerous Dossiers: Exposing the Secret War Against America's Greatest Authors*. New York: Donald L. Fine, 1988.

Morgan, Chester M. *Dearly Bought, Deeply Treasured: The University of Southern Mississippi, 1912–1987*. Jackson: University of Mississippi Press, 1987.

Morris, Willie. *New York Days*. Boston: Little, Brown, 1993.

Newsham, Joseph P. "The New Chapel." In *Twice Remembered: Moments in the History of Spring Hill College*, edited by Charles J. Boyle. Mobile: The Friends of the Spring Hill Library, 1993.

O'Neil, Thomas. *The Grammys for the Record*. New York: Penguin Books, 1993.

Official WSM Grand Ole Opry History-Picture Book. Vol. 2, No. 1. Nashville: WSM, 1961.

Old Town 2031 Old Natchez Trace. Nashville: Fridrich & Clark Realty [1994].

Pear, Nancy. "Jimmy Buffett: Singer, Songwriter, Guitarist." In *Contemporary Musicians: Profiles of the People in Music*, edited by Michael L. LeBlanc, Vol. 4. Detroit: Gale Research, 1991.

Pearty, Danny. "Carmen Miranda, 1909–55." In *Cult Movie Stars*. New York: Simon & Schuster, 1991.

Rees, Dafydd, and Luke Crampton. "Jimmy Buffett." In *Rock Movers & Shakers.* New York: Watson-Guptill, 1991.

Rider, Fremont, ed. *The American Genealogical-Biographical Index.* Vol. 21. Middletown, Conn.: Godfrey Memorial Library, 1957.

Rolling Stone eds. *Rolling Stone Rock Almanac: The Chronicles of Rock & Roll.* New York: Collier Books/Macmillan, 1983.

Rose, Al. *Storyville, New Orleans: Being an Authentic, Illustrated Account of the Notorious Red-Light District.* Tuscaloosa: University of Alabama Press, 1974.

Sanjek, Russell, and David Sanjek. "The 1980s, etc." In *American Popular Music Business in the 20th Century.* New York: Oxford University Press, 1991.

Saxon, Lyle. *Lafitte the Pirate.* New York: The Century Co., 1930. Reprint. Gretna, La.: Pelican, 1989.

Scheuer, Steven, and Robert J. Pardi. "Key West." In *Movies on TV, 1988–1989.* New York: Bantam Books, 1987.

Seeger, Pete. *The Incompleat Folksinger,* edited by Jo Metcalf Schwartz. New York: Simon and Schuster, 1972.

Shactman, Tom. *Decade of Shocks: Dallas to Watergate, 1963–1974.* New York: Poseidon Press, 1983.

Shaw, Arnold. *Belafonte: An Unauthorized Biography.* New York: Pyramid Books, 1960.

Skates, John R. "Hattiesburg: The Early Years." In *Hattiesburg: A Pictorial History,* edited by Kenneth G. McCarty, Jr. Hattiesburg, Miss.: Woodland Enterprises, 1989.

Smith, Joe. "Irving Azoff," "Dan Fogelberg," "Mitch Miller." In *Off the Record,* edited by Mitchell Fink. New York: Warner Books, 1988.

Snow, Hank, the Singing Ranger, with Jack Ownbey and Bob Burris. *The Hank Snow Story.* Music in American Life Series. Urbana: University of Illinois Press, 1994.

Spitz, Bob. *Dylan: A Biography.* New York: W. W. Norton, 1989.

Stambler, Irwin, and Grelun Landon. "Buffett, Jimmy." In *The Encyclopedia of Folk, Country & Western Music,* 2nd ed. New York: St. Martin's Press, 1984.

Sweet, Brian. *Steely Dan: Reelin' in the Years.* London: Omnibus Press, 1994.

Swenson, John. "Jimmy Buffett." In *The Rolling Stone Record Guide: Reviews and Ratings,* edited by Dave Marsh with John Swenson. New York: Random House, 1979. Reprinted in *The New Rolling Stone Record Guide: Revised.* New York: Random House, 1983.

"Tom Dooley." In *The Viking Book of Folk Ballads of the English-Speaking World.* New York: Viking, 1956.

Tosches, Nick. "Cecil Gant: Owl Stew and All That." In *Unsung Heroes of Rock 'n' Roll.* Rev. ed. New York: Harmony Books, 1991.

Trott, Walt. Introduction to *The Country Music World of Charlie Lamb.* Nashville: Infac Publications, 1986.

———. *The Honky Tonk Angels: The Kitty Wells—Johnny & Jack Story.* Nashville: Nova Books, 1993.

United States Senate. "Cuba." *Alleged Assassination Plots Involving Foreign Leaders.* New York: W. W. Norton, 1976.

Unger, Irwin, and Debi Unger. *Turning Point 1968.* New York: Scribner's, 1988.

Urban Cowboy: Music from the Original Motion Picture Soundtrack [VF0797]. New York: Warner Bros., 1980.

Vollers, Maryanne. *Ghosts of Mississippi: The Murder of Medger Evers, the Trials of Byron De la Beckweth, and the Haunting of the New South.* Boston: Little, Brown, 1995.

Wacholtz, Larry E. "Travis Turk." In *Inside Country Music.* New York: Billboard Publications, 1986.

Wahlroos, Sven. *Mutiny and Romance in the South Seas: A Companion to the Bounty Adventure.* Topsfield, Mass.: Salem House, 1989.

Ward, Ed. "The Fifties and Before." In *Rock of Ages: The Rolling Stone History of Rock & Roll.* New York: Summit Books, 1986.

White, Timothy. "Sting" and "James Taylor." In *Rock Lives: Profiles & Interviews.* New York: Henry Holt, 1990.

Whitmer, Peter O. *When the Going Gets Weird: The Twisted Life and Times of Hunter S. Thompson.* New York: Hyperion, 1993.

Woliver, Robbie. *Bringing It All Back Home: 25 Years of American Music at Folk City.* New York: Pantheon Books, 1986.

Woodward, Bob. *The Short Life and Fast Times of John Belushi.* New York: Simon and Schuster, 1984.

Wyden, Peter. *Bay of Pigs: The Untold Story.* New York: Simon and Schuster, 1979.

Zalkind, Ronald. "Best American Recording Studios 1979." In *Contemporary Music Almanac 1980/81.* New York: Macmillan, 1980.

PERIODICALS AND NEWSPAPERS

"A & E Interview: Elliot Forrest Talks with Jimmy Buffett." *A & E Monthly,* August 1994.

Aiges, Scott. "Club Says No to Buffett Bid." *Times-Picayune* (New Orleans), 29 June 1990.

"Album Reviews: *Living and Dying in 3/4 Time.*" *Cash Box,* 9 February 1974.

[Allred, Ron]. "An Interview with Steve Eng." *The 3/4 Times Lone Star Parrot Head Club* (Watauga, Tex.), June 1996.

Anderson, Bob. "Interview: Jimmy Buffett." *High Times: The Magazine of High Society,* December 1976.

Armstrong, Darren. "Twenty Years and 18 Albums Later, Walker Continues to Break the Mold." *Denver Clarion,* 25 September 1986.

"Azoff Says MCA Country Division Has Been Carrying Label." *Variety,* 22 June 1983.

Baker, George. "Listen to the Mocking Birds." *The Nashville Tennessean,* 22 August 1965.

Balling, Joshua. "Jimmy Buffett OK After Seaplane Nosedives." *The Inquirer and Mirror* (Nantucket, Mass.), 1 September 1994.

Bane, Michael. "The Wry World of Jimmy Buffett." *Country Rambler,* 7 October 1976.

Biederman, Patricia Ward. "A Pirate Looks at 40." *The Atlanta Constitution,* 24 June 1984.

Bird, Rick. "Freewheeling Buffett Shrewd Businessman." *The Mississippi Press,* (Pascagoula), 15–16 July 1994.

Bogner, Steve. "Jimmy Buffett: Commercial—To an Extent." *Austin American Statesman,* 15 April 1975.

"Bonzai." "Lunching with Bonzai—Jimmy Buffett: You'll Never Work in This Business Again." *Mix,* June 1986.

Booth, William. "Squabble in Margaritaville over the Manatee." *The Washington Post,* 3 May 1992.

Boyer, Peter J. "Buffett Earned Reputation as Rock Rowdy. Associated Press uncredited clipping, 14 July 1978.

Bransford, Helen. "Jimmy Buffett." *Interview*, April 1986.

Braudy, Susan. "I, Claudine [Longet]." *Crawdaddy*, February 1978.

Broili, Susan. "Buffett Concert Changes Attitudes." *Durham Sun* (North Carolina), 6 February 1988.

Budhansky, Stephen, Erica E. Goode, and Ted Gest. "The Cold War [LSD] Experiments." *U.S. News and World Report*, 24 January 1994.

"Buffett." Obituary (Capt. James Delaney Buffett). *Mississippi Press* (Pascagoula) 3 January 1970.

"Buffett: Mrs. Hilda N. Buffett." Obituary, uncredited clipping, re: death of 6 April 1989 [Hilda Seymour].

Buffett, Jimmy. "Antigua Blowout: Wasting Away in the Lesser Antilles." *Outside*, July–August 1978.

———. "Beyond the Low-Water Mark." *Rolling Stone*, August 1992.

———. "Boomerang Love." *Ladies' Home Journal*, April 1990.

———. "Everything in the Woods Wants to Eat a Quail (Including Me)." *Esquire* [Sportsman's Issue], Fall 1992. Reprinted in *The Coconut Telegraph*, January–February 1993.

———. "From the Music Capitals of the World: Nashville." *Billboard*, 24 January 1970; 7 February 1970; 21 February 1970; 7 March 1970; 11 April 1970; 25 April 1970; 16 May 1970; 30 May 1970.

———. "The Making of 'Tales from Margaritaville.'" *The Coconut Telegraph*, September–October 1992.

———. *The Coconut Telegraph*, Christmas 1991.

———. "The Studio That Jack Built." *Billboard*, 25 April 1970.

———. "Talent in Action: Tony Joe White," *Billboard*, 14 February 1970; "Talent in Action: Isaac Hayes." *Billboard*, 16 May 1970; "Talent in Action: Ronnie Millsaps [sic]." *Billboard*, 30 May 1970.

———. "Talent Traffic." *Amusement Business*, 7 February 1970; 21 February 1970; 28 February 1970; 14 March 1970.

———. "'There's Booze in the America's Cup.'" *The Coconut Telegraph*, April 1987.

———. "You Can Take It with You." *The Coconut Telegraph*, May 1987.

———. "Words to Live By." *Esquire*, October 1993.

Buffett, John. "A Narrative of 20 Years' Residence on Pitcairn's Island." *The Friend* (Honolulu), vol. 4 (1846). [Providence Public Library, Providence, R.I.].

Buffett, Peets. "A Sailor's Life." *Mobile Bay Monthly*, September 1986.

"Buffett Brigade: Concertgoers Party in Summer Ritual." *Nashville Banner*, 20 July 1989.

"Buffett Coming to Austin." *American-Statesman* (Austin, Tex.), 17 January 1979.

"Buffett Salts Coast with Club." *Pensacola Journal*, 20 June 1984.

"Buffett Singing, Writing Way to Top in Nashville." *The Mobile Register*, 3 July 1970.

"Buffett to Enter Georgia Music Hall of Fame?" *The Atlanta Constitution*, 13 July 1990.

"Buffett Writes Novel." *Mississippi Press* (Pascagoula), 23 August 1992.

"Buffett's Suds." *Rolling Stone*, 6 September 1982.

Burger, Frederick. "About Buffett's New Paradise." *The Miami Herald*, 24 October 1982.

————. "Buffeted by Fame and a Broken Leg, Jimmy Is Not Wasting Away Again." *The Miami Herald,* 12 May 1978.

————. "Jimmy Buffett." *The Miami Herald,* 20 January 1980.

————. "No More Reefer Madness: Fingers Taylor Happily Playing Blues on His Own." *The Atlanta Constitution,* 12 January 1985.

"Burglars Take Magazine Files." *Oregonian,* 8 April 1967.

"C & W Singles Reviews—Picks of the Week: Jimmy Buffett." *Cash Box,* 1 August 1970.

Cackett, Alan. "Jimmy Buffett." *Country Music People* (U.K.), September 1983.

Cain, Carol. *"The Jimmy Buffett Scrapbook," Mobile Press Register,* 17 January 1994.

Calloway, James. "Buffett Felled by Poor Sound System." *News and Observer* (Raleigh, N.C.), 11 March 1980.

Campbell, Mary. "Pop: Jimmy Buffett, Changing His Latitudes." *Chicago Daily News,* 11 September 1977.

————. "Buffett Plays to Full House with Books and Music." Associated Press uncredited clipping, 8 October 1992.

"Capt. Buffett Dies at 82." *Mississippi Press* (Pascagoula), 3 January 1970.

"Caribbean Country Boy." *Time,* 18 April 1977.

Chaplin, Gordon. "So Long, Key West: Jimmy Buffett Moves into the Washington Limelight." *The Washington Post,* 20 March 1977.

Childress, Mark. "Monday Pace: Jimmy Buffett—Sailing Along, Searching for Songs." *Birmingham News,* 18 February and 5 March 1979.

Cieply, Michael. "New Spin: MCA Records' Chief Turns the Firm Around By being Aggressive." *The Wall Street Journal,* March 31, 1988.

Cieply, Michael, and Steve Hochman. "Azoff Resigns as Head of MCA Music Unit to Form Own Firm." *Los Angeles Times,* 6 September 1989.

"Concert for the Homeless." *The Coconut Telegraph,* November 1988.

"Concert Reviews: Eagles, Jimmy Buffett." *Variety,* 23 March 1977.

Cooley, Alvin. *"Living and Dying in 3/4 Time." Zoo World,* 28 March 1974.

————. "Nashville Underground." *Zoo World,* 6 June 1974.

Cooper, Daniel. "Mono Nashville: Everlasting Hits." *Nashville Scene,* 23 February 1995.

Coppage, Noel. "Jimmy Buffett: 'About Ninety Per Cent Factual.' " *Stereo Review,* September 1974.

————. "Popular Discs and Tapes: Recording of Special Merit: Jimmy Buffett, *Changes in Attitudes, Changes in Latitudes." Stereo Review,* July 1977.

Corcoran, Tom. "Wastin' Away in Marijuanaville." *Crawdaddy,* December 1977.

Cosford, Bill. "Rock: Something for Everyone—Bluesy, Folk and Conch." *The Miami Herald,* 1 August 1975.

"Country Goes Pop." *Music Journal,* January 1978.

Crowe, Bill. "Margaritaville: A Feast for the Ears, Buffett Eyes Video." *Evansville Press* (Ind.), 27 June 1988.

Crowe, Cameron. "They Call Him Big Shorty." *Rolling Stone,* 15 June 1978.

Crozier, Natalie. "Rising Singer Proud of Childhood Here." *Mobile Press,* 11 July 1974.

————. "Rising Mobile Singer Appears on National TV." *Mobile Press,* 14 August 1974.

Cuzzort, Robin. "Buffett's Array of Players Reveals a Wild Imagination." *Nashville Banner,* 2 October 1992.

Davis, Doug. "Austin City Limits: Good Time Music." *Greensboro Daily News* (N.C.), 5 June 1977.

Dawson, Walter. "Record Reviews: Staking His Claim on High Ground." *Memphis Commercial Appeal,* 26 March 1978.

"Deaths: William 'Billy' Buffett." Unidentified clipping, October 1991.

Dove, Ian. "Andy Pratt at Max's Kansas City." *The New York Times,* 18 June 1973.

Drake, Kerry. "Jimmy Buffett Welcome to Sing Here Anytime." *Cheyenne State Tribune* (Wyo.), 10 April 1978.

Duffy, Thom. "Dawn Patrol: Jungle Decor, Animal Skins—Club Livingston's We Presume." *Orlando Sentinal* (Fla.), 30 November 1986.

Elwood, Phillip. "Horny Rock Buffets Boarding House." *The San Francisco Examiner,* 11 September 1975.

Eng, Steve. Nashville's William Walker." *The Monocle,* September 1988.

———. "Profile: John Gawsworth." *Night Cry,* Spring 1988.

———. Review of *Hit Men: Power Brokers and Fast Money Inside the Music Business* by Frederic Dannen. *Bookpage,* August 1991.

———. Review of *The Jimmy Buffett Scrapbook* by Mark Humphrey, with Horace Lewine. *Bookpage,* March 1994.

———. "Wasted Away Again in Jimmy Buffettville." *Entertainment Express,* December 1993.

Erickson, Michael. Review. "Jimmy Buffett, *Somewhere Over China,*" *Nashville Banner,* 4 February 1982.

Evans, Bill. "Jimmy Buffett's Peaking at 32." *Gainsville Scene* (Fla.), 26 October 1979.

Everett, Todd. "King of the Parrot-Heads." *Los Angeles Herald Examiner,* 29 July 1986.

———. "Music Between My Ears: Jimmy Buffett at Troubadour." *Los Angeles Free Press,* 3 May 1974.

"Fan Fair Festivities June 6–10." *Amusement Business,* 2 July 1983.

Fast, Doug. "Jimmy Buffett's in Top Form." *Grand Rapids Press* (Mich.), 5 April 1983.

Ferguson, Hayes. "Jimmy Buffett." *Times-Picayune* (New Orleans), 29 April 1989.

Fleming, Michael, Karen Freifield, and Susan Mulcahy. "A Mixer of a Movie." *Newsday,* 24 February 1988.

Flippo, Chet. "Jimmy Buffett Catches Coral-Reefer Madness." *Rolling Stone,* 27 September 1977.

———. "Jimmy Buffett Goes to Paradise." *Look,* July 1979.

———. "Misadventures in Paradise: Keeping up with Jimmy Buffett in the Land of Sunshine, Greenies, Fins and Bikinis." *Rolling Stone,* 4 October 1979.

Gieson, John C. "Jimmy Buffett." *Tallahassee Sentinal Star,* uncredited clipping, 1982.

Gillette, Becky. "Stories to Send You [J. Buffett]." *Mississippi,* March–April 1993.

Gleason, Holly. "Jimmy Buffett: Adults Have Fun, Too." *Country Song Roundup,* January 1986.

Goldberg, Michael. "MCA Buys Azoff Firms." *Rolling Stone,* 3 July 1986.

———. "Grand Juries Investigate Mob Ties to Record Biz." *Rolling Stone,* 8 May 1986.

Goldsmith, Thomas. "Acoustic Buffett Benefits W. O. Smith Music School." *The Tennessean,* 21 March 1992.

———. "Buffett Book Links Tunes, Fictional Tales." *The Tennessean,* 26 August 1989.

———. "Jimmy Buffett Captains Lively Ship." *The Tennessean,* 25 July 1988.

———. Travis Tritt." *The Tennessean,* 9 June 1991.

Goldstein, Patrick. "MCA in the Front Line of a New Controversy." *Los Angeles Times,* 18 May 1986.

———. "MCA Layoffs—First Cut the Deepest?" *Los Angeles Times,* 6 September 1989.

"The Governor Stone: Singer Named Honorary Captain." *Mississippi Press* (Pascagoula), 30 August 1987.

Graff, Gary. "Buffett Deserts Key West, but Not Margaritaville." Knight-Ridder Newspapers, uncredited clipping, 1994.

Graham, Evaleah. "Buffett Fans Ignore Common Courtesies." *The Aspen Times* (Colo.), 25 August 1977.

Grayden, Robin. "Albums: Jimmy Buffett, *Changes in Latitudes, Changes in Attitudes." Melody Maker* (U.K.), 28 May 1977.

———. "Albums: Jimmy Buffett, *Son of a Son of a Sailor." Melody Maker* (U.K.), 13 May 1978.

Hager, George. "Jimmy Buffett on a Binge." *Times-Picayune* (New Orleans), 9 April 1977.

Hall, Douglas Kent. "Mr. Bojangles' Dance: The Odyssey and Oddities of Jerry Jeff Walker." *Rolling Stone,* 19 December 1974.

Hance, Mary. "Hostess Serves Up More than Burgers at Rotier's." *Nashville Banner,* 5 May 1995.

"Hank," "Pickin'." *Hank,* January 1976.

"Happy: While Wasting Away in Margaritaville, Jimmy Buffett Finds a Wife Worth His Salt." *People Weekly,* 3 October 1977.

Harrington, Richard. "Jimmy Buffett: Oh, the Stories He Can Tell." *The Washington Post,* 17 December 1989.

Hartberg, Lucretias. "Island-Hopping with Jimmy Buffett: There's Adventure and Intrigue in the Search for Joe Merchant." *The Tennessean,* 4 October 1992.

Hayes, Paul. "Decibels for Deaf Children: Jimmy Buffett Stars at the Picnic." *The Aspen Times* (Colo.), 18 June 1981.

Hayes, Paul, and Susan Pettit. "Buffett, Deaf Camp Picnic Draw 5,000." *The Aspen Times* (Colo.), 25 June 1981.

Hetzer, Michael. "Buffett Doesn't Change His Attitude at UNC." *Raleigh News and Observer* (N.C.), 8 February 1988.

Heyman, Richard. "Buffett, Mayor, Open 'Margaritaville.' " *The Key West Citizen,* 29 January 1985.

Hickey, Dave. "A Night of 'Hillbilly Reality' with Tompall Glaser." *Country Music,* December 1973.

Hilburn, Robert. "Hey, Parrot Heads, Guess Who's No. 1 on the Book List?" *Los Angeles Tribune,* 20 September 1992.

Hines, Regina. *Governor Stone:* Countians, Kin Share Special Bond with Link to 1880s Sailing Vessel." *Mississippi Press* (Pascagoula), 30 August 1987.

Hoekstra, Dave. "Buffett Finds No Changes in Attitude." *Chicago Sun-Times,* 28 June 1987.

Hollander, Sarah. "It's Official: Capt. Tony Given Mayor's Title for Life." *The Key West Citizen,* 17 August 1994.

"Honor Mr. and Mrs. J. D. Buffett with Dance" and "Post-Nuptial Festivity for Newly-Weds." Uncredited clipping, 2 April 1943.

Howie, Allen. "Tim Krekel." *Louisville Music News* (Ky.), January 1993.

Huffstickler, Albert. "Jimmy Buffett: Writing Away in Margaritaville." *Clockwatch Review: A Journal of the Arts* 3, no. 2 (1986).

Hughes, John. "Jimmy Buffett Has a Plan to Keep Margaritaville Alive." *Louisville Times* (Ky.), 29 June 1985.

Hunt, Dennis. "A Little Country Sunshine." *Los Angeles Times*, 17 October 1974.

Hunt, Lee Ann. "Names & Faces: Buffett Visits Ole Miss." *Cocoa Today* (Fla.), 6 August 1982.

"Jimmy Buffett: 'Banana Wind' to Blow Online." *Nashville Banner*, 29 May 1996.

"Jimmy Buffett, Band Slated for Concert Tonight at City Park." *The Daily Oklahoman* (Oklahoma City), 23 July 1976.

"Jimmy Buffett: Beertown Becomes Margaritaville." *Emerald City Chronicle* (Wis.), 4–18 April 1978.

"Jimmy Buffett Has a Lot in Common with Faulkner." *Commercial Dispatch* (Columbus, Miss.), 5 August 1982.

"Jimmy Buffett Helps Save Manatees." *Stockton Record* (Calif.), 4 December 1981.

"Jimmy Buffett Opens Margaritaville Store." *The Coconut Telegraph*, February 1985.

"Jimmy Buffett Sings for Florida Salt Ponds." Uncredited clipping (Associated Press), 25 November 1986.

"Jimmy Buffett Trying to Save Sparrows." *Mobile Press*, 18 March 1983.

"Jimmy Buffett Visits Faulkner Conference." *Starkville Daily News* (Miss.), 5 August 1982.

"Jimmy Buffet Wows 'em in Margaritaville." Uncredited clipping, 2 December 1981.

"Jimmy's Mermaids: Sometimes I See Me as an Old Manatee . . ." *The Coconut Telegraph*, April 1986.

Johnson, Rheta Grimsley. "Buffett's Concert Not Free." Uncredited clipping, 28 July 1986.

"The Jolly Mon." *Publishers Weekly*, 12 February 1988.

"The Jolly Mon." *South Florida Parenting*, April 1992.

Jordan, Pat. "The Cult of Jimmy Buffett." *Southern Living*, May 1988.

Joyce, Mike. "Performing Arts: Jimmy Buffett." *The Washington Post*, 13 July 1981.

Jumper, Kathy. "Fan Wants to Help Buffett Save Ponds." *Mobile Press Register*, 6 August 1987.

Katz, Lee Michael. "Inquiry: We'd Be Miserable Without Our Music." *USA Today*, 26 July 1985.

Kent, Mark R. "Concert by Buffett Labeled Outstanding." Uncredited clipping, 17 November 1974, Country Music Foundation Library, Nashville, Tenn.

Kenton, Gary. "Jimmy Buffett: *Riddles in the Sand*." *Country Rhythms*, April 1985.

King, Larry. Interview with Jimmy Buffett. *The Coconut Telegraph*, November–December 1989.

Kirby, Kip. "Inside Creative Workshop." *Hank*, April 1978 (Buzz Cason).

Kirsch, Bob. "Talent in Action: Delaney Bramlett, Jimmy Buffett." *Billboard*, 29 September 1973.

―――. "Talent in Action: Jimmy Buffett, Byron Keith Daugherty." *Ibid.*, 7 June 1975.

Knoblauch, Jim. "Jimmy Buffett: *Somewhere Over China*." *Prairie Sun*, 6 March 1982.

Kronke, David. "Buffett Still the Beach Bum." *Nightbeat (The Atlanta Journal/The Atlanta Constitution)*, 17 August 1985.

Lammers, Bill. "Rock Spotlight: Buffett Adrift Within Songs." *Kingsport Times-News* (Tenn.), 29 January 1982.

Lansden, Pamela. "Take One." *People Weekly,* 11 November 1986.

Latham, Aaron. "The Ballad of the Urban Cowboy: America's Search for True Grit." *Esquire,* 12 September 1978.

Lawrence, Tom. "Buffett's Still Crazy Fun." *Friendswood Journal* (Pearland, Tex.), 14 August 1987.

Lerner, Michael A. "The Hit Man of the Record Business: MCA's Abrasive Wizard." *Newsweek,* 8 February 1988.

Levine, Beth. "Trades: HBJ and Jimmy Buffett: Together Again for a New Novel." *Publishers Weekly,* 12 October 1990.

———. "Where's 'Margaritaville'?" In "Bookselling: No Doom, No Gloom, No Blockbusters," *Publishers Weekly,* 2 February 1990.

Lomartire, Paul. "Buffett's Midas Touch: Key West's Golden Boy Isn't Wasting Away in Margaritaville." *The Miami News,* 31 May 1988.

———. "Changes in Latitudes: Jimmy Buffett Set His Sails for Broadway and Best Sellers." *The Palm Beach Post* (Fla.), 26 October 1989.

———. "Inside: Palm Beach County Living—Changes in Latitude." *The Palm Beach Post* (Fla.), 26 October 1989.

Lomax, John, III. "President's Profile: Jimmy Bowen—Producing the Lion's Share of Success with No. 1 Flair." *Billboard,* 13 February 1988.

Lombardi, John. "King of the Schmooze." *Esquire,* November 1986.

Lowe, Richard H. "Buffett Draws Cast for Film Venture." Associated Press uncredited clipping, 17 December 1976.

"MCA-Matsushita Deal." *The Tennessean,* 3 December 1990.

McCall, Michael. "Fast Tracks: Radio's Closed Minds Frustrate Buffett." *Nashville Banner,* 13 July 1989.

———. "Music City New Margaritaville?" *Nashville Banner,* 19 October 1984.

McKnight, Gail. "Buffett Proves Life's a Beach." *The Tennessean,* 22 July 1989.

"Manatee Update." *The Coconut Telegraph,* July–August 1989.

"Margaritaville Cafe." *The Coconut Telegraph,* January 1988.

"Margaritaville Records: A State of Mind Is Now a State of Recording." *The Coconut Telegraph,* March–April 1992.

MarLyn. "Jimmy Buffett Wastin' Away in Old Snowmass." *Colorado Homes and Lifestyles,* September–October 1981.

"*Marsala* and *Monfalcone*, Wood Ships, Were Built in Pascagoula in Old Days." Uncredited clipping, 2 April 1943.

Mason, Tom. "Jimmy Buffett—From Mobile to Paradise." *Mobile Press,* 29 February 1980.

Matthews, Jay, and Stephen J. Lynton. "Va. Officer Describes CIA Break-In." *The Washington Post,* 14 June 1975.

Menton, Eddie. "Jimmy Buffett Won't Be Wasting Away." *Mobile Press Register,* 17 June 1984.

Miller, Patricia. "Kicked Back in Key West." *Books and Bookmen,* February 1986.

Mitchell, Garry. "Mobile Songwriter's Career Goes Any Which Way But Down." *Mobile Press Register,* 10 March 1985.

Modderno, Craig. "Jimmy Buffett: A Long Way from Margaritaville." *USA Today,* 15 August 1986.

Molloy, Pat. "A View from the Door." *The Coconut Telegraph,* May–June 1989.

Morris, Chris. " '60 Minutes' Explores Alleged MCA Mob Ties." *Billboard,* 2 December 1989.

Morris, Edward. "Buffett's Back: Monarch of Margaritaville Gives Nashville New Chance." *Billboard,* 19 May 1984.

———. "Talent in Action: Jimmy Buffett." *Billboard,* 3 April 1982.

Morse, Steve. "A Hippie Musical by Jimmy Buffett." *The Boston Globe,* 17 August 1991.

———. "A Pirate Looks at 48, Amazed by His Ongoing Success." *The Boston Globe,* August 29, 1993.

———. "Dear Jimmy: Keep Your Night Job." *Los Angeles Tribune,* 13 October 1992.

Moulder, John. "Jerry Jeff Walker, Hell-Raising Poet." *Country Rambler,* 7 October 1976.

Murphy, George. "Lime Wedge." "Who's Responsible for the Perfect Margarita? Omigod, It's Me!" *The Coconut Telegraph,* February 1988.

Nadler, Susan. "Nobody Owns a Mercedes." *Florida Keys Magazine,* March 1986.

Nash, Robert. "Club Review: Pratt, Buffett Impressive at Max's." *Record World,* 7 July 1973.

———. "Talent on Stage: Jimmy Buffett." *Cash Box,* 23 June 1973.

"Nashville ASCAP Post Goes to Gerry Wood." *Cash Box,* 11 October 1969.

"Nashville Scene." *Billboard,* 7 July 1973.

Neese, Sandy. "Buffett Sails In—On a Surge of New Wind." *The Tennessean,* 25 June 1983.

Neff, James. "Jimmy Buffett: Changing His Attitude Spells Success." *Country Style,* November 1977.

Nightbyrd, Jeff. "Jimmy Buffett: Everything Begins with a Tale." *Zoo World,* 6 June 1974.

Nixon, Bruce. "Jimmy Buffett's Back: 'Mr. Margaritaville' Feels Refreshed After Regrouping." *Dallas Times-Herald,* 3 November 1983.

O'Reilly, Jane. "In Key West: Where Writers Get Top Billing." *Time,* 6 February 1984.

Oermann, Robert K. "Buffett Benefits Music City. *The Tennessean,* 22 April 1992.

———. "Buffett Gets Parrot Heads Squawking." *The Tennessean,* 5 June 1987.

———. "Jimmy Buffett's Back in Town, This Time He Means Business." *The Tennessean,* 29 April 1984.

———. "The New Jimmy Buffett." *The Tennessean,* 19 June 1992.

———. "New MCA Regime Takes Over." *The Tennessean,* May 30, 1984.

———. "The Queen of the Parrot Heads." *The Tennessean,* 19 June 1992.

———. "Sunny Jimmy Buffett 'Loves the Now.' " *The Tennessean,* 16 August 1986.

Parker, Jerry. "Margaritaville: Jimmy Buffett Brings 'Pure Key West' Sound to the Arie Crown, While Rosalyn Carter Wears His T-shirt." *Newsday,* 23 March 1978.

Parsons, Clark. "Buffett's Concert Was Like Homecoming." *Nashville Banner,* 25 July 1988.

———. "Exit/In." *The Tennessean,* 1 April 1994.

———. "The Return of Pot: Is It Time to Rethink Marijuana and Its Prohibitions?" *The Tennessean,* 30 October 1994.

"Pas Captain [James Buffett] Recalls Sailing to Cuba in '22." *Mississippi Press,* undated clipping in the collection of Jackson County Public Library, Pascagoula Branch, Pascagoula, Miss.

Peck, Abe. "Planet of the Tapes." *Rolling Stone,* 23 September 1976.

Pendergrast, Lolo. "Jimmy Buffett 'Done Good' at Auditorium." *Mobile Press,* 5 March 1980.

"People in the News: A1A His Favorite." *Nashville Banner*, 27 May 1981.

"People in the News: Jimmy Buffett—Seaplane Flips on Takeoff; Singer Uninjured." *Nashville Banner*, 26 August 1994.

"People in the News: Jimmy Buffett—Singer Aids Paralyzed Woman." *Nashville Banner*, 1 September 1993.

Pollock, Dale. "Irving Azoff Ties Films to Music and Winds Up in Lotsa Projects." *Variety*, 22 August 1979.

Powell, Tom. "T. P. on AB." *Amusement Business*, 25 June 1983.

Puterbaugh, Parke. "Records: Somewhere Over China, Jimmy Buffett." *Rolling Stone*, 1 April 1982.

Racine, Marty. "Review: Buffett Provides 'Harbour' Tour at Performance Here." *Houston Chronicle*, 7 November 1983.

Radel, Cliff. "Capt. Buffett Takes Off, and the Flight Is Smooth." Uncredited clipping, 1991.

"Random Notes." *Rolling Stone*, 6 October 1977; 6 April 1978; 20 April 1978; 18 May 1978.

Raymond, Paulie. "Susan Nadler: One Good Girl Who Went Bad, But Who Has Gone Straight." *The Key West Citizen*, 3 April 1988.

Reeves, Garland. "Writing Away Again in Margaritaville." *Mobile Press Register*, 12 October 1989.

Reilly, Peter. "Jimmy Buffett: Growing Up." *Stereo Review*, January 1980.

———. "Jimmy Buffett: Lovably Unique, Uniquely Lovable." *Stereo Review*, July 1976.

Rhodes, Larry. "Country Finds Buffett." *Country News*, December 1984.

Risley, Ford. "After Flunking Out in '64, Buffett Gets High Marks from Audience." *The Auburn Plainsman*, 19 April 1979.

Robins, Wayne. "In Review: TV Troubadour." *Newsday*, 26 October 1976.

Rockwell, Curtis. "A Parrot Head Speaks." *Mississippi Press* (Pascagoula), 17 January 1992.

Rockwell, John. "The Pop Life." *The New York Times*, 10 March 1978.

Rogers, Joe. "Et Cetera: Mississippi Catching Up to Reality." *The Tennessean*, 21 February 1995.

Rohter, Larry. "Buffett: Witty Light-Heartedness." *The Washington Post*, 20 June 1975.

Roland, Tom. "Music: W. O. Smith Students Make Joyful Noise." *The Tennessean*, 25 November 1995.

Rosco, Freddy. "The Cowboy Sociologist Sings a Song at Ebbetts." *Rocky Mountain News*, 20 August 1975.

Rose, Frank. Review of *Son of a Son of a Sailor*. In *Rolling Stone*, 23 March 1978.

Rose, Terry. Interview with Jimmy Buffett. *The Coconut Telegraph*, May–June 1993.

Ross, Penelope. "Life as 'A Tire Swing.'" *The Music Gig*, May 1976.

Ruhlmann, William. "Jimmy Buffett in Margaritaville: The Beach Bum Who Broke the Bank." *Goldmine*, 4 February 1994.

"Rumble in Manateeville." *People Weekly*, 18 May 1992.

Russell, Candice. "The Troubadour of Key West." *The Miami Herald*, 23 June 1974.

Rutkoski, Rex. "Jimmy Buffett Is Mending Fences in Nashville." *Music City News*, February 1984.

"Sailing Singer Changes Latitude." *The Tennessean*, 28 July 1985.

"Saving the Manatee." *The Coconut Telegraph*, October 1985.

Schwed, Mark. "Golden Oldie? No, Jimmy Buffett Has Just Moved from Margaritaville to Nashville." *Baltimore News American*, 1 July 1984.

Shaugnessy, Carol. "Hobbit: A Caribbean Soul." *The Coconut Telegraph*, June 1986.

———. "Saving the Salt Ponds." *The Coconut Telegraph*, December 1986.

Shewey, Don. "Jimmy Buffett: Somebody's Taking Us All to the Cleaners, and I've Already Had My Shirts Done." *Unicorn Times*, November 1976.

———. "Not Hot." *Rolling Stone*, 15 November 1979.

Silver, Vernon. "How He Got There He Hasn't a Clue." *The New York Times*, 16 May 1993.

"Singer Buffet [sic] Marries." *Greenville Piedmont* (S.C.), 29 August 1977.

Sims, Judith. "Jimmy Buffett, Rock's Rowdy Comickaze." *Rolling Stone*, 17 July 1975.

"Singer Named Honorary Captain." *Mississippi Press* (Pascagoula), 30 August 1987.

"Single Reviews: 'Saxophones.'" *Cash Box*, 16 February 1974.

"Skipper Jimmy Buffet Looks over the Ship." Uncredited clipping, 15 September 1987.

"Slow, Slow, Slow Your Boat: 1994 Manatee Mortalities." *Save the Manatee Club Newsletter*, September 1994.

Smith, Donna K. "Sunshine," "New Orleans Margaritaville." *The Coconut Telegraph*, November–December 1992.

Spear, Susie. "'Parrot Heads' Flock to Buy Idol's Book." *Clarion-Ledger* (Jackson, Miss.), 15 October 1992.

Spears, Gregory. "Buffett Sings the Praises of Endangered Species Act." *Tallahassee Democrat* (Fla.), 8 April 1987.

"Special Guest." *Mobile Press Register*, 4 July 1976.

"Special Merit Spotlight: 'The Christian?'" *Billboard*, 6 June 1970.

"Specials." *The Columbia Record* (S.C.), 2 August 1975.

Spera, Keith. "Evangeline, Evangeline." *Offbeat*, March 1993.

———. "Jimmy Buffett Comes Home." *Offbeat*, March 1993.

"Spring Hill Is Tradition with Washichek Family." *Mobile Register*, 27 June 1966.

"Star Tracks: Ashley Gets Buffetted." *People Weekly*, 26 April 1982.

Stearns, David Patrick. "Jimmy Buffett Is Broadway Bound." *USA Today*, 24 August 1994.

Stein, Beth. "Off the Record: Christmas Comes Early for These Young Musicians." *Nashville Banner*, 20 November 1995.

Stokes, Geoffrey. "Jimmy Buffett's Venial Sins." *The Village Voice*, 31 March 1980.

Surette, Yvonne. "Jimmy Buffett Plays It Mellow." *Boston Globe*, 19 February 1976.

Sutherland, Sam. "Talent in Action: Andy Pratt, Jim Buffet [sic]." *Billboard*, 23 June 1973.

Tisserand, Michael. "Iguanas of the Night." *Offbeat*, March 1993.

"Toolen Urges Spring Hill SGA to Cancel Leary Invitation." *Mobile Register*, 27 September 1968.

Trocheck, Kathy Hogan. "Tropical Troubadour." *The Atlanta Constitution*, 22 July 1989.

Uncle Tom. "Jimmy Buffett." *The Great Speckled Bird*, 5 July 1971.

Van Gieson, John C. "Jimmy Buffett." Uncredited clipping, ca. 1982.

Van Matre, Lynn. "The Other Side of Jimmy Buffett." *The Orlando Sentinal* (Fla.), 18 November 1983.

———. "Singer Jimmy Buffett: If the Phone Doesn't Ring, It's Probably Hollywood." *Chicago Tribune*, 6 April 1986.

Warren, Jill. "Nightlife: King of Margaritaville Records LP in Nashville." *Indianapolis Star,* 22 June 1984.

West, Jim. "Showman and Misfit, Jimmy Buffett's Back." *Durham Herald* (N.C.), 5 February 1988.

"Will Rock Foot Democrats' Campaign Bills?" *Rolling Stone,* 15 September 1983.

Williams, Bill. "Nashville Scene." *Billboard,* 8 November 1969.

Williams, Thomas. "From the Music Capitals of the World: Nashville." *Billboard,* 11 December 1971.

Willson, Elizabeth. "Making Millions in Margaritaville." *Florida Trend,* May 1991.

"Witness to Kennedy Murder Is Attacked." *Hattiesburg American* (Miss.), 11 January 1968.

Wood, Gerry. "Boats, Beaches, Bars, Ballads & Tales You'll Never Hear at Margaritaville." *Island Life,* September 1992.

———. "Closeup: Jimmy Buffett—Volcano." *Island Life,* 8 September 1979.

———. "Nashville Scene: Buffett Makes Bucks with Margaritaville Mart." *Billboard,* 22 November 1986.

———. "Talent in Action: Jimmy Buffett." *Billboard,* 20 March 1976.

———. "That Key/Nashville Sound Goes Down Smooth." *Billboard,* 8 December 1990.

Woods, William C. "From Jimmy Buffett, a Way of Marking Time." *The Washington Post,* 17 March 1976.

Wright, Lawrence. "The Life and Death of Richard Brautigan." *Rolling Stone,* 11 April 1985.

"You Can Help." *The Coconut Telegraph,* December 1988.

Young, Charles M. "Hell Is for Heroes: The Eagles' Slow Burn in Rock & Roll Inferno." *Rolling Stone,* 29 November 1979.

Zaslow, Jeffrey. "Florida Roots Still Strong in Buffett's Music." *Tallahassee Sentinal Star,* 3 March 1981.

Zimmerman, David. "In the Buffett Zone, Life Couldn't Be Better." *USA Today,* 7 December 1989.

Index

■